自动化国家级特色专业系列规划教材指导委员会

孙优贤　吴　澄　郑南宁　柴天佑

俞金寿　周东华　李少远　王红卫

陈　虹　荣　冈　苏宏业

21世纪普通高等教育电气信息类规划教材

自动化专业英语
第三版

王树青　主编

化学工业出版社

·北京·

本书共分 6 章和 2 个附录。第 1 章是自动控制基础知识，介绍反馈控制原理、自动控制系统稳定性分析、设计及控制器参数整定；第 2 章是测量和执行器，包括压力、液面、流量、温度的测量和执行阀；第 3 章是先进控制系统，介绍前馈、比值、串级、自适应和模型预测控制；第 4 章是计算机控制系统，包括计算机控制基础、系统结构、PLC、DCS、现场总线以及计算机控制系统通信；第 5 章是自动控制系统，其中有物理系统建模，控制用的直流电动机，太阳能跟踪系统，电站控制以及工业机器人；第 6 章是人工智能技术及应用，包括神经元网络、模糊逻辑、专家系统以及应用。

　　本书可作为高等学校自动化及相关专业学生的教材，也可作为自动化科技人员的参考资料。

图书在版编目 (CIP) 数据

自动化专业英语/王树青主编. —3 版. —北京：
化学工业出版社，2010.6 (2022.4 重印)
自动化国家级特色专业系列规划教材
ISBN 978-7-122-08217-6

Ⅰ. 自… Ⅱ. 王… Ⅲ. 自动化-英语-高等学校-教材 Ⅳ. H31

中国版本图书馆 CIP 数据核字（2010）第 066480 号

责任编辑：郝英华　　　　　　　　　　　　装帧设计：张　辉
责任校对：陈　静

出版发行：化学工业出版社（北京市东城区青年湖南街 13 号　邮政编码 100011）
印　　装：北京印刷集团有限责任公司
787mm×1092mm　1/16　印张 18¾　字数 455 千字　2022 年 4 月北京第 3 版第 11 次印刷

购书咨询：010-64518888　　　　　　　　　　售后服务：010-64518899
网　　址：http://www.cip.com.cn
凡购买本书，如有缺损质量问题，本社销售中心负责调换。

定　　价：46.00 元　　　　　　　　　　　　　　　　　　　　版权所有　违者必究

总　　序

随着工业化、信息化进程的不断加快,"以信息化带动工业化、以工业化促进信息化"已成为推动我国工业产业可持续发展、建立现代产业体系的战略举措,自动化正是承载两化融合乃至社会发展的核心。自动化既是工业化发展的技术支撑和根本保障,也是信息化发展的主要载体和发展目标,自动化的发展和应用水平在很大意义上成为一个国家和社会现代工业文明的重要标志之一。从传统的化工、炼油、冶金、制药、机械、电力等产业,到能源、材料、环境、军事、国防等新兴战略发展领域,社会发展的各个方面均和自动化息息相关,自动化无处不在。

本系列教材是在建设浙江大学自动化国家级特色专业的过程中,围绕自动化人才培养目标,针对新时期自动化专业的知识体系,为培养新一代的自动化后备人才而编写的,体现了我们在特色专业建设过程中的一些思考与研究成果。

浙江大学控制系自动化专业在人才培养方面有着悠久的历史,其前身是浙江大学于1956 年创立的化工自动化专业,这也是我国第一个化工自动化专业。1961 年该专业开始培养研究生,1981 年以浙江大学化工自动化专业为基础建立的"工业自动化"学科点被国务院学位委员会批准为首批博士学位授予点,1984 年开始培养博士研究生,1988 年被原国家教委批准为国家重点学科,1989 年确定为博士后流动站,同年成立了工业控制技术国家重点实验室,1992 年原国家计委批准成立了工业自动化国家工程研究中心,2007 年启动了由国家教育部和国家外专局资助的高等学校学科创新引智计划("111"引智计划)。经过 50多年的传承和发展,浙江大学自动化专业建立了完整的高等教育人才培养体系,沉积了深厚的文化底蕴,其高层次人才培养的整体实力在国内外享有盛誉。

作为知识传播和文化传承的重要载体,浙江大学自动化专业一贯重视教材的建设工作,历史上曾经出版过很多优秀的教材和著作,对我国的自动化及相关专业的人才培养起到了引领作用。当前,加强工程教育是高等学校工科人才培养的主要指导方针,浙江大学自动化专业正是在教育部卓越工程师教育培养计划的指导下,对自动化专业的培养主线、知识体系和培养模式进行重新布局和优化,对核心课程教学内容进行了系统性重新组编,力求做到理论和实践相结合,知识目标和能力目标相统一,使该系列教材能和研讨式、探究式教学方法和手段相适应。

本系列教材涉及范围包括自动控制原理、控制工程、检测和传感、网络通信、信号和信息处理、建模与仿真、计算机控制、自动化综合实验等方面,所有成果都是在传承老一辈教育家智慧的基础上,结合当前的社会需求,经过长期的教学实践积累形成的。大部分教材和其前身在我国自动化及相关专业的培养中都具有较大的影响,例如《过程控制工程》的前身是过程控制的经典教材之一、王骥程先生编写的《化工过程控制工程》。已出版的教材,既有国家"九五"重点教材,也有国家"十五"、"十一五"规划教材,多数教材或其前身曾获得过国家级教学成果奖或省部级优秀教材奖。

本系列教材主要面向自动化(含化工、电气、机械、能源工程及自动化等)、计算机科学和技术、航空航天工程等学科和专业有关的高年级本科生和研究生,以及工作于相应领域和部门的科学工作者和工程技术人员。我希望,这套教材既能为在校本科生和研究生的知识拓展提供学习参考,也能为广大科技工作者的知识更新提供指导帮助。

本系列教材的出版得到了很多国内知名学者和专家的悉心指导和帮助,在此我代表系列教材的作者向他们表示诚挚的谢意。同时要感谢使用本系列教材的广大教师、学生和科技工作者的热情支持,并热忱欢迎提出批评和意见。

2011 年 6 月

第三版前言

《自动化专业英语》（前两版名为《工业自动化专业英语》）自 2001 年修订后已有近 10 年的时间了。在这 10 年里，自动化技术随着微电子、计算机等新技术的迅速发展，又前进了一大步。许多新的英语词汇不断出现在科技论文、专著和教科书中。因此，及时更新教材，使学生能尽快掌握日新月异的知识变化，极力促动着教材的修订工作。

在这次修订中，主要修改了计算机控制系统和测量与执行器两章的内容。其余部分内容几乎没有变更。经过修订后，全书内容共分 6 章和 2 个附录。第 1 章是自动控制基础知识，内容包括反馈控制、控制系统稳定性分析、过程控制系统设计和控制器参数整定；第 2 章是测量和执行器，内容有压力测量及传感器，液面测量及传感器，流量测量及流量仪表，温度测量及测量装置，以及执行器与流量控制执行阀；第 3 章是先进控制系统，内容有前馈、比值、串级控制，时滞补偿控制，选择性控制，自适应控制，统计质量控制，模型预测和监督控制；第 4 章是计算机控制系统，内容有计算机控制基础，计算控制结构，计算机集成控制，可编程控制器（PLC）及应用，集散型控制系统（DCS），现场总线，计算机控制系统通信；第 5 章是自动控制系统，内容有物理系统建模，控制系统直流电动机，太阳能跟踪控制系统，现代电站控制系统，工业机器人等；第 6 章是人工智能技术及应用，包括神经网络、模糊逻辑、专家系统以及人工智能在过程控制中的应用。

本书的结构和编排同前两版一致。

编　者

2010 年 6 月

修订版前言

《工业自动化专业英语》于 2000 年 6 月由化学工业出版社第一次印刷出版。由于该书填补了高等院校工业自动化专业高年级学生没有一本较完整专业英语教材的空缺，因此，受到各高等院校的欢迎，不到一年时间，此书就售空。同时，有许多教授和专家对此书提出了许多宝贵的建议，其中特别强调的一条是希望把教材内容进一步向机电工业自动化领域扩展。据此，本书的主编之一王树青教授在较短的时间内为本书增编了第七章自动控制系统的内容，其中包括 5 篇课文和 5 篇阅读材料，内容有实际系统（机电系统）数学模型，直流电动机控制系统，宇宙飞船太阳跟踪控制系统，现代电力系统和工业机器人导论等。希望读者批评指正。

编　者
2001 年 2 月 16 日

第一版前言

出版系列的专业英语教材，是许多院校多年来共同的愿望。在高等教育面向 21 世纪的改革中，学生基本素质和实际工作能力的培养受到了空前重视。专业英语水平是当今大学毕业生能力的重要组成部分。在此背景下，教育部（原国家教委）几次组织会议研究加强外语教学问题，制订有关规范，使外语教学更加受到重视。教材是教学的基本要素之一，与基础英语相比，专业英语教学的教材问题此时显得尤为突出。

国家主管部门的重视和广大院校的呼吁引起了化学工业出版社的关注，他们及时地与原化工部教育主管部门和全国化工类专业教学指导委员会请示协商后，组织全国十余所院校成立了大学英语专业阅读教材编委会。在经过必要的调研后，根据学校需求，编委会优先从各校教学（交流）讲义中确定选题，同时组织力量开展编审工作。本套教材涉及的专业主要包括化学工程与工艺、石油化工、机械工程、信息工程、工业自动化、应用化学及精细化工、生化工程、环境工程、制药工程、材料科学与工程、化工商贸等。

根据"全国部分高校化工类及相关专业大学英语专业阅读教材编审委员会"的要求和安排编写的《工业自动化专业英语》教材，可供工业自动化及相关专业本科生使用，也可以作为同等程度（通过大学英语四级）的专业技术人员自学教材。

本教材分为六章（Chapter），每章含有 5 个单元（Unit），每单元由一篇课文和一篇阅读材料构成。阅读材料提供与课文相关的背景知识，以进一步拓宽课文内容，为学生自学（开拓视野和训练阅读技能）提供合适的材料。根据课文和阅读材料的内容，配有相应的练习题。各篇课文之间、课文与所配阅读材料之间，既有一定的内在联系，又独立成章，可根据不同教学时数灵活选用。课文及阅读材料共计五十五篇，均选自原版英文教科书、科技报告、专著及专业期刊，大部分为国外 20 世纪 90 年代以来的出版物。其中：

Chapter 1 为工业过程控制原理，包括过程控制入门、反馈控制原理、自动控制系统稳定性分析、工业生产过程自动控制系统设计和控制器参数整定等；

Chapter 2 为工业过程参数测量和执行器，主要介绍工业生产过程参数的测量，如液面、压力、流量和温度的测量以及各种执行机构等；

Chapter 3 为工业过程模型化和系统辨识，其中包括数学模型的建立、系统辨识、最小二乘原理与迭代计算以及系统辨识实践步骤等；

Chapter 4 为复杂工业过程的先进控制，包括前馈和比值控制、纯滞后补偿控制、自适应控制、推理控制和模型预测控制等；

Chapter 5 为计算机与自动化，其中包括集散控制系统与可编程控制器、A/D 和 D/A 转换、微型计算机、数字化和基于 PC 控制器等；

Chapter 6 为智能控制，包括智能控制技术、神经网络控制、模糊逻辑应用、专家系统和人工智能在过程控制中应用等。

在专业英语阅读阶段，掌握一定数量的科技词汇（包括专业词汇）是教学的主要目的之一。本教材覆盖了控制、测量和计算机等的基本内容。整个教材注意前后呼应，词汇的复现率高，每个单元均有词汇练习，有利于学生比较牢固地掌握基本词汇。附录中列出总词汇表。

大纲中对专业英语阅读阶段的学习技能有明确的要求，有针对性的练习是训练阅读技能的有效手段。本教材在设计练习时，作了一些尝试，主要的练习形式如下。

① 课文前设问题或要求。根据课文内容设计的问题或要求，置于课文前面，以激发学生通过阅读获取信息的欲望，有利于学生调动背景知识，变被动阅读为主动阅读。

② 大部分课文配有摘要填空的练习形式，要求学生在规定时间内选用课文中的（一般不多于3个）词填空，培养学生通篇浏览（Surveying）、查找信息（Locating Information）及寻找关键词（Keywords）的能力，这是对阅读技能的一种强化训练，也是对学生语言能力和专业知识水平的一种有效考查方式。

③ 教材中没有指定英译中翻译练习，教师可从课文和阅读材料中选取。

书中第1、4、6章和附录由浙江大学王树青编写，第2、3和5章分别由北京化工大学韩建国、田水滢和李大字、王晶编写，全书的统稿工作由王树青和韩建国完成。

本教材从结构、内容到练习设计都是一种尝试，我们热诚希望使用本书的广大师生提出宝贵意见。

致谢 本教材在成书过程中得到了化学工业出版社大力支持，华东理工大学蒋慰孙教授审阅了全书，并提出了许多宝贵的意见，浙江大学陆建中老师对全书进行了认真的校核，来国妹女士出色完成了全书的录入和排版工作。对他们的热情帮助和指导谨在此一并表示衷心感谢。

编　者

1999年9月9日

目 录

CHAPTER 1　FUNDAMENTALS OF AUTOMATIC CONTROL ··· 1
    1.1　Introduction to Process Control ·· 1
    1.2　What is Feedback and What are Its Effects? ··· 12
    1.3　Stability of Closed-Loop Control Systems ··· 23
    1.4　The Design Process of Control System ··· 33
    1.5　Controller Tuning ·· 45

CHAPTER 2　MEASUREMENTS AND ACTUATORS ··· 57
    2.1　Pressure Measurements ·· 57
    2.2　Level Measurements ·· 66
    2.3　Flow Measurements ··· 74
    2.4　Temperature Measurement ··· 82
    2.5　Actuators ·· 90

CHAPTER 3　ADVANCED CONTROL SYSTEMS ··· 98
    3.1　Feedforward and Ratio Control ·· 98
    3.2　Time-Delay Compensation and Inferential Control ··· 107
    3.3　Adaptive Control Systems ·· 115
    3.4　Model Based Predictive Control ··· 125
    3.5　Supervisory Control Systems ··· 133

CHAPTER 4　COMPUTER CONTROL SYSTEMS ·· 138
    4.1　Fundamentals of Computer Control ·· 138
    4.2　Computer Control System Architecture ··· 148
    4.3　Programmable Controllers ·· 158
    4.4　Distributed Control System (DCS) ·· 167
    4.5　Computer Control System Communications(1) ·· 178

CHAPTER 5　AUTOMATIC CONTROL SYSTEMS ··· 188
    5.1　Mathematical Modeling of Physical Systems ··· 188
    5.2　DC Motors in Control Systems ··· 197
    5.3　Sun-Seeker System ·· 204

5.4	Modern Power Systems	213
5.5	Introduction to Industrial Robots	226

CHAPTER 6   ARTIFICIAL INTELLIGENCE TECHNIQUES AND APPLICATIONS ······ 237
- 6.1 Artificial Intelligence Techniques ······ 237
- 6.2 Use Neural Networks for Problem Solving ······ 242
- 6.3 Applications of Fuzzy Logic ······ 249
- 6.4 Expert systems ······ 254
- 6.5 AI in Process Control ······ 258

APPENDIXES ······ 264
- Appendix 1   Sources of Information in Automatic Control ······ 264
- Appendix 2   总词汇表 (INDEX) ······ 268

REFERENCES ······ 285

CHAPTER 1　FUNDAMENTALS OF AUTOMATIC CONTROL

1.1　Introduction to Process Control

Before reading the text below, try to answer the following questions:
1. What is the process control in a process plant?
2. What is the typical process control strategies?
3. Could you please give an example of process control?

In recent years the performance requirements for process plants have become increasingly difficult to satisfy. Stronger competition, tougher environmental and safety regulations, and rapidly changing economic conditions have been key factors in the tightening of plant product quality specifications. A further complication is that modern processes have become more difficult to operate because of the trend toward larger, more highly integrated plants with smaller surge capacities between the various processing units. Such plants give the operators little opportunity to prevent upsets from propagating from one unit to other interconnected units. In view of the increased emphasis placed on safe, efficient plant operation, it is only natural that the subject of *process control* has become increasingly important in recent years. In fact, without process control it would not be possible to operate most modern processes safely and profitably, while satisfying plant quality standards.

1.1.1　Illustrative Example

As an introduction to process control, consider the continuous stirred-tank heater shown in Figure 1.1.1 The inlet liquid stream has a mass flow rate w and a temperature T_i. The tank contents are well agitated and heated by an electrical heater that provides Q watts. It is assumed that the inlet and outlet flow rates are identical and that the liquid density ρ remains constant, that is, the temperature variations are small enough that the temperature dependence of ρ can be neglected. Under these conditions the volume V of liquid in the tank remains constant.

The control objective for the stirred-tank heater is to keep the exit temperature T at a constant reference value T_R. The reference value is referred to as a *set point*

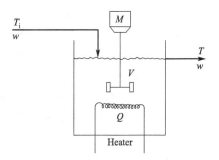

Figure 1.1.1　Continuous stirred-tank heater.

in control terminology. Next we consider two questions.

Question 1. *How much heat must be supplied to the stirred-tank-heater to heat the liquid from an inlet temperature T_i to an exit temperature T_R?*

To determine the required heat input for the design operating conditions, we need to write a steady-state energy balance for the liquid in the tank. In writing this balance, it is assumed that the tank is perfectly mixed and that heat losses are negligible. Under these conditions there are no temperature gradients within the tank contents and consequently, the exit temperature is equal to the temperature of the liquid in the tank. A steady-state energy balance for the tank indicates that the heat added is equal to the change in enthalpy between the inlet and exit streams:

$$\bar{Q} = \bar{w}C(\bar{T} - \bar{T}_i) \tag{1.1.1}$$

where $\bar{T}_i$, $\bar{T}$, $\bar{w}$, and $\bar{Q}$ denote the nominal steady-state design values of T_i, T, w, and Q, respectively, and C is the specific heat❶ of the liquid. We assume that C is constant. At the design conditions, $\bar{T} = T_R$ (the set point). Making this substitution in Eq. (1.1.1) gives an expression for the nominal heat input $\bar{Q}$:

$$\bar{Q} = \bar{w}C(T_R - \bar{T}_i) \tag{1.1.2}$$

Equation (1.1.2) is the design equation for the heater. If our assumptions are correct and if the inlet flow rate and inlet temperature are equal to their nominal values, then the heat input given by Eq. (1.1.2) will keep the exit temperature at the desired value, T_R. But what if conditions change? This brings us to the second question:

Question 2. *Suppose that inlet temperature T_i changes with time. How can we ensure that T remains at or near the set point T_R?*

As a specific example, assume that T_i increases to a new value greater than $\bar{T}_i$. If Q is held constant at the nominal value of $\bar{Q}$, we know that the exit temperature will increase so that $T > T_R$. (cf. Eq. (1.1.1)).

To deal with this situation, there are a number of possible strategies for controlling exit temperature T.

Method 1. Measure T and adjust Q. One way of controlling T despite disturbances in T_i is to adjust Q based on measurements of T. Intuitively, if T is too high, we should reduce Q; if T is too low, we should increase Q. This control strategy will tend to move T toward the set point T_R and could be implemented in a number of different ways. For example, a plant operator could observe the measured temperature and compare the measured value to T_R. The operator would then change Q in an appropriate manner. This would be an application of *manual control*. However, it would probably be more convenient and economical to have this simple control task performed automatically by an electronic device rather than a person, that is, to utilize *automatic control*.

Method 2. Measure T_i, adjust Q. As an alternative to Method 1, we could measure disturbance variable T_i and adjust Q accordingly. Thus, if T_i is greater than $\bar{T}_i$, we would decrease Q; for

---

❶ specific heat 比热，根据国际 GB 3100~3102.1993 已改为 specific heat capacity 比热容.——编者注

$T_i < \bar{T_i}$ we would set $Q > \bar{Q}$.

Method 3. Measure T, adjust w. Instead of adjusting Q, we could choose to manipulate mass flow rate w. Thus, if T is too high we would increase w to reduce the energy input rate in the stirred tank relative to the mass flow rate and thereby reduce the exit temperature.

Method 4. Measure T_i, adjust w. In analogy with Method 3, if T_i is too high, w should be increased.

Method 5. Measure T_i and T, adjust Q. This approach is a combination of Methods 1 and 2.

Method 6. Measure T_i and T, adjust w. This approach is a combination of Methods 3 and 4.

Method 7. Place a heat exchanger on the inlet stream. The heat exchanger is intended to reduce the disturbances in T_i and consequently reduce the variations in T. This approach is sometimes called "hog-tieing" an input.

Method 8. Use a larger tank. If a larger tank is used, fluctuations in T_i will tend to be damped out due to the larger thermal capacitance of the tank contents. However, increased volume of tankage would be an expensive solution for an industrial plant due to the increased capital costs of the larger tank. Note that this approach is analogous to the use of water baths in chemistry laboratories where the large thermal capacitance of the bath serves as a heat sink and thus provides an isothermal environment for a small-scale research apparatus.

1.1.2 Classification of Control Strategies

Next, we will classify the eight control strategies of the previous section and discuss their relative advantages and disadvantages. Methods 1 and 3 are examples of *feedback control* strategies. In feedback control, the process variable to be controlled is measured and the measurement is used to adjust another process variable which can be manipulated. Thus, for Method 1, the measured variable is T and the manipulated variable is Q. For Method 3, the measured variable is still T but the manipulated variable is now w. Note that in feedback control the disturbance variable T_i is not measured.

It is important to make a distinction between *negative feedback and positive feedback*. Negative feedback refers to the desirable situation where the corrective action taken by the controller tends to move the controlled variable toward the set point. In contrast, when positive feedback exists, the controller tends to make things worse by forcing the controlled variable farther away from the set point. Thus, for the stirred-tank heater, if T is too high we would decrease Q (negative feedback) rather than increase Q (positive feedback).

Methods 2 and 4 are *feedforward control strategies*. Here, the disturbance variable T_i is measured and used to manipulate either Q (Method 2) or w (Method 4). Note that in feedforward control, the controlled variable T is *not* measured. Method 5 is a feedforward-feedback control strategy since it is a combination of Methods 1 and 2. Similarly, Method 6 is also a feedforward-feedback control strategy since it is a combination of Methods 3 and 4. Methods 7 and 8 consist of equipment design changes and thus are not really control strategies. Note that Method 7 is somewhat inappropriate since it involves adding a heat exchanger to the inlet line of the stirred-tank heater which in itself was designed to function as a heat exchanger! The control strategies for the stirred-tank heater are summarized in Table 1.1.1.

Table 1.1.1 Temperature Control Strategies for the Stirred-Tank Heater

Method	Measured Variable	Manipulated Variable	Category
1	T	Q	FB
2	T_i	Q	FF
3	T	w	FB
4	T_i	w	FF
5	T_i and T	Q	FF/FB
6	T_i and T	w	FF/FB
7	—	—	Design change
8	—	—	Design change

So far we have considered only one source of process disturbances, fluctuations in T_i. We should also consider the possibility of disturbances in other process variables such as the ambient temperature, which would affect heat losses from the tank. Recall that heat losses were assumed to be negligible earlier. Changes in process equipment are another possible source of disturbances. For example, the heater characteristics could change with time due to scaling by the liquid. It is informative to examine the effects of these various types of disturbances on the feedforward and feedback control strategies discussed above.

First, consider the feedforward control strategy of Method 2 where the disturbances in T_i are measured and the measurements are used to adjust the manipulated variable Q. From a theoretical point of view, this control scheme is capable of keeping the controlled variable T exactly at set point T_R despite disturbances in T_i. Ideally, if accurate measurements of T_i were available and if the adjustments in Q were made in an appropriate manner, then the corrective action taken by the heater would cancel out the effects of the disturbances before T is affected. Thus, in principle, feedforward control is capable of providing *perfect control* in the sense that the controlled variable would be maintained at the set point.

But how will this feedforward control strategy perform if disturbances occur in other process variables? In particular, suppose that the flow rate w cannot be held constant but, instead, varies over time. In this situation, w would be considered a disturbance variable. If w increases, then the exit temperature T will decrease unless the heater supplies more heat. However, in the control strategy of Method 2 the heat input Q is maintained constant as long as T_i is constant. Thus *no* corrective action would be taken for unmeasured flow disturbances. In principle, we could deal with this situation by measuring *both* T_i and w and then adjusting Q to compensate for both of these disturbances. However, as a practical matter it is generally uneconomical to attempt to measure all potential disturbances. It would be more practical to use a combined feedforward-feedback control system, since feedback control provides corrective action for unmeasured disturbances, as discussed below. Consequently, in industrial applications feedforward control is normally used in combination with feedback control.

Next, we will consider how the feedback control strategy of Method 1 would perform in the presence of disturbances in T_i or w. If Method 1 were used, no corrective action would occur until after the disturbance had upset the process, that is, until after T differed from T_R. Thus, by its inherent nature, feedback control is not capable of perfect control since the controlled variable must deviate from the set point before corrective action is taken. However, an extremely important advantage of feedback control is that corrective action is taken regardless of the *source of the disturbance*. Thus, in Method 1, corrective action would be taken (by adjusting Q) after a disturbance in T_i or w caused T to deviate from the set point. The ability to handle unmeasured disturbances of unknown origin is a major reason why feedback controllers have been so widely used for process control.

Selected from *"Process Dynamics and Control, D. Seborg & T. Edgar, John Wiley & Sons, 1989"*

Words and Expressions

1. plant   [plɑ:nt]   *n.* 车间,工厂,系统
2. strategy   ['strætidʒi]   *n.* 策略
3. competition   [kɔmpə'tiʃən]   *n.* 竞赛,竞争
4. integrate   ['intigreit]   *v.* 使成整体;求……积分
5. surge capacity   [sə:dʒ kə'pæsiti]   *n.* 谐振能力
6. upset   ['ʌpset]   *n.*; *v.* 混乱,扰乱
7. propagate   ['prɔpəgeit]   *v.* 传播,宣传
8. process control   过程控制
9. quality   ['kwɔliti]   *n.* 质量
10. standard   ['stændəd]   *n.* 标准
11. stirred-tank   [stə:rid-tæŋk]   *n.* 搅拌槽
12. heater   ['hi:tə]   *n.* 加热器
13. inlet   ['inlet]   *n.* 入口,进口
14. agitate   ['ædʒiteit]   *v.* 搅动
15. watt   [wɔt]   *n.* 瓦特
16. variation   [vɛəri'eiʃən]   *n.* 变化量
17. constant   ['kɔnstənt]   *n.* 常数,恒量
18. set point   [set pɔint]   *n.* 设定值,给定值
19. terminology   [tə:mi'nɔlədʒi]   *n.* 术语
20. negligible   ['neglidʒib(ə)l]   *adj.* 可以忽略的,微不足道的
21. gradient   ['greidiənt]   *n.* 梯度
22. steady-state   ['stedi-steit]   *n.* 稳态
23. energy balance   能量平衡
24. enthalpy   [en'θælpi]   *n.* 焓,热函
25. intuitively   [in'tju:itivli]   *adv.* 直觉地
26. implement   ['impliment]   *v.* 实现,执行
27. manual control   手动控制,人工控制
28. automatic control   自动控制
29. hog   [hɔg]   *v.* (使)拱(弯、扭)曲,变形
30. tie   [tai]   *v.* 结;约束
31. fluctuation   [flʌktjueiʃən]   *vi.* 波动

32. damp   [dæmp]   v. 阻尼；衰减
33. isothermal   [aisəu'θə:məl]   n. 等温线; adj. 同温的
34. heat sink   [hi:t siŋk]   n. 散热片，散热装置
35. feedback control   反馈控制
36. manipulate   [mə'nipjuleit]   v. 处理
37. negative feedback   负反馈
38. positive feedback   正反馈
39. feedforward control   前馈控制
40. heat exchanger   热交换器
41. ambient   ['æmbiənt]   adj. 周围的, 外界的
42. heat loss   热损失
43. perfect control   完美控制
44. inherent   [in'hiərənt]   adj. 固有的, 内在的, 本征的

Exercises

1. *Complete the notes below with words taken from the text above.*
   (1) A further complication _____ modern processes _____ more difficult to operate because of the trend toward larger, more highly integrated plants _____ smaller surge capacities between the various processing units.
   (2) _____ determine the required heat input _____ the design operating conditions, we need _____ a steady-state energy balance _____ the liquid in the tank.
   (3) Important to make a distinction _____ and _____ refers to the desirable situation where the _____ taken by the _____ tends to move the _____ toward the set point.

2. *Put the following into Chinese:*
   performance   process plant   process control
   reference   operating conditions   disturbance
   automatic control   manual control   perfect control
   feedback control   set point   controlled variable

3. *Put the following into English:*
   带搅拌加热器   密度   比热容   热容   热损失
   负反馈   正反馈   前馈控制策略   控制器

Reading Material:

Overview of Control Engineering

   The goal of control engineering is to improve, or in some cases enable, the performance of a system by the addition of *sensors*, *control processors*, and *actuators*. The sensors measure or sense various signals in the system and operator commands; the control processors process the sensed signals and drive the actuators, which affect the behavior of the system. A schematic diagram of a general *control system* is shown in Figure 1.1.2.

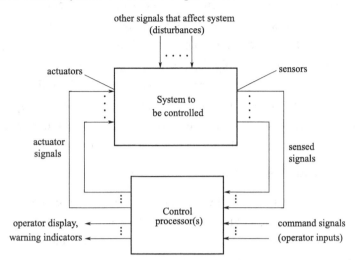

Figure 1.1.2   A schematic diagram of a general control system.

This general diagram can represent a wide variety of control systems. The system to be controlled might be an aircraft, a large electric power generation and distribution system, an industrial process, a head positioner for a computer disk drive, a data network, or an economic system. The signals might be transmitted via analog or digitally encoded electrical signals, mechanical linkages, or pneumatic or hydraulic lines. Similarly the control processor or processors could be mechanical, pneumatic, hydraulic, analog electrical, general-purpose or custom digital computers.

Because the sensor signals can affect the system to be controlled (via the control processor and the actuators), the control system shown in Figure 1.1.2 is called a *feedback* or *closed-loop* control system, which refers to the signal "loop" that circulates clockwise in this figure. In contrast, a control system that has no sensors, and therefore generates the actuator signals from the command signals alone, is sometimes called an *open-loop* control system[①]. Similarly, a control system that has no actuators, and produces only operator display signals by processing the sensor signals, is sometimes called a *monitoring system*.

In industrial settings, it is often the case that the sensor, actuator, and processor signals are *boolean, i.e.* assume only two values. Boolean sensors include mechanical and thermal limit switches, proximity switches, thermostats, and pushbutton switches for operator commands. Actuators that are often configured as Boolean devices include heaters, motors, pumps, valves, solenoids, alarms, and indicator lamps. Boolean control processors, referred to as *logic controllers*, include industrial relay systems, general-purpose microprocessors, and commercial *programmable logic controllers*.

In this book, we consider control systems in which the sensor, actuator, and processor signals assume real values, or at least digital representations of real values. Many control systems include both types of signals: the real-valued signals that we will consider, and Boolean signals, such as fault or limit alarms and manual override switches, that we will not consider.

1. System Design and Control Configuration

Control configuration is the selection and placement of the actuators and sensors on the system to be controlled, and is an aspect of system design that is very important to the control engineer. Ideally, a control engineer should be involved in the design of the system itself, even before the control configuration. Usually, however, this is not the case: the control engineer is provided with an already designed system and starts with the control configuration. Many aircraft, for example, are designed to operate without a control system; the control system is intended to improve the performance (indeed, such control systems are sometimes called *stability augumentation* systems, emphasizing the secondary role of the control system).

Actuator Selection and Placement

The control engineer must decide the type and placement of the actuators. In an industrial process system, for example, the engineer must decide where to put actuators such as pumps, heaters, and valves. The specific actuator hardware (or at least, its relevant characteristics) must also be chosen. Relevant characteristics include cost, power limit or authority, speed of response, and accuracy of response. One such choice might be between a crude, powerful pump that is slow to respond, and a more accurate but less powerful pump that is faster to respond.

Sensor Selection and Placement

The control engineer must also decide which signals in the system will be measured or sensed, and with what sensor hardware. In an industrial process, for example, the control engineer might decide which temperatures, flow rates, pressures, and concentrations to sense. For a mechanical system, it may be possible to choose *where* a sensor should be placed, $e.g$[2]., where an accelerometer is to be positioned on an aircraft, or where a strain gauge is placed along a beam. The control engineer may decide the particular type or relevant characteristics of the sensors to be used, including the type of transducer, and the signal conditioning and data acquisition hardware. For example, to measure the angle of a shaft, sensor choices include a potentiometer, a rotary variable differential transformer, or an 8-bit or 12-bit absolute or differential shaft encoder. In many cases, sensors are smaller than actuators, so a change of sensor hardware is a less dramatic revision of the system design than a change of actuator hardware.

There is not yet a well-developed theory of actuator and sensor selection and placement, possibly because it is difficult to precisely formulate the problems, and possibly because the problems are so dependent on available technology. Engineers use experience, simulation, and trial and error to guide actuator and sensor selection and placement.

2. Modeling

The engineer develops mathematical models of
- the system to be controlled,
- noises or disturbances that may act on the system,
- the commands the operator may issue,
- desirable or required qualities of the final system.

These models might be deterministic (*e.g.*, ordinary differential equations (ODE's), partial differential equations (PDE's), or transfer functions), or stochastic or probabilistic (*e.g.*, power spectral densities).

Models are developed in several ways. *Physical modeling* consists of applying various laws of physics (*e.g.*, Newton's equations, energy conservation, or flow balance) to derive ODE or PDE models. *Empirical modeling* or *identification* consists of developing models from observed or collected data. The a priori assumptions used in empirical modeling can vary from weak to strong: in a "black box" approach, only a few basic assumptions are made, for example, linearity and time-invariance of the system, whereas in a physical model identification approach, a physical model structure is assumed, and the observed or collected data is used to determine good values for these parameters. Mathematical models of a system are often built up from models of subsystems, which may have been developed using different types of modeling.

Often, several models are developed, varying in complexity and fidelity. A simple model might capture some of the basic features and characteristics of the system, noises, or commands; a simple model can simplify the design, simulation, or analysis of the control system, at the risk of inaccuracy. A complex model could be very detailed and describe the system accurately, but a complex model can greatly complicate the design, simulation, or analysis of the system.

3. Controller Design

The *controller* or *control law* describes the algorithm or signal processing used by the control processor to generate the actuator signals from the sensor and command signals it receives.

Controllers vary widely in complexity and effectiveness. Simple controllers include the *proportional* (P), the *proportional plus derivative* (PD), the *proportional plus integral* (PI), and the *proportional plus integral plus derivative* (PID) controllers, which are widely and effectively used in many industries. More sophisticated controllers include the *linear quadratic regulator* (LQR), the estimated-state-feedback controller, and the *linear quadratic Gaussian* (LQG) controller. These sophisticated controllers were first used in state-of-the-art aerospace systems, but are only recently being introduced in significant numbers.

Controllers are designed by many methods. Simple P or PI controllers have only a few parameters to specify, and these parameters might be adjusted empirically, while the control system is operating, using "tuning rules". A controller design method developed in the 1930's through the 1950's, often called *classical controller design*, is based on the 1930's work on the design of vacuum tube feedback amplifiers. With these heuristic (but very often successful) techniques, the designer attempts to synthesize a compensation network or controller with which the closedloop system performs well (the terms "synthesize", "compensation", and "network" were borrowed from amplifier circuit design).

In the 1960's through the present time, state-space or "modern" controller design methods have been developed. These methods are based on the fact that the solutions to some optimal control problems can be expressed in the form of a feedback law or controller, and the development of efficient computer methods to solve these optimal control problems.

Over the same time period, researchers and control engineers have developed methods of controller design that are based on extensive computing, for example, numerical optimization.

4. Controller Implementation

The signal processing algorithm specified by the controller is implemented on the control processor. Commercially available control processors are generally restricted to logic control and specific types of control laws such as PID. Custom control processors built from general-purpose microprocessors or analog circuitry can implement a very wide variety of control laws. General-purpose *digital signal processing* (DSP) chips are often used in control processors that implement complex control laws. Special-purpose chips designed specifically for control processors are also now available.

5. Control System Testing, Validation and Tuning

Control system testing may involve:
- extensive computer simulations with a complex, detailed mathematical model,
- real-time simulation of the system with the actual control processor operating ("hardware in the loop"),
- real-time simulation of the control processor, connected to the actual system to be controlled,
- field tests of the control system.

Often the controller is modified after installation to optimize the actual performance, a process known as tuning.

Selected from: *Stephen P. Boyd, Craig H. Barratt,* "*Linear Controller Design*", *Prentice-Hall, Inc,* 1991

Words and Expressions

1. sensor   ['sensə]   *n.* 传感器
2. actuator   ['æktjueitə]   *n.* 执行器
3. schematic   [ski'mætik]   *adj.* 示意性的
4. aircraft   ['ɛəkrɑːft]   *n.* 航空器，飞行器
5. positioner   [pə'ziʃənə]   *n.* 定位器
6. encode   [in'kəud]   *v.* 编码，译码
7. mechanical linkage   机械连接
8. pneumatic   [njuː'mætik]   *adj.* 气动的
9. hydraulic   [hai'drɔːlik]   *adj.* 水力的，液动的
10. monitor   ['mɔnitə]   *n.* 监视器
11. boolean   ['buːljən]   *adj.* 布尔的
12. switch   ['switʃ]   *n.* 开关
13. proximity   [prɔk'simiti]   *n.* 近似，接近
14. thermostat   ['θeməstæt]   *n.* 自动调温器，温度调节装置
15. pushbutton   ['puʃbʌtn]   *n.* 按钮
16. solenoid   ['səulənɔid]   *n.* (电)螺线管
17. motor   ['məutə]   *n.* 电机，马达

18. pump [pʌmp] *n.* 泵
19. valve [vælv] *n.* 阀
20. relay ['riːlei] *n.* (电工) 继电器
21. override switch　过载开关
22. control configuration　控制组态
23. stability augmentation　*n.* 稳定性增益
24. concentration [kɔnsen'treiʃən] *n.* 浓度
25. accelerometer [æksələ'rɔmitə] *n.* 加速度表
26. strain gauge　应变仪, 拉力计
27. transducer [trænz'djuːsə] *n.* 传感器
28. acquisition [ækwi'ziʃən] *n.* 获取, 采集
29. potentiometer [pətenʃi'ɔmitə] *n.* 电位器
30. stochastic [stə'kæstik] *adj.* 随机的
31. probabilistic [prɔbəbi'listik] *adj.* 概率的
32. physical modeling　物理模型
33. empircal modeling　经验模型
34. identification [aidentifi'keiʃən] *n.* 辨识
35. parameter [pə'ræmitə] *n.* 参数
36. fidelity [fi'deliti] *n.* 保真性
37. proportional plus derivative　比例加微分
38. proportional plus integral　比例加积分
39. sophisticated [sə'fistikeitid] *adj.* 复杂的, 高级的；非常有经验的
40. linear quadratic regulator　线性二次型调节器
41. linear quadratic Gaussian　线性二次型高斯
42. state-of-the-art　技术水平, 科学发展动态, 现代化的
43. tuning rules　*n.* 整定规则
44. classical ['klæsikl] *adj.* 经典的
45. heuristic [hjuə'ristik] *adj.* 启发式的
46. optimal ['ɔptiml] *adj.* 最优的, 最佳的
47. algorithm ['ælgəriðəm] *n.* 算法
48. validation [væli'deiʃnə] *n.* 有效, 证实
49. field test　现场测试, 现场试验

Notes

① 此句中"a control system that…, therefore…"是主语, 其中"that…,therefore…"是由"that"引导的一个定语从句, 用来修饰主语, 显然此从句的结构是"因为……所以……"; "is sometimes called…"是本句的谓语。

② e.g.: exampli gratia, (拉丁语)例如。

1.2 What is Feedback and What are Its Effects?

> *During reading the following section, try to answer following questions:*
> 1. What is the feedback control?
> 2. What are the effects of feedback on a control system?

The motivation of using feedback, illustrated by the examples in Section (1), is somewhat oversimplified. In these examples, the use of feedback is shown to be for the purpose of reducing the error between the reference input and the system output. However, the significance of the effects of feedback in control systems is more complex than is demonstrated by these simple examples. The reduction of system error is merely one of the many important effects that feedback may have upon a system. We show in the following sections that feedback also has effects on such system performance characteristics as **stability, bandwidth, overall gain, disturbance,** and **sensitivity**.

To understand the effects of feedback on a control system, it is essential that we examine this phenomenon in a broad sense. When feedback is deliberately introduced for the purpose of control, its existence is easily identified. However, there are numerous situations wherein a physical system that we normally recognize as an inherently nonfeedback system turn out to have feedback when it is observed in a certain manner. In general, we can state that whenever a closed sequence of **cause-and-effect relationships**[①] exists among the variables of a system, feedback is said to exist. The viewpoint will inevitably admit feedback in a large number of systems that ordinarily would be identified as nonfeedback systems. However, with the availability of the feedback and control system theory, this general definition of feedback enables numerous systems, with or without physical feedback, to be studied in a systematic way once the existence of feedback in the sense mentioned previously is established.

We shall now investigate the effects of feedback on the various aspects of system performance. Without the necessary mathematical foundation of linear-system theory, at this point we can only rely on simple static-system notation for our discussion. Let us consider the simple feedback system configuration shown in Figure 1.2.1, where r is the input signal, y the output signal, e the error, and b the feedback signal. The parameters G and H may be considered as constant gains. By simple algebraic manipulations, it is simple to show that the input-output relation of he system is

$$M = \frac{y}{r} = \frac{G}{1+GH} \quad (1.2.1)$$

Using this basic relationship of the feedback system structure, we can uncover some of the significant effects of feedback.

1.2.1 Effect of Feedback on Overall Gain

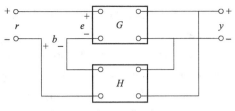

Figure 1.2.1 Feedback system.

As seen Eq. (1.2.1), feedback affects the gain G of a nonfeedback system by a factor $1+GH$. The system of Figure 1.2.1 is said to have **negative feedback,** since a minus sign is assigned to the feedback signal. The quantity GH may itself include a minus sign, so *the general effect of feedback is that is may increase or decrease the gain G*. In a practical control system, G and H are functions of frequency, so the magnitude of $1+GH$ may be greater than 1 in one frequency range but less than 1 in another. Therefore, *feedback could increase the system gain in one frequency range but decrease it in another.*

1.2.2 Effect of Feedback on Stability

Stability is a notion that describes whether the system will be able to follow the input command, or be useful in general. In a nonrigorous manner, *a system is said to be unstable if its output is out of control*. To investigate the effect of feedback on stability, we can again refer to the expression in Eq. (1.2.1). If $GH=-1$, the output of the system is infinite for any finite input, and the system is said to be unstable. Therefore, we may state that *feedback can cause a system that is originally stable to become unstable.* Certainly, feedback is a two-edged sword;

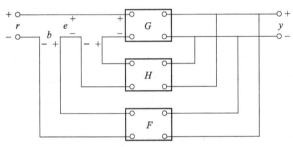

Figure 1.2.2 Feedback system with two feedback loops.

when used improperly, it can be harmful. It should be pointed out, however, that we are only dealing with the static case here, and in general, $GH=-1$ is not the only condition for instability.

It can be demonstrated that one of the advantages of incorporating feedback is hat it can stabilize an unstable system. Let us assume that the feedback system in Figure 1.2.1 is unstable because $GH=-1$. If we introduce another feedback loop through a negative feedback gain of F, as shown in Figure 1.2.2, the input-output relation of the overall system is

$$\frac{y}{r} = \frac{G}{1+GH+GF} \qquad (1.2.2)$$

It is apparent that although the properties of G and H are such that the inner-loop feedback system is unstable, because $GH=-1$, the overall system can be stable by proper selection of the outer-loop feedback gain F. In practice, GH is a function of frequency, and the stability condition of the closed-loop system depends on the **magnitude** and **phase** of GH. The bottom line is that *feedback can improve stability or be harmful to stability if it is not applied properly.*

1.2.3 Effect of Feedback on Sensitivity

Sensitivity considerations often are important in the design of control systems. Since all physical elements have properties that change with environment and age, we cannot always consider the parameters of a control system to be completely stationary over the entire operating life of the system. For instance, the winding resistance of an electric motor changes as the temperature of the motor rises during operation. The electronic typewriter described in Section (1) sometimes may not operate normally when first turned on due to the still-changing system parameters during warm-up. This phenomenon is sometimes called "morning sickness". Most duplicating machines have a warm-up period during which operation is blocked out when first turned on.

In general, a good control system should be very insensitive to parameter variations but sensitive to the input commands. We shall investigate what effect feedback has on the sensitivity to parameter variations. Referring to the system shown in Figure 1.2.1, we consider G to be a gain parameter that may very. The sensitivity of the gain of the overall system, M, to the variation in G is defined as

$$S_G^M = \frac{\partial M / M}{\partial G / G} = \frac{\text{percentage change in } M}{\text{percentage change in } G} \qquad (1.2.3)$$

where ∂M denotes the incremental change in M due to the incremental change in G, ∂G. By using Eq.(1.2.1), the sensitivity function is written

$$S_G^M = \frac{\partial M}{\partial G} \cdot \frac{M}{G} = \frac{1}{1+GH} \qquad (1.2.4)$$

This relation shows that if GH is a positive constant, the magnitude of the sensitivity function can be made arbitrarily small by increasing GH, provided[2] that the system remains stable. It is apparent that in an open-loop system, the gain of the system will respond in a one-to-one fashion to the variation in G (i.e., $S_G^M = 1$). We again remind you that in practice, GH is a function of frequency; the magnitude of $1+GH$ may be less than unity over some frequency ranges, so that feedback could be harmful to the sensitivity to parameter variations in certain cases. In general, the sensitivity of the system gain of a feedback system to parameter variations depends on where the parameter is located. The reader can derive the sensitivity of the system in Figure 1.2.1 due to the variation of H.

1.2.4 Effect of Feedback on External Disturbance or Noise

All physical systems are subject to some types of extraneous signals or noise during operation. Examples of these signals are thermal-noise voltage in electronic circuits and brush or commutator noise in electric motors. External disturbance, such as wind gust acting on an antenna, is also quite common in control systems. Therefore, in the design of a control system, considerations should be given so that the system is insensitive to noise and disturbances and sensitive to input commands.

The effect of feedback on noise and disturbance depends greatly on where these extraneous signals occur in the system. No general conclusions can be reached, but in many situations, *feedback can reduce the effect of noise and disturbance on system performance*. Let us refer to the system shown in Figure 1.2.3, in which r denotes the command signal and n is the noise signal. In the absence of feedback, $H=0$, the output y due to n acting alone is

$$y = G_2 n \qquad (1.2.5)$$

With the presence of feedback, the system output due to n acting alone is

$$y = \frac{G_2}{1+G_1G_2H}n \qquad (1.2.6)$$

Comparing Eq.(1.2.6) with Eq.(1.2.5) shows that the noise component in the output of Eq.(6) is reduced by the factor $1+G_1G_2H$ if the latter is greater than unity and the system is kept stable.

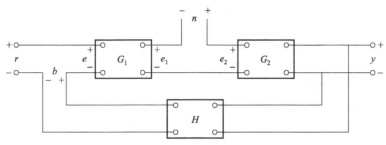

Figure 1.2.3 Feedback system with a noise signal.

In Chapter 4 the feedforward and forward controller configurations are used along with feedback to reduce the effects of disturbance and noise inputs. In general, feedback also has effects on such performance characteristics as bandwidth, impedance, transient response, and frequency response. These effects will become known as we continue.

Selected from "*Automatic Control System, Seventh Edition, Benjamin C.Kuo, Prentice-Hall Inc*, 1995"

Words and Expressions

1. motivation   [məuti'veiʃən]   *n.* 动机
2. oversimplify   ['əuvə'simplifai]   *vt.* 过于简化
3. bandwidth   ['bəndwið]   *n.* 带宽; 误差范围
4. gain   [gein]   *n.* 增益
5. sensitivity   [sensi'tiviti]   *n.* 灵敏度
6. sense   [sens]   *n.v.* 感受, 检测
7. inevitable   [in'evitəbl]   *adj.* 不可避免的
8. numerous   ['nju:mərəs]   *adj.* 众多的, 大量的
9. static-system   静态系统
10. algebraic   ['ældʒibrik]   *adj.* 代数的
11. nonrigorous   [nɔn'rigərəs]   *adj.* 不严密的
12. infinite   ['infənit]   *adj.* 无穷大
13. two-edged   [tu:'edʒd]   *adj.* 双刃的
14. magnitude   ['mægnitju:d]   *n.* 大小, 幅值
15. phase   [feiz]   *n.* 相角, 相位
16. stationary   ['steiʃnəri]   *adj.* 静止的, 平稳的
17. winding   ['waindiŋ]   *adj.* 卷绕的; *n.* 线圈, 绕组
18. resistance   [ri'zistəns]   *n.* 电阻, 阻抗
19. incremental   ['inkrimɛntəl]   *adj.* 增加的; *n.* 增量
20. duplicate   ['dju:plikeit]   *vt.* 加倍, 复写, 复制

21. thermal-noise ['θə:məl-nɔiz] n. 热噪声
22. voltage ['vəultidʒ] n. 电压,伏特数
23. brush [brʌʃ] n. 电刷
24. commutator ['kɔmjuteitə] n. 整流器
25. gust [gʌst] n. 冲击
26. antenna [æn'tenə] n. 天线
27. impedance [im'pi:dəns] n. 阻抗
28. transient [trænsiənt] adj. 瞬时的
29. transient response 瞬时响应
30. frequency response 频率响应

Notes

① 因果关系,指的是系统输出只和当前时刻及其以前各时刻的输入有关,而与当前时刻以后的各个时刻输入无关。这是系统物理可实现的一个基本要求。
② "provided" 连接词,与"that"连用表示"只要……,以……为条件"。

Exercises

1. *Complete the notes below with words taken from the text above.*
   (1) In a nonrigorous manner, _____ is said to be _____ if its output is _____. To investigate the effect of feedback on _____, we can again refer to the expression in Eq. (1.2.1). _____, the output of the system is _____ for any finite _____, and the system is said _____.
   (2) Control configuration is the _____ and _____ of the actuators and sensors on _____ to be controlled, and is an aspect of system design that is very important.
   (3) _____ are developed in several ways. _____ consists of applying various laws of physics (e.g., Newton's equations, energy conservation, or flow balance) to derive ODE or PDE models. _____ or _____ consists of developing models from observed or collected _____.
   (4) Simple controllers include the _____ (P), the _____ (PD), the _____, and the _____ controllers, which are widely and effectively used in many industries.

2. *Put the following into Chinese:*
   stability   sensitivity   actuator   sensor
   transducer   linear quadratic regulator (LQR)   linear quadratic controller
   simulation   temperature   flow rate   pressure
   concentration   level

3. *Put the following into English:*
   幅值   相角   闭环   开环   可编程逻辑控制器
   模型   黑箱   经验模型   比例   比例加微分
   比例加积分

Reading Material:

Root-Locus Technique

1. Introduction

We have demonstrated the importance of the poles and zeros of the closed-loop transfer function of a linear control system on the dynamic performance of the system. The roots of the characteristic equation, which are the poles of the closed-loop transfer function, determine the absolute and the relative stability of linear SISO systems. Keep in mind that the transient properties of the system also depend on the zeros of the closed-loop transfer function.

An important study in linear control systems is the investigation of the trajectories of the roots of the characteristic equation—or, simply, the root loci—when a certain system parameter varies.

The basic properties and the systematic construction of the root loci are first due to W.R.Evans. In this material we show how to construct these loci by following some simple rules. For plotting the root loci accurately, one can always use a root-locus program and a digital computer. For example, the programs ROOTLOCI in the ACSP package, **rlplot** in the CSAD toolbox, and ROOT LOCUS of the Program CC, just to name a few, can all be used to generate the data and plots of the root loci given the loop transfer function. If we were learning to be a technician, all we have to do is get familiar with the application of one of these programs. However, it is far more important to learn the basics of the root loci, their properties, as well as how to interpret the data provided by the root loci for analysis and design purposes. As an intelligent engineer, we must know if the data provided by the root loci are indeed correct, and be able to derive vital information from the root loci. The material is prepared with these objectives in mind.

The root-locus technique is not confined to the study of control systems. In general, the method can be applied to study the behavior of roots of any algebraic equation with variable parameters. The general root-locus problem can be formulated by referring to the following algebraic equation of the complex variable, say, s:

$$F(s)=P(s)+KQ(s)=0 \qquad (1.2.7)$$

Where $P(s)$ is an nth-order polynomial of s,

$$P(s)=s^n + a_{n-1}s^{n-1} + \cdots + a_1 s + a_0 \qquad (1.2.8)$$

and $Q(s)$ is an mth-order polynomial of s; n and m are positive integers.

$$Q(s)=s^m + b_{m-1}s^{m-1} + \cdots + b_1 s + b_0 \qquad (1.2.9)$$

For the present, we do not place any limitations on the relative magnitudes between n and m. K in Eq.(1.2.7) is a real constant that can vary from $-\infty$ to $+\infty$.

The coefficients $a_0, a_2, \cdots, a_{n-1}, b_1, b_2, \cdots, b_{m-1}$ are considered to be real and fixed.

Root loci of multiple-variable parameters can be treated by varying one parameter at a time. The resultant loci are called the **root contours**. By replacing s with z in Eqs. (1.2.7) through

(1.2.9), we can construct the root loci of the characteristic equation of a linear discrete-data system in a similar fashion.

For the purpose of identification, we define the following categorie of root loci based on the sign of K:

① RL: the portion of the root loci when K is positive; $0 \leqslant K < \infty$.
② CRL (complementary root loci): the portion of the root loci when K is negative.
③ RC (root contours): contour of roots when more than one parameter varies.
④ Root loci: refers to the total root loci for $-\infty < K < \infty$.

2. Basic Properties of the Root Loci

Since our main interest is control systems, let us consider the closed-loop transfer function of a single-loop control system:

$$\frac{Y(s)}{R(s)} = \frac{G(s)}{1+G(s)H(s)} \quad (1.2.10)$$

Keeping in mind that the transfer function of multiple-loop SISO systems can also be expressed in a similar form. The characteristic equation of the closed-loop system is obtained by setting the denominator polynomial of $Y(s)/R(s)$ to zero. Thus the roots of the characteristic equation must satisfy

$$1+G(s)H(s)=0 \quad (1.2.11)$$

Suppose that $G(s)H(s)$ contains a variable parameter K as a multiplying factor, such that the rational function can be written as

$$G(s)H(s) = \frac{KQ(s)}{P(s)} \quad (1.2.12)$$

where $P(s)$ and $Q(s)$ are polynomials as defined in Eqs.(1.2.8) and (1.2.9), respectively. Equation (1.2.11) is written

$$1 + \frac{KQ(s)}{P(s)} = \frac{P(s)+KQ(s)}{P(s)} = 0 \quad (1.2.13)$$

The numerator polynomial of Eq. (1.2.13) is identical to Eq. (1.2.7). Thus by considering that the loop transfer function $G(s)H(s)$ can be written in the form of Eq. (1.2.12), we have identified the root loci of a control system with the general root-locus problem.

When the variable parameter K does not appear as a multiplying factor of $G(s)H(s)$, we can always condition the functions in the form of Eq. (1.2.7). As an illustrative example, consider that the characteristic equation of a control system is

$$s(s+1)(s+2) + s^2 + (3+2K)s + 5 = 0 \quad (1.2.14)$$

To express the last equation in the form of Eq. (1.2.13), *we divide both sides of the equation by the terms that do not contain K*, and we get

$$1 + \frac{2Ks}{s(s+1)(s+2)+s^2+3s+5} = 0 \quad (1.2.15)$$

Comparing the last equation with Eq. (1.2.13), we get

$$\frac{Q(s)}{P(s)} = \frac{2s}{s^3+4s^2+5s+5} \quad (1.2.16)$$

Now K is isolated as a multiplying factor to the function $Q(s)/P(s)$.

We shall show that the root loci of Eq. (1.2.11) can be constructed based on the properties of $Q(s)/P(s)$. In case where $G(s)H(s)=KQ(s)/P(s)$, the root-locus problem is another example in which the characteristics of the closed-loop system, in this case represented by the roots of the characteristic equation, are determined from the knowledge of the loop transfer function $G(s)H(s)$.

Now we are ready to investigate the conditions under which Eq. (1.2.11) or Eq. (1.2.13) is satisfied. Let us express $G(s)H(s)$ as

$$G(s)H(s)=KG_1(s)H_1(s) \tag{1.2.17}$$

Where $G_1(s)H_1(s)$ does not contain the variable parameter K. Then Eq. (1.2.11) is written

$$G_1(s)H_1(s) = -\frac{1}{K} \tag{1.2.18}$$

To satisfy Eq. (1.2.18), the following conditions must be satisfied simultaneously:

Condition on Magnitude

$$|G_1(s)H_1(s)| = \frac{1}{|K|} \quad -\infty < K < \infty \tag{1.2.19}$$

Condition on Angles

$$\angle G_1(s)H_1(s)=(2i+1)\pi \quad K \geq 0$$
$$=\text{odd multiples of } \pi \text{ radians or } 180° \tag{1.2.20}$$
$$\angle G_1(s)H_1(s)=2i\pi \quad K \leq 0$$
$$=\text{even multiples of } \pi \text{ radians or } 180° \tag{1.2.21}$$

where $i=0, \pm 1, \pm 2, \cdots$ (any integer).

In practice, the conditions stated in Eqs. (1.2.19) through (1.2.21) play different roles in the construction of the root loci.

- The conditions on angles in Eq. (1.2.20) or Eq. (1.2.21) are used to determine the trajectories of the root loci in the s-plane.
- Once the root loci are drawn, the values of K on the loci are determined by using the condition on magnitude in Eq. (1.2.19).

The construction of the root loci is basically a graphical problem, although some of the properties are derived analytically. The graphical construction of the root loci is based on knowledge of the poles and zeros of the function $G(s)H(s)$. In other words, $G(s)H(s)$ must first be written as

$$G(s)H(s) = KG_1(s)H_1(s) = \frac{K(s+z_1)(s+z_2)\cdots(s+z_m)}{(s+p_1)(s+p_2)\cdots(s+p_n)} \tag{1.2.22}$$

where the zeros and poles of $G(s)H(s)$ are real or in complex-conjugate pairs.

Applying the conditions in Eqs. (1.2.19), (1.2.20), and (1.2.21) to Eq. (1.2.22), we have

$$|G_1(s)H_1(s)| = \frac{\prod_{k=1}^{m}|s+z_k|}{\prod_{j=1}^{n}|s+p_j|} = \frac{1}{|K|} \quad -\infty<K<\infty \tag{1.2.23}$$

For $0 \leqslant K \leqslant \infty$ (RL):

$$\angle G_1(s)H_1(s) = \sum_{k=1}^{m}\angle(s+z_k) - \sum_{j=1}^{n}\angle(s+p_j) = (2i+1)\times 180° \qquad (1.2.24)$$

For $-\infty < K \leqslant 0$ (CRL):

$$\angle G_1(s)H_1(s) = \sum_{k=1}^{m}\angle(s+z_k) - \sum_{j=1}^{n}\angle(s+p_j) = 2i\times 180° \qquad (1.2.25)$$

where $i=0, \pm 1, \pm 2, \cdots$

The graphical interpretation of Eq. (1.2.24) is that any point s_1 on the RL that corresponds to a positive value of K must satisfy the condition:

The difference between the sums of the angles of the vectors drawn from the zeros and those from the poles of $G(s)H(s)$ to s_1 is an odd multiple of $180°$.

For negative values of K, any point s_1 on the CRL must satisfy the condition:

The difference between the sums of the angles of the vectors drawn from the zeros and those from the poles of $G(s)H(s)$ to s_1 is an even multiple of $180°$.

Once the root loci are constructed, the values of K along the loci can be determined by writing Eq. (1.2.23) as

$$|K| = \frac{\prod_{j=1}^{n}|s+p_j|}{\prod_{k=1}^{m}|s+z_k|} \qquad (1.2.26)$$

The value of K at any point s_1 on the root loci is obtained from Eq. (1.2.26) by substituting the value of s_1 into the equation. Graphically, the numerator of Eq. (1.2.26) represents the product of the lengths of the vectors drawn from the poles of $G(s)H(s)$ to s_1, and the denominator represents the product of lengths of the vectors drawn from the zeros of $G(s)H(s)$ to s_1. If the point s_1 is on the RL, K is positive; if s_1 is on the CRL, then K is negative.

To illustrate the use of Eqs. (1.2.24) to (1.2.26) for the construction of the root loci, let us consider the function

$$G(s)H(s) = \frac{K(s+z_1)}{s(s+p_2)(s+p_3)} \qquad (1.2.27)$$

The location of the poles and zero of $G(s)H(s)$ are arbitrarily assigned as shown in Figure 1.2.4. Let us select an arbitrary trial point s_1 in the s-plane and draw vectors directed from the poles and zeros of $G(s)H(s)$ to the point. If s_1 is indeed a point on the RL (K is positive), it must satisfy Eq. (1.2.24); that is, the angles of the vectors shown in Figure 1.2.4 must satisfy

$$\angle(s_1+z_1) - \angle s_1 - \angle(s_1+p_2) - \angle(s_1+p_3)$$
$$= \theta_{z1} - \theta_{p1} - \theta_{p2} - \theta_{p3} = (2i+1)\times 180° \qquad (1.2.28)$$

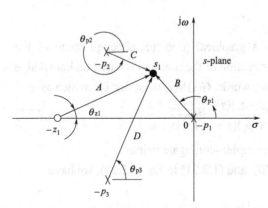

Figure 1.2.4 Pole-zero configuration of $G(s)H(s)=K(s+z_1)/[s(s+p_2)(s+p_3)]$.

where $i=0, \pm 1, \pm 2, \cdots$. As shown in Figure 1.2.4, the angles of the vectors are measured with the positive real axis as reference. Similarly, if s_1 is a point on the CRL (K is negative), it must satisfy Eq. (1.2.25); that is,

$$\angle(s_1+z_1)-\angle s_1-\angle(s_1+p_2)-\angle(s_1+p_3) \\ =\theta_{z1}-\theta_{p1}-\theta_{p2}-\theta_{p3}=2i\times 180° \quad (1.2.29)$$

where $i=0, \pm 1, \pm 2, \cdots$.

If s_1 is found to satisfy either Eq. (1.2.28) or Eq. (1.2.29), Eq. (1.2.26) is used to find the magnitude of K at the point. As shown in Figure 1.2.4 the lengths of the vectors are represented by A, B, C, and D. The magnitude of K is

$$|K|=\frac{|s_1||s_1+p_2||s_1+p_3|}{|s_1+z_1|}=\frac{BCD}{A} \quad (1.2.30)$$

The sign of K depends on whether s_1 is on the RL or the CRL. Thus, given the function $G(s)H(s)$ with K as a multiplying factor and the poles and zeros are known, the construction of the root loci of the zeros of $1+G(s)H(s)$ involves the following two steps:

① A search for all the s_1 points in the s-plane that satisfy Eq. (1.2.24) for positive K. If the root loci for negative values of K are required, Eq. (1.2.25) must be satisfied.

② Use Eq. (1.2.26) to find the magnitude of K on the root loci.

We have established the basic conditions on the construction of the root-locus diagram. However, if we were to use the trial-and-error method just described, the search for all the root-locus points in the s-plane that satisfy Eq. (1.2.24) or Eq. (1.2.25) and Eq. (1.2.26) would be a very tedious task. Years ago, when Evans first invented the root-locus technique, digital computer technology was still at its infancy; he had to devise a special tool, called the **Spirule,** which can be used to assist in adding and subtracting angles of vectors quickly, according to Eq. (1.2.24) or Eq. (1.2.25), Even with the Spirule, for the device to be effective, the user still has to know the general proximity of the roots in the s-plane.

With the availability of digital computers and efficient root-finding subroutines, the Spirule and the trial-and-error method have long become obsolete. Nevertheless, even with a high-speed computer and an effective root-locus program, the analyst should still have an in-depth understanding of the properties of the root loci in order to be able to manually sketch the root loci of simple and moderately complex systems and to interpret the computer results correctly, when applying the root loci for analysis and design of control systems.

Selected from "*Automatic Control Systems, Benjamin C. Kuo, Prentice Hall, 1995*"

Words and Expressions

1. characteristic equation　特征方程
2. absolute stability　绝对稳定性
3. relative stability　相对稳定性
4. trajectory　[trædʒiktəri]　*n.* 轨道；轨线
5. loci　['ləusai]　*n.* 轨迹 (pl.locus)

6. vital ['vaitl] adj. 重要的
7. complex variable 复变量
8. positive integer 正整数
9. root contours 根轨线
10. discrete-data 离散数据
11. multiplying factor 乘号
12. rational function 有理函数
13. denominaton polynomial 分母多项式
14. numerator polynomial 分子多项式
15. divide by 用……除以
16. isolate ['aisəleit] v. 使隔离,使孤立
17. magnitude ['mægnitju:d] n. 幅值
18. angles ['æŋgəls] n. 幅角
19. graphical [græfikəl] adj. 图表的,绘图的
20. complex-conjugate pairs 共轭复数对
21. assign [ə'sain] v. 配置
22. s-plane s 平面
23. tedious ['ti:djəs] adj. 乏味的,沉闷的
24. infancy [in'fənsi] n. 初期,幼年
25. subtract [səb'trækt] v. 减去
26. proximity [prɔk'simiti] n. 近似
27. subroutine [sʌb'ru:ti:n] n. 子程序
28. obsolete ['ɔbsəli:t] adj. 过时的,陈旧的
29. sketch [sketʃ] v. 拟定,勾画
30. moderate ['mɔdərit] adj. 中等的,适度的

1.3 Stability of Closed-Loop Control Systems

Before reading the text below, try to answer the following questions:
1. What is the important consequence in a closed-loop control system?
2. Do you know the general stability criterion?
3. What is the definition of stability for a linear control system?

An important consequence of feedback control is that it can cause oscillatory responses. If the oscillation has a small amplitude and damps out quickly, then the control system performance is generally considered to be satisfactory. However, under certain circumstances the oscillations may be undamped or even have an amplitude that increases with time until a physical limit is reached, such as a control valve being fully open or completely shut. In these situations, the closed-loop system is said to be *unstable*.

In this unit we analyze the stability characteristics of closed-loop systems and present several useful criteria for determining whether a system will be stable. Additional stability criteria based on frequency response analysis are not discussed here. But first we consider an illustrative example of a closed-loop system that can become unstable.

EXAMPLE

Consider the feedback control system shown in Figure 1.3.1 with the following transfer functions:

$$G_c = K_c \qquad G_v = \frac{1}{2s+1} \qquad (1.3.1)$$

$$G_p = G_L = \frac{1}{5s+1} \qquad G_m = \frac{1}{s+1} \qquad (1.3.2)$$

Show that the closed-loop system produces unstable responses if controller gain K_c is too large.

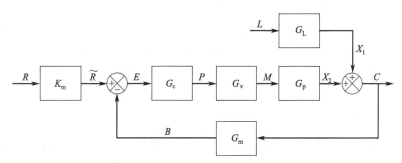

Figure 1.3.1   Standard block diagram of a feedback control system.

Solution

To determine the effect of K_c on the closed-loop response $c(t)$, we consider a unit step change in set point, $R(s) = 1/s$. We have derived the closed-loop transfer function for set-point changes:

$$\frac{C}{R} = \frac{K_m G_c G_v G_p}{1 + G_c G_v G_p G_m} \tag{1.3.3}$$

Substituting (1.3.1) and (1.3.2) into (1.3.3) and rearranging gives

$$C(s) = \frac{1}{s} \frac{K_c(s+1)}{10s^3 + 17s^2 + 8s + 1 + K_c} \tag{1.3.4}$$

After K_c is specified, $c(t)$ can be determined from the inverse Laplace transform of Eq. (1.3.4). But first the roots of the cubic polynomial in s must be determined before performing the partial fraction expansion. These roots can be calculated using standard root-finding techniques.

The unstable response for Example is an oscillation where the amplitude grows in each successive cycle. In contrast, for an actual physical system the amplitudes would increase until a physical limit is reached or an equipment failure occurs. Since the final control element usually has saturation limits, the unstable response would manifest itself as a sustained oscillation with a constant amplitude instead of a continually increasing amplitude.

Clearly, a feedback control system must be stable as a prerequisite for satisfactory control. Consequently, it is of considerable practical importance to be able to determine under what conditions a control system becomes unstable. For example, what values of the PID controller parameters K_c, τ_I, and τ_D keep the controlled process stable?

1.3.1 General Stability Criterion

Most industrial processes are stable without feedback control. Thus, they are said to be *open-loop stable* or *self-regulating*. An open-loop stable process will return to the original steady state after a transient disturbance (one that is not sustained) occurs. By contrast there are a few processes, such as exothermic chemical reactors, that can be *open-loop unstable*. These processes are extremely difficult to operate without feedback control.

Before presenting various stability criteria, we introduce the following definition for unconstrained linear systems. We use the term "unconstrained" to refer to the ideal situation where there are no physical limits on the output variable.

Definition of stability[①]. *An unconstrained linear system is said to be stable if the output response is bounded for all bounded inputs. Otherwise it is said to be unstable.*

By a bounded input, we mean an input variable that stays within upper and lower limits for all values of time. For example, consider a variable $x(t)$ that varies with time. If $x(t)$ is a step or sinusoidal function, then it is bounded. However, the functions $x(t) = t$ and $x(t) = e^{3t}$ are not bounded.

Characteristic Equation

As a starting point for the stability analysis, consider the block diagram in Figure 1.3.1. Using block diagram algebra, we obtain

$$C = \frac{K_m G_c G_v G_p}{1+G_{OL}} R + \frac{G_L}{1+G_{OL}} L \qquad (1.3.5)$$

where G_{OL} is the open-loop transfer function, $G_{OL}=G_c G_v G_p G_m$.

For the moment consider set-point changes only, in which case Eq. (1.3.5) reduces to the closed-loop transfer function,

$$\frac{C}{R} = \frac{K_m C_c G_v G_p}{1+G_{OL}} \qquad (1.3.6)$$

If G_{OL} is a ratio of polynomials in s (i.e., a *rational function*), then the closed-loop transfer function in Eq. (1.3.6) is also a rational function. After a rearrangement it can be factored into poles (p_i) and zeroes (z_i) as

$$\frac{C}{R} = K' \cdot \frac{(s-z_1)(s-z_2)\cdots(s-z_m)}{(s-p_1)(s-p_2)\cdots(s-p_n)} \qquad (1.3.7)$$

where K' is a multiplicative constant selected to give the correct steady-state gain. To have a physically realizable system, the number of poles must be greater than or equal to the number of zeroes, that is, $n \geq m$, Note that a *pole-zero cancellation* occurs if a zero and a pole have the same numerical value.

Comparing Eqs. (1.3.6) and (1.3.7) indicates that the poles are also the roots of the following equation which is referred to as the *characteristic equation* of the closed-loop system:

$$1 + G_{OL} = 0 \qquad (1.3.8)$$

The characteristic equation plays a decisive role in determining system stability, as discussed later.

For a unit change in set point, $R(s) = 1/s$, and Eq. (1.3.7) becomes

$$C = \frac{K'}{s} \frac{(s-z_1)(s-z_2)\cdots(s-z_m)}{(s-p_1)(s-p_2)\cdots(s-p_n)} \qquad (1.3.9)$$

If there are no repeated poles (i.e., if they are all *distinct poles*), then the partial fraction expansion of Eq. (1.3.9) has the form

$$C(s) = \frac{A_0}{s} + \frac{A_1}{s-p_1} + \frac{A_2}{s-p_2} + \cdots + \frac{A_m}{s-p_n} \qquad (1.3.10)$$

where the $\{A_i\}$ can be determined. Taking the inverse Laplace transforms of Eq. (1.3.10) gives

$$c(t) = A_0 + A_1 e^{p_1 t} + A_2 e^{p_2 t} + \cdots + A_n e^{p_n t} \qquad (1.3.11)$$

Suppose that one of the poles is a positive real number, that is $p_k > 0$. Then it is clear from Eq. (1.3.11) that $c(t)$ is unbounded and thus the closed-loop system in Figure 1.3.1 is unstable. If p_k is a complex number, $p_k = a_k + jb_k$, with a positive real part ($a_k > 0$), then the system is also unstable. By constrast, if all of the poles are negative (or have negative real parts), then the system is stable. These considerations can be summarized in the following stability criterion:

General Stability Criterion. *The feedback control system in Figure* 1.3.1 *is stable if and only if all roots of the characteristic equation are negative or have negative real parts. Otherwise, the system is unstable.*

1.3.2 Routh Stability Criterion

In 1905 Routh published an analytical technique for determining whether any roots of a polynomial have positive real parts. According to the General Stability Criterion, a closed-loop system will be stable only if all of the roots of the characteristic equation have negative real parts. Thus, by applying Routh's technique to analyze the coefficients of the characteristic equation, we can determine whether the closed-loop system is stable. This approach is referred to as the Routh Stability Criterion. It can be applied only to systems whose characteristic equations are polynomials in s. Thus, the Routh Stability Criterion is not directly applicable to systems containing time delays, since an $e^{-\theta s}$ term appears in the characteristic equation where θ is the time delay. However, if $e^{-\theta s}$ is replaced by a Pade approximation then an *approximate* stability analysis can be performed. An *exact* stability analysis of systems containing time delays can be performed by direct root-finding or by using a frequency response analysis.

The Routh Stability Criterion is based on a characteristic equation that has the form

$$a_n s^n + a_{n-1} s^{n-1} + \cdots + a_1 s + a_0 = 0 \tag{1.3.12}$$

We arbitrarily assume that $a_n > 0$. If $a_n < 0$, we simply multiply Eq. (1.3.12) by -1 to generate a new equation that satisfies this condition. A *necessary* (but not sufficient) condition for stability is that all of the coefficients (a_0, a_1, $\cdots$, a_n) in the characteristic equation must be positive. If any coefficient is negative or zero, then at least one root of the characteristic equation lies to the right of, or on, the imaginary axis, and the system is unstable. If all of the coefficients are positive, we next construct the following Routh array:

Row				
1	a_n	a_{n-2}	a_{n-4}	$\cdots$
2	a_{n-1}	a_{n-3}	a_{n-5}	$\cdots$
3	b_1	b_2	b_3	$\cdots$
4	c_1	c_2		$\cdots$
$\vdots$	$\vdots$			
$n+1$	z_1			

The Routh array has $n + 1$ rows where n is the order of the characteristic equation, Eq. (1.3.12). The Routh array has a roughly triangular structure with only a single element in the last row. The first two are merely the coefficients in the characteristic equation, arranged according to odd and even powers of s. The elements in the remaining rows are calculated from the formulas:

$$b_1 = \frac{a_{n-1} a_{n-2} - a_n a_{n-3}}{a_{n-1}} \tag{1.3.13}$$

$$b_2 = \frac{a_{n-1} a_{n-4} - a_n a_{n-5}}{a_{n-1}} \tag{1.3.14}$$

$$c_1 = \frac{b_1 a_{n-3} - a_{n-1} b_2}{b_1} \tag{1.3.15}$$

$$c_2 = \frac{b_1 a_{n-5} - a_{n-1} b_3}{b_1} \tag{1.3.16}$$

Note that the expressions in the numerators of Eqs. (1.3.13) to (1.3.15) are similar to the calculation of a determinant for a 2×2 matrix except that the order of subtraction is reversed. Having constructed the Routh array, we can now state the Routh Stability Criterion:

Routh Stability Criterion. *A necessary and sufficient condition for all roots of the characteristic equation in Eq.* (1.3.12) *to have negative real parts is that all of the elements in left column of the Routh array are positive.*

Selected from *"Process Dynamics and Control, Dale E. Seborg etc. John Wiley & Sonsi, 1989"*

Words and Expressions

1. criterion [krai'tiəriən] *n.* 判据，准则
2. oscillatory ['ɔsileitəri] *adj.* 振动的
3. amplitude ['æmplitjuːd] *n.* 振幅，振荡
4. undamped [ʌn'dæmpt] *adj.* 无阻尼的，无衰减的
5. inverse [in'vəːs] *adj.* 逆的，相反的
6. cubic ['kjuːbik] *adj.* 立方的
7. polynomial [pɔli'nəumjəl] *n.* 多项式
8. partial ['pɑːʃəl] *adj.* 部分的，偏的
9. fraction ['frækʃən] *n.* 分数
10. successive [sək'sesiv] *adj.* 连续的
11. cycle ['saikl] *n.* 周期，循环
12. saturation [sætʃə'reiʃən] *n.* 饱和
13. manifest ['mænifest] *vt.* 表明，显示
14. prerequisite ['priːrekwizit] *adj.* 先决条件的，首先的
15. exothermic [eksəu'θəːmik] *adj.* 放热的
16. unconstrained [ʌnkən'streind] *adj.* 自由的，无约束的
17. sinusoidal [sainə'sɔidəl] *adj.* 正弦波的
18. rational function 有理函数
19. multiplicative [mʌlti'plikətiv] *n.* 乘法，乘子
20. cancellation [kænsə'leiʃən] *n.* 相消，删去
21. characteristic equation 特征方程
22. distinct pole [di'stiŋkt pəul] *n.* 孤立极点
23. coefficient [kəui'fiʃənt] *n.* 系数
24. imaginary axis [i'mædʒinəri 'ækis] *n.* 虚轴
25. triangular [trai'æŋgjulə] *adj.* 三角形的
26. odd [ɔd] *adj.* 奇的
27. even ['iːvən] *adj.* 偶的
28. power ['pauə] *n.* 幂
29. numerator ['njuːməreitə] *n.* 分子
30. matrix ['meitriks] *n.* 矩阵

Note

① 此类稳定性又称作外部稳定性，或有界输入、有界输出稳定性(bounded input bounded output stability)。

Exercises

1. *Complete the notes below with words taken from the text above.*
   (1) An important consequence of _____ is _____ can cause _____ responses. If the oscillation has a small _____ and _____ out quickly, then the control system performance is generally considered to be satisfactory.
   (2) The unstable response _____ Example 1 _____ an oscillation _____ the amplitude grows in each _____. In contrast, _____ an actual physical system the amplitudes would increase _____ a physical limit _____ reached _____ an equipment failure occurs.
   (3) An unconstrained linear system is said _____ if the output response is bounded _____. Otherwise it is said _____.

2. *Put the following into Chinese:*

   oscillatory   damp   unstable
   complex number   controlled variable   manipulated variable
   load variable   error
   process transfer function   pole-zero cancellation   self-regulating

3. *Put the following into English:*

   判据   拉氏变换   零点   极点   特征方程   系数
   偏差变量   比较器   伺服问题   给定变化   负载变化

Reading Material:

Frequency-Domain Analysis

1. Introduction

In practice the performance of a control system is measured more realistically by its time-domain characteristics. The reason is that the performance of most control systems is judged based on the time responses due to certain test signals. This is in contrast to the analysis and design of communication systems for which the frequency response is of more importance, since most of the signals to be processed are either sinusoidal or composed of sinusoidal components. We learned that the time response of a control system is usually more difficult to determine analytically, especially for high-order systems. In design problems there are no unified methods of arriving at a designed system that meets the time-domain performance specifications, such as maximum overshoot, rise time, delay time, settling time, and so on. On the other hand, in the frequency domain a wealth of graphical methods are available that are not limited to low-order systems. It is important to realize that there are correlating relations between the frequency-and time-domain performances in a linear system, so that the time-domain properties of the system can be predicted based on the frequency-domain characteristics. The frequency domain is also more convenient for measurements of system sensitivity to noise and parameter variations. With these in mind, we may consider the primary motivation of conducting control systems analysis and design in the frequency domain to be convenience and the availability of the existing analytical tools. Another reason is that it presents an alternative point of view to control system problems, which often provides valuable or crucial information in the complex analysis and design of control systems. Therefore, to conduct frequency-domain analysis of a linear control system does not imply that the system will be subject only to a sine-wave input. It may never be. Rather, from the frequency-response studies, we will be able to project the time-domain performance of the system.

The starting point for frequency-domain analysis of a linear system is its transfer function. It is well known from linear system theory that when the input to a linear time-invariant system is sinusoidal with amplitude R and frequency ω_0.

$$r(t) = R\sin\omega_0 t \quad (1.3.17)$$

the steady-state output of the system, $y(t)$, will be a sinusoid with the same frequency ω_0, but possibly with different amplitude and phase; that is,

$$y(t) = Y\sin(\omega_0 t + \phi) \quad (1.3.18)$$

where Y is the amplitude of the output sine wave and ϕ is the phase shift in degrees or radians.

Let the transfer function of a linear SISO system be $M(s)$; then the Laplace transforms of the input and the output are related through

$$Y(s) = M(s)R(s) \quad (1.3.19)$$

For sinusoidal steady-state analysis, we replace s by $j\omega$, and Eq. (1.3.19) becomes

$$Y(j\omega) = M(j\omega)R(j\omega) \quad (1.3.20)$$

By writing the function $Y(j\omega)$ as

$$Y(j\omega) = |Y(j\omega)|\angle Y(j\omega) \quad (1.3.21)$$

with similar definitions for $M(j\omega)$ and $R(j\omega)$, Eq. (1.3.20) leads to the magnitude relation between the input and the output:

$$|Y(j\omega)| = |M(j\omega)||R(j\omega)| \quad (1.3.22)$$

and the phase relation:

$$\angle Y(j\omega) = \angle M(j\omega) + \angle R(j\omega) \quad (1.3.23)$$

Thus for the input and output signals described by Eqs. (1.3.17) and (1.3.18), respectively, the amplitude of the output sinusoid is

$$Y = R|M(j\omega_0)| \quad (1.3.24)$$

and the phase of the output is

$$\phi = \angle M(j\omega_0) \quad (1.3.25)$$

Thus, by knowing the transfer function $M(s)$ of a linear system, the magnitude characteristic, $|M(j\omega)|$ and the phase characteristic, $\angle M(j\omega)$, completely describe the steady-state performance when the input is a sinusoid. The crux of frequency-domain analysis is that the amplitude and phase characteristics of a closed-loop system can be used to predict both time-domain transient and steady-state system performances.

2. Frequency Response of Closed-Loop Systems

For the single-loop control system configuration studied, the closed-loop transfer function is

$$M(s) = \frac{Y(s)}{R(s)} = \frac{G(s)}{1+G(s)H(s)} \qquad (1.3.26)$$

Under the sinusoidal steady-state, $s=j\omega$, Eq. (1.3.27) becomes

$$M(j\omega) = \frac{Y(j\omega)}{R(j\omega)} = \frac{G(j\omega)}{1+G(j\omega)H(j\omega)} \qquad (1.3.27)$$

The sinusoidal steady-state transfer function $M(j\omega)$ may be expressed in terms of its magnitude and phase; that is,

$$M(j\omega) = |M(j\omega)| \angle M(j\omega) \qquad (1.3.28)$$

Or $M(j\omega)$ can be expressed in terms of its real and imaginary parts:

$$M(j\omega) = \text{Re}[M(j\omega)] + j\text{Im}[M(j\omega)] \qquad (1.3.29)$$

The magnitude of $M(j\omega)$ is

$$|M(j\omega)| = \left|\frac{G(j\omega)}{1+G(j\omega)H(j\omega)}\right| = \frac{|G(j\omega)|}{\|1+G(j\omega)H(j\omega)\|} \qquad (1.3.30)$$

and the phase of $M(j\omega)$ is

$$\angle M(j\omega) = \phi_M(j\omega) = \angle G(j\omega) - \angle[1+G(j\omega)H(j\omega)] \qquad (1.3.31)$$

If $M(s)$ represents the input-output transfer function of an electric filter, the magnitude and phase of $M(j\omega)$ indicate the filter characteristics on the input signal. Figure 1.3.2 shows the gain and phase characteristics of an ideal low-pass filter that has a sharp cutoff frequency at ω_c. It is well known that an ideal filter characteristic is physically unrealizable. In many ways the design of control systems is quite similar to filter design, and the control system is regarded as a signal processor. In fact, if the ideal low-pass-filter characteristics shown in Figure 1.3.2 were physically realizable, they would be highly desirable for a control system, since all signals would be passed without distortion below the frequency ω_c, and eliminated completely at frequencies above ω_c, where noise may lie.

If ω_c is increased indefinitely, the output $Y(j\omega)$ would be identical to the input $R(j\omega)$ for all frequencies. Such a system would follow a step-function input in the time domain exactly. From Eq. (1.3.31) we see that for $|M(j\omega)|$ to be unity at all frequencies, the magnitude of $G(j\omega)$ must be infinite. An infinite magnitude of $G(j\omega)$ is, of course, impossible to achieve in practice, nor would it be desirable, since most control systems become unstable when their loop gains become very high. Furthermore, all control systems are subject to noise during operation. Thus, in addition to responding to the input signal, the system should be able to reject

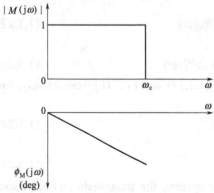

Figure 1.3.2 Gain-phase characteristics of an ideal low-pass filter.

and suppress noise and unwanted signals. For control systems with high-frequency noise, such as air-frame vibration of an aircraft, the frequency response should have a finite cutoff frequency ω_c. The phase characteristics of the frequency response of a control system are also of importance, as we shall see that they affect the stability of the system.

Figure 1.3.3 illustrates typical gain and phase characteristics of a control system. As shown by Eqs. (1.3.31) and (1.3.32), the gain and phase of a closed-loop system can be determined from the foreward-path and loop transfer functions. In practice, the frequency

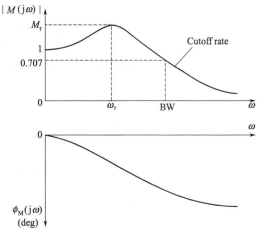

Figure 1.3.3 Typical gain-phase characteristics of a feedback control system.

responses of $G(s)$ and $H(s)$ can often be determined by applying sine-wave inputs to the system and sweeping the frequency from 0 to a value beyond the frequency range of the system.

3. Frequency-Domain Specifications

In the design of linear control systems using frequency-domain methods, it is necessary to define a set of specifications so that the performance of the system can be identified. Specifications such as the maximum overshoot, damping ratio, and so on, used in the time domain, can no longer be used directly in the frequency domain. The following frequency-domain specifications are often used in practice.

Resonant Peak M_r

The resonant peak M_r is the maximum value of $|M(j\omega)|$.

In general, the magnitude of M_r gives indication of the relative stability of a stable closed-loop system. Normally, a large M_r corresponds to a large maximum overshoot of the step response. For most control systems, it is generally accepted in practice that the desirable value of M_r should be between 1.1 and 1.5.

Resonant Frequency ω_r

The resonant frequency ω_r is the frequency at which the peak resonance M_r occurs.

Bandwidth BW

The bandwidth BW is the frequency at which $|M(j\omega)|$ drops to 70.7 percent of, or 3 dB down from, its zero-frequency value.

In general, the bandwidth of a control system gives an indication of the transient-response properties in the time domain. A large bandwidth corresponds to a faster rise time, since higher-frequency signals are more easily passed through the system. Conversely, if the bandwidth is small, only signals of relatively low frequencies are passed, and the time response will be slow and sluggish. Bandwidth also indicates the noise-filtering characteristics and the robustness of the system. The robustness represents a measure of the sensitivity of a system to parameter variations. A robust system is one that is insensitive to parameter variations.

Cutoff Rate. Often, bandwidth alone is inadequate to indicate the ability of a system in distinguishing signals from noise. Sometimes it may be necessary to look at the slope of $|M(j\omega)|$, which is called the cutoff rate of the frequency response, at high frequencies. Apparently, two systems can have the same bandwidth, but the cutoff rates may be different. The performance criteria for the frequency domain defined above are illustrated in Figure 1.3.3.

Selected from *"Automatic Control Systems, Benjamin C.Kuo, Prentice Hall, 1995"*

Words and Expressions

1. frequency-domain 频率域
2. time-domain 时间域
3. realistically [riə'listikli] *adv.* 实际地
4. high-order system 高阶系统
5. unified ['juːnifaid] *adj.* 统一的
6. maximum overshoot 最大超调
7. rise time 上升时间
8. delay time 滞后时间
9. settling time 建立 (置位, 稳定) 时间
10. low-order system 低阶系统
11. convenient [kən'viːniənt] *adj.* 方便的, 便利的
12. parameter variation 参数摄动
13. sine-wave [sain-weiv] *n.* 正弦波
14. crux [krʌks] *n.* 症结
15. low-pass filter 低通滤波器
16. signal processor 信号处理器
17. distortion [di'stɔːʃən] *n.* 失真, 变形
18. step-function 阶跃函数
19. unity ['juːniti] *n.* 一致, 联合
20. cutoff frequency 切断频率
21. damping ratio 衰减率
22. resonant peak ['rezənənt piːk] *n.* 共振尖峰
23. sluggish ['slʌgiʃ] *adj.* 迟滞的
24. cutoff rate 切断速率
25. slope [sləup] *n.* 斜面, 倾斜

1.4 The Design Process of Control System

> *During reading the following section, try to find out the answers for:*
> 1. Do you know the design process of a control system?
> 2. What factors may be influence the control system design?

Good design eludes definition, but you can usually recognize something that is well designed. One characteristic of good design is that it is exactly right for the specific application. Everything necessary is present, but everything unnecessary is absent.

The skills needed for good design entail experience, intuition, and esthetic sensibility. They are not easily learned from books. The most you ought to expect from any textbook on design (including this one) is to learn about some useful tools.

Like most books on control system design, this book presents tools that can be reduced to mathematical equations: analysis and simulation. Skill in the other aspects of design (such as conceptualization of the overall system, selection of components, dealing with constraints on time and money), which is as important as the mathematical analysis, is acquired and perfected through practical experience.

In practice one learns that most systems develop through evolution: not only biological systems, but also human inventions such as the automobile and the airplane. The sleek, high-performance automobile can be traced to the humble model T; the advanced tactical fighter, still on the contractors drawing boards, has its roots at Kitty Hawk.

Much of engineering is modifying existing designs. A new model of an existing product is designed to incorporate new technological advances: a new or improved sensor or actuator, a digital processor to replace an analog controller.

Imitation (often called "reverse engineering") is another common design technique. In its most obvious and least creative form you dissect an existing product, and copy the design. The process is legal unless the product copied has patent protection. A more creative use of imitation is to borrow ideas from one application and use them in another. You need to control the level of the liquid in a vessel; consider how it is done in your toilet tank. You must control the temperature of the liquid in the vessel; think of how it is done in your tropical fish tank.

Innovation is often limited by codes, standards, and engineering conservatism. The aircraft industry, for example, took many years to accept the "fly-by-wire" concept, by which the mechanical connections (rods or cables) between the pilot's controls (the stick and pedals) and the moveable aerodynamic control surfaces (the rudder, elevator, and ailerons) are replaced by electric wires carrying signals from the pilot's controls to a flight control computer and from the computer to actuators located at the control surfaces[1]. While engineering standards may retard progress, they are nevertheless necessary to prevent technological anarchy.

For all these reasons, you rarely get the opportunity to design an entirely new control system. But suppose the opportunity does arise. How would you proceed? The procedure you might follow is depicted in the form of a flow chart in Figure 1.4.1. As this figure shows, much of the design process falls outside the realm of analysis and simulation.

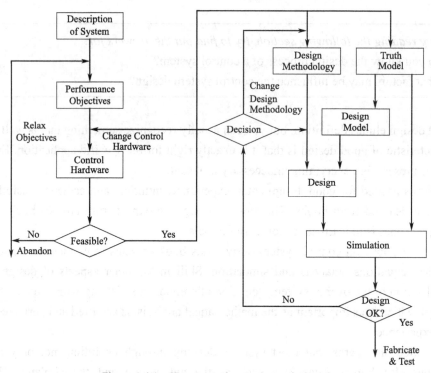

Figure 1.4.1 How control systems are designed.

First you need a physical appreciation of the problem by determining the physical quantity or quantities that must be controlled, and the level of performance required. A consideration that could determine how to proceed might be whether a system similar to the one in question has already been designed. If so, what improvements are you expected to make? If not, is the design perceived as being a difficult problem? Why? What resources (time, money) are at your disposal?

Obtaining a clear statement of the performance requirements is usually more difficult than you might think. In addition to those performance requirements that are explicitly specified (e.g., speed of response, tracking accuracy, disturbance rejection, stability margins), there may also be implicit requirements that are normally met by "conventional" control system designs. Being unaware of implicit performance requirements, you might be tempted to adopt a nonstandard and seemingly innovative design approach leading to a control system that fails to meet these requirements. In certain applications, for example, it may be known that high frequency noise is present from a variety of physical sources. With a conventional design approach it may be appropriate to ignore this noise because experience with this approach has shown that the effect of the noise is negligible. A different (unconventional) design approach that fails to account for the presence of the noise, however, might prove unsatisfactory.

It is often necessary to take nontechnical factors into consideration. Such factors may include economics, esthetics, schedules, or even the internal politics of the manufacturer. Consider, for example, the following scenarios:

- Your company produces a machine that includes a simple analog position servo costing a few dollars. The performance of the servo is adequate for many tasks, but an improved servo would make the machine more versatile and hence potentially worth a higher price. Eager to incorporate "high tech" into the company's product line and knowing that you are knowledgeable in the methods of modern control theory, the director of engineering assigns you the task of designing an improved control system using a microprocessor. You perform a design study (using, for example, the methods of this book) and determine that a microprocessor-based controller can indeed improve performance significantly, but would cost upwards of $100. What would you recommend?
- Suppose you find in your design study that the analog servo was not well designed. In particular, you find that the existing analog servo can be easily modified at no significant cost to yield essentially the same performance as the microprocessor-based system. Now what would you recommend?
- What if the director of engineering, before having been promoted to his present position, was the engineer who designed the original analog servo?
- You are engaged as a control system consultant to a building contractor, who wants to produce a controlled environment. Your fee is a percentage of the cost of the control system. After a detailed design and simulation study you determine that an inexpensive, commercial thermostat will perform nearly as well as a custom computer control costing several thousand dollars. Your recommendation?

As you see, factors other technical merit can influence engineering design choices.

After satisfying yourself that you understand the technical and nontechnical issues, you make a tentative selection of appropriate hardware. Only after the hardware is selected does the analytic phase of the design process begin.

The first step is to select an appropriate design methodology. (Here a knowledge of the methods discussed in this book would be helpful.) Concurrently you might begin developing a "truth model" of the dynamics of the process—a set of differential and algebraic equations that you are confident adequately represents the behavior of the process. The truth model, which can be used in a simulation for evaluating the performance of the design, is usually too complicated for design purposes. Hence you will probably want to develop a "design model" by simplifying the truth model. The design model should be simple enough to work with but must retain the essential features of the process. Striking the right balance between simplicity and verisimilitude is often a matter of insight and experience.

Having adopted a design methodology and developed a design model, you proceed to perform the design calculations. A generation ago, this step usually entailed laborious hand calculations and curve plotting. Nowadays extensive software is available to assist in performing the calculations, so this step is rarely burdensome.

The final step in the analytical phase of the design is to evaluate the performance of the system by means of a simulation based on the truth model. If the initial design appears to meet the performance and other requirements, fabrication and testing a prototype of the system design would be in order.

Rarely, however, will the starting design satisfy all the objectives, and it will generally be necessary to modify some aspect of the approach. Depending on the perceived deficiencies of the starting design, it might be necessary to change the control hardware. For example, it might be necessary to increase the "authority," i.e., the maximum effort level, of the actuator. Or to add an additional sensor.

On the other hand, it may be found that the design methodology used for the starting design was inappropriate. An example of this would be the decision to base the design on a continuous-time control, with a plan to implement an approximation to the continuous-time control using digital components, and the subsequent discovery that a discrete-time design approach, leading directly to a digital implementation, would have been a better choice of method. After making the appropriate changes, the relevant steps of the design process are repeated as many times as necessary to achieve the desired objectives.

Sometimes you may have to admit defeat: After repeating the design process over and over using different combinations of hardware and design approaches, you may conclude that you don't know how to design a system to meet the requirements. You may have to report that to the best of your knowledge and ability, the required performance requires a breakthrough in hardware or methodology—an invention that does not exist.

As you can see, the selection of the control algorithm is usually only a small part of the overall design process. Experience teaches that the control algorithm is rarely a critical factor in the overall system performance. If you succeed in designing a system (by any method) that works, it is unlikely that a different control algorithm can alone achieve as much as an order of magnitude improvement in performance or reduction in cost. Nevertheless, improvements of less than an order of magnitude may still not be inconsequential and may be worth pursuing.

An unfamiliar process may appear overwhelming unless you are familiar with some of the standard design techniques and conventional approaches. Consider, for example, the problem of controlling the motion of an aircraft so that it proceeds from a given starting point to a specified destination subject to a variety of constraints such as permissible trajectories, available fuel, safety, etc.(Specific instances of this problem include manned aircraft, cruise missiles, and remotely piloted vehicles. Needless to say, each of these applications differs widely in its details from the others.) Problems in aircraft flight control have mostly been solved, but it is instructive to speculate on how you would approach the problem if you didn't know that the solution exists.

In principle, the flight control problem could be formulated as a general optimization problem: to minimize a mathematically specified performance index subject to mathematical constraints. In practice, however, this approach is all but doomed to failure, for many reasons, including the following:
- *Multiple objectives and hidden constraints:* It is rare that everything you want a system to do can be expressed in a single performance criterion to be optimized. Often you only want a system to perform well enough, to be cost effective, and to be reliable. These verbal criteria resist quantitative formulation. Moreover, you may be unaware of all the

constraints. The only constraints you may know about are those that have been encountered with similar processes using conventional design approaches. A new design approach, however, may satisfy the known constraints but may create problems not previously encountered.
- *Number of state variables:* The number of state variables in a physical system is often larger than you want or need to deal with.
- *Disparate time scales:* Many processes entail phenomena that occur at widely disparate time scales. In a cruise aircraft application, for example, the position changes on a time scale of minutes or hours; the attitude, on the other hand, changes on a time scale of seconds; and the time scale for the dynamics of the actuators may be in milliseconds.
- *Uncertain dynamics:* The dynamics of the process are generally not as well known as you would like. Although you need some sort of model with which to evaluate performance of the system, your confidence in the model is not high enough to entrust to a brute-force mathematical optimization.
- *Failure to provide insight:* Even with confidence in the dynamics and a mathemati-cally justifiable performance criterion, you may be unwilling to entrust the solution of the problem to a computer-generated optimization, because you may not be able to get an intuitive appreciation of the solution.

For these reasons, among others, a prudent engineer would take a less radical approach. Experienced control system designers make use of such approaches often without conscious knowledge. In some application areas the approaches are virtually "canonical"; no one working in the area would consider any other design approach.

Selected from "*Advanced Control System Design*, *Bernard Friedland*, *Prentice Hall Inc*, 1996"

Words and Expressions

1. elude   [i'lu:d]   vt. 避免
2. entail   [in'teil]   vt. 需要，必需
3. intuition   [intju:'iʃən]   n. 直觉
4. esthetic   [i:s'θetik]   adj. 感觉的
5. conceptualization   [kən'septjuəlizeiʃən]   n. 概念化
6. sleek   [sli:k]   adj. 光滑的
7. humble   ['hʌmbl]   adj. 低级的
8. tactical   ['tæktikl]   adj. 战术的
9. contractor   [kən'træktə]   n. 承包者，合同户
10. analog   ['ænəlɔg]   n. 模拟量，相似体
11. reverse engineering   反转工程
12. dissect   [di'sekt]   v. 切成碎片；仔细研究；解剖
13. innovation   [inəu'veiʃən]   n. 改革，创新
14. pedal   ['pedl]   n. 踏板

15. rudder   ['rʌdə]   n. 方向舵
16. aileron   ['eilərɔn]   n. 副翼
17. retard   [ri'tɑ:d]   v. 延迟
18. anarchy   ['ænəki]   n. 混乱
19. depict   [di'pikt]   vt. 描述，描写
20. realm   [relm]   n. 区域
21. perceive   [pə'si:v]   v. 感知，察觉
22. disposal   [dis'pəuzəl]   n. 处理，安排
23. implicit   [im'plisit]   adj. 隐含的，内含的
24. scenario   [si'nɑ:riəu]   n. 假定；情节；方案
25. esthetics [i:s'θetikz]   n. 美学
26. versatile ['və:sətail]   adj. 通用的
27. consultant [kən'sʌltənt] n. 顾问
28. tentative ['tentətiv]   adj. 试验性的，尝试性的
29. methodology [meθə'dɔlədʒi] n. 方法论
30. verisimilitude [verisi'militju:d] n. 逼真
31. laborious [lə'bɔ:riəs]   adj. 艰苦的，费力的
32. burdensome ['bə:dnsəm]   adj. 繁重的，艰难的
33. prototype ['prəutətaip] n. 样机；标准，范例
34. deficiency [di'fiʃənsi]   n. 不定，故障
35. inconsequential [inkɔnsi'kwenʃəl] adj. 无意义的，不重要的
36. pursue   [pə'sju:]   vt. 追赶，追求
37. cruise missile [kru:z 'misail] n. 巡航导弹
38. vehicle   [vi'ikl]   n. 飞行器
39. doom   [du:m]   vt. 注定要
40. verbal   ['və:bəl]   adj. 口头的
41. constraint [kən'streint] n. 约束；强制
42. disparate ['dispərit]   adj. 不同的，不等的，不相称的
43. brute-force 强力
44. entrust   [in'trʌst]   v. 委托
45. intuitive [in'tju:itiv] adj. 直觉的
46. prudent   ['pru:dənt]   adj. 谨慎的，精明的
47. canonical [kə'nɔnikəl]   adj. 规范的

Note

① 此句主干为"The aircraft industry took many years to accept the fly-by-wire concept"，"by which"引导的状语从句，且在此从句中主语是"connections"，谓语结构是"are replaced by electric wires"，其中"carrying…"是动名词短语，作修饰"wires"的定语。

Exercises

1. Complete the notes below with words taken from the text above.

(1) The _____ needed for good _____ entail experience, _____ , and _____. They are not easily learned from books. The most you ought to expect from any textbook on _____ (including this one) is to learn about some useful _____.

(2) _____ unaware of implicit performance requirements, you _____ tempted to adopt a nonstandard and _____ innovative design approach _____ to a control system that fails to meet these requirements. _____ certain applications, for example, it _____ known that high frequency noise _____ present from a variety of physical sources. _____ a conventional design approach it may be appropriate to ignore this noise because experience _____ this approach _____ shown _____ the effect of the noise is negligible.

(3) Modern manufacturing generally can be classified _____ number of major industrial sectors such as oil, _____, power, _____, paper, _____, textile, _____, auto, _____, machine, _____, electronics, and _____, etc. The common _____ of these industries _____ that they _____ production plants.

(4) In general, the mathematical model _____ control purposes _____ identify the process variables (such as temperature, pressure, flow rate, composition, etc.) to determine _____ of these variables are _____ to the process or _____ from the process.

2. *Put the following into Chinese:*

design	decision	methodology	productivity
investment	fundamental	evaluating	benefit
distillation column	overhead	process dynamic	
manipulatable input	observable output	measurable disturbance	

3. *Put the following into English:*

控制系统设计	设计模型	炼油	化工	电力
造纸	水泥	纺织	塑料	钢铁
航空航天	再沸器			

Reading Material:

Control System Design Considerations

We described a general strategy for control system design (see Unit 1.4 and Figure 1.4.1). In this section we focus attention on two important steps:(1) specification of the control system objectives, and (2) selection of the control system configuration via the choice of controlled, manipulated, and measured variables.

The formulation of the control system objectives is strongly dependent on the objectives of the processing plant. The primary plant objective is to maximize profits by transforming raw

materials into useful products while satisfying a number of important criteria:
① **Safety.** It is essential that the plant be operated safely to protect the well-being of plant personnel and nearby communities. For example, safety considerations may limit the allowable temperature and pressure for a process vessel while explosion limits may restrict the hydrocarbon-to-oxygen ratio.
② **Environmental Regulations.** Processing plants must be operated so as to comply with environmental regulations concerning air and water quality as waste disposal.
③ **Product Specifications.** For the plant to sell its products, there are usually product specifications that must be met concerning product quality and production rate.
④ **Operational Constraints.** In addition to the above three criteria, it is necessary that process variables satisfy certain other operating constraints. For example, distillation columns are operated so as to avoid conditions such as flooding and weeping; reactor temperatures are often limited so as to prevent degradation of the catalyst or the onset of undesirable side reactions.

The plant objectives, in turn, determine the objectives for the control system as well as the controller set points.

1. Classification of Process Variables

For purposes of control system design, it is convenient to classify process variables as either inputs or outputs, as is shown in Figure 1.4.2. The output variables ($y_1, y_2, \cdots, y_N$) are process variables that ordinarily are associated with exit streams of a process or conditions inside a process vessel (e.g., compositions, temperatures, levels, and flow rates). A subset of the output variables is selected as variables to be controlled (i.e., *controlled variables*) in order to satisfy the plant and control objectives. The process inputs ($x_1, x_2, \cdots, x_M$) are physical variables that affect the process outputs. Typically, the inputs are associated with inlet streams (e.g., feed composition or feed flow rate) or environmental conditions (e.g., ambient temperature). However, an exit flow rate from a process can also be an "input" from a control point of view if the flow rate is used as a manipulated variable or if the magnitude of the flow rate is determined by downstream units. For example, the flow rate of an exit stream from a storage tank may be adjusted by a downstream unit if the stream serves as a feed to that unit. Some of the process inputs are specified as manipulated variables, while the other inputs are considered to be disturbance variables, specified by the external environment.

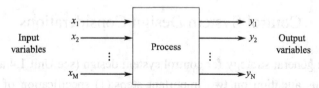

Figure 1.4.2 Process with multiple inputs and multiple outputs.

In general, it is not feasible to control all of the output variables for a number of reasons:
① It may not be possible or economical to measure all of the outputs, especially compositions.
② There may not be enough manipulated variables.

③ Potential control loops may be impractical because of slow dynamics, a low sensitivity to available manipulated variables, or interactions with other control loops.

In general, controlled variables are measured on-line and the measurements are used for feedback control. However, it is theoretically possible to control a process variable that is not measured by using a mathematical model of the process to calculate the value of the unmeasured controlled variable. This inferential control strategy was proposed by Brosilow and co-workers to control product composition of a distillation column by inferring mole fraction from flow rate and temperature measurements. Inferential control schemes have also been used for product dryness and digester control in pulp mills.

2. Selection of Controlled Variables

The consideration of plant and control objectives has led to a number of suggested guidelines for the selection of controlled variables from the available output variables:

Guideline 1.

Select variables that are not self-regulating. A common example is liquid level in a storage vessel with a pump in the exit line.

Guideline 2.

Choose output variables that may exceed equipment and operating constraints (e.g., temperatures, pressures, and compositions).

Guideline 3.

Select output variables that are a direct measure of product quality (e.g., composition, refractive index) or that strongly affect it (e.g., temperature, pressure).

Guideline 4.

Choose output variables that seriously interact with other controlled variables. The steam header pressure for a plant boiler that supplies several downstream units is an example of this type of output variable.

Guideline 5.

Choose output variables that have favorable dynamic and static characteristics. Ideally, there should be at least one manipulated variable that has a significant, direct, and rapid effect on each controlled variable.

These five guidelines should not be considered to be hard and fast rules. Also, for a particular application the guidelines may be inconsistent and thus result in a conflict. As an example of their use, an output variable such as temperature must be kept in limits (Guideline 2). Temperature could also affect other output variables (e.g., composition, pressure) and thus also should be selected according to Guideline 4. If there were a conflict, Guideline 2 would be the overriding concern in this situation.

3. Selection of Manipulated Variables

Based on the plant and control objectives, a number of guidelines have been proposed for the selection of manipulated variables from among the input variables:

Guideline 6.

Select inputs that have large effects on the controlled variables.

Thus, for each control loop it is desirable that the steady-state gain between the manipulated variable and the controlled variable be as large as possible. Also, it is important that the manipulated variable have a large enough range. For example, if a distillation column operates at a steady-state reflux ratio of five, it will be much easier to control the level in the reflux drum by using the reflux flow rather than the distillate flow rate, since the reflux flow rate is five times larger. However, the effect of this choice on the product compositions must also be considered in making the final decision.

Guideline 7.

Choose inputs that rapidly affect the controlled variables.

Clearly, it is desirable the a manipulated variable affect the corresponding controlled variable as quickly as possible. Also, any time delays or time constants that are associated with the manipulated variable should be small relative to the dominant process time constant.

Guideline 8.

The manipulated variables should affect the controlled variables directly rather than indirectly.

Compliance with this guideline usually results in a control loop with favorable static and dynamic characteristics. For example, consider the problem of controlling the exit temperature of a process stream that is heated by steam in a shell and tube heat exchanger. It is preferable to throttle the steam flow to the heat exchanger rather than the condensate flow from the shell, since the steam flow rate has a more direct effect on the steam pressure inside the shell and thus on the steam saturation temperature and the rate of heat transfer.

Guideline 9.

Avoid recycling of disturbances.

As Newell and Lee have noted, it is preferable *not* to manipulate an inlet stream or a recycle stream, because disturbances tend to be propagated forward or recycled back to the process. This problem can be avoided by manipulating a utility stream to absorb disturbances or an exit stream that allows the disturbances to be passed downstream, provided that the exit stream changes do not upset downstream process units.

Note that these guidelines may be in conflict. For example, a comparison of the effects of two inputs on a single controlled variable may indicate that one has a larger steady-state gain (Guideline 6) but slower dynamics (Guideline 7). In this situation a trade-off between static and dynamic considerations must be made in selecting the appropriate manipulated variable from the two input candidates.

4. Selection of Measured Variables

Safe, efficient operation of processing plants is made possible by the on-line measurement of key process variables. Clearly, output variables that are used as controlled variables should be measured. Other output variables are measured to provide additional information to the plant operators or for use in model-based control schemes such as supervisory control or inferential control[1]. It is also desirable to measure selected input variables as well as output variables, since recorded measurements of manipulated inputs provide useful information for tuning controllers and troubleshooting control loops. Also, measurements of disturbance inputs can be used in feedforward control schemes.

In choosing which outputs to measure and in locating measurement points, both static and dynamic considerations are important.

Guideline 10.

Reliable, accurate measurements are essential for good control.

There is ample evidence in the literature that inadequate measurements are a key contributor to poor control. Hughart and Kominek cite common measurement problems that they observed in distillation column control problems: orifice runs without enough straight piping, sample lines with too much time delay, temperature probes located in insensitive regions, and flow measurements of liquids at saturation temperatures (e.g., distillate and bottoms streams) that involve liquid flashing in the orifice. They note that these measurement problems can be readily resolved during the process design stage but that improving a measurement location after the process is operating is extremely difficult.

Guideline 11.

Select measurement points that have an adequate degree of sensitivity.

For example, in distillation columns a product composition is often controlled indirectly by regulating a temperature near the end of the column if an analyzer is not available. However, for high-purity separations the location of the temperature measurement point can be important. If a tray near an end of the column is selected, the tray temperature tends to be insensitive, since the tray composition can vary significantly even though the tray temperature changes very little. By contrast, if the temperature measurement point is moved closer to the feed tray, the temperature sensitivity is improved, but disturbances entering the column at the ends(e.g., condenser, reboiler) are not sensed as quickly.

Guideline 12.

Select measurement points that minimize time delays and time constants.

Reducing dynamic lags and time delays associated with process measurements improves closed-loop stability and response characteristics. Hughart and Kominek have observed distillation columns with the sample connection for the bottoms analyzer located 200 feet downstream from the column. This distance introduces a significant time delay and makes the column difficult to control, even more so because the time delay varies with the flow rate.

Selected from "*Process Dynamics and Control*, Dale E. Seborg & T. Edgar, John Wiley & Sonsi, 1989"

Words and Expressions

1. vessel ['vesəl] *n.* 容器,导管
2. hydrocarbon-to-oxygen ['haidrəu'kɑːbən-tu-ɔksidʒən] *n.* 碳氢化合物的氧化
3. flooding ['flʌdiŋ] *n.* 泛滥; 溢流
4. weeping ['wiːpiŋ] *n.* 渗漏; 分泌
5. degradation [degrə'deiʃən] *n.* 降低; 降解

6. catalyst ['kætəlist] n. 催化剂
7. subset ['sʌbset] n. 子集
8. downstream ['daun'stri:m] n. 下游
9. storage tank ['stɔ:ridʒ tæŋk] n. 存储器
10. inferential control n. 推断控制
11. digester [di'dʒestə] n. 蒸煮
12. pulp [pʌlp] n. 纸浆
13. guideline [gaidlain] n. 方针
14. reflux ['ri:flʌks] n. 回流；分馏
15. drum [drʌm] n. 室
16. throttle ['θrɔtl] v. 扼杀
17. condensate [kən'denseit] n. 冷凝物
18. propagate ['prɔpəgeit] v. 繁殖；宣传，传播
19. troubleshooting control loop 故障排除控制回路
20. orifice ['ɔrifis] n. 孔口
21. tray [trei] n. 塔盘

Note

① 本句中"to provide..."与"for use..."是由 or 引导的两个并列短语结构，表示"be measured"的目的。

1.5 Controller Tuning

> *Before reading the text, try to answer these questions*:
> 1. What are the commonly encountered process control system in a chemical plant?
> 2. What must be adjusted after a control system is installed?
> 3. What method is often used for tuning of a controller?
> 4. Could you please give the typical approach and steps?

After a control system is installed the controller settings must usually be adjusted until the control system performance is considered to be satisfactory. This activity is referred to as *controller tuning* or field tuning of the controller. Because controller tuning is usually done by trial and error, it can be quite tedious and time-consuming. Consequently, it is desirable to have good preliminary estimates of satisfactory controller settings. A good first guess may be available from experience with similar control loops. Alternatively, if a process model or frequency response data are available, some special design methods can be employed to calculate controller settings. However, field tuning may still be required to fine tune the controller, especially if the available process information is incomplete or not very accurate.

1.5.1 Guidelines for Common Control Loops

General guidelines for selection of controller type (P,PI,etc.) and choice of settings are available for commonly encountered process variables: flow rate, liquid level. gas pressure, temperature, and composition. The guidelines discussed below are useful for situations where a process model is not available. However, they should be used with caution because exceptions do occur. Similar guidelines are available for selecting the initial controller settings for the startup of a new plant.

Flow Control

Flow and liquid pressure control loops are characterized by fast responses (on the order of seconds), with essentially no time delays. The process dynamics are due to compressibility (in a gas stream) or inertial effects (in a liquid). The sensor and signal transmission line may introduce significant dynamic lags if pneumatic instruments are used. Disturbances in flow-control systems tend to be frequent but generally not of large magnitude. Most of the disturbances are high-frequency noise (periodic or random) due to stream turbulence, valve changes, and pump vibration. PI flow controllers are generally used with intermediate values of the controller gain K_c. The presence of recurring high-frequency noise rules out the use of derivative action.

Liquid Level

A typical non-self-regulating liquid-level process has been discussed. Because of its integrating nature, a relatively high-gain controller can be used with little concern about instability of the control system. In fact, an increase in controller gain often brings an increase in system stability, while low controller gains can increase the degree of oscillation. Integral control action is normally used but is not necessary if small offsets in the liquid level (±5%) can be tolerated. Derivative action is not normally employed in level control, since the level measurements often contain noise due to the splashing and turbulence of the liquid entering the tank.

In many level control problems, the liquid storage tank is used as a surge tank to damp out fluctuations in its inlet streams. If the exit flow rate from the tank is used as the manipulated variable, then conservative controller settings should be applied to avoid large, rapid fluctuations in the exit flow rate. This strategy is referred to as *averaging control*. If level control also involves heat transfer, such as in a vaporizer or evaporator, the process model and controller design become much more complicated. In such situations special control methods can be advantageous.

Gas Pressure

Gas pressure is relatively easy to control, except when the gas is in equilibrium with a liquid. A gas pressure process is self-regulating: the vessel (or pipeline) admits more feed when the pressure is too low and reduces the intake when the pressure becomes too high. PI controllers are normally used with only a small amount of integral control action (i.e., τ_I large). Usually the vessel volume is not large, leading to relatively small residence times and time constants. Derivative action is normally not needed because the process response times are usually quite small compared to other process operations.

Temperature

General guidelines for temperature control loops are difficult to state because of the wide variety of processes and equipment involving heat transfer (and their different time scales). For example, the temperature control problems are quite different for heat exchangers, distillation columns, chemical reactors, and evaporators. Due to the presence of time delays and/or multiple thermal capacitances, there will usually be a stability limit on the controller gain. PID controllers are commonly employed to provide more rapid responses than can be obtained with PI controllers.

Composition

Composition loops generally have characteristics similar to temperature loops, but with several differences:
① Measurement noise is a more significant problem in composition loops.
② Time delays due to analyzers may be a significant factor.

These two factors can limit the effectiveness of derivative action. Due to their importance and the difficulty of control, composition and temperature loops often are prime candidates for the advanced control strategies.

1.5.2 Trial and Error Tuning

Controller field tuning is often performed using trial and error procedures suggested by controller manufacturers. A typical approach for PID controllers can be summarized as follows:

Step 1. Eliminate integral and derivative action by setting τ_D at its minimum value and τ_I at its maximum value.

Step 2. Set K_c at a low value (e.g., 0.5) and put the controller on automatic.

Step 3. Increase the controller gain K_c by small-increments until continuous cycling occurs after a small set-point or load change. The term "continuous cycling" refers to a sustained oscillation with constant amplitude.

Step 4. Reduce K_c by a factor of two.

Step 5. Decrease τ_I in small increments until continuous cycling occurs again. Set τ_I equal to three times this value.

Step 6. Increase τ_D until continuous cycling occurs. Set τ_D equal to one-third of this value.

The value K_c that results in continuous cycling in Step 3 is referred to as the *ultimate gain* and will be denoted by K_{cu}. In performing the experimental test, it is important that the controller output does not saturate. If saturation does occur, then a sustained oscillation can result even though $K_c > K_{cu}$.

Because the concept of an ultimate gain plays such a key role in control system design and analysis, we present a more formal definition:

Definition. *The* ultimate gain K_{cu} is the largest value of the controller gain K_c that results in closed-loop stability when a proportional-only controller is used.

If a process model is available, then K_{cu} can be calculated theoretically using the stability criteria. The trial and error tuning procedure described above has a number of disadvantages:

① It is quite time-consuming if a large number of trials is required to optimize K_c, τ_I, and τ_D or if the process dynamics are quite slow. Unit control loop testing may be expensive because of lost productivity or poor product quality.

② Continuous cycling may be objectionable since the process is pushed to the stability limit. Consequently, if external disturbances or a change in the process occurs during controller tuning, unstable operation or a hazardous situation could result (e.g., a "runaway" chemical reactor).

③ This tuning procedure is not applicable to processes that are open-loop unstable because such processes typically are unstable at both high and low values of K_c, but are stable for an intermediate range of values.

④ Some simple processes do not have an ultimate gain (e.g., processes that can be accurately modeled by first-order or second-order transfer functions without time delays).

1.5.3 Continuous Cycling Method

Trial and error tuning methods based on a sustained oscillation can be considered to be variations of the famous *continuous cycling* method that was published by Ziegler and Nichols in 1942. This classic approach is probably the best known method for tuning PID controllers. The continuous cycling approach has also been referred to as *loop tuning* or the *ultimate gain method*. The first step is to experimentally determine K_{cu} as described in the previous section. The period of the resulting sustained oscillation is referred to as the *ultimate period* P_u. The PID controller settings are then calculated from K_{cu} and P_u using the Ziegler-Nichols (Z-N) tuning relations in Table 1.5.1. The Z-N tuning relations were empirically developed to provide a 1/4 decay ratio. These tuning relations have been widely used in industry and serve as a convenient base case for comparing alternative control schemes. However, controller tuning examples presented later in this section indicate that Z-N tuning can be inferior to settings obtained by other methods and should be used with caution[①].

Table 1.5.1 Ziegler-Nichols Controller Settings Based on the Continuous Cycling Method

Controller	K_c	τ_I	τ_D
P	$0.5K_{cu}$	—	—
PI	$0.45K_{cu}$	$P_u/1.2$	—
PID	$0.6K_{cu}$	$P_u/2$	$P_u/8$

Note that the Z-N setting for proportional control provides a significant safety margin since the controller gain is one-half of the stability limit K_{cu}. When integral action is added, K_c is reduced to $0.45K_{cu}$ for PI control. However, the addition of derivative action allows the gain to be increased to $0.6K_{cu}$ for PID control.

For some control loops, the degree of oscillation, associated with the 1/4 decay ratio and the corresponding large overshoot for set-point changes are undesirable. Thus, more conservative settings are often preferable, such as the modified Z-N settings in Table 1.5.2.

Although widely applied, the Ziegler-Nichols continuous cycling method has some of the same disadvantages as the trial and error method. However, the continuous cycling method is less time-consuming than the trial and error method because it requires only one trial and error search. Again, we wish to emphasize that the controller settings in Tables 1.5.1 and 1.5.2 should be regarded as first estimates. Subsequent fine tuning via trial and error is often required, especially if the "original settings" in Table 1.5.1 are selected. Alternatively, the continuous cycling autotuning method discussed at the end of this section may be used.

Table 1.5.2 Original and Modified Ziegler-Nichols Settings for PID Controllers

	K_c	τ_I	τ_D
Original (1/4 decay ratio)	$0.6K_{cu}$	$P_u/2$	$P_u/8$
Some overshoot	$0.33K_{cu}$	$P_u/2$	$P_u/3$
No overshoot	$0.2K_{cu}$	$P_u/2$	$P_u/3$

1.5.4 Process Reaction Curve Method

In their famous paper, Ziegler and Nichols proposed a second on-line tuning technique, the process reaction curve method. This method is based on a single experimental test that is made with the controller in the manual mode. A small step change in the controller output is introduced and the measured process response $B(t)$ is recorded. This step response is also referred to as the *process reaction curve*. It is characterized by two parameters: S, the slope of the tangent through the inflection point, and θ, the time at which the tangent intersects the time axis.

Two different types of process reaction curves are shown in Figure 1.5.1 for step changes occurring at $t=0$. The response for Case (a) is unbounded, which indicates that this process is not self-regulating. In contrast, the hypothetical process considered in Case (b) is self-regulating since the process reaction curve reaches a new steady state. Note that the slope-intercept characterization can be used for both types of process reaction curves.

The Ziegler-Nichols tuning relations for the process reaction curve method are shown in Table 1.5.3. S^* denotes the normalized slope, $S=S/\Delta p$ where Δp is the magnitude of the step change that was introduced in controller output p. These tuning relations were developed empirically to give closed-loop responses with 1/4 decay ratios. The tuning relations in Table 1.5.3 can be used for both self-regulating and non-self-regulating processes.

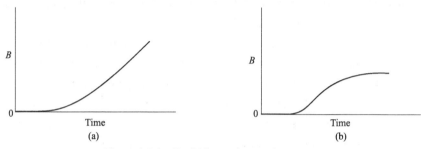

Figure 1.5.1 Typical process reaction curves:
(a) non-self-regulating process, (b) self-regulating process.

Table 1.5.3 **Ziegler-Nichols Tuning Relations (Process Reaction Curve Method)**

Controller Type	K_c	τ_I	τ_D
P	$\dfrac{1}{\theta S^*}$	—	—
PI	$\dfrac{0.9}{\theta S^*}$	3.33θ	—
PID	$\dfrac{1.2}{\theta S^*}$	2θ	0.5θ

If the process reaction curve has the typical sigmoidal shape shown in Case (b) of Figure.1.5.1, the following model usually provides a satisfactory fit:

$$\frac{B'(s)}{P'(s)} = G_v G_p G_m = \frac{Ke^{-\theta s}}{\tau s + 1} \tag{1.5.1}$$

Where B' is the measured value of the controlled variable and P' is the controller output, both expressed as deviation variables. Note that this model includes the transfer functions for the final control element and sensor-transmitter combination, as well as the process transfer function. Model parameters K, τ, and θ can be determined from the process reaction curve.

The process reaction curve (PRC) method offers several significant advantages:
① Only a single experimental test is necessary.
② It does not require trial and error.
③ The controller settings are easily calculated.

However, the PRC method also has several disadvantages:

① The experimental test is performed open-loop conditions. Thus, if a significant load change occurs during the test, no corrective action is taken *and* the test results may be significantly distorted.

② It may be difficult to determine the slope at the inflection point accurately, especially if the measurement is noisy and a small recorder chart is used.

③ The method tends to be sensitive to controller calibration errors. By contrast, the Z-N method is less sensitive to calibration errors in K_c since the controller gain is adjusted during the experimental test.

④ The recommended settings in Table 1.5.2 and Table 1.5.3 tend to result in oscillatory responses since they were developed to provide a 1/4 decay ratio.

⑤ The method is not recommended for processes that have oscillatory open-loop responses since the process model in Eq.(1.5.1) will be quite inaccurate.

Closed-loop versions of the process reaction curve method have been proposed as a partial remedy for the first disadvantage. In this approach, a process reaction curve is generated by making a step change in set point during proportional-only control. The model parameters in Eq.(1.5.1) are then calculated in a novel manner from the closed-loop response. A minor disadvantage of these closed-loop process reaction methods is that the model parameter calculations are more complicated than for the standard open-loop method.

Selected from "*Process Dynamics and Control*, Dale E. Seborg Q T. Edgar, *John Wiley & Sonsi*, 1989"

Words and Expressions

1. controller tuning 控制器整定
2. trail and error 试差法
3. tedious [ˈtiːdjəs] *adj.* 费时的
4. time-consuming 耗时的
5. startup [staːtˈʌp] *n.* 启动
6. inertial [iˈnəʃəl] *adj.* 惯性的
7. vibration [vaiˈbreiʃən] *n.* 振动
8. turbulence [ˈtəˈbjuləns] *n.* 湍流
9. recur [riˈkəː] *n.* 重复；递归
10. splashing [splæʃiŋ] *n.* 喷溅物
11. fluctuation [ˈflʌktjueiʃən] *n.* 波动起伏
12. vaporizer [ˈveipəraizə] *n.* 蒸馏器
13. evaporator [iˈvæpəreitə] *n.* 蒸发器，脱水器
14. residence time 滞留时间
15. ultimate [ˈʌltimət] *adj.* 最终的；临界的
16. loop tuning 回路整定
17. decay ratio 衰减比

18. be inferior to   较……差, 在……下面
19. overshoot   [ˈəuvəˈʃuːt]   *n.* 超调
20. slope   [sləup]   *n.* 斜率; 倾斜
21. tangent   [ˈtændʒənt]   *n.* 切线; 正切
22. intersect   [intəˈsekt]   *v.* 相交, 交叉
23. hypothetical   [haipəˈθetikl]   *adj.* 假设的, 假定的
24. intercept   [intəˈsept]   *v.* 截止
25. sigmoidal   [ˈsigmɔidl]   *adj.* S 形的
26. chart   [tʃɑːt]   *n.* 图表
27. calibration   [ˈkælibreiʃən]   *n.* 刻度, 标度; 标准

Note

① 在"that…"引导的宾语从句中,主语是"Z-N tuning",谓语部分有两个,一个是"be inferior to settings obtained by other methods",另一个是"should be used with caution",其中"obtained…"是过去分词短语作修饰"settings"的定语。

Exercises

1. *Complete the notes below with words taken from the text above.*
   (1) _____ a control system is installed the controller _____ must usually be adjusted _____ the control system performance is considered to be satisfactory. This activity is referred to as _____ or _____ of the controller. Because controller tuning is usually done by _____, it can be quite _____ and _____.
   (2) Disturbances _____ systems tend to be frequent _____ generally _____ of large magnitude. Most of the disturbances are _____ (periodic or random) due to stream turbulence, _____, and pump vibration.
   (3) General guidelines for _____ are difficult _____ because of the wide variety of _____ and _____ involving _____ (and their different time scales). For example, the temperature control problems are quite different for heat exchangers, _____, _____, and evaporators.
   (4) _____ and _____ methods based on a _____ can be considered to be variations of the famous _____ method that was published by _____ and _____ in 1942. This classic approach is probably the best known method for _____. The continuous cycling approach has also been referred to as _____ or the _____.
2. *Put the following into Chinese:*
   setting   tuning   trial and error   guideline
   averaging control   residence time   eliminate   ultimate gain
   time-consuming   continuous cycling method   decay ratio
   process reaction curve method   Ziegler-Nichols tuning

3. *Put the following into English:*

流量控制　　液面控制　　压力控制　　温度控制
成分控制　　临界增益法　临界周期　　超调
热交换器　　化学反应器　汽化器

4. *Complete the following close test.*

For purposes of control system design, _____ convenient to classify process variables _____ inputs _____ outputs. The output variables ($y_1, y_2, \cdots, y_N$) _____ process variables _____ ordinarily _____ associated _____ exit streams of a process _____ conditions inside a process vessel (e.g., compositions, temperatures, levels, and flow rates). _____ subset of the output variables _____ selected _____ variables to be controlled (i.e., controlled variables) _____ satisfy the plant and control objectives. The _____ ($x_1, x_2, \cdots, x_M$) are physical variables _____ affect the _____. Typically, _____ are associated _____ inlet streams (e.g.,temperature). However, _____ from a process _____ an "input" from a control point of view _____ the flow rate _____ a manipulated variable _____ the magnitude of the flow rate is determined by _____. For example, _____ of an exit stream from a _____ may be adjusted by _____ if the stream serves _____ to that _____. _____ of the process inputs are specified as _____, _____ the other inputs are considered _____ disturbance variables, specified by the _____.

Reading Material:

Autotuning

1. Introduction

By combining the methods for determination of process dynamics with the methods for computing the parameters of a PID controller, methods for automatic tuning of PID controllers can be obtained. Practical controllers with such features have only recently appeared on the market. There are several reasons for this. The recent development of microelectronics has made it possible to incorporate the additional program code needed for the autotuning at a reasonable cost. The interest in autotuning at universities is also quite new. Most of the research effort has been devoted to the related but more difficult problem of adaptive control.

The chapter presents an overview of approaches to autotuning. Some commercial products are then examined: the Foxboro EXACT^{TM} controller, which is based on transient response analysis, an autotuner based on relay feedback experiments and manufactured by Satt Control Instruments; and two controllers based on parameter estimation and manufactured by Leeds & Northrup and Turnbull Control Systems. The last controllers also have a pretuning mode that is based on transient response analysis.

2. Approaches to Autotuning

A block diagram of a PID controller with automatic tuning is shown in Figure 1.5.2. When the tuning is performed, an extra loop is introduced. This loop consists of a process identification scheme and a design procedure that computes the PID parameters. An additional perturbation signal (V) may be added to ensure proper excitation of the process. The tuning can be performed either in closed loop or in open loop. The tuning procedure is characterized by:

① The underlying process model
② The identification procedure
③ The design method

The previous chapters thus provide the basis for discussing autotuning methods. Since there are several identification and design

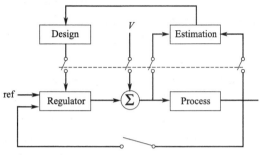

Figure 1.5.2 Block Diagram of a PID Controller with Automatic Tuning.

procedures, there are numerous ways to perform autotuning. Apart from the classification above, the autotuners can also be characterized by their operating modes. Tuning can be performed on operator demand or it can be initiated automatically.

Methods Based on Transient Responses

Autotuners can be based on open-loop or closed-loop transient response analysis. The most common methods are based on step or pulse responses, but there are also methods that can use a wide variety of transients.

Open-Loop Tuning

A simple process model can be obtained from an open-loop transient response experiment. A step or a pulse is injected at the process input, and the response is measured. To perform such an experiment, the process must be stable. If a pulse test is used, the process may include an integrator. It is necessary that the process be in equilibrium when the experiment is begun. There are, in principle, only one or two parameters that must be set *a priori*: the amplitude and the duration of a pulse or the amplitude of a step. These parameters must be chosen so that the response is well visible above the noise level, but not so large that the process nonlinearities become significant.

Many methods can be used to extract process characteristics from a transient response experiment. Periods of oscillation and damping can be determined from simple zero crossing and peak detectors. The method of moments discussed in the same section can also be used to determine process models directly. More elaborate signal processing methods, such as parameter estimation or the fast Fourier transform, can also be used.

The transient response methods are often used as a pretuning mode in more complicated tuning devices. The main advantage of the methods (they require little prior knowledge) is then exploited. The drawback with the transient response methods is that they are sensitive to disturbances. This drawback is less important if they are used only in the pretuning phase.

Closed-Loop Tuning

Automatic tuning based on transient response identification can also be performed on line. The steps or pulses are then introduced in the reference signal. They can be introduced by the controller for identification purposes. There are also autotuners that do not introduce any transient disturbances. Instead, large disturbances caused by set point changes or load disturbances are detected and the closed-loop responses are considered. The Foxboro EXACT controller, which is described in the next section, is an example of such a scheme.

Since a proper closed-loop transient response is the goal for the design, it is appealing to base the tuning methods directly on the properties of the closed-loop transient responses. It is easy to give design specifications in terms of the closed-loop transient response, e.g., damping, overshoot, closed-loop time constants, etc. The drawback is that the relation between these specifications and the PID parameters is normally quite involved. Heuristics and logic are therefore required for these kinds of tuning devices.

Methods Based on Frequency Responses

Since frequency response methods can also be used to determine the process dynamics, autotuners can be based on this methodology.

Use of the Relay Method

In traditional frequency response methods, the transfer function of a process is determined by measuring the steady-state response to a sinusoidal input. A difficulty with this method is that appropriate frequencies of the input signal must be specified. A special method can be used to generate automatically an appropriate frequency of the input signal The idea was simply to introduce a nonlinear feedback of the rely type so that there would be a limit cycle oscillation. With an ideal relay the method gives an input signal to the process whose period is close to the crossover frequency of the open-loop system.

A block diagram of an autotuner based on the relay method is shown in Figure 1.5.3. Notice that there is a switch that selects either relay feedback or ordinary PID feedback. When it is desired to tune the system, the PID function is disconnected and the system is connected to relay control. The system then starts to oscillate. The period and the amplitude of the oscillation are determined when steady-state oscillation is obtained. This gives the ultimate period and the ultimate gain. The parameters of a PID controller can then be determined from these values, e.g., using the Ziegler-Nichols frequency response method. The PID controller is then automatically switched in again, and the control is executed with the new PID parameters.

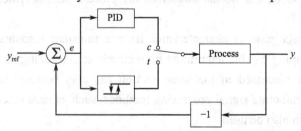

Figure 1.5.3 Block Diagram of an Autotuner Based on the Relay Method for System Identification (The system operates as a relay controller in the tuning mode (t) and as an ordinary PID controller in the control mode (c).)

This tuning device has one parameter that must be specified in advance, namely, the initial amplitude of the relay. A feedback loop from measurement of the amplitude of the oscillation to the relay amplitude can be used to ensure that the output is within reasonable bounds during the oscillation. It is also useful to introduce hysteresis in the relay. This reduces the effects of measurement noise and also increases the period of the oscillation. With hysteresis there is an additional parameter, which can, however, be set automatically based on a determination of the measurement noise level. Notice that there is no need to know time scales *a priori* since the crossover frequency is determined automatically.

In this method, an oscillation with suitable frequency is generated by a static nonlinearity. Even the order of the time constant of the process can be unknown. Therefore, this method is not only suitable as a tuning device; it can also be used in a pretuning phase in other tuning procedures where the time constant of the system has to be known, e.g., to decide a suitable sampling period.

This tuning method can also be modified to identify several points on the Nyquist curve. This can be accomplished by making several experiments with different values of the amplitude and the hysteresis of the relay. A filter with known characteristics can also be introduced in the loop to identify other points on the Nyquist curve. If two points are known, design methods based on two points can be used, e.g., the dominant pole design method or the M_p circle design.

Frequency response analysis can also be used for on-line tuning of PID controllers. By introducing bandpass filters, the signal content at different frequencies can be investigated. From this knowledge, a process model give in terms of points on the Nyquist curve can be identified on line. A crucial choice in this autotuner is the choice of frequencies in the bandpass filters. This choice can perhaps be simplified by using the tuning procedure described above in a pretuning phase.

Methods Based on Parametric Models

Perhaps the most common tuning procedure is to use a recursive parameter estimation to determine a low-order discrete time model of the process. The parameters of the low-order model obtained are then used in some design scheme to obtain the controller parameters. An autotuner of this type can also be operated as an adaptive regulator that will change the regulator parameters continuously. Autotuners based on this idea, therefore, often have an option for continuous adaptation.

A drawback with autotuners of this type is that they require significant prior information. A sampling period for the identification procedure must be specified; it should be related to the time constants of the closed-loop system. Since the identification is performed on line, a controller that at least manages to stabilize the system is required. Therefore, the available products based on this identification procedure often have a pretuning phase, which can be based on the methods presented in the previous sections.

Selected from "*Automation Tuning of PID Controllers*, Rurl Johan Astrom and Tore Hagglund, *ISA*, 1991"

Words and Expressions

1. autotuning [ɔːtəˈtjuːniŋ] n. 自动整定
2. microelectronic [maikrəuiːlekˈtrɔniks] n. 微电子学
3. perturbation [pəːtəˈbeiʃən] n. 干扰
4. pulse [pʌls] n. 脉冲
5. inject [inˈdʒekt] vt. 注射
6. equilibrium [iːkwiˈlibriəm] n. 平衡点，平衡状态
7. duration [djuəˈreiʃən] n. 持续时间
8. extract [iksˈtrækt] n. 提取
9. elaborate [iˈlæbəreit] adj. 详细的，精确的
10. fast fourier transform 快速傅里叶变换
11. heuristic [hjuəˈristik] adj. 启发式的
12. hysteresis [histəˈriːsis] n. 滞后
13. filter [ˈfiltə] n. 滤波器
14. dominant [ˈdɔminənt] adj. 主要的
15. bandpass [ˈbændpɑːs] adj. 带通的
16. crucial [ˈkruːʃəl] adj. 决定性的
17. recursive [riˈkəːsiv] adj. 循环的，递归的

CHAPTER 2 MEASUREMENTS AND ACTUATORS

2.1 Pressure Measurements

Discussed in this unit are as follows:
1. The terms of pressure
2. The difference between atmospheric, absolute, gauge, and differential pressure values
3. Various pressure units in use, i.e., British units versus SI(metric) units
4. Various types of pressure measuring devices

2.1.1 Introduction

Pressure is the force exerted by gases and liquids due to their weight, such as the pressure of the atmosphere on the surface of the earth and the pressure containerized liquids exert on the bottom and walls of a container.

Pressure units are a measure of the force acting over a specified area. It is most commonly expressed in pounds per square inch (psi), sometimes pounds per square foot (psf) in English units, or pascals (Pa or kPa) in metric units.

$$\text{Pressure} = \frac{\text{force}}{\text{area}}$$

2.1.2 Pressure Measurement

There are six terms applied to pressure measurements. They are as follows:

Total vacuum—which is zero pressure or lack of pressure, as would be experienced in outer space.

Vacuum is a pressure measurement made between total vacuum and normal atmospheric pressure (14.7 psi).

Atmospheric pressure is the pressure on the earth's surface due to the weight of the gases in the earth's atmosphere and is normally expressed at sea level as 14.7 psi or 101.36 kPa. It is however, dependant on atmospheric conditions. The pressure decreases above sea level and at an elevation of 5000 ft drops to about 12.2 psi (84.122 kPa).

Absolute pressure is the pressure measured with respect to a vacuum and is expressed in pounds per square inch absolute (psia).

Gauge pressure is the pressure measured with respect to atmospheric pressure and is normally expressed in pounds per square inch gauge (psig). Figure 2.1.1(a) shows graphically the relation between atmospheric, gauge, and absolute pressures.

Differential pressure is the pressure measured with respect to another pressure and is expressed as the difference between the two values. This would represent two points in a pressure or flow system and is referred to as the *delta p* or Δp. Figure 2.1.1(b) shows two situations, where differential pressure exists across a barrier and between two points in a flow system.

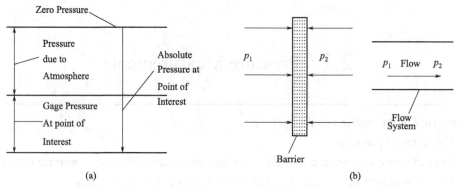

Figure 2.1.1 Illustration of (a) gauge pressure versus absolute pressure and (b) delta or differential pressure.

Table 2.1.1 Pressure Conversions

	Water		Mercury‡			
	in*	cm$^+$	Mm	Ins	kPa	psi
1 psi	27.7	70.3	51.7	2.04	6.895	1
1 psf	0.19	0.488	0.359	0.014	0.048	0.007
1 kPa	4.015	10.2	7.5	0.295	1	0.145
Atmospheres	407.2	1034	761	29.96	101.3	14.7
Torr	0.535	1.36	1	0.04	0.133	0.019
Millibar	0.401	1.02	0.75	0.029	0.1	0.014

* At 39° F.
$^+$ At 4°C.
‡ Mercury at 0°C.

2.1.3 Pressure Instruments

Diaphragms, capsules, and bellows

Gauges are a major group of pressure sensors that measure pressure with respect to atmospheric pressure. Gauge sensors are usually devices that change their shape when pressure is applied. These devices include diaphragms, capsules, bellows, and Bourdon tubes.

A diaphragm consists of a thin layer or film of a material supported on a rigid frame and is shown in Figure 2.1.2(a). Pressure can be applied to one side of the film for gauge sensing or pressures can be applied to both sides of the film for differential or absolute pressure sensing. A wide range of materials can be used for the sensing film, from rubber to plastic for low-pressure devices, silicon for medium pressures, to stainless steel for high pressures. When pressure is applied to the diaphragm, the film distorts or becomes slightly spherical. This movement can be sensed using a strain gauge, piezoelectric, or changes in capacitance techniques (older techniques included magnetic and carbon pile devices). The deformation in the above sensing devices uses transducers to give electrical signals. Of all these devices the micromachined silicon diaphragm is

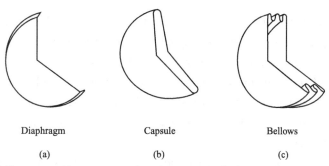

Figure 2.1.2 Various types of pressure-sensing elements: (a) diaphragm, (b) capsule, and (c) bellows.

the most commonly used industrial pressure sensor for the generation of electrical signals.

A silicon diaphragm uses silicon, which is a semiconductor. This allows a strain gauge and amplifier to be integrated into the top surface of the silicon structure after the diaphragm was etched from the back side. These devices have built-in temperature-compensated piezoelectric strain gauge and amplifiers that give a high output voltage (5V FSD [volt full scale reading or deflection]). They are very small, accurate (2 percent FSD), reliable, have a good temperature operating range, are low cost, can withstand high overloads, have good longevity, and are unaffected by many chemicals. Commercially made devices are available for gauge, differential, and absolute pressure sensing up to 200 psi (1.5 MPa). This range can be extended by the use of stainless steel diaphragms to 100,000 psi (700 MPa).

Figure 2.1.3(a) shows the cross sections of the three configurations of the silicon chips (sensor dies) used in microminiature pressure sensors, i.e., gauge, absolute, and differential. The given dimensions illustrate that the sensing elements are very small. The die is packaged into a plastic case (about 0.2 in thick×0.6 in diameter). A gauge assembly is shown in Figure 2.1.3(b). The sensor is used in blood pressure monitors and many industrial applications, and is extensively used in automotive pressure-sensing applications, i.e., manifold air pressure, barometric air pressure, oil, transmission fluid, break fluid, power steering, tire pressure and the like.

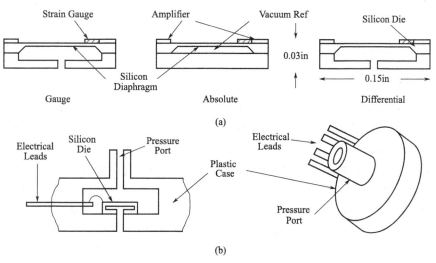

Figure 2.1.3 Cross section of (a) various types of microminiature silicon pressure sensor die and (b) a packaged microminiature gauge sensor.

Capsules are two diaphragms joined back to back, as shown in Figure 2.1.2(b). Pressure can be applied to the space between the diaphragms forcing them apart to measure gauge pressure. The expansion of the diaphragm can be mechanically coupled to an indicating device. The deflection in a capsule depends on its diameter, material thickness, and elasticity. Materials used are phosphor bronze, stainless steel, and iron nickel alloys. The pressure range of instruments using these materials is up to 50 psi (350 kPa). Capsules can be joined together to increase sensitivity and mechanical movement.

Bellows are similar to capsules, except that the diaphragms instead of being joined directly together, are separated by a corrugated tube or tube with convolutions, as shown in Figure 2.1.2(c). When pressure is applied to the bellows it elongates by stretching the convolutions and not the end diaphragms. The materials used for the bellows type of pressure sensor are similar to those used for the capsule, giving a pressure range for the bellows of up to 800 psi (5 MPa). Bellows devices can be used for absolute and differential pressure measurements.

Differential measurements can be made by connecting two bellows mechanically, opposing each other when pressure is applied to them, as shown in Figure 2.1.4(a). When pressures p_1 and p_2 are applied to the bellows a differential scale reading is obtained. Figure 2.1.4(b) shows a bellows configured as a differential pressure transducer driving a *linear variable differential transformer* (LVDT) to obtain an electrical signal, p_2 could be the atmospheric pressure for gauge measurements. The bellows is the most sensitive of the mechanical devices for low-pressure measurements, i.e., 0 to 210 kPa.

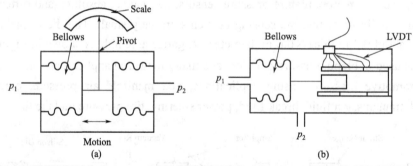

Figure 2.1.4 Differential bellows pressure gauges for (a) direct scale reading and (b) as a pressure transducer.

Bourdon tubes

Bourdon tubes are hollow, cross-sectional beryllium, copper, or steel tubes, shaped into a three quarter circle, as shown in Figure 2.1.5(a). They may be rectangular or oval in cross section, but the operating principle is that the outer edge of the cross section has a larger surface than the inner portion. When pressure is applied, the outer edge has a proportionally larger total force applied because of its larger surface area, and the diameter of the circle increases. The walls of the tubes are between 0.01 and 0.05 in thick. The tubes are anchored at one end so that when pressure is applied to the tube, it tries to straighten and in doing so the free end of the tube moves. This movement can be mechanically coupled to a pointer, which when calibrated, will indicate pressure as a line of sight indicator, or it can be coupled to a potentiometer to give a resistance value proportional to the pressure for electrical signals. Figure 2.1.5(b) shows a helical pressure tube.

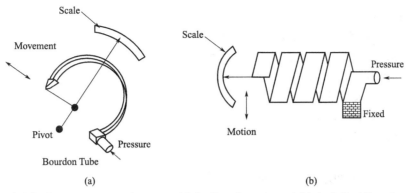

Figure 2.1.5 Pressure sensors shown are (a) the Bourdon tube and (b) the helical Bourdon tube.

This configuration is more sensitive than the circular Bourdon tube. The Bourdon tube dates from the 1840s. It is reliable, inexpensive, and one of the most common general purpose pressure gauges.

Bourdon tubes can withstand overloads of up to 30 to 40 percent of their maximum rated load without damage, but if overloaded may require recalibration. The tubes can also be shaped into helical or spiral shapes to increase their range. The Bourdon tube is normally used for measuring positive gauge pressures, but can also be used to measure negative gauge pressures. If the pressure on the Bourdon tube is lowered, then the diameter of the tube reduces. This movement can be coupled to a pointer to make a vacuum gauge. Bourdon tubes can have a pressure range of up to 100,000 psi (700 MPa). Figure 2.1.6 shows the Bourdon-tube type of pressure gauge when used for measuring negative pressure (vacuum) (a) and positive pressure (b). Note the counterclockwise movement in (a) and the clockwise movement in (b).

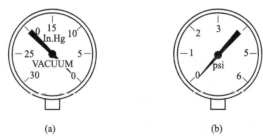

Figure 2.1.6 Bourdon-tube type pressure gauges for (a) negative and (b) positive pressures.

Selected from *"Fundamentals of Industrial Instrumentation and Process Control, William C. Dunn, McGraw-Hill Inc, 2005"*

Words and Expressions

1. container   [kən'teinə]   *n.* 容器
2. metric unit   公[米]制单位
3. vacum   ['vækjuəm]   *n.* 真空,真空度,真空状态
4. atmospheric pressure   大气压
5. absolute pressure   绝压
6. gauge pressure   表压

7. differential pressure　差压
8. diaphragm　['daiəfræm]　*n.* 膜片, 膜盒, 膜层, 薄膜
9. capsule　['kæpsjuːl]　*n.* 小盒, 膜盒, 容器
10. bellows　['beləuz]　*n.* 风箱, 波纹管, 弹簧皱纹管, 膜盒
11. Bourdon tube　波登管
12. silicon　['silikən]　*n.* 硅
13. stainless steel　不锈钢
14. distort　[disˈtɔːt]　*vt.* 使……变形, 弯曲, 扭曲
15. spherical　[sferik(əl)]　*adj.* 球形的, 圆的
16. strain gauge　应变仪, 应变电阻片
17. piezoelectric　[pai,iːzəuiˈlektrik]　*adj.* 压电的
18. capacitance　[kəˈpæsitəns]　*n.* 容量, 电容
19. deformation　[,diːfɔːˈmeiʃən]　*n.* 变形, 扭曲
20. semiconductor　[,semikənˈdʌktə]　*n.* 半导体
21. longevity　[lɔnˈdʒeviti]　*n.* 长寿命, 耐久性
22. manifold　['mænifəuld]　*adj.* 各种各样的, 形形色色的
23. barometric　[,bærəˈmetrik]　*adj.* 气压的, 大气的
24. deflection　[diˈflekʃən]　*n.* 偏转, 偏移, 偏角
25. elasticity　[,elæsˈtisəti]　*n.* 弹性, 弹力
26. phosphor bronze　磷青铜
27. iron nickel alloys　铁镍合金
28. corrugated　['kɔrə,geitid]　*adj.* 波纹状的, 波纹形的
29. corrugated tube　波纹管
30. elongate　['iːlɔŋgeit]　*adj.* 拉长的, 延伸的
31. convolution　[,kɔnvəˈluːʃən]　*n.* 回旋, 旋转
32. stretch　[stretʃ]　*vt.* 伸长, 拉长, 展开
33. hollow　['hɔləu]　*adj.* 空心的, 中空的
34. beryllium copper　铍青铜
35. rectangular　[rekˈtæŋgjulə]　*adj.* 矩形的, 长方形的
36. oval　['əuvəl]　*adj.* 椭圆形的
37. strainghten　['streitn]　*v.* 变直, 伸直
38. potentiometer　[pə,tenʃiˈɔmitə]　*n.* 电位器, 电位计
39. helical　['helikəl]　*adj.* 螺旋形的
40. clockwise　['klɔkwaiz]　*adj.* 顺时针的, 顺时针方向的
41. counterclockwise　[,kauntəˈklɔkwaiz]　*adj.* 逆时针的, 逆时针方向的
42. psi　*abbr.* 磅/每平方英寸
43. Pascal (Pa or kPa)　帕斯卡（帕或千帕）

Exercises

1. *Put the following into Chinese:*

　　atmospheric pressure　　absolute pressure　　gauge pressure　　differential pressure

total vacuum	diaphragm	capsule	bellow
Bourdon tube	silicon diaphragm		

2. *Put the following into English:*

英制　　　　　　　公制　　　　　　　扩散硅压力传感器　　　　压力传感器
差压变送器　　　　压力传感元件　　　波登管压力表

Reading Material:

Pressure Transmitters

Signal Transmissions

In the process plant, it is impractical to locate the control instruments out in the plant near the process. It is also true that most measurements are not easily transmitted from some remote location. Pressure measurement is an exception, but if a high pressure measurement of some dangerous chemical is to be indicated or recorded several hundred feet from the point of measurement, a hazard will be created. The hazard may be from the pressure and/or from the chemical carried in the line.

To eliminate this problem, a signal transmission system was developed. In process instrumentation, this system is usually either pneumatic (air pressure) or electrical. Because this chapter deals with pressure, the pneumatic, or air pressure system, will be discussed first. Later it will become evident that the electrical transmitters perform a similar function.

Using the transmission system, it will be possible to install most of the indicating, recording, and control instruments in one location. This makes it practical for a minimum number of operators to run the plant efficiently.

When a transmission system is employed, the measurement is converted to a pneumatic signal by the transmitter scaled from 0 to 100 percent of the measured value. This transmitter is mounted close to the point of measurement in the process. The transmitter output—air pressure for a pneumatic transmitter—is piped to the recording or control instrument. The standard output range for a pneumatic transmitter is 3 to 15 psi, 20 to 100 kPa; or 0.2 to 1.0 bar or kg/cm^2. These are the standard signals that are almost universally used.

Let us take a closer look at what this signal means. Suppose we have a field-mounted pressure transmitter that has been calibrated to a pressure range of 100 psi to 500 psi (689.5 to 3447.5 kPa).

When the pressure being sensed is 100 psi (69 kPa), the transmitter is designed to produce an output of 3 psi air pressure (or the approximate SI equivalent 20 kPa). When the pressure sensed rises to 300 psi (2068.5 kPa), or midscale, the output will climb to 9 psi, or 60 kPa, and at top scale, 500 psi (3447.5 kPa), the signal output will be 15 psi, or 100 kPa.

This signal is carried by tubing, usually 1/4-inch copper or plastic, to the control room, where it is either indicated, recorded, or fed into a controller.

The receiving instrument typically employs a bellows element to convert this signal into pen or pointer position. Or, if the signal is fed to a controller, a bellows is also used to convert the signal for the use of the controller. The live zero makes it possible to distinguish between true zero and a dead instrument.

The top scale signal is high enougth to be useful without the possibility of creating hazards.

Mechanical Pressure Seals

Application

A sealed pressure system is used with a pressure measuring instrument to isolate corrosive or viscous products, or products that tend to solidify, from the measuring element and its connective tubing.

Definition

A sealed pressure system consists of a conventional pressure measuring element or a force-balance pressure transmitter capsule assembly connected, either directly or by capillary tubing, to a pressure seal as seen in Figure 2.1.7. The system is solidly filled with a suitable liquid transmission medium.

The seal itself may take many forms, depending on process conditions, but consists of a pressure sensitive flexible member, the diaphragm, functioning as an isolating membrane, with a suitable method of attachment to a process vessel or line.

Principle of Operation

Process pressure applied to the flexible member of the seal assembly forces some of the filling fluid out of the seal cavity into the capillary tubing and pressure measuring element, causing the element to expand in proportion to the applied process pressure, thereby actuating a pen, pointer, or transmitter mechanism. A sealed pressure system offers high resolution and rapid response to pressure changes at the diaphragm. The spring rate of the flexible member must be

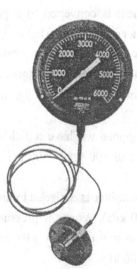

Figure 2.1.7 Seal connected to 6-inch pressure gauge.

Figure 2.1.8 Seals connected to differential pressure transmitter.

low when compared with the spring rate of the measuring element to ensure that the fill volume displacement will full stroke the measuring element for the required pressure range. A low-diaphragm spring rate, coupled with maximum fill volume displacement, is characteristic of the ideal system.

A sealed pressure system is somewhat similar to a liquid-filled thermometer, the primary differences being a flexible rather than rigid member at the process, and no initial filling pressure. The flexible member of the seal should ideally accommodate any thermal expansion of the filling medium without perceptible motion of the measuring element. A very stiff seal member, such as a Bourdon tube, combined with a low-pressure (high-volume change) element, will produce marked temperature effects from both varying ambient or elevated process temperatures.

The Foxboro 13DMP Series pneumatic d/p Cell transmitters with pressure seals (Figure 2.1.8) measure differential pressures in ranges of 0 to 20 to 0 to 850 inches of water or 0 to 5 to 0 to 205 kPa at static pressures from full vacuum up to flange rating. They transmit a proportional 3 to 15 psi or 20 to 100 kPa or 4 to 20 mA dc signal to receivers located up to several hundred yards or meters from the point of measurement.

Selected from *"Instrumentation for Process Measurement and Control, NORMAN A. ANDERSON, CHILTON COMPANY, 1998"*

Words and Expressions

1. impractical   [imˈpræktikəl]   *adj.* 不实用的，做不到的，不切实际的
2. transmitter   [trænzˈmitə]   *n.* 变送器，变换器
3. exception   [ikˈsepʃən]   *n.* 除外，例外，异常
4. dangerous   [ˈdeindʒərəs]   *adj.* 危险的
5. pneumatic   [njuːˈmætik]   *adj.* 气动的，压力的
6. indicate   [ˈindikeit]   *vt.* 显示，指示
7. live zero   实际零点，实时零点
8. seal   [siːl]   *vt.* 封闭，密封
9. isolate   [ˈaisəleit]   *vt.* 隔离
10. solidify   [səˈlidifai]   *v.* 充实，固化，充满
11. capillary   [kæˈpiləri]   *n.* 毛细管
12. flexible member   柔性部件
13. cavity   [ˈkæviti]   *n.* 内腔，中空
14. resolution   [ˌrezəˈluːʃən]   *n.* 分辨率，清晰度
15. accommodate   [əˈkɔmədeit]   *vt.* 调节，提供，适应
16. perceptible   [pəˈseptəbl]   *adj.* 明显的，易感知的
17. stiff   [stif]   *adj.* 刚性的，非弹性的，不易弯的
18. elevate   [ˈeliveit]   *vt.* 升高，增加，提高
19. flange   [flændʒ]   *n.* 法兰盘
20. force-balance pressure transmitter   力平衡压力变送器

2.2 Level Measurements

> *Topics discussed in this unit are as follows:*
> 1. The formulas used in level measurements
> 2. The difference between direct and indirect level measuring devices
> 3. The difference between continuous and single-point measurements
> 4. The various types of instruments available for level measurements

2.2.1 Introduction

This unit discusses the measurement of the level of liquids and free flowing solids in containers. The detector is normally sensing the interface between a liquid and a gas, a solid and a gas, a solid and a liquid, or possibly the interface between two liquids. Sensing liquid levels fall into two categories; firstly, single-point sensing and secondly, continuous level monitoring. In the case of single-point sensing the actual level of the material is detected when it reaches a predetermined level, so that the appropriate action can be taken to prevent overflowing or to refill the container.

Continuous level monitoring measures the level of the liquid on an uninterrupted basis. In this case the level of the material will be constantly monitored and hence, the volume can be calculated if the cross-sectional area of the container is known.

Level measurements can be direct or indirect; examples of these are using a float technique or measuring pressure and calculating the liquid level. Free flowing solids are dry powders, crystals, rice, grain and so forth.

2.2.2 Level Formulas

Pressure is often used as an indirect method of measuring liquid levels. Pressure increases as the depth increases in a fluid. The pressure is given by

$$\Delta p = \gamma \Delta h \tag{2.2.1}$$

Where Δp=change in pressure
    γ=specific weight
    Δh=depth

Note the units must be consistent, i.e., pounds and feet, or newtons and meters.

Buoyancy is an indirect method used to measure liquid levels. The level is determined using the buoyancy of an object partially immersed in a liquid. The buoyancy B or upward force on a body in a liquid can be calculated from the equation

$$B = \gamma \times \text{area} \times d \tag{2.2.2}$$

Where area is the cross-sectional area of the object and d is the immersed depth of the object.

The liquid level is then calculated from the weight of a body in a liquid W_L, which is equal to its weight in air ($W_A - B$), from which we get

$$d = \frac{W_A - W_L}{\gamma \times \text{area}} \tag{2.2.3}$$

The weight of a container can be used to calculate the level of the material in the container. In Figure 2.2.1(a) the volume V of the material in the container is given by

$$V = \text{area} \times \text{depth} = \pi r^2 \times d \tag{2.2.4}$$

Where r is the radius of the container and d is the depth of the material.

The weight of material W in a container is given by

$$W = \gamma V \tag{2.2.5}$$

Capacitive probes can be used in nonconductive liquids and free flowing solids for level measurement. Many materials, when placed between the plates of a capacitor, increase the capacitance by a factor μ called the dielectric constant of the material. For instance, air has a dielectric constant of 1 and water 80. Figure 2.2.1(b) shows two capacitor plates partially immersed in a nonconductive liquid. The capacitance (Cd) is given by

$$Cd = Ca\mu\frac{d}{r} + Ca \tag{2.2.6}$$

Where Ca=capacitance with no liquid

μ=dielectric constant of the liquid between the plates

r=height of the plates

d=depth or level of the liquid between the plates

There are large variations in dielectric constant with temperature so that temperature correction may be needed. In Eq. (2.2.6) the liquid level is given by

$$d = \frac{(Cd - Ca)}{\mu Ca}r \tag{2.2.7}$$

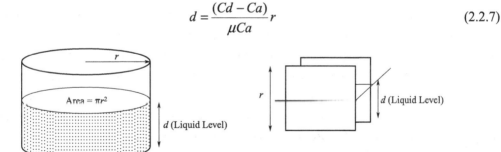

(a)   (b)

Figure 2.2.1   Shows the relation between (a) volume of liquid and the cross-sectional area and the liquid depth and (b) liquid level, plate capacitance, and a known dielectric constant in a nonconducting liquid.

2.2.3 Level Sensing Devices

There are two categories of level sensing devices. They are direct sensing, in which case the actual level is monitored, and indirect sensing where a property of the liquid such as pressure is sensed to determine the liquid level.

Direct Level Sensing

Sight glass (open end/differential) or gauge is the simplest method for direct visual reading. As shown in Figure 2.2.2 the sight glass is normally mounted vertically adjacent to the container.

The liquid level can then be observed directly in the sight glass. The container in Figure 2.2.2(a) is closed. In this case the ends of the glass are connected to the top and bottom of the tank, as would be used with a pressurized container (boiler) or a container with volatile, flammable, hazardous, or pure liquids. In cases where the tank contains inert liquids such as water and pressurization is not required, the tank and sight glass can both be open to the atmosphere as shown in Figure 2.2.2(b). The top of the sight glass must have the same pressure conditions as the top of the liquid or the liquid levels in the tank and sight glass will be different. In cases where the sight glass is excessively long, a second inert liquid with higher density than the liquid in the container can be used in the sight glass (see Figure 2.2.2(c)).

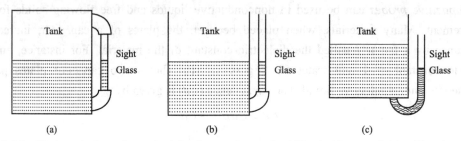

Figure 2.2.2 Various configurations of a sight glass to observe liquid levels (a) pressurized or closed container, (b) open container, and (c) higher density sight glass liquid.

Floats (angular arm or pulley) are shown in Figure 2.2.3. The figure shows two types of simple float sensors. The float material is less dense than the density of the liquid and floats up and down on top of the material being measured. In Figure 2.2.3(a) a float with a pulley is used; this method can be used with either liquids or free flowing solids. With free flowing solids, agitation is sometimes used to level the solids. An advantage of the float sensor is that it is almost independent of the density of the liquid or solid being monitored. If the surface of the material being monitored is turbulent, causing the float reading to vary excessively, some means of damping might be used in the system. In Figure 2.2.3(b) a ball float is attached to an arm; the angle of the arm is measured to indicate the level of the material (an example of the use of this type of sensor is the monitoring of the fuel level in the tank of an automobile). Although very simple and cheap to manufacture, the disadvantage of this type of float is its nonlinearity as shown by the line of sight scale in Figure 2.2.4(a). The scale can be replaced with a potentiometer to obtain an electrical signal that can be linearized for industrial use.

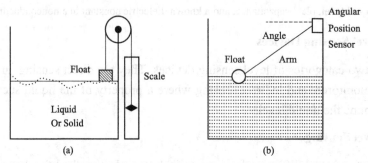

Figure 2.2.3 Methods of measuring liquid levels using (a) a simple float with level indicator on the outside of the tank and (b) an angular arm float.

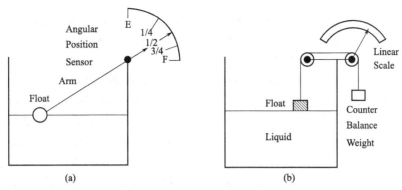

Figure 2.2.4 Scales used with float level sensors (a) nonlinear scale with angular arm float and (b) linear scale with a pulley type of float.

Figure 2.2.4(b) shows an alternative method of using pulleys to obtain a direct visual scale that can be replaced by a potentiometer to obtain a linear electrical output with level.

Probes for measuring liquid levels fall into three categories, i.e., conductive, capacitive, and ultrasonic.

Conductive probes are used for single-point measurements in liquids that are conductive and nonvolatile as a spark can occur. Conductive probes are shown in Figure 2.2.5(a). Two or more probes as shown can be used to indicate set levels. If the liquid is in a metal container, the container can be used as the common probe. When the liquid is in contact with two probes the voltage between the probes causes a current to flow indicating that a set level has been reached. Thus, probes can be used to indicate when the liquid level is low and to operate a pump to fill the container. Another or a third probe can be used to indicate when the tank is full and to turn off the filling pump.

Capacitive probes are used in liquids that are nonconductive and have a high μ and can be used for continuous level monitoring. The capacitive probe shown in Figure 2.2.5(b) consists of an inner rod with an outer shell; the capacitance is measured between the two using a capacitance bridge. In the portion out of the liquid, air serves as the dielectric between the rod and outer shell. In the immersed section, the dielectric is that of the liquid that causes a large capacitive change, if the tank is made of metal it can serve as the outer shell. The capacitance change is directly proportional to the level of the liquid. The dielectric constant of the liquid must be known for this type of measurement. The dielectric constant can vary with temperature so that temperature correction may be required.

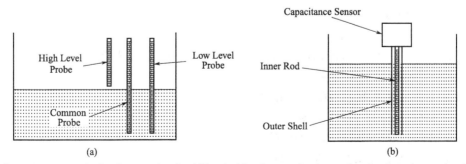

Figure 2.2.5 Methods of measuring liquid levels (a) using conductive probes for detecting set levels and (b) a capacitive probe for continuous monitoring.

Ultrasonics can be used for single point or continuous level measurement of a liquid or a solid. A single ultrasonic transmitter and receiver can be arranged with a gap as shown in Figure 2.2.6(a) to give single-point measurement. As soon as liquid fills the gap, ultrasonic waves from the transmitter reach the receiver. A setup for continuous measurement is shown in Figure 2.2.6(b). Ultrasonic waves from the transmitter are reflected by the surface of the liquid to the receiver; the time for the waves to reach the receiver is measured. The time delay gives the distance from the transmitter and receiver to the surface of the liquid, from which the liquid level can be calculated knowing the velocity of ultrasonic waves. As there is no contact with the liquid, this method can be used for solids and corrosive and volatile liquids. In a liquid the transmitter and receiver can also be placed on the bottom of the container and the time measured for a signal to be reflected from the surface of the liquid to the receiver to measure the depth of the liquid.

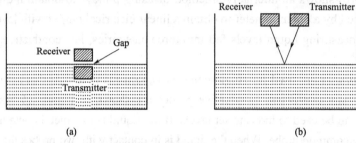

Figure 2.2.6　Use of ultrasonics for (a) single-point liquid level measurement and (b) continuous liquid level measurements made by timing reflections from the surface of the liquid.

Selected form *"Fundamentals of Industrial Instrumentation and Process Control, William C.Dunn, McGraw-Hill Ine., 2005"*

Words and Expressions

1. flowing　　['fləuiŋ]　　*adj.* 流动的
2. predetermine　　[ˌpriːdiˈtəːmin]　　*vt.* 预定，预置
3. overflow　　[ˌəuvəˈfləu]　　*vi.* 溢出，溢流
4. uninterrupted　　[ˈʌnˌintəˈrʌptid]　　*adj.* 不停的，不间断的，连续的
5. specific weight　　比重
6. buoyancy　　['bɔiənsi]　　*n.* 浮力，浮动性
7. immerse　　[iˈməːs]　　*vt.* 浸没，沉入
8. capacitive probe　　电容电极
9. nonconductive　　[ˈnɔnkənˈdʌktiv]　　*adj.* 不传导的，不导电的，非导电
10. dielectric constant　　介电常数
11. sight glass　　玻璃液面计，观察玻璃，观察孔
12. pressurized container　　带压容器，带压储罐
13. flammable　　[ˈflæməbl]　　*adj.* 易燃的
14. hazardous　　[ˈhæzədəs]　　*adj.* 危险的，易爆的
15. float　　[fləut]　　*n.* 浮体，浮球，浮标，沉桶

16. dense [dens] *adj.* 密集的，稠密的，厚的
17. pulley ['puli] *n.* 滑轮
18. conductive [kən'dʌktiv] *adj.* 传导的，导电的，传热的
19. ultrasonic [ˌʌltrə'sɔnik] *adj.* 超声的，超音的，超音速的
20. nonvolatile [nɔn'vɔlətail] *adj.* 永久的，不挥发的，非挥发性的
21. spark [spɑːk] *n.* 火花，电火花
22. rod [rɔd] *n.* 拉杆，连杆

Exercise

1. *Put the following into Chinese:*

Level measurement   container   interface   buoyancy   immersed
radium   capacitive probe   nonconductive   dielectric constant
sight glass   float   level formula

2. *Put the following into English:*

密度   浮力式液面计   浮球   标尺   电位计   导电电极
电容电极   超声波   张力式仪表   应变仪   荷重传感器

Reading Material:

Indirect Level Sensing

The most commonly used method of indirectly measuring a liquid level is to measure the hydrostatic pressure at the bottom of the container. The depth can then be extrapolated from the pressure and the specific weight of the liquid can be calculated using Eq.(2.2.1). The pressure can be measured by any of the methods given in the section on pressure. The dial on the pressure gauge can be calibrated directly in liquid depth. The depth of liquid can also be measured using bubblers, radiation, resistive tapes, and by weight measurements.

Example 1 A pressure gauge located at the base of an open tank containing a liquid with a specific weight of 54.5 lb/ft^3 registers 11.7 psi. What is the depth of the fluid in the tank?

From Eq.(2.2.1)

$$h = \frac{p}{\gamma} = \frac{11.7\text{psi} \times 144}{54.5 \text{lb/ft}^3} = 30.9 \text{ft}$$

Bubbler devices require a supply of clean air or inert gas. The setup is shown in Figure 2.2.7(a). Gas is forced through a tube whose open end is close to the bottom of the tank. The specific weight of the gas is negligible compared to the liquid and can be ignored. The pressure required to force the liquid out of the tube is equal to the pressure at the end of the tube due to the liquid, which is the depth of the liquid multiplied by the specific weight of the liquid. This method can be used with corrosive liquids as the material of the tube can be chosen to be corrosion resistant.

Example 2 How far below the surface of the water is the end of a bubbler tube, if bubbles

start to emerge from the end of the tube when the air pressure in the bubbler is 148 kPa?
From Eq. (2.2.1)

$$h = \frac{p}{\gamma} = \frac{148 \text{ kPa} \times 10^{-4}}{1 \text{ gm/cm}^3} = 14.8 \text{ cm}$$

Radiation methods are sometimes used in cases where the liquid is corrosive, very hot, or detrimental to installing sensors. For single-point measurement only one transmitter and a detector are required. If several single-point levels are required, a detector will be required for each level measurement as shown in Figure 2.2.7(b). The disadvantages of this system are the cost and the need to handle radioactive material.

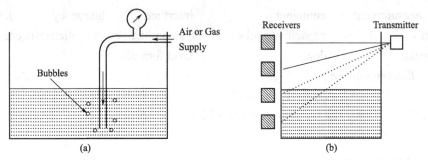

Figure 2.2.7 Liquid level measurements can be made (a) using a bubbler technique or (b) using a radiation technique.

Resistive tapes can be used to measure liquid levels (see Figure 2.2.8). A resistive element is placed in close proximity to a conductive strip in an easily compressible nonconductive sheath;

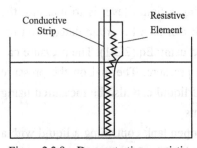

Figure 2.2.8 Demonstrating a resistive tape level sensor.

the pressure of the liquid pushes the resistive element against the conductive strip, shorting out a length of the resistive element proportional to the depth of the liquid. The sensor can be used in liquids or slurries, it is cheap but is not rugged or accurate, it is prone to humidity problems, and measurement accuracy depends on material density.

Load cells can be used to measure the weight of a tank and its contents. The weight of the container is subtracted from the reading, leaving the weight of the contents of the container. Knowing the cross-sectional area of the tank and the specific weight of the material, the volume and/or depth of the contents can be calculated. This method is well suited for continuous measurement and the material being weighed does not come into contact with the sensor. Figure 2.2.9(a) shows two elements that can be used in load sensors for measuring force. Figure shows a cantilever beam used as a force or weight sensor. The beam is rigidly attached at one end and a force is applied to the other end, a strain gauge attached to the beam is used to measure the strain in the beam, a second strain gauge is used for temperature compensation. Figure 2.2.9(b) shows a piezoelectric sensor used to measure force or weight. The sensor gives an output voltage proportional to the force applied.

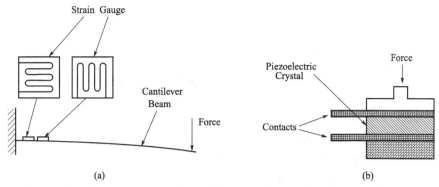

Figure 2.2.9 Force sensors can be used for measuring weight using (a) strain gauge technique or (b) a piezoelectric technique.

Example 3 What is the depth of the liquid in a container, if the specific weight of the liquid is 82 lb/ft^3; the container weights 45 lb and is 21 in in diameter? A load cell measures a total weight of 385 lb.

Using Eq.(2.2.4) and (2.2.5) we get the following:

$$\text{Weight of liquid} = 385 - 45 = 340 \text{ lb}$$

$$\text{Volume of liquid} = \frac{3.14 \times 21 \times 21 \times d}{12 \times 12 \times 4} \text{ ft} = \frac{340 \text{ lb}}{82 \text{ lb/ft}^3}$$

$$\text{Depth } (d) = \frac{4.15 \times 576}{1384.7} \text{ ft} = 1.73 \text{ ft} = 20.7 \text{ in}$$

Selected from "*Fundamentals of Industrial Instrumentation and Process Control, William C. Dunn, McGraw-Hill Ins, 2005*"

Words and Expressions

1. indirect   [,indi'rekt]   *adj.* 间接的，非直接的
2. hydrostatic   [,haidrəu'stætik]   *adj.* 静力学的，流体静力学的，水压的
3. extrapolate   [ik'stræpəleit]   *vt.* 推断，推知，外推
4. dial   ['daiəl]   *n.* 表盘，表面，钟面，指针，刻度盘
5. bubble   ['bʌbl]   *n.* 水泡，气泡，冒泡
6. radiation   [,reidi'eiʃən]   *n.* 发射，放射，放射线
7. resistive   [ri'zistiv]   *adj.* 电阻的，抵抗的，有阻力的
8. register   ['redʒistə]   *n.* 登记表，自动记录器
9. ignore   [ig'nɔː]   *vt.* 不管，忽略，不计
10. corrosive   [kə'rəusiv]   *adj.* 腐蚀性的，生锈的，侵蚀的
11. load cell   荷重元件，载荷传感器
12. cantilever   ['kæntiliːvə]   *n.* 悬臂梁
13. rigidity   [ri'dʒiditi]   *n.* 刚性，刚度，硬度
14. beam   [biːm]   *n.* 横梁，秤杆，天平梁

2.3 Flow Measurements

This unit covers the following topics:
1. Reynolds number and ist application to flow patterns
2. Formulas used in follow measurements
3. Bernoulli equation and its applications
4. Flow measurements using differential pressure measuring devices and their characteristics

2.3.1 Introduction

This unit discusses the basic terms and formulas used in flow measurements and instrumentation. The measurement of fluid flow is very important in industrial applications. Optimum performance of some equipment and operations require specific flow rates. The cost of many liquids and gases are based on the measured flow through a pipeline making it necessary to accurately measure and control the rate of flow for accounting purposes.

2.3.2 Basic Terms

This unit will be using terms and definitions from previous units as well as introducing a number of new definitions related to flow and flow rate sensing.

Velocity is a measure of speed and direction of an object. When related to fluids it is the rate of flow of fluid particles in a pipe. The speed of particles in a fluid flow varies across the flow, i.e., where the fluid is in contact with the constraining walls (the boundary layer) the velocity of the liquid particles is virtually zero; in the center of the flow the liquid particles will have the maximum velocity. Thus, the average rate of flow is used in flow calculations. The units of flow are normally feet per second (fps), feet per minute (fpm), meters per second (mps), and so on. Previously, the pressures associated with fluid flow were defined as static, impact, or dynamic.

Laminar flow of a liquid occurs when its average velocity is comparatively low and the fluid particles tend to move smoothly in layers, as shown in Figure 2.3.1(a). The velocity of the particles

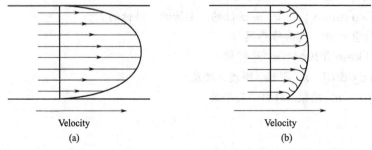

Figure 2.3.1   Flow velocity variations across a pipe with (a) laminar flow and (b) turbulent flow.

across the liquid takes a parabolic shape.

Turbulent flow occurs when the flow velocity is high and the particles no longer flow smoothly in layers and turbulence or a rolling effect occurs. This is shown in Figure 2.3.1(b). Note also the flattening of the velocity profile.

Viscosity is a property of a gas or liquid that is a measure of its resistance to motion or flow. A viscous liquid such as syrup has a much higher viscosity than water and water has a higher viscosity than air. Syrup, because of its high viscosity, flows very slowly and it is very hard to move an object through it. Viscosity (dynamic) can be measured in poise or centipoise, whereas kinematic viscosity (without force) is measured in stokes or centistokes. Dynamic or absolute viscosity is used in the Reynolds and flow equations.

The *Reynolds number R* is a derived relationship combining the density and viscosity of a liquid with its velocity of flow and the cross-sectional dimensions of the flow and takes the form

$$R = \frac{VD\rho}{\mu} \tag{2.3.1}$$

Where V=average fluid velocity
D=diameter of the pipe
ρ=density of the liquid
μ=absolute viscosity

Flow patterns can be considered to be laminar, turbulent, or a combination of both. Osborne Reynolds observed in 1880 that the flow pattern could be predicted from physical properties of the liquid. If the Reynolds number for the flow in a pipe is equal to or less than 2000 the flow will be laminar. From 2000 to about 5000 is the intermediate region where the flow can be laminar, turbulent, or a mixture of both, depending upon other factors. Beyond 5000 the flow is always turbulent.

The *Bernoulli equation* is an equation for flow based on the law of conservation of energy, which states that the total energy of a fluid or gas at any one point in a flow is equal to the total energy at all other points in the flow.

Energy factors. Most flow equations are based on the law of energy conservation and relate the average fluid or gas velocity, pressure, and the height of fluid above a given reference point. This relationship is given by the Bernoulli equation. The equation can be modified to take into account energy losses due to friction and increase in energy as supplied by pumps.

Energy losses in flowing fluids are caused by friction between the fluid and the containment walls and by fluid impacting an object. In most cases these losses should be taken into account. Whilst these equations apply to both liquids and gases, they are more complicated in gases because of the fact that gases are compressible.

Flow rate is the volume of fluid passing a given point in a given amount of time and is typically measured in gallons per minute (gpm), cubic feet perminute (cfm), liter per minute, and so on. Table 2.3.1 gives the flow rate conversion factors.

Total flow is the volume of liquid flowing over a period of time and is measured in gallons, cubic feet, liters and so forth.

Table 2.3.1 Flow Rate Conversion Factors

1 gal/min=6.309×10⁻⁵m³/s	1 L/min=16.67×10⁻⁶m³/s
1 gal/min=3.78 L/min	1 cu ft/sec=449 gal/min
1 gal/min=0.1337ft³/min	1 gal/min=0.00223ft³/s
1 gal water=231 in³	1 cu ft water=7.48 gal

1 gal water=0.1337 ft³=231 in³; 1 gal water=8.35 lb; 1ft³ water=7.48 gal; 1000 liter water=1 m³; 1 litter water=1 kg

2.3.3 Flow Formulas

Continuity equation

The continuity equation states that if the overall flow rate in a system is not changing with time (see Figure 2.3.2(a)), the flow rate in any part of the system is constant. From which we get the following equation:

$$Q=VA \tag{2.3.2}$$

Where Q=flow rate

V=average velocity

A=cross-sectional area of the pipe

The units on both sides of the equation must be compatible, i.e., English units or metric units.

Example 1 What is the flow rate through a pipe 9 in diameter, if the average velocity is 5 fps?

$$Q=\frac{5 \text{ ft/s} \times \pi \times 0.75^2 \text{ ft}^2}{4}=2.21 \text{ cfs}=\frac{2.21 \text{ gps}}{0.137}=16.1 \text{ gps}=16.1\times 60 \text{ gpm}=968 \text{ gpm}$$

If liquids are flowing in a tube with different cross section areas, i.e., A_1 and A_2, as is shown in Figure 2.3.2(b), the continuity equation gives

$$Q=V_1A_1=V_2A_2 \tag{2.3.3}$$

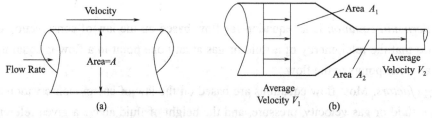

Figure 2.3.2 Flow diagram used for use in the continuity equation: (a) fixed diameter and (b) effects of different diameters on the flow rate.

Bernoulli equation

The Bernoulli equation gives the relation between pressure, fluid velocity, and elevation in a flow system. The equation is accredited to Bernoulli (1738). When applied to Figure 2.3.3(a) the following is obtained:

$$\frac{p_A}{\gamma_A}=\frac{V_A^2}{2g}+Z_A=\frac{p_B}{\gamma_B}=\frac{V_B^2}{2g}+Z_B \tag{2.3.4}$$

where p_A and p_B=absolute static pressures at points A and B, respectively

γ_A and γ_B =specific weights

V_A and V_B=average fluid velocities

g=acc of gravity

Z_A and Z_B=elevations above a given reference level, i.e., Z_A–Z_B is the head of fluid.

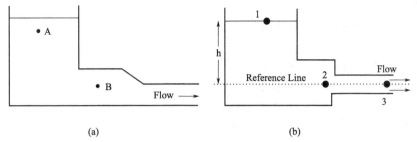

Figure 2.3.3 Container diagrams (a) the pressures at points A and B are related by the Bernoulli equation and (b) application of the Bernoulli.

The units in Eq. (2.3.4) are consistent and reduce to units of length (feet in the English system and meter in the SI system of units) as follows:

$$\text{Pressure energy} = \frac{p}{\gamma} = \frac{\text{lb/ft}^2 (\text{N/m}^2)}{\text{lb/ft}^3 (\text{N/m}^3)} = \text{ft(m)}$$

$$\text{Kinetic energy} = \frac{V^2}{g} = \frac{(\text{ft/s})^2 (\text{m/s}^2)}{\text{ft/s}^2 (\text{m/s}^2)} = \text{ft(m)}$$

$$\text{Potential energy} = Z = \text{ft(m)}$$

This equation is a conservation of energy equation and assumes no loss of energy between points A and B. The first term represents energy stored due to pressure, the second term represents kinetic energy or energy due to motion, and the third term represents potential energy or energy due to height. This energy relationship can be seen if each term is multiplied by mass per unit volume which cancels as the mass per unit volume is the same at points A and B. The equation can be used between any two positions in a flow system. The pressures used in the Bernoulli equation must be absolute pressures.

In the fluid system shown in Figure 2.3.3(b) the flow velocity V at point 3 can be derived from Eq.(2.3.4) and is as follows using point 2 as the reference line.

$$\frac{p_1}{\gamma_1} + 0 + h = \frac{p_3}{\gamma_3} + \frac{V_3^2}{2g} + 0 \tag{2.3.5}$$

$$V_3 = \sqrt{2gh}$$

Point 3 at the exit has dynamic pressure but no static pressure above 1 atm, and hence, p_3=p_1=1 atm and γ_1=γ_3. This shows that the velocity of the liquid flowing out of the system is directly proportional to the square root of the height of the liquid above the reference point.

Selected from *"Fundamentals of Industrial Instrumentation and Process Control, William C.Dunn, McGraw-Hill Inc., 2005"*

Words and Expressions

1. accounting   [əˈkauntiŋ]   *n.* 统计, 计算, 结算
2. velocity   [viˈlɔsiti]   *n.* 速度

3. particle ['pɑ:tikl] n. 粒子，质点，颗粒
4. virtually ['və:tjuəl:] adv. 实际上
5. laminar flow 层流
6. parabolic shape 抛物线型，抛物线状
7. turbulent flow 湍流
8. viscosity [vis'kɔsiti] n. 黏性，黏度，内摩擦
9. syrup ['sirəp] n. 浆，糖浆，糖汁
10. poise [pɔiz] n. 平衡剂，缓冲剂，泊（黏度单位）
11. centipoise ['senti,pɔiz] 厘泊（黏度单位），10^{-2} 泊
12. kinematics [kaini'mætiks] n. 运动学
13. stock [stɔk] n. 存料，原料，树干，库存，股票
14. centistoke ['senti,stɔk] 厘沱（动力黏度单位）
15. Reynolds number R 雷诺数 R
16. flow patterns 流型，流动型式
17. Bernoulli equation 伯努利方程
18. energy factors 能量因素，品质因素
19. energy losses 能量损失
20. flow rate 流率，流速
21. total flow 总体流量
22. continuity equation 连续方程
23. acc of gravity 重力加速度

Exercise

1. *Put the following into Chinese:*

   flow rate   accounting   laminar flow   energy losses
   total flow   Pressure energy   kinetic energy   potential energy
   restriction   orifice plate   Venturi tube   flow nozzle
   elbow   rotameter   mass flow

2. *Put the following into English:*

   雷诺数   流型   伯努利方程   流速   湍流   黏度
   能量守恒   摩擦力   参考点   重力加速度   连续性方程

Reading Material:

Flow Measurement Instruments

Flow measurements are normally indirect measurements using differential pressures to measure the flow rate. Flow measurements can be divided into the following groups: flow rate, total flow, and mass flow. The choice of the measuring device will depend on the required accuracy and fluid characteristics(gas, liquid, suspended particulates, temperature, viscosity, and so on.)

Flow rate

Differential pressure measurements can be made for flow rate determination when a fluid flows through a restriction. The restriction produces an increase in pressure which can be directly related to flow rate. Figure 2.3.4 shows examples of commonly used restrictions; (a) orifice plate, (b) Venturi tube, (c) flow nozzle.

The orifice plate is normally a simple metal diaphragm with a constricting hole. The diaphragm is normally clamped between pipe flanges to give easy access. The differential pressure ports can be located in the flange on either side of the orifice plate as shown in Figure 2.3.4(a), or alternatively, at specific locations in the pipe on either side of the flange determined by the flow patterns (named vena contracta). A differential pressure gauge is used to measure the difference in pressure between the two ports; the differential pressure gauge can be calibrated in flow rates. The lagging edge of the hole in the diaphragm is beveled to minimize turbulence. In fluids the hole is normally centered in the diaphragm, see Figure 2.3.5(a). However, if the fluid contains particulates, the hole could be placed at the bottom of the pipe to prevent a build up of particulates as in Figure 2.3.5(b). The hole can also be in the form of a semicircle having the same diameter as the pipe and located at the bottom of the pipe as in Figure 2.3.5(c).

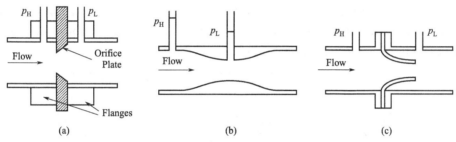

Figure 2.3.4　Types of constrictions used in flow rate measuring devices
(a)orifice plate, (b)Venturi tube, (c)flow nozzle.

The Venturi tube shown in Figure 2.3.4(a) uses the same differential pressure principle as the orifice plate. The Venturi tube normally uses a specific reduction in tube size, and is not used in larger diameter pipes where it becomes heavy and excessively long. The advantages of the Venturi tube are its ability to handle large amounts of suspended solids, it creates less turbulence and hence less insertion loss than the orifice plate. The differential pressure taps in the Venturi tube are located at the minimum and maximum pipe diameters. The Venturi tube has good accuracy but has a high cost.

The flow nozzle is a good compromise on the cost and accuracy between the orifice plate and the Venturi tube for clean liquids. It is not normally used with suspended particles. Its main use is the measurement of steam flow. The flow nozzle is shown in Figure 2.3.4(c).

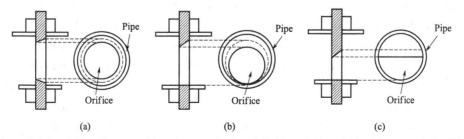

Figure 2.3.5　Orifice shapes and locations used (a) with fluids and (b) and (c) with suspended solids.

To summarize, the orifice is the simplest, cheapest, easiest to replace, least accurate, more subject to damage and erosion, and has the highest loss. The Venturi tube is more difficult to replace, most expensive, most accurate, has high tolerance to damage and erosion, and the lowest losses of all the three tubes. The flow nozzle is intermediate between the other tow and offers a good compromise. The Dall tube has the advantage of having the lowest insertion loss but cannot be used with slurries.

The elbow can be used as a differential flow meter. Figure 2.3.6(a) shows the cross section of an elbow. When a fluid is flowing, there is a differential pressure between the inside and outside of the elbow due to the change in direction of the fluid. The pressure difference is proportional to the flow rate of the fluid. The elbow meter is good for handling particulates in solution, with good wear and erosion resistance characteristics but has low sensitivity.

The pilot static tube shown in Figure 2.3.6(b) is an alternative method of measuring the flow rate, but has some disadvantages in measuring flow, in that it really measures the fluid velocity at the nozzle. Because the velocity varies over the cross section of the pipe, the Pilot static tube should be moved across the pipe to establish an average velocity, or the tube should be calibrated for one area. Other disadvantages are that the tube can become clogged with particulates and the differential pressure between the impact and static pressures for low flow rates may not be enough to give the required accuracy. The differential pressures in any of the above devices can be measured using the pressure measuring sensors discussed in Unit1.

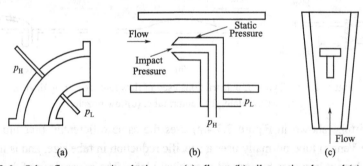

Figure 2.3.6 Other flow measuring devices are (a) elbow, (b) pilot static tube, and (c) rotameter.

Variable-area meters, such as the rotameter shown in Figure 2.3.6(c) are often used as a direct visual indicator for flow rate measurements. The rotameter is a vertical tapered tube with a T (or similar) shaped weight. The tube is graduated in flow rate for the characteristics of the gas or liquid flowing up the tube. The velocity of a fluid or gas flowing decreases as it goes higher up the tube, due to the increase in the bore of the tube. Hence, the buoyancy on the weight reduces the higher up the tube it goes. An equilibrium point is eventually reached where the force on the weight due to the flowing fluid is equal to that of the weight, i. e., the higher the flow rate the higher the weight goes up the tube. The position of the weight is also dependent on its size and density, the viscosity and density of the fluid, and the bore and taper of the tube. The Rotameter has a low insertion loss and has a linear relationship to flow rate. In cases where the weight is not visible, i, e., an opaque tube used to reduce corrosion and the like, it can be made of a magnetic material and tracked by a magnetic sensor on the outside of the tube. The rotameter can be used to measure differential pressures across a constriction or flow in both liquids and gases.

Selected from "*Fundamentals of Industrial Instrumentation and Process Control, William C. Dunn, McGraw-Hill Inc., 2005*"

Words and Expressions

1. restriction   [ris'trikʃən]   *n.* 节流，限制，油门
2. arifice plate   孔板
3. venturi tube   文丘里管
4. flow nozzle   测流嘴
5. constricting hole   节流孔
6. clamp   ['klæmp]   *n.* 夹板，压板，夹紧
7. port   [pɔ:t]   *n.* 气门，出品，入口，孔，空气口
8. vena contracta   缩脉，收缩断面
9. lagging edge   后沿下降边，后沿，脉冲后沿
10. bevel   ['bevəl]   *n.* 斜角，斜边
11. insertion   [in'sə:ʃən]   *n.* 插入，插放，安置
12. compromise   ['kɔmprəmaiz]   *n.* 折衷，综合平衡
13. ratio   ['reiʃiəu]   *n.* 比率，比值
14. elbow   ['elbəu]   *n.* 肘，弯管接头，弯管，弯头，弯管流量计
15. pilot static tube   测量静力管，导向静力管
16. rotameter   ['rəutə,mi:tə]   *n.* 转子流量计，转子式测速仪
17. buoyancy   ['bɔiənsi]   *n.* 浮力
18. bore   [bɔ:]   *n.* 腔，中心孔
19. taper   ['te:pə]   *n.* 圆锥形，尖锥形
20. opaque   [əu'pe:k]   *adj.* 不透明的，不传导的，不传热的

2.4 Temperature Measurement

> *Topics covered in this unit are as follows:*
> 1. The principles of temperature measurement
> 2. The principle of thermocouple
> 3. The wide variety of temperature measuring devices

2.4.1 Principles of temperature measurement

Temperature measurement is very important in spheres of life and especially so in the process industries. However, it poses particular problems, since temperature measurement cannot be related to a fundamental standard of temperature in the same way that the measurement of other quanities can be related to the primary standards of mass, length and time.

This is a root cause of the fundamental difficulties that exist in establishing an absolute standard for temperature in the form of a relationship between it and other measurable quantities for which a primary standard unit exists. In the absence of such a relationship, it is necessary to establish fixed, reproducible reference points for temperature in the form of freezing and boiling points of substances,where the transition between solid,liquid and gaseous states is sharply defined.The International Practical Temperature Scale (IPTS)* uses this philosophy and designes six primary fixed points for reference temperatures in terms of:

- The triple point of equilibrium hydrogen $-259.34\,°C$
- The boiling point of oxygen $-182.962\,°C$
- The boiling point of water $100.0\,°C$
- The freezing point of zinc $419.58\,°C$
- The freezing point of silver $961.93\,°C$
- The freezing point of gold $1064.43\,°C$

(all at standard atmospheric pressure)

The freezing points of certain other metals are also used as secondary fixed points to provide additional reference points during calibration procedures.

Instruments to measure temperature can be divided into separate classes according to the physical principle on which they operate.The main principles used are:

- The thermoelectric effect
- Resistance change
- Sensitivity of semiconductor device
- Radiative heat emission
- Thermography

- Thermal expansion
- Resonant frequency change
- Sensitivity of fiber optic devices
- Acoustic thermometry
- Colour change
- Change of state of material

2.4.2 Thermocouples

Thermoelectric effect sensors rely on the physical principle that,when any two different metals are connected together,an e.m.f., which is a function of the temperature, is generated at the junction between the metals. The general form of this relationship is:

$$e = a_1T + a_2T^2 + a_3T^3 + \cdots + a_nT^n$$

Where e is the e.m.f. generated and T is the absolute temperature.

This is clearly non-linear,which is inconvenient for measurement applications. Fortunately, for certain pairs of materials, the terms involving squared and higher powers of T (a_2T^2, a_3T^3, etc.) are approximately zero and the e.m.f.–temperature relationship is approximately linear according to:

$$e \approx a_1T$$

Wires of such pairs of materials are connected together at one end, and in this form are known as thermocouples. Thermocouples are a very important class of divice as they provide the most commonly used method of measuring temperatures in industry.

Atypical thermocouple, made from one chromel wire and one constantan wire, is shown in Figure 2.4.1(a). For analysis purposes, it is useful to represent the thermocouple by its equivalent electrical circuit, shown in Figure 2.4.1(b). The e.m.f. generated at the point where the different wires are connected together is represented by a voltage source, E_1, and the point is known as the hot iunction. The temperature of the hot junction is customarily shown as T_h on the diagram. The e.m.f. generated at the hot junction is measured at the open ends of the thermocouple,which is known as the reference junction.

Thermocouple wires are manufactured to close tolerances and tend to be expensive. Their use is thus limited to the probe itself. Thermocouple extension wires,compatible with the T/C wires, are used as the link between the T/C and the measuring device or transducer.

The evolution of modern electronics has created transducer small enough to fit inside the T/C box (or head). The major advantage of this arrangement is the avoidance of long-distance transmission of a very low T/C voltage signal.Such a low voltage signal is prone to electrical noise (as opposed to the 4~20 mA signal).

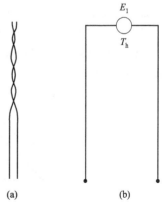

Figure 2.4.1 (a) Thermocuple; (b) equivalent circuit.

Application Notes

The three basic types of T/C construction are:
- Ceramic beaded,
- Insulated (plastic, glass, or ceramic fiber); they are generally extruded (Figure 2.4.2),

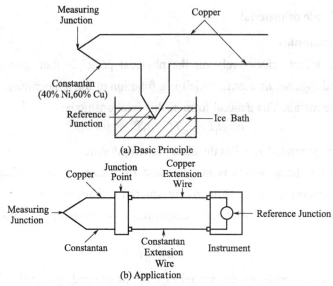

Figure 2.4.2   Thermocouples(using copper-constantan)2.

- Metal-sheathed mineral-insulated (MSMI); the sheath is generally stainless steel or Inconel, and mineral insulation is generally magnesium oxide or aluminum oxide. Sheathed material can give the T/C excellent protection from outside chemical and mechanical effects. However, sheathed T/Cs, since they are a one-piece construction, are more difficult to strip and terminate than other types. The junction should be welded and insulated.

Thermocouples can be constructed to be protected or exposed. If protected, they can be grounded or ungrounded. When grounded they give a faster response (since good temperature transfer is obtained); however, they are susceptible to electrical noise (due to stray electrical signal pickup). When T/Cs are ungrounded, they are slower to respond but are electrically isolated. In addition, a T/C may be spring-loaded in the thermowell so that the tip and well surface remain in contact to ensure good heat transfer. If exposed, the fastest response is provided, but the wires are totally unprotected.

Typical thermocouple assembly is showed in Figure 2.4.3.

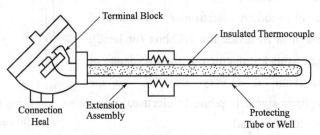

Figure 2.4.3   Typical thermocouple assembly.

Thermocouples are self-powered and of single and rugged (shock-resistant) construction. They are inexpensive (half the price of an RTD), come in a wide choice of physical forms, and provide a wide temperature range. In addition, they can be calibrated to generate a specific curve (for an extra cost) and are easy to interchange. They provide a fast response and measurement at one specific point.

Selected from "*The Condensed Handbook of Measurement and Control*", *Battikha. N.E., Instrument Society of America*, 1997, *and* "*Measurement and Instrumentation principles, Alans. Morris, Butterworth-Heineman*, 2001"

Words and Expressions

1. sphere [sfiə] *n.* 范围，球体，球形
2. triple point 三态点
3. boiling point 沸点
4. freezing point 凝点
5. zinc [ziŋk] *n.* 锌
6. thermoelectric effect 热电势效应
7. thermography 热像仪
8. fiber optic 光纤
9. Acoustic thermometry 声测温技术
10. thermocouple ['θəːməukʌpl] 热电偶 (T/C)
11. e.m.f 电动势
12. IPTS (International Practicl Temperature Scale) 国际实用温标
13. transducer [træns'djusə] 变速器，传感器
14. thermowell [θəːməu'wel] *n.* 热电偶套管，测温插套
15. liquid-in-glass thermometer *n.* 充液管式温度计
16. capillary [kə'piləri] *adj.* 毛细的
17. rugged [rʌgid] *adj.* 坚固的
18. susceptible [sə'septibl] *adj.* 易受影响的
19. be compatible with 与……一致；与……兼容
20. junction ['dʒʌŋkʃən] *n.* 接触点，接触端
21. ceramic beaded 陶制珠状的
22. extrude [ek'struːd] *v.* 挤压；突出
23. sheath [ʃiːθ] *n.* 鞘；护套
24. magnesium oxide [mæg'niːziəm 'ɔksaid] *n.* 氧化镁
25. aluminum oxide [ə'luːminəm 'ɔksaid] *n.* 氧化铝
26. weld [weld] *v.* 焊接
27. grounded [graundid] *adj.* 接地的
28. deterioration [di'tiəriəreiʃən] *n.* 变坏，恶化；退化
29. oxidize ['ɔksidaiz] *v.* 氧化，生锈
30. irrelevant [i'relivənt] *adj.* 不相关的，不切题的

Exercise

1. *Answer the questions bellow:*
   (1) How many parts does a typical temperature assembly consist of and what are they?
   (2) Which of the following descriptions is not true for the filled-system thermometer?
       a. Special ambient temperature is not required for the system which is slow to respond.
       b. The filled bulb transducers temperature to volumetric expansion of the fluid directly.
       c. Being used, the bulb must be immersed sufficiently.
       d. Is is still useful although its drawbacks restrict its application.
   (3) Why are there thermocouple extension wires more than T/C wires used as the link between the T/C and the measuring device or transducer?
   (4) What is the advantage of small transducers that can be fit inside the T/C head?

2. *Put the following into Chinese:*

   Sphere   fundamental standard   absolute standard
   thermoelectric effect resistance change   thermography
   thermal expansion   resonant frequency   fiber optic
   acoustic thermometry colour change   expensive
   ceramic beaded   junction

3. *Put the following into English:*

   热电偶   热电阻   冰点   沸点   固态
   液态   气态   国际实际温标   物理原理   电动势
   不锈钢   接地的   隔离

Reading Material:

Temperature Measuring Devices

> *There are several methods of measuring temperature that can be categorized as follows:*
> 1. Expansion of a material to give visual indication, pressure, or dimensional change
> 2. Electrical resistance change
> 3. Semiconductor characteristic change
> 4. Voltage generated by dissimilar metals
> 5. Radiated energy
>
> Thermometer is often used as a general term given to devices for measuring temperature. Examples of temperature measuring devices are described below.

1. Thermometers

Mercury in glass was by far the most common direct visual reading thermometer (if not the only one). The device consisted of a small bore graduated glass tube with a small bulb containing a reservoir of mercury. The coefficient of expansion of mercury is several times greater than the coefficient of expansion of glass, so that as the temperature increases the mercury rises up the tube giving a relative low cost and accurate method of measuring temperature. Mercury also has the advantage of not wetting the glass, and hence, cleanly traverses the glass tube without breaking into globules or coating the tube. The operating range of the mercury thermometer is from −30 to 800℉ (−35 to 450℃) (freezing point of mercury −38℉ [−38℃]). The toxicity of mercury, ease of breakage, the introduction of cost effective, accurate, and easily read digital thermometers has brought about the demise of the mercury thermometer.

Bimetallic strip is a type of temperature measuring device that is relatively inaccurate, slow to respond, not normally used in analog applications to give remote indication, and has hystersis. The bimetallic strip is extensively used in ON/OFF applications not requiring high accuracy, as it is rugged and cost effective. These devices operate on the principle that metals are pliable and different metals have different coefficients of expansion. If two strips of dissimilar metals such as brass and invar (copper-nickel alloy) are joined together along their length, they will flex to form an arc as the temperature changes; this is shown in Figure 2.4.4(a). Bimetallic strips are usually configured as a spiral or helix for compactness and can then be used with a pointer to make a cheap compact rugged thermometer as shown in Figure 2.4.4(b). Their operating range is from −180 to 430℃ and can be used in applications from oven thermometers to home and industrial control thermostats.

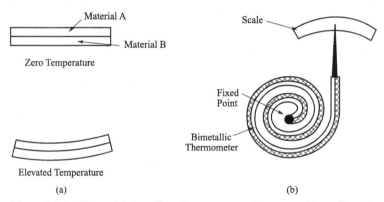

Figure 2.4.4　Shows (a) the effect of temperature change on a bimetallic strip and (b) bimetallic strip thermometer.

2. Pressure-Spring Thermometers

These thermometers are used where remote indication is required, as opposed to glass and bimetallic devices which give readings at the point of detection. The pressure-spring device has a metal bulb made with a low coefficient of expansion material with a long metal tube, both contain material with a high coefficient of expansion; the bulb is at the monitoring point. The metal tube is terminated with a spiral Bourdon tube pressure gage (scale in degrees) as shown in Figure 2.4.5. The pressure system can be used to drive a chart recorder, actuator, or a potentiometer wiper to obtain an electrical signal. As the temperature in the bulb increases, the pressure in the system rises. the pressure rise being proportional to the temperature change. The change in pressure is sensed by the Bourdon tube and converted to a temperature scale. These devices can be accurate to 0.5 percent and can be used for remote indication up to 100m but must be calibrated, as the stem and Bourdon tube are temperature sensitive.

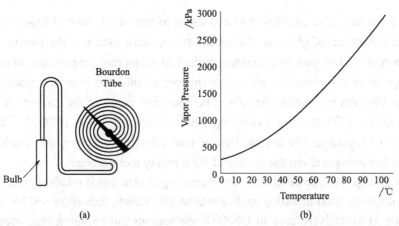

Figure 2.4.5   Illustrates (a) pressure filled thermometer and (b) vapor pressure curve for methyl chloride.

3. Resistance Temperature Devices

Resistance temperature devices (RTD) are either a metal film deposited on a former or are wire-wound resistors. The devices are then sealed in a glassceramic composite material. The electrical resistance of pure metals is positive, increasing linearly with temperature. Table 2.4.1 gives the temperature coefficient of resistance of some common metals used in resistance thermometers. These devices are accurate and can be used to measure temperatures from -300 to $1400\,°F$ (-170 to $780\,°C$).

In a resistance thermometer the variation of resistance with temperature is given by

$$R_{T2} = R_{T1}(1 + \text{Coeff.}[T_2 - T_1]) \tag{2.4.1}$$

where R_{T2} is the resistance at temperature T_2 and R_{T1} is the resistance at temperature T_1.

Example 1 What is the resistance of a platinum resistor at 250 ℃, if its resistance at 20 ℃ is 1050 Ω ?

$$\text{Resistance at 250\,°C} = 1050(1+0.00385\,[250-20])$$
$$=1050(1+0.8855)$$
$$=1979.775\,\Omega$$

Resistance devices are normally measured using a Wheatstone bridge type of system, but are supplied from a constant current source. Care should also be taken to prevent electrical current from heating the device and causing erroneous readings. One method of overcoming this problem is to use a pulse technique. When using this method the current is turned ON for say 10 ms every 10 s, and the sensor resistance is measured during this 10 ms time period. This reduces the internal heating effects by 1000 to 1 or the internal heating error by this factor.

Table 2.4.1   Temperature Coefficient of Resistance of Some Common Metals

Material	Coeff.per degree Celsius	Material	Coeff.per degree Celsius
Iron	0.006	Tungsten	0.0045
Nickel	0.005	Platinum	0.00385

Selected from "*Fundamentals of Industrial Instrumentation and Process Control, William C.Dunn, McGraw-Hill Inc.* 2005"

Words and Expressions

1. expansion [iks'pænʃən] *n.* 扩张，膨胀，延长
2. visual ['vizjuəl] *adj.* 可视的，可见的，光学的
3. dimensional [di'menʃənəl] *adj.* 尺寸的，量纲的，因次的
4. dissimilar [di'similə] *adj.* 不相似的，不同的，不一样的
5. thermometer [θə'mɔmitə] *n.* 温度计，温度表
6. Mercury ['məːkjuri] *n.* 汞，水银，水银温度计
7. wetting ['wetiŋ] *n.* 浸湿，润湿
8. traverse ['trævəːs] *vi.* 横过，通过，往返运动，上下来回
9. demise [di'maiz] *n.* 死亡，让位
10. bimetallic strip 双层金属片，双金属片
11. hysteresis [histə'riːsis] *n.* 磁滞，现象，滞后，迟滞
12. ragged ['rʌgid] *adj.* 结实的，坚固的，稳定的
13. pliable ['plaiəbl] *adj.* 易弯的，可弯的
14. brass [brɑːs] *n.* 黄铜
15. invar [in'vɑː] *n.* 镍铁合金，殷钢
16. helix ['hiːliks] *n.* 螺旋管，螺旋弹簧
17. compactness [kəm'pæktnis] *n.* 致密，紧密
18. oven ['ʌvən] *n.* 烘箱，烤炉，干燥箱
19. pressure-spring thermometer 压力-弹簧式温度计，压力式温度计
20. RTD 热电阻
21. deposit [di'pɔzit] *v.* 沉积，镀，涂
22. wire-wound resistor 绕线电阻，线绕电阻
23. Wheatstone bridge 惠斯登电桥
24. former ['fɔːmə] *n.* 样板，模型，线圈框架

2.5 Actuators

> *Topics covered in this unit are as follows:*
> 1. The valve actuator
> 2. The valve positioner
> 3. The electric Motor actuators
> 4. Flow control actuators and valve characteristics

Operation of the closed-loop control system depends on the performance of each loop component, including the final control element, whether it be damper, variable speed pump, motor relay, saturable reactor, or valve.Each of these elements requires an actuator that will make the necessary conversion from controller output signal to element input.This controller output may be pneumatic or electric and in some cases hydraulic or mechanical.The first need, then, is a device, an actuator, that will convert this control signal into a force that will position the final control element.From economic and performance standpoints, the most popular final operator is the pneumatic diaphragm actuator.A typical actuator is shown in Figure 2.5.1.

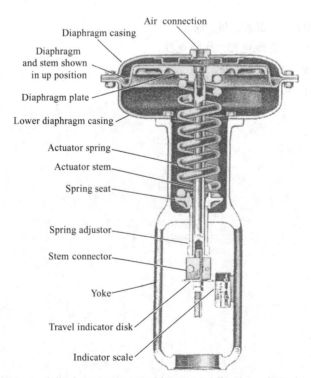

Figure 2.5.1　Spring and diaphragm actuator with an "up" fail-safe mode.Spring adjuster allows slight alteration of bench set. (*Courtesy Fisher Controls International LLC.*)

2.5.1 Valve Actuator

The pneumatic signal is applied to a large flexible diaphragm backed by a rigid diaphragm plate.The force created is opposed by a coil spring with a fixed spring rate.Thus, the stem position is an equilibrium of forces that depends on diaphragm area, pneumatic pressure, and spring characteristic.The spring tension is adjusted to compensate for line pressure on the valve and to produce a full valve stroke with signal changes from bottom to top scale value.The mechanical designs employed vary from one manufacturer to another Figure 2.5.1 illustrates the Foxboro Series Pactuator.

Pneumatic spring-diaphragm actuators have many applications, the most common of which is the operation of a control valve.They have been adapted to globe, Saunders-patent, butterfly, and ball valves.Spring-diaphragm actuators convert air signal pressure to force and motion and can be adapted to a large number of industrial requirements when precise loading of positioning is required.

On loss of air signal, the spring will cause the actuator to return to the zero pressure position.This feature provides fail-safe action.First, in order to provide maximum safety, the function of the valve is determined.Second, the action—air-to-open or air-to-close—that will allow the spring to put the valve in that position if the energy supply (air pressure) should fail is selected.The actuator shown can be reversed for either air-to-open or air-to-close action by simply removing the cap, turning over the actuator, and replacing the cap.

The motion of the valve stem positioned by a diaphragm actuator is not exactly linear for uniform changes in air pressure (pneumatic signal). The nonlinearity is caused by the diaphragm material, variations in spring rate, the moving pieces, and packing box friction.(Packing box friction varies with fluid pressure and the type and compression of packing.)

One of the effects of friction and nonlinear diaphragm characteristics is hysteresis. This is the difference between position on increasing versus position on decreasing pneumatic signal pressure. With compression on the packing and fluid pressure on the valve, the hysteresis could possibly be as high as 10 percent of the total travel. In control applications with low-gain or high-proportional band, hysteresis can produce an insensitive area or dead zone in the control loop.This would make precise control difficult.The solution to this problem is (1) good design of the actuator; (2) careful choice of low-friction packing, such as Teflon rings:and (3) use of a valve positioner.

2.5.2 Valve Positioner

If the diaphragm actuator does not supply sufficient force to position the valve accurately and overcome any opposition that flowing conditions create a positioner may be required. If the change in controller air pressure is small. The change in force available to reposition the valve stem might be too small to reposition it accurately. In this situation, a valve positioner (Figure 2.5.2) will prove helpful. Positioners are used to overcome the factors previously listed, along with other things, such as the effects of highly viscous fluids, gumming, or sedimentation.

Figure 2.5.2　Valv actor positioner provides fast precise valve positioning proportional to 20 to 100 kPa or 3 to 15 psi.

Positioners provide precise positioning and also increase the response speed of the valve.There are times, however, when a positioner should not be used:when the process responds faster than the valve (such as in a flow process), and when use of a positioner makes it necessary to set the proportional band of the process controller three-to-five times wider than if would be set if a positioner were not used.In many applications, this is not possible.Two typical applications of valve positioners are temperature control and pH control.

2.5.3　Electrical Signals

When the output of the controller is an electrical signal. additional equipment is required to position the valve or operators. One approach is to convert the electrical signal into a pneumatic signal at the valve location and use a pneumatic actuator. This is a very common solution. The second method is to utilize an all electrical system.Both methods will be discussed below.

Fortunately, the standards for electrical and pncumatic signals are in the same ratio.Both have a live zero and the zero lever multiplied by five equals the upper or full-scale value.This simplifies the conversion from one system to the other.The converters may be either rack-or field-mounted.However.when used with valves, the field-mounted type is generally employed. There are two types:one a current-to-pneumatic converter, and the other a positioner. The converter accepts a current signal, usually 4 to 20 mA de, and converts it into 3 to 15 psi C20 to (100 kPa) or other suitable pncumatic output.The positioner mounted on the valve yoke is a device that converts a current input signal to a proportional stem position.The pneumatic output of the positioner supplies air pressure to a pneumatic actuator.The valve stem is mechanically linked to a shaft on the positioner.

Split input ranges are available when a less than full-scale input current will provide a full-scale pneumatic output or full-scale valve movement, for example, a 4 to 12 mA dc input produces a 3 to 15 psi (20 to 100 kPa) output.Reverse action,in which an increasing current input causes a decreasing output, is also available.

2.5.4 Electric Motor Actuators

If compressed air is not available, it may be advantageous to use an electric motor actuator.An example of this mechanism is shown in Figure 2.5.3. Proportional control of actuator output or stem position is achieved through a feedback slide wire along with an internal servoamplifier. The 4 to 20 mA de analog signal from the controller is applied directly to the actuator.Depending on the gear ratios used, full stroke may take from 15 to 51 seconds.

Figure 2.5.3 Electric motor actuator.

Electric motor actuators generally cost more than ten times as much as pneumatic actuators, operate at a much slower speed, and are not, therefore, generally the first choice when one is selecting an actuator.

In addition to electric motor actuators, there are electrical solenoid operators.The solenoid actuator is simple, small, and inexpensive.However, its application is limited to the on off or two-position action.

Selected from "*Instrumentation for Process Measurement and Control, Norman A.Anderson, Chikton Company,* 1998"

Words and Expressions

1. damper ['dæmpə] *n.* 阻尼器，调节板，制动器，风门，气闸
2. variable speed pump 可变速泵
3. motor relay 电动继电器
4. saturable reactor 饱和电抗器，饱和式磁力仪，饱和扼流圈
5. pneumatic diaphragm actuator 气动薄膜执行器

6. yoke ['jəuk] n. 支架
7. Saunders-patent 桑托斯专利
8. butterfly valve 蝶阀
9. ball valve 球阀
10. packing box 密封盒, 填料盒
11. Teflon ring 聚四氟乙烯填圈, 特氟隆填圈
12. positioner [pə'ziʃənə] n. 定位器, 控制阀反馈装置
13. valve positioner 阀门定位器
14. proportional band 比例带
15. shaft [ʃɑ:ft] n. 连接轴, 传动轴
16. split [splɪt] n. 迁移
17. gear [giə] n. 齿轮
18. stroke [strəuk] n. 行程, 冲程
19. solenoid ['səulinɔid] n. 电磁线圈, 螺线管, 圆柱形

Exercise

1. *Put the following into Chinese:*

   Control valve   valve position   electric motor actuator   damper
   variable speed pump   diaphragm area   pneumatic pressure
   fail-safe action   air-to-open   packing box friction   hysteresis
   converters   gear ratio

2. *Put the following into English:*

   控制性能   最终控制元件   控制器输出   阀驱动器
   气动   电动   液动   弹簧圈
   不灵敏区   死区   电磁阀   阀特性

Reading Material:

Flow Control Actuators

When a change in a measured variable with respect to a reference has been sensed, it is necessary to apply a control signal to an actuator to make corrections to an input controlled variable to bring the measured variable back to its preset value. In most cases any change in the variables, i e., temperature, pressure, mixing ingredients, and level, can be corrected by controlling flow rates. Hence, actuators are in general used for flow rate control and can be electrically, pneumatically, or hydraulically controlled. Actuators can be self-operating in local feedback loops in such applications as temperature sensing with direct hydraulic or pneumatic valve control, pressure regulators, and float level controllers. There are two common types of variable aperture actuators used for flow control; they are the globe valve and the butterfly valve.

1. Globe Valve

The globe valve's cross section is shown in Figure 2.5.4 (a).The actuator can be driven electrically using a solenoid or motor, pneumatically or hydraulically.The actuator determines the speed of travel and distance the valve shaft travels.The globe type valve can be designed for quick opening, linear, or equal percentage operation.In equal percentage operation the flow is proportional to the percentage the valve is open,or there is a log relationship between the flow and valve travel.The shape of the plug determines the flow characteristics of the actuator and is normally described in terms of percentage of flow versus percentage of lift or travel.

The valve plug shown in Figure 2.5.4 (a) gives a linear relationship between flow and lift.The characteristic is given if Figure 2.5.4 (b).Also shown in the graph are the characteristics for a quick opening plug and an equal percentage plug to illustrate some of the characteristics that can be obtained from the large number of plugs that are available.The selection of the type of control plug should be carefully chosen for any particular application.The type will depend on a careful analysis of the process characteristics, i.e., if the load changes are linear a linear plug should be used.Conversely, if the load changes are nonlinear a plug with the appropriate nonlinear characteristic should be used.

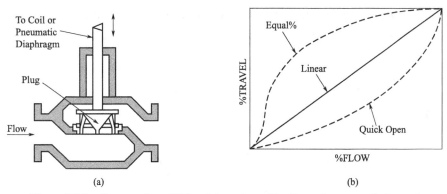

Figure 2.5.4　Cross section of (a) a globe valve with a linear flow control plug and (b) different flow patterns for various plugs versus plug travel.

The globe valve cna be straight through with single seating as illustrated in Figure 2.5.4(a) or can be configured with double seating, which is used to reduce the actuator operating force, but is expensive, difficult to adjust and maintain,and does not have a tight seal when shutoff.Angle valves are also available, i.e., the output port is at right angles or 45° to the input port.

Many other configurations of the globe valve are avaiable.Illustrated in Figure 2.5.5 (a) is a two-way valve (diverging type) , which is used to switch the incoming flow from one exit to another.When the valve stem is up the lower port is closed and the incoming liquid exits to the right, and when the valve is down the upper port is closed and the liquid exits from the bottom.Also available is a converging-type valve, which is used to switch either of the two in coming flows to a single output.Figure 2.5.5 (b) illustrates a three-way valve.In the neutral position both exit ports are held closed by the spring.When the valve stem moves down the top port is opened and when the valve stem moves up from the neutral position the lower port is opened.

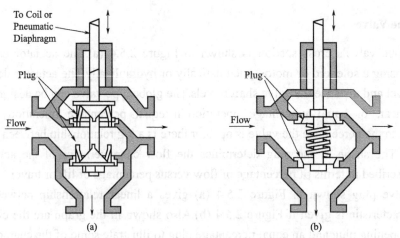

Figure 2.5.5 Cross sections of globe valve configurations:(a) two-way valve and (b) three-position valve.

Butterfly valve

The butterfly valve is shown in Figure 2.5.6 (a) and its flow versus travel characteristics are shown in Figure 2.5.6 (b) .The relation between flow and lift is approximately equal percentage uq to about 50 percent open, after which it is linear.Butterfly valves offer high capacity at low cost, are simple in design, easy to install, and have tight closure.The torsion force on the shaft increases until open up to 70° and then reverses.

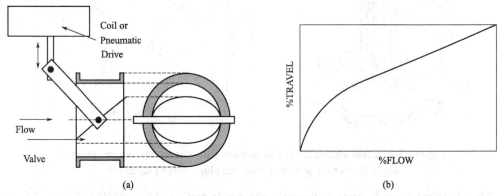

Figure 2.5.6 Cross sections of (a) a butterfly valve and (b) its flow versus travel characteristic.

2. Valve Characteristics

Other factors that determine the choice of valve type are corrosion resistance, operating temperature ranges, high and low pressures, velocities, and fluids containing solids.Correct valve installation is essential; vendor recommendations must be carefully followed. In situations where sludge or solid particulates can be trapped upstream of a valve, a means of purging the pipe must be available. To minimize disturbances and obtain good flow characteristics a clear run of 1 to 5 pipe diameters up an down stream should be allowed.

Valve sizing is based on pressure loss.Valves are given a C_V number that is based on test results.The C_V number is the number of gallons of water flowing per minute through a fully open valve at 60°F (15.5°C) that will cause a pressure drop of 1 psi (6.9kPa). It implies that when flowing through the fully opened valve, it will have a pressure drop of 1 psi (6.9kPa), i.e., a valve with a C_V of 25 will have a pressure drop of 1 psi when 25 gal of water per minute is flowing through it. For liquids, the relation between pressure drop P_d (pounds per square inch), flow rate Q (gallon per minute), and C_V is given by

$$C_V = Q \times \sqrt{(SG/P_d)} \tag{2.5.1}$$

where SG is the specific gravity of the liquid.

Example 1 What is the C_V of a valve, if there is a pressure drop of 3.5 psi when 2.3 gal per second of a liquid with a specific weight (SW) of 60 lb/ft^3 is flowing?

$$C_V = 2.3 \times 60 \sqrt{\frac{60}{62.4 \times 3.5}} = 138 \times 0.52 = 72.3$$

Table 2.5.1 gives a comparison of some of the valve characteristics; the values shown are typical of the devices available and may be exceeded by some manufacturers with new designs and materials.

Table 2.5.1 Valve Characteristics

Parameter	Globe	Diaphragm	Ball	Butterfly	Rotary plug
Size	1 to 36 in	1 to 20 in	1 to 24 in	2 to 36 in	1 to 12 in
Slurries	No	Yes	Yes	No	Yes
Temperature range(℃)	−200 to 540	−40 to 150	−200 to 400	−50 to 250	−200 to 400
Quick-opening	Yes	Yes	No	No	No
Linear	Yes	No	Yes	No	Yes
Equal%	Yes	No	Yes	Yes	Yes
Control range	20:1 to 100:1	3:1 to 15:1	50:1 to 350:1	15:1 to 50:1	30:1 to 100:1
Capacity(C_V) (d=Dia.)	10 to 12×d^2	14 to 22×d^2	14 to 24×d^2	12 to 35×d^2	12 to 14×d^2

Selected form "*Fundamentals of Industrial Instrumentation and Control, William C.Dum, McGraw-Hill Inc., 2005*"

Words and Expression

1. ingredient   [inˈgriːdiənt] *n.* 成分,配料,组成部分
2. mixing ingredients   混合配料
3. self-operating   自力式操作,自力式控制
4. pressure regulator   压力调节器
5. globe valve   球形阀
6. equal percentage   等百分比
7. single seating   单座
8. double seating   双座
9. vendor   [ˈvendə] *n.* 厂商,卖主,售货商
10. sludge   [slʌdʒ] *n.* 污泥,污水,沉积物
11. trap   [træp] *n.& vt.* 捕获,收集,截留,使分离
12. purging   [ˈpəːdʒing] *n.* 清洗,净化
13. C_V number   阀流通能力
14. pressure drop   压力降

CHAPTER 3   ADVANCED CONTROL SYSTEMS

3.1   Feedforward and Ratio Control

> *After completing this unit, you should be able to answer the following questions*:
> 1. What are the advantages and disadvantages of feedback control?
> 2. What is the feedforward control?
> 3. What is the ratio control?

It was emphasized that feedback control is an important technique that is widely used in the process industries. Its main advantages are:

① Corrective action occurs as soon as the controlled variable deviates from the set point, regardless of the source and type of disturbance.

② It requires minimal knowledge about the process to be controlled; in particular, a mathematical model of the process is *not* required, although it is useful for control system design.

③ The ubiquitous PID controller is both versatile and robust. If process conditions change, retuning the controller usually produces satisfactory control.

Feedback control also has certain inherent disadvantages:

① No corrective action is taken until after a deviation in the controlled variable occurs.

Thus, perfect control, where the controlled variable does not deviate from the set point during load or set-point changes, is theoretically impossible.

② It does not provide predictive control action to compensate for the effects of known or measurable disturbances.

③ It may not be satisfactory for processes with large time constants and/or long time delays. If large and frequent disturbances occur, the process may operate continually in a transient state and never attain the desired steady state.

④ In some applications the controlled variable cannot be measured on-line and, consequently, feedback control is not feasible.

For situations in which feedback control by itself is not satisfactory, significant improvements in control can be achieved by adding feedforward control. But to use feedforward control, the disturbances must be measured (or estimated) on-line. In this unit, we consider the design and analysis of feedforward control systems. We begin with an overview of feedforward control and ratio control, a special type of feedforward control, is introduced next.

3.1.1 Introduction to Feedforward Control

With feedforward control the basic idea is to measure important load variables and take corrective action before they upset the process. In contrast, a feedback controller does not take corrective action until after the disturbance has upset the process and generated an error signal. Simplified block diagrams for feedforward and feedback control are shown in Figure 3.1.1.

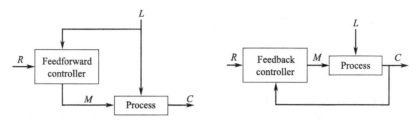

Figure 3.1.1 Block diagrams for feedforward and feedback control.

Feedforward control has several disadvantages:

① The load disturbances must be measured on-line. In many applications this is not feasible.

② To make effective use of feedforward control, at least a crude process model should be available. In particular, we need to know how the controlled variable responds to changes in both the load and manipulated variables. The quality of feedforward control depends on the accuracy of the process model.

③ Ideal feedforward controllers that are theoretically capable of achieving perfect control may not be physically realizable. Fortunately, practical approximations of these ideal controllers often provide very effective control.

Feedforward control was not widely used in the process industries until the 1960s. However, the basic concept is much older and was applied as early as 1925 in the three-element level control system for boiler drums. We will use this control application to illustrate the use of feedforward control.

The boiler drum and a conventional feedback control system are shown in Figure 3.1.2. The level of the boiling liquid is measured and used to adjust the feedwater flow rate. This control system tends to be quite sensitive to rapid changes in the load variable, steam flow rate, due to the small liquid capacity of the boiler drum. Rapid load changes can occur due to steam demands made by downstream processing units. Another difficulty is that large controller gains cannot be used since level measurements exhibit rapid fluctuations for boiling liquids. Thus, a high controller gain would tend to amplify the measurement noise and produce unacceptable variations in the feedwater flow rate.

The feedforward control scheme in Figure 3.1.3 can provide better control of the liquid level. Here the steam flow rate is measured and the feedforward controller adjusts the feedwater flow rate so as to balance the steam demand. Note that the controlled variable, liquid level, is not measured. As an altern-ative, steam pressure could be measured instead of steam flow rate.

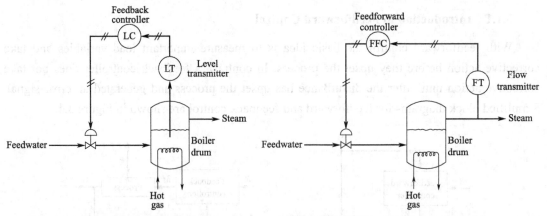

Figure 3.1.2　The feedback control of the liquid level in a boiler drum.

Figure 3.1.3　The feedback control of the liquid level in a boiler drum.

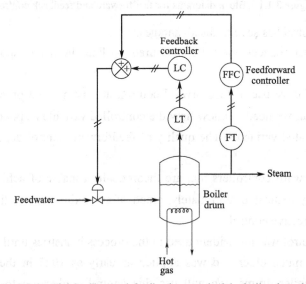

Figure 3.1.4　The feedforward-feedback control of the boiler drum level.

In practical applications, feedforward control is normally used in combination with feedback control. Feedforward control is used to reduce the effects of measurable disturbances while *feedback trim* compen-sates for inaccuracies in the process model, measurement errors, and unmeasured disturbances. The feedforward and feedback controllers can be combined in several different ways. One popular configuration is shown in Figure 3.1.4, where the outputs of the feedforward and feedback controllers are added together and the combined signal is sent to the control valve.

3.1.2　Ratio Control

Ratio control is a special type of feedforward control that has been widely used in the process industries. In ratio control, the objective is to maintain the ratio of two variables at a specified value. Thus, the variable R_a, the actual ratio of the two process variables,

$$R_a = \frac{M}{L} \tag{3.1.1}$$

is controlled rather than controlling the individual variables, M and L. The process variables are usually flow rates. The calculation of R_a in Eq. (3.1.1) is performed in terms of the original physical variables, rather than deviation variables.

Typical applications of ratio control include (1) blending operations, (2) maintaining a stoichiometric ratio of reactants to reactor, (3) keeping a specified reflux ratio for a distillation column, and (4) holding the fuel-air to a furnace at the optimum value.

Ratio control can be implemented in two basic schemes. In Method I, which is shown in Figure 3.1.5, the flow rates for both the load stream and the manipulated stream are measured and the calculated ratio $R_m = M_m/L_m$ is computed using a *divider* element. Special computing elements such as dividers and multipliers are available as off-the-shelf items for both pneumatic and electronic control systems. The output of the divider is sent to a ratio controller (RC) which compares the calculated ratio R_m to the desired ratio R_d and adjusts the manipulated flow M accordingly. The ratio controller would normally be a PI controller with a set point equal to the desired ratio.

The main advantage of Method I is that the actual ratio R_m is calculated. A key disadvantage is that a divider element must be included in the loop and this element makes the process gain vary in a nonlinear fashion. From Eq.(1), the process gain is

$$K_p = \left(\frac{\partial R_a}{\partial M}\right)_L = \frac{1}{L} \tag{3.1.2}$$

which is inversely related to load flow rate L. Because of this significant disadvantage, the preferred scheme for implementing ratio control is Method II, which is shown in Figure 3.1.6.

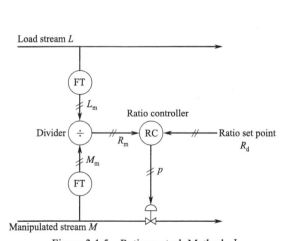
Figure 3.1.5 Ratio control, Method I.

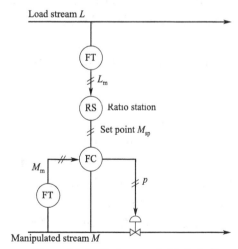
Figure 3.1.6 Ratio control, Method II.

In Method II the flow rate of the load stream is measured and the measurement is transmitted to the ratio station (RS), which multiplies this signal by an adjustable gain. The value of this gain K_R is the desired ratio. The output signal from the ratio station is then used as the set point for the flow controller, which adjusts the flow rate of the manipulated stream. The chief advantage of Method II is that the open-loop gain remains constant since a divider is not used.

Note that load variable L is measured in both ratio control schemes (cf. Figure 3.1.5 and

3.1.6). Thus, ratio control is, in essence, a very simple form of feedforward control. Regardless of how ratio control is implemented, the process variables must be scaled correctly. For example, in Method II the gain setting for the ratio station must take into account the spans of the two flow transmitters. Thus, the gain for the ratio station K_R should be set at

$$K_R = R_d \frac{K_m}{K_t} \tag{3.1.3}$$

where R_d is the desired ratio, and K_m and K_t are the spans of the flow transmitters for the manipulated and load streams, respectively. If orifice plates are used with differential-pressure transmitters, then the transmitter output is proportional to the square of the flow. Consequently, the gain of the ratio station should then be proportional to R_d^2 rather than R_d, unless square root extractors are used to convert each transmitter output to a signal that is proportional to flow.

Selected from "*Process Dynamics and Control, Dale E. Seborg & T. Edgar, John Wiley & Sonsi*, 1989"

Words and Expressions

1. deviate ['diːvieit] *v.* 偏离
2. theoretically [θiə'retikli] *adv.* 理论上
3. transient ['trænziənt] *adj.* 短暂的
4. overview ['əuvəvjuː] *n.* 纵览
5. boiler drum ['bɔilə drʌm] *n.* 汽鼓
6. downstream ['daun'striːm] *adj.; adv.* 下流的(地); 顺流的(地)
7. controller gain 控制器增益
8. alternative [ɔːl'tænətiv] *n.* 选择; *adj.* 选择性的, 二中选一的
9. configuration [kən,figju'reiʃən] *n.* 构造, 结构, 外形
10. ratio control 比率控制
11. stoichiometric [stɔikiə'metrik] *adj.* 化学计算的
12. implement ['implimənt] *vt.* 执行
13. pneumatic [njuː'mætik] *n.* 气体学
14. deviation [,diːvi'eiʃən] *n.* 偏差
15. transmit [trænzmit] *vt.* 传送
16. orifice ['ɔrifis] *n.* 口, 孔
17. extractor [iks'træktə] *n.* 提取器

Exercises

1. *Complete the notes below with words taken from the text above.*

    (1) For situations _____ feedback control by itself _____ satisfactory, significant improvements in control can be achieved by adding _____. _____ use feedforward control, _____ must be measured (or estimated) on-line.

    (2) In practical applications, feedforward control ____ normally _____ combination with _____. Feedforward control is used _____ the effects of

measurable disturbances _____ feedback trim compensates _____ inaccuracies in the process model, _____, and unmeasured disturbances.

(3) _____ is a special type of feedforward control that _____ in the process industries. In ratio control, _____ is to maintain _____ of two variables at a specified value.

2. *Put the following into Chinese:*

autotuning	open-loop tuning	closed-loop tuning
transient response	frequency response	relay method
Nyquist curve	dominant pole	boiler drum
blending operation	holding	

3. *Put the following into English:*

在线	离线	滤波器	自适应调节器	比值控制
可测扰动	测量误差	回流比	差压变送器	

Reading Material:

Cascade Control

A disadvantage of conventional feedback control is that corrective action for disturbances does not begin until after the controlled variable deviates from the set point. As discussed in text, feedforward control offers large improvements over feedback control for processes that have large time constants or time delays. However, feedforward control requires that the disturbances be measured explicitly and a model must be available for calculating the controller output. An alternative approach which improves the dynamic response to load changes is to use a secondary measurement point and a secondary feedback controller. The secondary measurement point is located so that it recognizes the upset condition sooner than the controlled variable, but the disturbance is not necessarily measured. This approach utilizes multiple feedback loops and is called *cascade control*. It is particularly useful when the disturbances are associated with the manipulated variable or when the final control element exhibits nonlinear behavior.

Figure 3.1.7 shows a stirred chemical reactor where cooling water is passed through the reactor jacket to regulate the reactor temperature. The reactor temperature is affected by changes in disturbance variables such as reactant feed temperature or composition. The simplest control strategy would handle such disturbances satisfactorily by adjusting a control valve on the cooling water inlet stream. However, an increase in the inlet cooling water temperature may cause unsatisfactory performance. The resulting increase in the reactor temperature, due to a reduction in heat removal rate, may occur slowly. If there are appreciable dynamic lags in the jacket as well as in the reactor, the corrective action taken by the controller will be delayed. To circumvent this disadvantage, a feedback controller for the jacket temperature with its set point determined by the reactor temperature controller could be added to provide cascade control, as shown in Figure 3.1.7. This approach measures the jacket temperature, compares it to a set point, and uses the resulting error

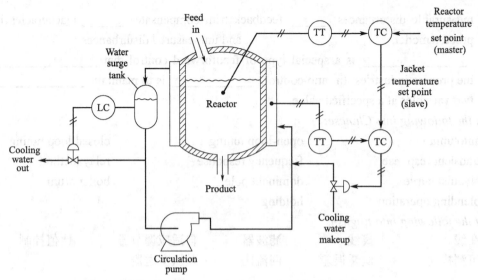

Figure 3.1.7 Cascade control of an exothermic chemical reactor.

signal as the input to a controller for the cooling water makeup, thus maintaining the heat removal rate from the reactor at a constant level. The controller set point and both measurements are used to adjust a single manipulated variable, the cooling water makeup rate. The principal advantage of the cascade control strategy is that a second measured variable is located close to a potential disturbance to improve the closed-loop response.

Cascade control is widely used in the process industries and has two distinguishing features:

① The output signal of the *master controller* serves as the set point for the *slave* controller.

② The two feedback control loops are nested, with the *secondary control loop* (for the slave controller) located inside the *primary control loop* (for the master controller).

In the reactor example the primary measurement is the reactor temperature, which is used by the master controller. The secondary measurement is the jacket temperature, which is transmitted to the slave controller.

As a second example of cascade control, consider the natural draft furnace temperature control problem reported by Johnson and shown in Figure 3.1.8. The conventional feedback control system in Figure 3.1.8 may do a satisfactory job of regulating the hot oil temperature despite disturbances in oil flow rate or cold oil temperature. But if a disturbance occurs in the fuel gas supply pressure, the fuel gas flow changes, which upsets the furnace operation, thus changing

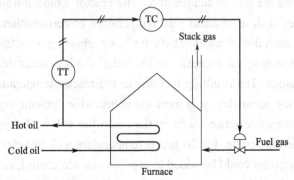

Figure 3.1.8 A furnace temperature control that uses conventional feedback control.

the hot oil temperature. Only then will the temperature controller (TC) begin to take corrective action by adjusting the fuel gas flow via the control valve. Thus, we anticipate that conventional feedback control would result in very sluggish responses to changes in fuel gas supply pressure. This disturbance is clearly associated with the manipulated variable.

The cascade control scheme of Figure 3.1.9 provides improved performance because the control valve will be adjusted as soon as the change in supply pressure is detected. The performance improvements for disturbances in oil flow rate or inlet temperature may not be as large, in which case feedforward control may be desirable for those disturbances. For the cascade control scheme, the master (or primary) controller is the temperature controller that adjusts the set point of the slave (or secondary) controller in the pressure control loop. If a disturbance in supply pressure occurs, the pressure controller will act very quickly to hold the fuel gas pressure at its set point. Since the pressure control loop responds rapidly, the supply pressure disturbance will have little effect on furnace operation and exit oil temperature. Alternatively, flow control, rather than pressure control, could be employed in the slave loop to achieve essentially the same result.

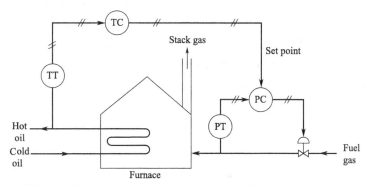

Figure 3.1.9　A furnace temperature control using cascade control.

The block diagram for a general cascade control system is shown in Figure 3.1.10. Subscript 1 refers to the primary control loop while subscript 2 refers to the secondary control loop. Thus, for the furnace temperature control example:

C_1＝hot oil temperature

C_2＝fuel gas pressure

L_1＝cold oil temperature (or cold oil flow rate)

L_2＝supply pressure of fuel gas

B_1＝measured value of hot oil temperature

B_2＝measured value of fuel gas pressure

R_1＝set point for C_1

R_2＝set point for C_2

All of the above variables represent deviations from the nominal steady state. Since load disturbances can occur in both the primary and secondary control loops, two load variables (L_1 and L_2) and two load transfer functions (G_{L1} and G_{L2}) are shown in Figure 3.1.10.

It is clear from Figure 3.1.9 and 3.1.10 that cascade control will effectively eliminate the effects of pressure disturbances entering the secondary loop (i.e., L_2 in Figure 3.1.10). But what about the effects of disturbances such as L_1 which enter the primary loop? Cascade control can

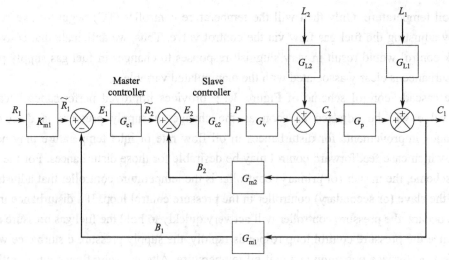

Figure 3.1.10 Block diagram of the cascade control system.

provide an improvement over conventional feedback control when both controllers are well tuned. The cascade arrangement will reduce the response time of the elements in the secondary loop, which will in turn affect the primary loop, but the improvement may be slight. As mentioned previously, feedforward control can be employed to reduce errors in C_1, but L_1 must be measured directly and a model relating L_1, C_1, and C_2 should be available.

Selected from "*Process Dynamics and Control, Dale E. Seborg & T. Edgar, John Wiley & Sonsi,* 1989"

Words and Expressions

1. casecade   [kæs'keid]   *n.* 串级
2. exothermic   [,eksəu'θə:mik]   *adj.* 放热的
3. explicitly   [iksp'lisitli]   *adj.* 明白的
4. multiple   ['mʌltipl]   *adj.* 复合的
5. lag   [læg]   *vi.* 落后；延缓
6. circumvent   [,sə:kəm'vent]   *vt.* 躲避；避免
7. transmiter   [trænz'mitə]   *n.* 传送器；变送器
8. master controller   主控制器
9. nest   [nest]   *vt.* 组合
10. slave controller   从属控制器
11. via   ['vaiə]   *prep.* 经由；经过
12. subscript   ['sʌbskript]   *n.* 下标

3.2 Time-Delay Compensation and Inferential Control

> *During reading the following unit, try to find the answers for*:
> 1. Why the time delays commonly occur?
> 2. What is the best know strategy for time-delay compensation?
> 3. What is the inferential control?

In this section we discuss two advanced control techniques that deal with problematic areas in process control; namely, the occurrence of significant time delays and the lack of on-line measurements for feedback control. The first problem is handled by *time-delay compensation* and the second problem can be solved by a technique called *inferential control*.

3.2.1 Time-Delay Compensation

Time delays commonly occur in the process industries because of the presence of distance velocity lags, recycle loops, and the *dead time* associated with composition analysis. The presence of time delays in a process limits the performance of a conventional feedback control system. From a frequency response perspective, a time delay adds phase lag to the feedback loop, which adversely affects closed-loop stability. Consequently, the controller gain must be reduced below the value that could be used if no time delay were present, and the response of the closed-loop system will be sluggish compared to that of the control loop with no time delay.

To improve the performance of time-delay systems, special control strategies have been developed to provide time-delay compensation. The Smith predictor technique is the best known strategy and is discussed here. The Smith predictor is often referred to as a *model-based* controller, as is Internal Model Control. This is because the control strategy utilizes the model parameters directly. A related method, the analytical predictor, has been developed for digital control applications. Various investigators have found that the performance of the Smith predictor for set-point changes can be as much as 30% better than a conventional controller based on an integral squared error criterion.

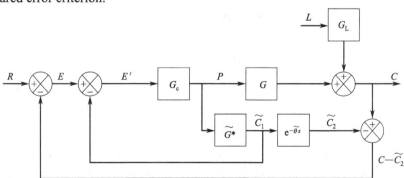

Figure 3.2.1　Block diagram of the Smith predictor.

A block diagram of the Smith predictor is shown in Figure 3.2.1 with $G_c=G_m=1$ for simplicity. Here the model of the process transfer function $\widetilde{G}(s)$ is divided into two parts: the part without a time delay, $\widetilde{G}*(s)$, and the time-delay term, $e^{-\widetilde{\theta}s}$. Thus, the total transfer function model is $\widetilde{G}(s)=\widetilde{G}*(s)e^{-\widetilde{\theta}s}$. The model of the process without the time delay, $\widetilde{G}*(s)$, is used to predict the effect of the control action on the process output. The controller uses this predicted response $\widetilde{C}_1$ to calculate its output. The predicted process output is also delayed by the amount of the time delay $\widetilde{\theta}$ for comparison with the actual process output C. This corrects for modeling errors and for load disturbances entering the process. This delayed model output is denoted by $\widetilde{C}_2$ in Figure 3.2.1. From the block diagram,

$$E' = E - \widetilde{C}_1 = R - \widetilde{C}_1 - (C - \widetilde{C}_2) \qquad (3.2.1)$$

If the process model is perfect and the disturbance is zero, then $\widetilde{C}_2 = C$ and

$$E' = R - \widetilde{C}_1 \qquad (3.2.2)$$

In this case the controller acts on the error signal that would occur if no time delay were present.

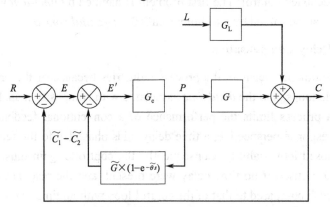

Figure 3.2.2 An alternative block diagram of a Smith predictor.

Figure 3.2.2 shows an alternative (equivalent) configuration for the Smith predictor that includes an inner feedback loop, similar to that is cascade control. Assuming there is no model error ($\widetilde{G}=G$), the inner loop has the effective transfer function

$$G'_c = \frac{P}{E} = \frac{G_c}{1+G_c G^*(1-e^{-\theta s})} \qquad (3.2.3)$$

where G^* is defined analogous to $\widetilde{G}*$ that is, $G = G^* e^{-\theta s}$. After some rearrangement, the closed-loop servo transfer function is obtained:

$$\frac{C}{R} = \frac{G_c G^* e^{-\theta s}}{1+G_c G^*} \qquad (3.2.4)$$

By contrast, for conventional feedback control

$$\frac{C}{R} = \frac{G_c G^* e^{-\theta s}}{1+G_c G^* e^{-\theta s}} \qquad (3.2.5)$$

Comparison of Eqs.(3.2.4) and (3.2.5) indicates that the Smith predictor has the theoretical advantage of eliminating the time delay from the characteristic equation. Unfortunately, this advantage is lost if the process model is very inaccurate. However, the Smith predictor can still provide improvement over conventional feedback control if the model errors are not too large (i.e., if the model parameters are within about ±30% of the actual values).

One drawback of the Smith predictor approach is that it is *model-based*; namely a dynamic model of the process is required. If the process dynamics change significantly, the predictive model will be inaccurate and the controller performance will deteriorate, perhaps to the point of instability. For such processes, the controller should be tuned conservatively to accommodate possible model errors. Schleck and Hanesian performed a detailed study analyzing the effect of model errors on the Smith predictor for a first-order plus time-delay model. They found that if the assumed time delay is not within 30% of the actual process time delay, the predictor is inferior to a PI controller with no time-delay compensation. If the time delay varies significantly, it may be necessary to use some sort of adaptive controller to achieve satisfactory performance.

The Smith predictor configuration generally is beneficial for load changes. However, the simulation study of Meyer et al. indicated that a conventional PI controller can provide better regulatory control than the Smith predictor for certain conditions. This somewhat anomalous behavior can be attributed to the closed-loop transfer function, which is

$$\frac{C}{L} = \frac{G_L[1+G_c G^*(1-e^{-\theta s})]}{1+G_c G^*} \tag{3.2.6}$$

where G_L is the load transfer function. The denominators of C/L and C/R in Eq.(3.2.4) are the same, but the numerator terms are quite different in form.

3.2.2 Inferential Control

The previous discussion of time-delay compensation assumed that measurements of the controlled variable were available. In some control problems, the process variable that is to be controlled cannot be conveniently measured on-line. For example, product composition measurement may require that a sample be sent to the plant analytical laboratory. In this situation, measurements of the controlled variable are not available frequently enough nor quickly enough to be used for feedback control.

One solution to this problem is to use inferential control, whereby process measurements that can be obtained rapidly are used to infer the value of the controlled variable. For example, if the overhead product stream in a distillation column cannot be analyzed on-line, sometimes measurement of the top tray temperature can be used to infer the actual composition. For a binary mixture, the Gibbs phase rule indicates that there is a unique relation between composition and temperature if pressure is constant. Therefore, a thermodynamic equation could be employed to relate the temperature of the top tray to overhead composition.

On the other hand, for the separation of multicomponent mixtures, approximate methods to estimate compositions must be used. Based on process models and plant data, simple algebraic correlation can be developed to relate the mole fraction of the heavy key component to several different tray temperatures (usually near the top of the column). The overhead composition then can be inferred from the available temperature measurements and used in the control algorithm. The parameters in the correlation may be updated, if necessary, as actual composition measurements become available. For example, if samples are sent to the plant's analytical laboratory once per hour, the correlation parameters can be adjusted so that the predicted values agree with the measured values.

The concept of inferential control can be employed for other process operations, such as chemical reactors, where composition is normally the controlled variable. Selected temperature measurements can be used to estimate the outlet composition if it cannot be measured on-line. However, when inferential control does not perform satisfactorily, incentive exists to introduce other on-line measurements for feedback control. Consequently, there is considerable interest in the development of new instrumentation, such as process analyzers, which can be used on-line and which exhibit very short response times.

Selected from "Process Dynamics and Control, Dale E. Seborg & T. Edgar, John Wiley & Sonsi, 1989"

Words and Expressions

1. time-delay [taim-di'lei] n. 时间滞后
2. occurrence [ə'kʌrəns] n. 发生
3. compensation [kɔmpen'seiʃən] n. 补偿
4. inferential [infə'renʃəl] control 推理控制
5. velocity [vi'ləsiti] n. 速率，速度
6. closed-loop stability 闭环稳定性
7. smith predictor technique 史密斯预估器技术
8. model-based controller 基于模型的控制器
9. internal model control 内部模型控制
10. set-point [set'pɔint] n. 设定值
11. error criterion ['erə,krai'tiəriən] n. 误差标准
12. integral square 求平方积分
13. predictor [pri'diktə] n. 预估器
14. denote [di'nəut] vt. 指示
15. simplicity [sim'plisiti] n. 简单
16. equivalent [i'kwivələnt] a. 等价的，相等的
17. analogous [ə'næləgəs] a. 类似的
18. comparison [kəm'pærisn] n. 比较
19. theoretical [θiə'retikl] a. 理论的
20. analytical [,ænə'litikl] a. 分析的
21. correlation [,kɔri'leiʃən] n. 相关，交互作用
22. analyzer ['ænəlaizə] n. 分析器

Exercises

1. *Complete the notes below with words taken from the text above.*

   (1) In this section we discuss two advanced control techniques _____ problematic

areas in process control; _____, the occurrence of significant _____ and the lack of _____ for feedback control. The first problem is handled by _____ and the second problem can be solved _____ a technique called _____.

(2) _____ the performance of time-delay systems, special control strategies _____ developed _____ time-delay compensation. The _____ technique is the _____ strategy and is discussed here. The Smith predictor is often _____ as a _____ controller, _____ Internal Model Control.

(3) One drawback of the Smith predictor approach is that _____ model-based; namely a dynamic model of the process is required. If _____ change significantly, _____ will be inaccurate and _____ will deteriorate, perhaps to the point of instability. For such processes, the controller _____ conservatively _____ possible model errors.

(4) _____ some control problems, the process variable _____ controlled cannot conveniently _____ on-line. For example, product composition measurement _____ require _____ sample _____ to the plant analytical laboratory. _____ this situation, measurements of the controlled variable _____ available frequently _____ quickly _____ to be used for feedback control.

2. *Put the following into Chinese:*

time delay	inferential control	dead time
distance velocity	sluggish	Smith predictor
model-based	inferential model control	
predictive model	secondary feedback controller	

3. *Put the following into English:*

| 在线测量 | 相角(位)滞后 | 数字控制 | 串级控制 | 辅助测量变量 |
| 冷却水 | 夹套 | 主控制器 | 副控制器 | 燃料气 |

Reading Material:

Selective Control/Override Systems

Most process control problems have an equal number of controlled variables and manipulated variables. If there are fewer manipulated variables than controlled variables, then it is not possible to eliminate offset in all the controlled variables for arbitrary load or set-point changes. This assertion is evident from a steady-state model and a degrees-of-freedom analysis. For control problems with more controlled variables than manipulated variables, a strategy is needed for sharing the manipulated variables among the controlled variables. In other applications the opposite situation occurs, namely there are more manipulated variables than controlled variables.

Selectors

When there are more controlled variables than manipulated variables, a common solution to this problem is to use a *selector* to choose the appropriate process variable from among a number of available measurements. Alternatively, a multivariable control system can be employed. Selectors can be based on either multiple measurement points, multiple final control elements, or multiple controllers, as discussed below. Selectors are used to improve the control system performance as well as to protect equipment from unsafe operating conditions.

One type of selector device chooses as its output signal the highest (or lowest) of two or more input signals. This approach is often referred to as *auctioneering*. On instrumentation diagrams the symbol HS denotes high selector and LS a low selector. For example, a high selector can be used to determine the *hot spot* temperature in a fixed-bed chemical reactor as shown in Figure 3.2.3. In this case the output from the high selector is the input to the temperature controller. In an exothermic catalytic reaction, the process may "run away" due to disturbances or changes in the reactor. Immediate action should be taken to prevent a dangerous rise in temperature. Because a hot spot may potentially develop at one of several possible locations in the reactor, multiple (redundant) measurement points should be employed. This approach minimizes the time required to identify when a temperature has risen too high at some point in the bed. With a median selector, the selector output is the median of three or more input signals. These devices are useful for situations in which redundant sensors are used to measure a single process variable. By selecting the median input, maximum reliability is obtained since a single sensor failure will not result in loss of control.

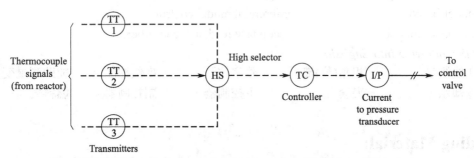

Figure 3.2.3 Control of a reactor hot spot temperature by using a high selector.

The use of high or low limits for process variables is another type of selective control, called an *override*. The feature of anti-reset windup in feedback controllers is a type of override. Another example is a distillation column which has lower and upper limits on the heat input to the column reboiler. The minimum level ensures that liquid will remain on the trays, while the upper limit is determined by the onset of flooding. Overrides are also used in forced draft combustion control systems to prevent an imbalance between air flow and fuel flow, which could result in unsafe operating conditions.

Other types of selective systems employ multiple final control elements or multiple controllers. Stephanopoulos has described applications where several manipulated variables are used to control a single process variable (also called *split-range control*). Typical examples include the adjustment of both inflow and outflow from a chemical reactor in order to control reactor pressure or the use of both acid and base to control pH in wastewater treatment. For the multiple controller case, the controllers are generally employed in parallel rather than in series, as was the situation for the cascade configuration of Figure 3.2.3. In this approach the selector chooses from several controller outputs which final control element should be adjusted.

Consider the selective control system shown in Figure 3.2.4, which is used to regulate level and exit flow rate in a pumping system for a sand-water slurry. During normal operation, the level controller (LC) adjusts the slurry exit flow by changing the pump speed. A variable speed pump is used rather than a control valve due to the abrasive nature of the slurry. The slurry velocity in the exit line must be kept above a minimum value at all times to prevent the line from sanding up. Consequently, the selective control system is designed so that as the flow rate approaches the lower limit, the flow controller takes over from the level controller and speeds up the pump. The strategy is implemented in Figure 3.2.4 using a high selector and a reverse-acting flow controller with a high gain. The set point and gain of the flow controller are chosen so that the controller output is at the maximum value when the measured flow is near the constraint.

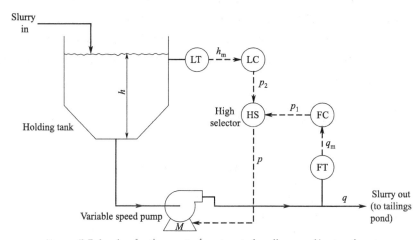

Figure 3.2.4 A selective control system to handle a sand/water slurry.

The block diagram for the selector control loop used in the slurry example is shown in Figure 3.2.5. The selector compares signals P_1 and P_2, both of which have the same units (e.g., voltage or current). There are two parallel feedback loops. Note that G_v is the transfer function for the final control element, the variable speed drive pump. A stability analysis of Figure 3.2.5 would be rather complicated because the high selector introduces a nonlinear element into the control system. Typically the second loop (pump flow) will be faster than the first loop (level) and uses proportional plus integral control (although reset windup protection will be required). Proportional control could be employed on the slower loop (liquid level) because tight level control is not required.

One alternative arrangement to Figure 3.2.4 would be to employ a single controller, using the level and flow transmitter signals as inputs to a high selector, with its output signal sent to the controller. The controller output would then adjust the pump speed. This scheme has a lower capital cost since only one controller is needed. However, it suffers from an important operational

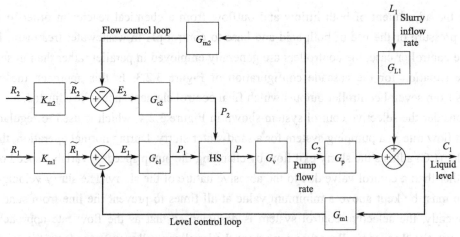

Figure 3.2.5 Block diagram for the selective control loop with two measurements and two controllers (variables in Figure 3.2.4 are identified).

disadvantage, namely, it may not be possible to tune the single controller to meet the needs of both the level and flow control loops. In general, these control loops and their transmitters will have very different dynamic characteristics. A second alternative would be to replace the flow transmitter and controller with a constant (override) signal to the high selector whose value corresponds to the minimum allowable flowrate. However, this scheme would be susceptible to changing pump characteristics.

Selected from "*Process Dynamics and Control, Dale E. Seborg & T. Edgar, John Wiley & Sonsi*, 1989"

Words and Expressions

1. override [ˌəuvəˈraid] *v.*; *n.* 越限, 超驰, 过载
2. arbitrary [ˈɑːbitrəri] *adj.* 任意的
3. assertion [əˈsəːʃən] *n.* 要求
4. auctioneer [ɔːkʃəˈniər] *vi.* 最大脉冲输出
5. exothermic catalytic reaction 放热催化作用
6. potential [pəˈtenʃəl] *adj.* 潜在的; 可能的
7. anti-reset windup 防积分饱和
8. reboiler [riːˈbɔilə] *n.* 重沸器
9. split-range control 滑动区间控制
10. sand-water slurry [sændwɔtəˈsləːri] *n.* 砂水浆
11. abrasive [əˈbreisiv] *adj.* 具有磨蚀性的
12. complicate [ˈkɔmplikeit] *vt.* 使复杂
13. allowable [əˈləuəbl] *adj.* 可允许的
14. susceptible [ˌsəˈseptəbl] *adj.* 灵敏的, 易感的, 易受影响

3.3 Adaptive Control Systems

> *After reading this unit, you should be able to answer*:
> 1. What is the adaptive control system?
> 2. Which industrial processes may require adaptive control?
> 3. Could you please describe the two general categories of adaptive control applications?

Process control problems inevitable require on-line tuning of the controller settings to achieve a satisfactory degree of control. If the process operating conditions or the environment changes significantly, the controller may have to be retuned. If these changes occur frequently, then adaptive control techniques should be considered. An *adaptive control system* is one in which the controller parameters are adjusted automatically to compensate for changing process conditions. A variety of adaptive control techniques have been proposed for situations where the process changes are largely unknown or for the easier class of problems where the changes are known or can be anticipated[①]. In this section we are principally concerned with automatic adjustment of feedback controller settings.

Catalytic reaction systems are a notable example of an important process where changes occur that are not directly measurable. As Lee and Weekman have noted,

Catalytic processes are notorious for changes in catalyst behavior, and adaptive loops are found quite commonly in such applications. The ad hoc development of an adaptive loop has probably saved more advanced control projects from failure than any other single technique.

Other causes of changing process conditions that may require controller retuning or adaptive control are:

① Heat exchanger fouling

② Unusual operational status, such as failures, start-up, and shutdown, or batch operations

③ Large, frequent disturbances (feed composition, fuel quality, etc.)

④ Ambient variations (rain storms, daily cycles, etc.)

⑤ Changes in product specifications (grade changes) or flow rates

⑥ Inherent nonlinear behavior (e.g., the dependence of chemical reaction rates on temperature)

It is convenient to distinguish between two general categories of adaptive control applications. The first category consists of situations where the process changes can be anticipated or measured directly. If the process is reasonably well understood, then it may be feasible to adjust the controller settings in a systematic fashion (called *programmed adaptation*) as process conditions change or as disturbances enter the system. The second category consists of situations where the process changes cannot be measured or predicted. In this more difficult situation the adaptive control strategy must be implemented in a feedback manner since there is little opportunity for a feedforward type of strategy such as programmed adaptation. Many such controllers are referred to as *self-tuning controllers*; they are generally implemented via digital computer control.

3.3.1 Programmed Adaptation

If a process is operated over a range of conditions, improved control can be achieved by using a different set of controller settings for each operating condition. Alternatively, a relation can be developed between the controller settings and the process variables that characterize the process conditions. These strategies are examples of programmed adaptation. Programmed adaptation is limited to applications where the process dynamics depend on known, measurable variables and the necessary controller adjustments are not too complicated. Usually the adaptation is simple enough in structure that it can be implemented with some analog and all digital controllers. The most popular type of programmed adaptation is gain scheduling, where the controller gain is adjusted so that the openloop gain $K_{OL}=K_cK_vK_pK_m$ remains constant.

As an example of a control problem where programmed adaptation has been proposed, consider a once-through boiler. Here feedwater passes through a series of heated tube sections before emerging as superheated steam, the temperature of which must be accurately controlled. The feedwater flow rate has a significant effect on both the steady-state and dynamic behavior of the boiler. For example, Figure 3.3.1 shows typical open-loop responses to a step change in flow rate for two different feedwater flow rates, 50% and 100% of the maximum flow. Suppose an empirical first-order plus delay model is chosen to approximate the process. The steady-state gain, time delay, and dominant time constant are all twice as large at 50% flow as the corresponding values at 100% flow. The proposed solution to this control problem is to make the PID controller settings vary with w, the fraction of full-scale flow ($0 \leqslant w \leqslant 1$), in the following manner:

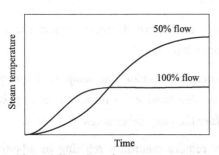

Figure 3.3.1 Open-loop step responses for a once-through boiler.

$$K_c = w\bar{K}_c$$
$$\tau_I = \bar{\tau}_I/w \quad (3.3.1)$$
$$\tau_D = \bar{\tau}_D/w$$

where $\bar{K}_c$, $\bar{\tau}_I$, and $\bar{\tau}_D$ are the controller settings for 100% flow. Note that this recommendation for programmed adaptation is qualitatively consistent with the Cohen and Coon rules for tuning controllers and assumes that the effect of flow changes is proportionally related to flow rate over the full range of operation.

In this example, step responses were available to categorize the process behavior for two different conditions. In other problems dynamic response data are not available but we have some knowledge of process nonlinearities. For pH control problems involving a strong acid and/or a strong base, the pH curve can be very nonlinear, with gain variations over several orders of magnitude. Consequently, special nonlinear controllers, both adaptive and nonadaptive, have been developed for pH control problems. In this case the process gain changes dramatically with the operating conditions, necessitating the use of gain scheduling (K_cK_p=constant) to maintain consistent stability margins.

For some types of adaptive control problems, the changes in steady-state and dynamic response characteristics can be related to the value of the controlled variable. For example, in a temperature control loop where the process gain varies with temperature, the controller gain could be made a function of the controlled variable, temperature. Feedback controllers are now commercially available which allow the user to vary K_c as a piecewise linear function of the error signal e, as shown in Figure 3.3.2. If the process gain K_p varies in a known manner, we should vary K_c so that the product K_cK_p is constant. This strategy would tend to keep the open-loop gain constant and thus maintain a specified margin of stability (assuming the process dynamics do not change also).

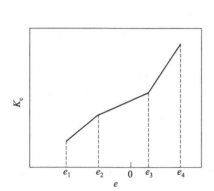

Figure 3.3.2 An adaptive controller where K_c varies with error signal e.

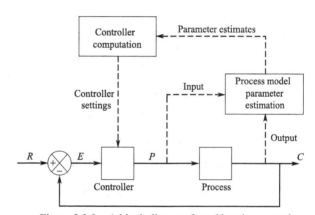

Figure 3.3.3 A block diagram for self-tuning control.

3.3.2 Self-tuning Control

If process changes can be neither measured nor anticipated, programmed adaptation cannot be used. An alternative approach is to update the parameters in a process model as new data are acquired (on-line estimation) and then base the control calculations on the updated model. For example, the controller settings could be expressed as a function of the parameters in the process model and the estimates of these parameters updated on-line as process input/output data are received. This type of controller is referred to as *self-tuning* or *self-adaptive*. Selftuning controllers generally are implemented as shown in Figure 3.3.3.

In Figure 3.3.3, three sets of computations are employed: estimation of the process model parameters, calculation of the controller settings, and implementation of the settings in a feedback loop. Most real-time parameter estimation techniques require that an external forcing signal occasionally be introduced to allow accurate estimation of process model parameters. Such an input signal can be deliberately introduced through the set point or added to the controller output.

The first type of self-tuning adaptive controller, called the *self-tuning regulator*, was proposed

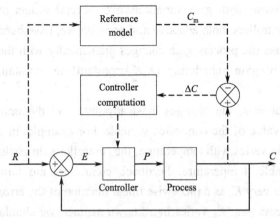

Figure 3.3.4 A block diagram for model-reference adaptive control.

in 1973 by Åström and Wittenmark and has since been implemented in several industrial applications. Subsequent modifications, the *self-tuning controller* and the *generalized predictive controller*, have also been used with industrial process. These controllers are based on a difference equation (digital) model of the process, and the self-tuning regulator and self-tuning controller utilize a minimum variance criterion to reduce the error in the controlled variable. The self-tuning regulator particularly is oriented towards applications where the process disturbances are stochastic in nature (i.e., random) rather than deterministic. Detailed discussion of these self-tuning methods is beyond the scope of this book.

A related type of adaptive control strategy, model reference adaptive control, attempts to achieve a closed-loop response that is as close as possible to a desired (or reference) response. The discrepancy or difference between actual response and the desired model reference ($\Delta C = C - C_m$) is used in the control law calculation (Figure 3.3.4). The boldface blocks in Figures 3.3.3 and 3.3.4 indicate functions carried out by a digital computer. While the controller can be implemented with analog or digital equipment, normally the latter is used.

3.3.3 Commercial Adaptive Control Systems

Several adaptive controllers have been field-tested and commercialized in the United States and abroad. The ASEA adaptive controller, called Novatune, was announced in 1983 and is based on the minimum variance-stochastic control algorithms mentioned above. Both feedforward and feedback contrl capabilities reside in the hardware, which can be configured for as many as 16 control loops. Novatune has been tested successfully in reactor and paper machine control applications in pH control of wastewater in the United States.

Another commercial adaptive controller (Leeds and Northrup) is based on making step changes in the set point and has been used successfully in process heating applications. This self-tuning controller is designed to provide exponential responses to set-point changes, with no overshoot. During the tuning procedure, a specified change in the set point (as large as feasible) is introduced to obtain the process gain and time constants. Controller settings are determined directly from a derived second-order process model and the desired closed-loop response time (time to reach 90% response) specified by the user. Additional testing may be required if the response exhibits some overshoot, which indicates that the model parameters are incorrect.

The Foxboro Company has developed a self-tuning PID controller that is based on an "expert system" approach for adjustment of the controller setting. The on-line tuning of K_c, τ_I, and τ_D is based on the closed-loop transient response to a step change in set point. By evaluating the salient characteristics of the response (e.g., the decay ratio, overshoot, and closed-loop period), the controller settings can be updated without actually finding a new process model. The details of the technique, however, are proprietary.

The Satt controller, which is marketed in the United States by Fisher Controls, has an autotuning function that is based on placing the process in a controlled oscillation at very low amplitude, comparable with that of the noise level of the process. Using process data, the autotuner identifies the ultimate gain and period and automatically calculates K_c, τ_1, and τ_D using the Ziegler-Nichols rules. Gain scheduling can also be implemented with this controller, using up to three sets of PID controller parameters.

The subject of adaptive control is one of great current interest. Many new algorithms are presently under development, but these need to be fieldtested before industrial acceptance can be expected. It is clear, however, that digital techniques are required for implementation of self-tuning controllers due to their complexity.

Selected from "*Process Dynamics and Control, Dale E. Seborg & T. Edgar, John Wiley & Sonsi,* 1989"

Words and Expressions

1. adaptive [ə'dæptiv] *adj.* 适应性的
2. adaptive control system 自适应控制系统
3. notorious [nəu'tɔːriəs] *adj.* 名声极坏的
4. catalytic [ˌkætə'litik] *adj.* 催化的
5. adaptive loop 适应性环路
6. single technique 单一性技术
7. start-up [staːtʌp] *vi.* 启动
8. batch operation 批操作，批处理
9. ambient variation 环境变化
10. daily cycle 日常周期性变化
11. empirical [em'piəikl] *adj.* 经验的
12. fraction ['frækʃən] *n.* 部分；分数
13. recommendation [ˌrecəmen'deiʃən] *n.* 推荐；推荐技术指标
14. programmed adaptation 可编程自适应
15. nonlinearity [nɔnlini'æriti] *n.* 非线性度，非线性
16. full-scale 满尺度，满量程
17. necessitate [ni'sesiteit] *vt.* 需要；迫使
18. margin ['maːdʒin] *n.* 阈；限度；范围
19. forcing signal 强迫信号
20. self-tuning adaptive controller 自整定适应控制器
21. subsequent modification 后修正
22. self-tuning regulator 自整定式调节器
23. generalized predictive controller 广义预测控制器
24. minimum variance criterion 最小差异准则

25. control strategy　控制方案
26. control law　控制法则
27. boldface　['bəuldfeis]　n. 黑体字
28. field-test　对……做现场试验
29. commercialize　[kə'mə:ʃəlaiz]　vt. 商品化
30. minimum variance-stochastic control　最小差异随机控制
31. exponential response　[ekspəu'nenʃəl ri'spɔns]　n. 指数响应
32. transient response　['trænziənt ris'pɔns]　n. 瞬时响应
33. salient　['seiliənt]　adj. 显著的
34. update　[ʌp'deit]　vt. 更新

Exercises

1. *Complete the notes below with words taken from the text above.*

    (1) process control problems inevitably require _____ of the controller settings _____ a satisfactory degree of control. ____ the process operating conditions _____ the environment changes significantly, the controller _____ be retuned. _____ these changes occur frequently, _____ adaptive control techniques _____ considered.

    (2) It is convenient to _____ between _____ general categories of adaptive control applications. The first category consists of situations _____ the process changes _____ anticipated _____ measured directly. If the process is reasonably well understood, _____ it _____ feasible _____ the controller settings in a systematic fashion (called programmed adaptation) _____ process conditions change _____ disturbances enter the system. The second category consists of situations _____ the process changes _____ measured or predicted. In this more difficult situation _____ must be implemented _____ feedback manner _____ there is little opportunity for a feedforward type of strategy _____ programmed adaptation. Many such controllers _____ to as _____ they are generally implemented _____.

    (3) If process changes _____ be _____ measured _____ anticipated, programmed adaptation _____ used. _____ approach is to update _____ in a process model _____ are acquired (on-line estimation) _____ base the control calculations on the _____.

2. *Put the following into Chinese:*

    adaptive control　　　　self-tuning control　　　programmed adaptation
    updated model　　　　　self-tuning regulator
    generalized predictive controller　　　　　　　　model parameter
    commercial　　　　　　split-rang control　　　　redundant

3. *Put the following into English:*

    自整定控制器　　广义预测控制　　选择性控制　　余差
    选择器　　　　　超驰控制系统　　防积分饱和　　催化反应
    废水处理

Reading Material:

Statistical Quality Control

Statistical quality control (SQC), also called *statistical process control* (SPC), involves the application of statistical concepts to determine whether a process is operating satisfactorily. The basic concepts of statistical quality control are over fifty years old, but only recently with the growing worldwide focus on increased productivity have applications of SQC become widespread. If a process is operating satisfactorily (or *in control*), then the variation of product quality falls within acceptable bounds, usually the minimum and maximum values of a specific composition or property (product specification).

Figure 3.3.5 illustrates the variation of the controlled variable c, represented in the form of a *histogram*, that might be expected to occur under typical steadystate operating conditions. The

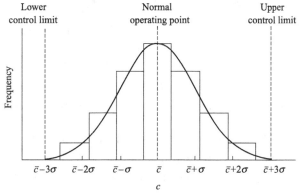

Figure 3.3.5 A histogram represents frequency of occurrence. (c=mean and σ=RMS deviation.)
Also shown is a normal probability distribution fit to the data.

mean $\bar{c}$ and root mean square (RMS) deviation σ are identified in Figure 3.3.5 and can be calculated from a series of J observations $c_1, c_2, \cdots, c_J$ as follows:

$$\bar{c} = \frac{1}{J}\sum_{i=1}^{J} c_i \tag{3.3.2}$$

$$\sigma = \left[\frac{1}{J}\sum_{i=1}^{J}(c_i - \bar{c})^2\right]^{1/2} \tag{3.3.3}$$

The RMS deviation, also called the standard deviation, is a measure of the spread of observations around the mean. A large value of σ indicates that wide variations in c occur. The probability that the controlled variable lies between two arbitrary values, c_1 and c_2, is given by the area under the histogram between c_1 and c_2. If the histogram follows a normal probability distribution (the curve in Figure 3.3.5), then 99.7% of all observations should lie within $\pm 3\sigma$ of the mean. These upper and lower control limits are used to determine whether the process is operating as expected. Note that the set point of the controlled variable should be selected near the mean $\bar{c}$ so that violations of the product specification are very unlikely (i.e., they have a low probability). In other words, both the upper and lower control limits should lie inside the operating constraints.

Figure 3.3.6 shows a process control chart for pH data taken over a time period of 50 days. Assume that $\bar{c}$ and σ have been calculated based on earlier observations. If all of the new data lie within the $\pm 3\sigma$ limits, then we conclude that nothing unusual has happened during the recorded time period. For this situation, the process environment is relatively unchanged and the product quality lies within specification. On the other hand, if repeated violations of the $\pm 3\sigma$ limits occur, then the process environment has changed and the process is *out of control*. This situation occurs in Figure 3.3.6 at $t=25$ days. Recall that if the normal probability distribution is valid, only 0.3% of the observations should violate the $\pm 3\sigma$ window. There are important economic consequences of a process being "out of control", for example, wasted product and customer dissatisfaction. Hence, SQC provides a systematic way to continuously monitor process performance and to improve product quality.

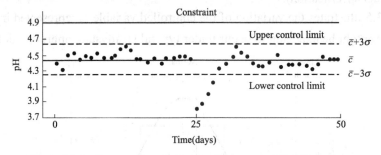

Figure 3.3.6 Process control chart for the average daily pH readings.

Statistical quality control is a diagnostic tool, that is, an indicator of quality problems, but is does not identify the source of the problem nor the corrective action to be taken. For example, suppose the data in Figure 3.3.6 were obtained from the monitoring of pH in a yarn-soaking kettle used in textile manufacturing. Because pH has a crucial influence on color and durability of the yarn, it is important to maintain pH within a range that gives the best results for both characteristics. The pH is considered to be in control between values of 4.25 and 4.64. At the 25th day, the data show that pH is out of control; this might imply that a property change in the raw material has occurred and must be corrected with the supplier. However, a real-time correction would be preferable. In Figure 3.3.6, the pH was adjusted by slowly adding more acid to the vats until it came back into control (Day 29).

In continuous processes where automatic feedback control has been implemented, the feedback mechanism theoretically ensures that product quality is at or near the set point, regardless of process disturbances. This, of course, requires that an appropriate manipulated variable has been identified for adjusting the product quality. However, even under feedback control, there may be daily variations of product quality because of disturbances or equipment or instrument malfunctions. These occurrences can be analyzed using the concepts of statistical quality control.

MacGregor has shown that the underlying theory of statistical quality control based on time-series models proves that feedback control is appropriate under certain assumptions. If (1) the cost of corrections in the manipulated variable is small compared to the cost of quality deviations, (2) process dynamics are important, and (3) corrections are made frequently by feedback control, SQC theory shows that a PI controller is optimal. On the other hand, when changes in the manipulated variable are infrequent because of their large cost (e.g., a unit shutdown), and the process is at steady-state, making hypothesis testing appropriate, the use of process control charts such as Figure 3.3.6 is optimal. Therefore process control charts should not be thought of as a general substitute for PID regulatory control and vice versa.

For a continuous plant some type of moving average can be employed to determine quality control. An average of the quality value for the past several days may be more meaningful than a single data point because of the blending that occurs in large product storage tanks. If the moving average exceeds the $\pm 3\sigma$ limits on a process control chart, then we conclude that some significant change in the process *not correctable by existing feedback control* has occurred; for example,

- Persistent disturbances from the weather
- An undetected grade change in raw materials
- A malfunctioning instrument or control system

In any case, further engineering analysis of the problem is indicated.

The subject of statistical quality control is quite broad and we have presented only the simplest concepts above. More details on process control charts, probability distributions, sampling, grouping of observations, and other related items have been provided by Grant and Leavenworth and Montgomery.

Selected from "*Process Dynamics and Control, Dale E. Seborg & T. Edgar, John Wiley & Sonsi*, 1989"

Words and Expressions

1. statistical quality control (SQC) 统计质量控制
2. application ['æpli'keiʃən] *n.* 应用，应用程序
3. productivity ['prədʌk'tiviti] *n.* 生产力
4. histogram ['histəgræm] *n.* 直方图，频率曲线
5. mean [mi:n] *n.* 平均(数)，平均(值)，中值
6. root mean square (RMS) 均方根
7. deviation ['di:vi'eiʃən] *n.* 背离；偏差
8. violation ['vaiə'leiʃən] *n.* 违反，违背
9. constraint [kən'streint] *n.* 强制，局促
10. systematic ['sisti'mætik] *adj.* 有系统的，体系的
11. diagnostic [daiəg'nɔstik] *adj.* 诊断的，特征的
12. yarn-soaking kettle 纱浸泡桶，染缸
13. textile ['tekstail] *adj.* 纺织的，织成的
14. durability [djuərə'biliti] *n.* 耐久性
15. vat [væt] *n.* 大桶

16. implement ['impliment] n. 工具; vt. 使生效, 执行
17. mechanism ['mekənizəm] n. 机构, 机理, 结构
18. malfunction ['mæl'fʌŋʃən] n. 故障; vi. 发生故障
19. underlying theory   支撑性的理论
20. time-series model   连续时间模型
21. vice versa   反过来也是这样
22. undetected grade   未发现的级别

3.4 Model Based Predictive Control

After completing this unit, you should be able to:
1. List the major ideas in the predictive control.
2. Describe the advantages of MPC over other methods.
3. Give the characterization of the MPC methodology.
4. Outline the basic structure of MPC.

3.4.1 Introduction

Model (Based) Predictive Control (MBPC or MPC), is not a specific control strategy but more of a very ample range of control methods developed around certain common ideas. These design methods lead to linear controllers which have practically the same structure and present adequate degrees of freedom. The ideas appearing in greater or lesser degree in all the predictive control family are basically:

- Explicit use of a model to predict the process output at future time instants (horizon).
- Calculation of a control sequence minimizing a certain objective function.
- Receding strategy, so that at each instant the horizon is displaced towards the future, which involves the application of the first control signal of the sequence calculated at each step.

The various MPC algorithms (also called long-range Predictive Control or LRPC) only differ amongst themselves in the model used to represent the process and the noises and the cost function to be minimized. This type of control is of an open nature within which many works have been developed, being widely received by the academic world and by industry. There are many applications of predictive control successfully in use at the present time, not only in the process industry but also applications to the control of a diversity of processes ranging from robot manipulators to clinical anesthesia. Applications in the cement industry, drying towers and in robot arms, are described, whilst developments for distillation columns, PVC plants, steam generators or servos are presented. The good performance of these applications shows the capacity of the MPC to achieve highly efficient control systems able to operate during long periods of time with hardly any intervention[①].

MPC presents a series of advantages over other methods, amongst which stand out:

- it is particularly attractive to staff with only a limited knowledge of control, because the concepts are very intuitive and at the same time the tuning is relatively easy.
- it can be used to control a great variety of processes, from those with relatively simple dynamics to other more complex ones, including systems with long delay times or of non-minimum phase or unstable ones.
- the multivariable case can easily be dealt with.

• it intrinsically has compensation for dead times.

• it introduces feed forward control in a natural way to compensate for measurable disturbances.

• the resulting controller is an easy to implement linear control law.

• its extension to the treatment of constraints is conceptually simple and these can be included systematically during the design process.

• it is very useful when future references (robotics or batch processes) are known.

• it is a totally open methodology based on certain basic principles which allow for future extensions.

As is logical, however, it also has its drawbacks. One of these is that although the resulting control law is easy to implement and requires little computation, its derivation is more complex than that of the classical PID controllers. If the process dynamic does not change, the derivation of the controller can be done beforehand, but in the adaptive control case all the computation has to be carried out at every sampling time. Although this, with the computing power available today, is not an essential problem one should bear in mind that many industrial process control computers are not at their best as regards their computing power and, above all, that most of the available time at the process computer normally has to be used for purposes other than the control algorithm itself (communications, dialogues with the operators, alarms, recording, etc)[2]. Even so the greatest drawback is the need for an appropriate model of the process to be available. The design algorithm is based on a prior knowledge of the model and it is independent of it, but it is obvious that the benefits obtained will depend on the discrepancies existing between the real process and the model used.

In practice, MPC has proved to be a reasonable strategy for industrial control, in spite of the original lack of theoretical results at some crucial points such as stability or robustness.

3.4.2 MPC Strategy

The methodology of all the controllers belonging to the MPC family is characterized by the following strategy, represented in Figure 3.4.1.

(1) The future outputs for a determined horizon N_1 called the prediction horizon, are predicted at each instant t using the process model. These predicted outputs $y(t+k\mid t)$ for $k=1, \cdots, N$. depend on the known values up to instant t (past inputs and outputs) and on the future control signals $u(t+k\mid t)$, $k=0, \cdots, N-1$, which are those to be sent to the system and to be calculated.

(2) The set of future control signals is calculated by optimizing a determined criterion in order to keep the process as close as possible to the reference trajectory $w(t+k)$ (which can be the set-point itself or a close approximation of it). This criterion usually takes the form of a quadratic function of the errors between the predicted output signal and the predicted reference trajectory. The control effort is included in the objective function in

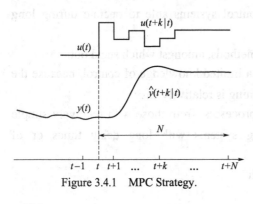

Figure 3.4.1　MPC Strategy.

most cases. An explicit solution can be obtained if the criterion is quadratic, the model is linear and there are no constraints, otherwise an iterative optimization method has to be used. Some assumptions about the structure of the future control law are also made in some cases, such as that it will be constant from a given instant.

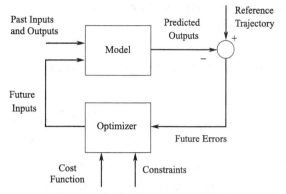

Figure 3.4.2   Basic structure of MPC.

(3) The control signal $u(t \mid t)$ is sent to the process whilst the next control signals calculated are rejected, because at the next sampling instant $y(t + 1)$ is already known and step (1) is repeated with this new value and all the sequences are brought up date. Thus the $u(t +1 \mid t + 1)$ is calculated (which in principle will be different to the $u(t + 1\mid t)$ because of the new information available) using the receding horizon concept.

In order to implement this strategy, the basic structure shown in Figure 3.4.2 is used. A model is used to predict the future plant outputs, based on past and current values and on the proposed optimal future control actions. These actions are calculated by the optimizer taking into account the cost function (where the future tracking error is considered) as well as the constraints.

The process model plays, in consequence, a decisive role in the controller. The chosen model must be capable of capturing the process dynamics so as to precisely predict the future outputs as well as being simple to implement and to understand. As MPC is not a unique technique but a set of different methodologies, there are many types of models used in various formulations.

One of the most popular in industry is the Truncated Impulse Response Model, which is very simple to obtain as it only needs the measurement of the output when the process is excited with an impulse input. It is widely accepted in industrial practice because it is very intuitive and can also be used for multivariable processes, although its main drawbacks are the large number of parameters needed and that only open-loop stable processes can be described this way. Closely related to this kind of model is the Step Response Model, obtained when the input is a step.

The Transfer Function Model is, perhaps, most widespread in the academic community and is used in most control design methods, as it is a representation that requires only a few parameters and is valid for all kind of processes. The State-Space Model is also used in some formulations, as it can easily describe multivariable processes.

The optimizer is another fundamental part of the strategy as it provides the control actions. If the cost function is quadratic, its minimum can be obtained as an explicit function (linear) of past inputs and outputs and the future reference trajectory. In the presence of inequality constraints the solution has to be obtained by more computationally taxing numerical algorithms. The size of the optimization problems depends on the number of variables and on the prediction horizons used and usually turn out to be relatively modest optimization problems which do not require sophisticated computer codes to be solved. However the amount of time needed for the constrained and robust cases can be various orders of magnitude higher than that needed for the unconstrained case and the bandwidth of the process to which constrained MPC can be applied is considerably reduced[③].

Selected from "Model Predictive Control in the process industry, Camacho, E.F. and C. Bordons, Spring Verlag, 1995"

Words and Expressions

1. methodology　[meθəˈdɔlədʒi]　*n.* 方法学, 方法论
2. ample　[ˈæmpl]　*adj.* 充足的, 丰富的
3. explicit　[iksˈplisit]　*adj.* 外在的, 清楚的
4. manipulator　[məˌnipjuˈleitə]　*n.* 机械手
5. clinical　[ˈklinikl]　*adj.* 临床的
6. anesthesia　[ˌænisˈθiːziə]　*n.* 麻醉, 麻痹
7. distillation　[ˈdistlˈeʃən]　*n.* 蒸馏
8. multivariable　[ˈmʌltiˈvɛəriəbl]　*n.* 多变量
9. intrinsically　[inˈtrinsikəli]　*adv.* 本质上
10. compensation　[ˈkɔmpenˈseiʃən]　*n.* 补偿
11. dead time　滞后
12. systematically　[ˈsistiˈmætikəli]　*adv.* 有条理地, 系统地
13. robotics　[rəˈbɔtiks]　*n.* 机器人学
14. batch process　批处理
15. extension　[iksˈtenʃən]　*n.* 扩展, 扩充
16. available time　空闲时间
17. discrepancy　[disˈkrepənsi]　*n.* 差异, 差别
18. robustness　[rəuˈbʌstnis]　*n.* 健壮性, 鲁棒性
19. quadratic　[kwɔˈdrætik]　*adj.* 二次的
20. iterative　[ˈitərətiv]　*adj.* 反复的
21. optimal　[ˈɔptəməl]　*adj.* 最佳的, 最理想的
22. future control action　未来控制行为
23. cost function　[kɔstˈfʌŋkʃən]　*n.* 成本函数
24. future tracking error　[ˈfjuːtʃəˈtrækiŋˈerə]　*n.* 未来的跟踪错误
25. unique　[juːˈnik]　*adj.* 独特的, 独一无二的
26. truncated　[ˈtrʌŋkeitid]　*adj.* 削去尖角的, 截短的
27. Impulse Response Model　脉冲响应模型
28. intuitive　[inˈtjuːitiv]　*adj.* 直觉的
29. constraint　[kənˈstreint]　*n.* 约束
30. optimizer　[ˈɔptəmaizə]　*n.* 最佳化器, 优化器
31. inequality　[iniˈkwɔliti]　*n.* 不等式
32. computationally　[kəmˌpjuːˈteiʃənəli]　*adv.* 计算上地
33. sophisticated　[səˈfistikeitid]　*adj.* 复杂的, 先进的
34. orders of magnitude　数量级

35. unconstrained [ˌʌnkənˈstreɪnd] *adj.* 不受约束的，自由的
36. bandwidth [ˈbændwɪdθ] *n.* 带宽

Notes

① "with hardly any intervention"：几乎没有什么干涉，介词短语。
② "with the…today"：插入语；
   "bear in mind that"：把……记在心上这个短语引出一个从句；
   "above all"：首先，首要，在本句中是插入语。
③ 这里的主句是 "the amount…can be various orders…and the bandwidth…is…reduced"。

Exercises

1. *Complete the notes below with words taken from the text above.*
   (1) model (Based) Predictive Control (MBPC or MPC), _____ specific control strategy _____ of a very ample range of control methods developed around _____. These design methods _____ linear controllers _____ practically the same structure and _____ adequate degrees of freedom.
   (2) The various MPC algorithms (also called long-range Predictive Control or LRPC) _____ differ amongst themselves in _____ used to represent _____ and _____ and _____ to be minimized. This type of control is _____ open nature _____ many works have been developed, _____ widely received by the _____ and by _____ many applications of _____ successfully _____ at the present time, _____ in the process industry _____ applications to the control of _____ of processes ranging _____ manipulators to _____.
   (3) _____ popular in industry is the Truncated Impulse Response Model, _____ very simple to obtain as _____ needs the measurement of the output _____ the process _____ excited _____ input. _____ widely accepted in _____ because _____ intuitive and _____ for multivariable processes, _____ its main drawbacks are the large number of _____ needed and _____ open-loop stable processes _____ this way. _____ related to this kind of model is _____, obtained when the input is _____.

2. *Put the following into Chinese:*
   model based predictive control   long-rang predictive control
   reference trajectory   prediction horizon   sampling instant
   receding horizon   cost function   tracking error
   statistical quality control   root mean square   histogram
   probability distribution   chart

3. *Put the following into English:*
   最小化   目标函数   机器人   非最小相位
   脉冲响应模型 阶跃响应模型   统计过程控制   标准偏差

Reading Material:

Model Predictive Cascade Control and IMC Cascade Control

Implementations of model predictive control (MPC) often use a cascade structure whereby the model predictive controller provides set points to lower level PID controllers which adjust the various process actuators. Such implementations provide greater security and better rejection of some process disturbances than would be possible when the model predictive controller directly adjusts the process actuators[①]. However, such implementations also present some conceptual difficulties, and can result in poorer dynamic performance if the lower level control system is not fast relative to the MPC system. The conceptual and practical difficulties arise from the fact that model predictive controllers need to know their control effort limits in order to function properly. What, however, are the limits on the set point to an inner loop? When the settling time of the inner loop is shorter than the sampling time of the model predictive controller, then the inner loop may be assumed to be always at steady state and the limits on the change in set point can be obtained by multiplying an estimate of the inner loop process gain by the difference between the current control effort and its limit. Unfortunately such estimates are sensitive to the gain of the inner loop process, which is apt to be quite variable. Further, it is not clear how to compute set point limits when the sampling time of the model predictive controller is shorter than the settling time of the inner loop.

The above problems led us to consider how one would implement a cascade system entirely within a MPC framework. These considerations led, in turn, to new structure for Internal Model Control (IMC) and PID cascade systems which allow a two level implementation of MPC which does not have the defects previously enumerated. Further, the new structures lead to new insights into the design and tuning of cascade systems.

Section II, which follows, presents a model predictive cascade structure and its IMC analog. The design of such systems is compared with classical design strategies, and new methods are presented for treating control effort saturation. Section III reviews briefly a new approach to tuning cascade systems which accounts for process uncertainty. Section IV compares the performance of the new IMC and PID cascade systems with each other and with single loop control for two uncertain processes where the variation in the inner loop process parameters is greater than the variations in the outer loop process parameters.

Model Predictive Cascade Control Structures

Figure 3.4.3 shows a MPC cascade structure.

The above structure differs from a single loop MPC systems in that 1) the process model is composed of two parts, $\tilde{p}_1$, and $\tilde{p}_2$, 2) the inner loop model, $\tilde{p}_2$, is used in conjunction with the secondary measurement, y_2, to obtain an estimate, $\tilde{d}_2$, of the effect of disturbances on the secondary measurement, and 3) disturbances, d_1, effecting the primary output, y_1, are assumed to be independent of the disturbances, d_2, which effect only the secondary process variable, y_2. A simple

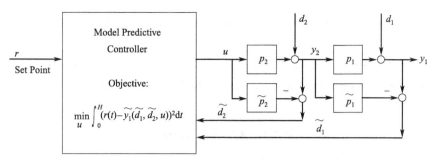

Figure 3.4.3 Model Predictive Cascade Control

formulation of the model predictive controller is to select the control effort, $u(t)$, to minimize an integral performance measure such as: $\int_0^H (r(t)-\tilde{y}_1(\tilde{d}_1,\tilde{d}_2,u))^2 \, dt$ (where $r(t)$ = set point) subject to saturation constraints on the control effort. The model, $\tilde{y}_1(\tilde{d}_1,\tilde{d}_2,u)$, is driven by disturbance estimates $\tilde{d}_1$ and $\tilde{d}_2$ and the computed control effort, and is used to predict the primary process variable over the time horizon, H. The minimization is repeated at each sampling instant. The simplest, and most common, method of predicting $\tilde{d}_1$ and $\tilde{d}_2$ into the future is to assume that they remain constant at the current estimate. To avoid overly aggressive control actions and to accommodate modeling errors it is common practice to allow the control effort to vary only over a period which is shorter than the time horizon H, and to impose limits on rate of change of the control effort.

The model predictive cascade controller of Figure 3.4.3 can be simplified into an IMC cascade controller given by Figure 3.4.4.

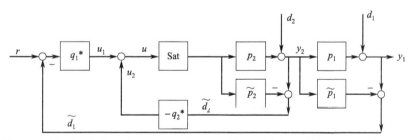

Figure 3.4.4 IMC Cascade Structure Suggested by Model Predictive Cascade Control

In Figure 3.4.4, the MPC controller is replaced by two controllers, q_1^* and $-q_2^*$, which together attempt to minimize the deviation of y_1, from its set point, r. The inner loop controller, $-q_2^*$, computes that part of the control effort which compensates for the effect of the inner loop disturbance, d_2, on the primary process variable y_1. The outer loop controller q_1^*, computes that part of the control effort which compensates for disturbances entering the outer loop and which causes the primary process variable to track its set point.

In the absence of control effort saturation, the structure of Figures 3.4.3 and 3.4.4 will perform identically provided that the controllers q_1^* and q_2^* are selected so as to minimize the same performance criterion as the model predictive controller. Garcia and Morari have shown the correspondence between IMC and MPC systems for single loop control systems. The extension of such a development for cascade systems should be straight forward, but will not be pursued here.

Rather, we next turn our attention to the selection of the IMC controllers for Figure 3.4.4.

Selected from "*Model Predictive Cascade Control and its Implications for Classical and IMC Cascade Control, C.Brosilow and N.Markale, Presented at the* 1992 *Annual AIChE meeting, Miamsi*"

Words and Expressions

1. model predictive casecade control   模型预测串级控制
2. implementation   [implimen'teiʃən]   *n.* 工具；安装，启用
3. apt   [æpt]   *adj.* 倾向于
4. enumerate   [inju:məreit]   *vt.* 列举，枚举
5. analog   ['ænəlɔg]   *n.* 类似物，相似体
6. saturation   [sætʃə'reiʃən]   *n.* 饱和，饱和度
7. sampling instant   抽样瞬间

Note

① "than would be possible"：这里省略了被比较的短语中的主要成分 "security and rejection" 或它们的代词；

"when the model…actuators"：这个从句描述了主句所要比较的对象原来所处的条件。

3.5　Supervisory Control Systems

> *During reading the following unit, try to answer*:
> 1. What is the supervisory control systems?
> 2. What is the application concept in supervisory control?

When digital computers were first used for on-line control applications in the 1960s, most of them were installed to enhance existing centralized control systems with a large number of analog controllers.

These enhancements added more "intelligence" to the control systems, so the operators could use these systems to maintain the process at a higher performance level than that achievable by using only analog controllers. These types of computer applications are called supervisory computer systems.

The hardware configuration of a supervisory control computer has been discussed elsewhere and will not be repeated. These earlier systems were expensive because of high hardware costs and the need for extensive software development for every installation. A detailed feasibility study was required to identify the cost and benefits before a project could be supported by management. However, past experience shows that after a project was completed, many of the benefits identified during the feasibility study would not be realized, while many side benefits or unexpected results helped to eventually justify the project economically. Some projects were reported as "technical successes, but economical failures," which implies that the cost of the project could not be recovered.

The most important contribution to the future of process control derived from these early supervisory control systems, whether they were economical successes or failures, was the technical know-how which they provided on the application of computer systems for on-line process control.

The wide acceptance of distributed control systems since the late 1970s has made the implementation of supervisory control much easier and less costly than ever before. As shown in previous chapters, a supervisory control computer can be connected to the common cautions network of a distributed control system and communicate directly with the data base. This eliminates the need for interface hardware and, thus, greatly reduces the supervisory control computer hardware cost.

The availability of high level programming languages and advanced operating systems has made the software development task easier than before. In addition, generalized supervisory control software packages are now offered by many vendors and software system houses. Software development tasks are now manageable in terms of cost and schedule.

With lower costs for both hardware and software, will the supervisory control system be considered as a low budget item which requires no detail cost/benefit analysis from management's point of view? The answer is maybe, but unlikely nor desirable. The fact is, today's large supervisory computer installations are many orders of magnitude faster and larger in memory capacity than early generation computers, and they are designed to provide much greater functionality than ever before, so the supervisory control computer system can cost even more than a computer purchased 20 years ago. On the other side of the spectrum, one can purchase a small computer and use it within a limited scope to control a process plant. This will be a low-cost computer, but the benefits will also be limited. In conclusion, the cost of supervisory computers today can range from a few thousand dollars to a few million dollars. A feasibility study is still needed for most applications, because even a low cost computer may require extensive software development, so the system with the lowest hardware cost may not be the best system.

The latest application concept in supervisory control is to combine several major computer functions, such as process control, on-line performance/cost analyses, and management information decision support into a network which consists of many computers. Note that several supervisory control computers and a "plant management system" are connected together to form an information network. The major goal for such a system is to optimize the plant's performance from both the technical and managerial points of view. The availability of realtime operating information to management may have a major impact on plant operating philosophy and even future plant organization. Some middle managers may no longer be needed to interpret plant operating data for senior managers, nor will they be needed for transmitting senior management decisions to plant personnel; all of these functions can be accomplished automatically. History has proven that fewer managerial levels improve overall effectiveness, so the potential savings from this type of system can be enormous. A manager now faces two questions; can he afford to have a computer, and, can he afford not to have a computer?

Selected from "*Modern Control Techniques for the Processing Industries T.H. TSAI, J.W. LANE, C.S.LIN, Marcel Dekker*, 1986"

Words and Expressions

1. supervisory [sju:pə'vaizəri] *adj.* 管理的, 监督的
2. enhance [in'hɑ:ns] *vt.* 提高, 加强
3. intelligence [in'telidʒəns] *n.* 智力, 情报
4. configuration [kənfigju'reiʃən] *n.* 结构, 形态, 配置
5. caution ['kɔ:ʃən] *n.* 警示, *vt.* 警告
6. feasibility [fi:zə'biliti] *n.* 可行性, 现实性
7. vendor ['vendə] *n.* 小贩, 卖主
8. budget ['bʌdʒit] *n.* 预算
9. spectrum ['spektrəm] *n.* 谱, 系列
10. potential [pə'tenʃəl] *n.* 潜力, *adj.* 潜在的
11. technical success   技术可行
12. economical failure   经济不可行

Exercises

1. *Complete the notes below with words taken from the text above.*

   (1) _____ digital computers _____ first _____ for on-line control applications in the 1960s, _____ were installed to enhance existing centralized control systems with _____ of analog controllers. These enhancements added more "intelligence" to the control systems, _____ the operators could use these systems to maintain the process at a higher performance level _____ achievable by using only analog controllers. These types of computer applications are called _____.

   (2) The wide acceptance of _____ since the late 1970s _____ the implementation of supervisory control _____ and _____ ever before. As shown in previous chapters, a supervisory control computer _____ connected to the _____ of a distributed control system and communicate directly _____ the _____. This eliminates the need for _____. And, _____, greatly reduces the supervisory control computer _____.

   (3) _____ application concept in supervisory control _____ several major computer functions, _____ process control, _____, and management information decision support into a network _____ consists of many computers _____ several supervisory control computers and a "_____" are connected together to form an _____. The major goal for such a system is _____ the plant's _____ from both the technical and managerial points of view.

2. *Put the following into Chinese:*

   supervisory control system analog controller
   performance distributed control system
   cost/benefit analysis management information system (MIS)
   decision support system (DSS) plant management system
   cascade structure internal model control

3. *Put the following into English:*

   可行性   通信网络   数据库   接口硬件   编程语言
   软件   硬件   内环   实时操作信息   计算机监控系统

4. *Complete the following close test:*

   Implementation of model predictive control (MPC) (Cutler and Ramaker, 1980, Prett and Garcia, 1988) often use _____ whereby the model predictive controller provides _____ to lower level PID controllers _____ adjust the various process _____. _____ implementations provide greater process _____ and better _____ of some process disturbances _____ possible _____ the model predictive controller directly adjusts the process actuators. _____, such implementations _____ present some conceptual difficulties, _____ result in poorer dynamic performance _____ the lower level control system _____. The conceptual and practical difficulties _____ the fact _____ model predictive controllers _____ their control effort limits _____ function properly.

Reading Material:

Intelligent Supervisory Control and Optimization

One of the most important problems in process control and management is intelligent supervisory control and optimization. Today, there are elaborate distributed control systems which are capable of providing base control technology such as proportional integral derivative control. They are capable of accessing data through instrumentation, manipulating process variables, and providing a foundation for optimization. However, these systems are not very flexible or adaptive to changing conditions in the plant environment.

For example, suppose we have a plant with a hundred PID loops. The coefficients in these PID loops are dependent on:
- What is being manufactured
- The goal of manufacturing
- The nature and state of disturbances
- The quality of raw materials
- The desired operating conditions of the plant

Because the plant is continually evolving, a particular parameter which is desirable at one point can be completely and totally undesirable, even detrimental, at another.

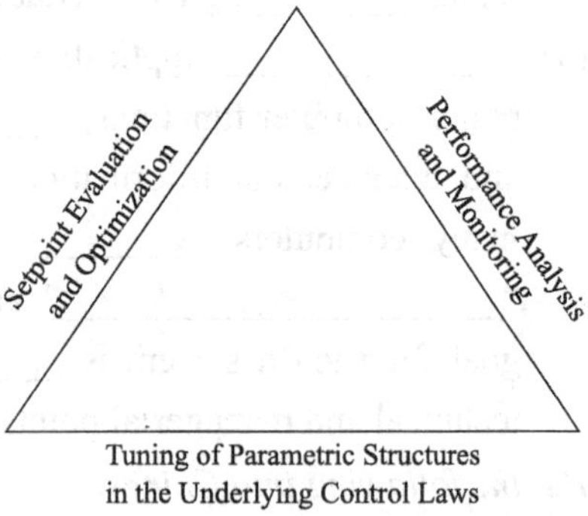

There are three major components to providing an intelligent supervisory control and optimization system which would be able to monitor, screen, and adjust the control and instrumentation layer based upon data and control from the plant and corporate layers. (See Figure 3.5.1) The areas of such a system are:
- Tuning of parametric structures in the underlying control laws
- Set-point evaluation and optimization
- Performance analysis and monitoring

Figure 3.5.1 Components of intelligent supervisory control and optimization system.

The tuning problem has plagued industry for a long time. Traditionally, when control technology is put into a plan, an audit is conducted. As part of the audit, the system is tuned and optimized values for the various proportional integral and derivative parameters are set. Since there is no plant-wide tuning system, it is left to the local plant personnel to maintain the parametric structure. The skill, judgment, and expertise required to do this are rare. Moreover, it is an important task which is highly time-consuming.

In general, in an average plant most of the loops are suboptimally tuned. It is not uncommon to find a loop so completely maltuned that it is actually detrimental to the goals of manufacturing. This problem has not been solved with purely traditional analytic approaches. Moreover, the construction of a plant-wide tuning system must be in line with the philosophy of CIM to be of maximum benefit and return value in a maintainable and controllable fashion. (See Figure 3.5.2) Another problem is set-point evaluation and optimization.

Each control law needs a reference set point. Depending upon what is being manufactured, the raw materials which are being used, the recipes and the goals, the set points can vary dramatically. Optimally setting the set points is again a nonanalytic problem which has a large heuristic content. The set points dramatically affect the alarm management strategy and philosophy in the plant and are dependent on the tuning coefficients for all the control laws.

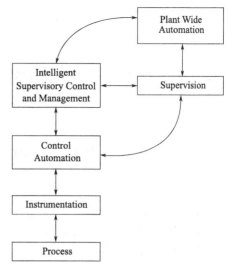

Figure 3.5.2 Intelligent supervisory control and management as part of a CIM architecture.

Determining how well the plant is operating and ascertaining poor control system design, as well as recommending areas for improved performance, are other aspects of constructing an intelligent supervisory control and optimization system. Usually, the requirements of control exceed the capabilities of simply adjusting tuning coefficients. Even with an optimal time-critical tuning environment, it is still possible for suboptimal plant performance to occur. Optimally tuned coefficients are not a substitute for poor control system design.

Intelligent supervisory control and optimization is a key opportunity in process control and management. Such a system can dramatically improve plant performance through the various levels of the automation pyramid. At the heart of the problem is constructing an intelligent plant-wide tuning system which would be the kernel of the supervisory control and optimization system.

Selected from "*AI in Process Control, Michael Stock, McGraw-Hill Book Company*, 1989"

Words and Expressions

1. intelligent supervisory control   智能监控
2. detrimental   ['detrə'mentl]   *adj.* 有害的
3. plague   [pleig]   *n.* 麻烦，灾害
4. audit   ['ɔːdit]   *n.* 检查; *v.* 决算，查账
5. suboptimally   [səb'ɔptiməli]   *adv.* 亚最佳地，次优地
6. recipe   ['resəpi]   *n.* 食谱，处方
7. heuristic   [hjuə'ristik]   *adj.* 启发式的，发展式的
8. ascertain   [æsə'tein]   *vt.* 确定，调查，弄清
9. kernel   ['kəːnl]   *n.* 核心，中心

CHAPTER 4 COMPUTER CONTROL SYSTEMS

4.1 Fundamentals of Computer Control

> *Topics covered in this unit are as follows:*
> 1. The black diagram for realisation of analogue control loop by computer control
> 2. Input and output interface
> 3. Input and output scaling
> 4. The PID control

Consider the level control system shown in schematic form in Figure 4.1.1. The plant consists of a tank with inlet and outlet pipes, the outlet pipeline containing a centrifugal pump and a control valve.

The flow rate f_1 of the inlet stream is determined by upstream conditions over which the level control system has no influence: f_1 is said to be wild. The level h is controlled by adjusting the flow rate f_0 of the outlet stream by means of a control valve. This is a typical feedback control system and is shown in block diagram form in Figure 4.1.2.

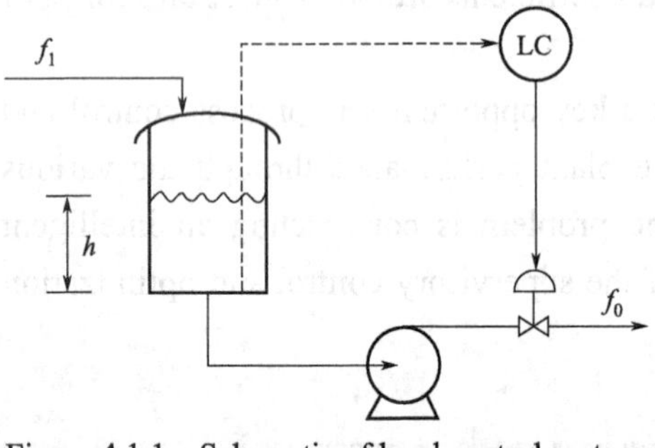

This unit explains how a typical analogue control loop is realised by means of computer control.

Consider again the level control loop depicted in Figure 4.1.1, the block diagram for which is shown in Figure 4.1.2, and whose implementation by computer control is depicted in Figure 4.1.3.

Figure 4.1.1 Schematic of level control system.

The signal is followed from the level transmitter, through the system and back out to the control valve. Both hardware and software aspects are covered.

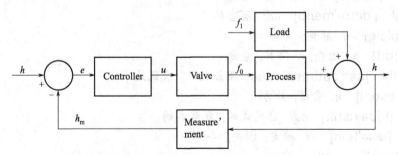

Figure 4.1.2 Block diagram of level control system.

This may be considered to consist of four sub systems:

① Process and load (F/H), and instrumentation comprising current to pressure (I/P) converter, valve (P/F) and dp cell (H/I).

② Input interface consisting of current to voltage (I/V) converter, sampler and analogue to digital converter (A/D).

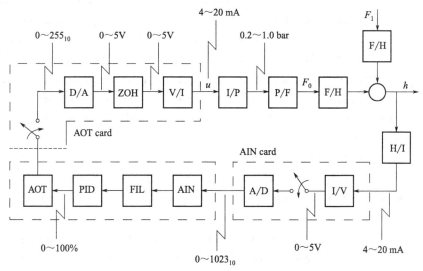

Figure 4.1.3 Block diagram for realisation of analogue control loop.

③ Function blocks for input scaling (AIN), filtering (FIL), control (PID) and output scaling (AOT).

④ Output interface consisting of sampler, digital to analogue converter (D/A), zero order hold (ZOH) and transmitter (V/I).

4.1.1 Input Interface

The three elements of I/V, sampler and A/D are all realised by the circuits of an AIN card. Assume that the dp cell's output is one of a number of 4～20 mA channels handled by the card, the circuit for which is as depicted in Figure 4.1.4.

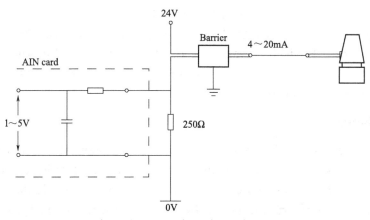

Figure 4.1.4 Analogue input channel.

The I/V conversion essentially consists of converting the 4~20 mA signal into a 0~5 V signal compatible with the input range of the A/D converter. The mA signal is dropped to earth across a 250 Ω resistor and converted into a 1~5 V signal. This is subsequently scaled into a 0~5 V signal by an op-amp circuit. The barrier depicted is external but on some systems is realised by circuits on the AIN card.

The sampling process, sometimes referred to as scanning, is necessary because the A/D converter is usually shared between all the input channels on the card. The sampler is often referred to as a multiplexer and sampled signals are said to be multiplexed. In operation, under control of the RTOS, the 0~5 V signal is switched through to the input of the A/D converter, and held there long enough for the A/D conversion to take place. The analogue signal must be sampled frequently enough for the samples to be a meaningful representation, but not so often as to cause unnecessary loading on the system. At the same time the sampling frequency must not be too low as to cause aliasing effects. The various input channels would be sampled at different frequencies, as appropriate.

The A/D converter is an integrated circuit chip. It converts the sampled 0~5 V signal into a bit pattern. Given that the original level measurement is from a dp cell, whose accuracy is ±1% at best, one would expect a 10-bit word with a range of $0 \sim 1023_{10}$ and a resolution of approximately ±0.1% to be adequate. However, this is insufficient resolution for some routines. For example, in PID control, the derivative action operates on the difference between successive input samples and, to avoid numerical instability, higher resolution is required. Therefore, it is not uncommon for A/D conversion to use at least 14 bit words with a range of $0 \sim 16383_{10}$ and a resolution of approximately ±0.006%.

4.1.2 Input Scaling

The AIN function block of Figure 4.1.3 represents an analogue input scaling routine. It operates on the output of the A/D converter. The following equation is used universally for linear scaling. For brevity, a 10-bit A/D converter is assumed:

$$\theta_0 = \text{bias} + \frac{\theta_1}{1023} \cdot \text{span}$$

where θ_1 is the decimal value of the binary output of the A/D converter.

A typical algorithm, written in structured text, for implementing it would be:

$$\text{OP} := \text{BI} + \text{SN} * \text{IP}/1023 \tag{4.1.1}$$

For example, a bit pattern of 1000011001_2 corresponds to $\theta = 537_{10}$ which, given a bias of -0.1 and a span of 2.1, yields a value for θ_0 of approximately 1.0 with a resolution of approximately 0.1%. The resultant value of 1.0012 is stored in slot 18 which obviously corresponds to the tank being half full.

4.1.3 Filtering

The FIL function block of Figure 4.1.3 represents a filter routine. It operates on the output of the AIN function block. Strictly speaking, given the high frequency filtering of the AIN card, this is only necessary if there is lower frequency noise, which is unlikely on the level in a buffer storage tank. The filter is nevertheless included as a typical example of signal processing.

The most common type of filter is the simple first order lag, which is of the form:

$$T\frac{d\theta_0}{dt} + \theta_0 = \theta_1$$

which may be rearranged:

$$\frac{d\theta_0}{dt} = \frac{\theta_1 - \theta_0}{T}$$

Using Euler's first order explicit method of numerical integration:

$$\theta_{0,j+1} = \theta_{0,j} + \left.\frac{d\theta_0}{dt}\right|_j \cdot \Delta t = \theta_{0,j} + \frac{\theta_{1,j} - \theta_{0,j}}{T} \cdot \Delta t$$

$$= \theta_{0,j} + k \cdot (\theta_{1,j} - \theta_{0,j})$$

A typical algorithm for implementing the filter would be

$$\text{OP:} = \text{OP} + \text{FC}*(\text{IP} - \text{OP}) \tag{4.1.2}$$

4.1.4 PID Control

The PID function block of Figure 4.1.3 represents the routine for a 3-term controller. It operates on the output of the FIL function block. In particular, a discretised version of the absolute form of the classical PID controller with derivative feedback was developed. Typical algorithms, written in structured text, for implementing this controller would be

```
        E = SP – IP
        if (OP = 0 or OP = 100) then goto L
        IA = IA + KI*E
L       OP = BI + (KC*E + IA – KD* (IP – PIP))
        if OP < 0 then OP = 0
        if OP > 100 then OP = 100
```
(4.1.3)

4.1.5 Output Scaling

The AOT function block of Figure 4.1.3 represents an analogue output scaling routine. It operates on the output of the PID function block. The output of the AOT function block is a decimal number whose binary equivalent is consistent with the input range of the D/A converter.

Given that the output signal is eventually used to position a valve, which can be done to within ±1% at best, one would expect an 8-bit word with a range of $0 \sim 255_{10}$ and a resolution of approximately ±0.25% to be adequate. However, in practice, most D/A converters use at least 10-bie words with a range of $0 \sim 1023_{10}$ and a resolution of approximately ±0.1%.

The following equation is used extensively for output scaling. The range of the controller output is normally $0 \sim 100\%$ and, for brevity, an 8-bit A/D converter is assumed:

$$\theta_0 = 255 \cdot \frac{(\theta_1 - \text{bias})}{\text{span}}$$

The output θ_0 is stored in the database as a bit pattern. The algorithm used for the output scaling is typically

$$\text{OP:} = 255*(\text{IP} - \text{BI})/\text{SN} \tag{4.1.4}$$

4.1.6 Output Interface

The four elements of sampler, D/A, ZOH and V/I are all realised by the circuits of an AOT card. Assume that the output is one of a number of $4 \sim 20$ mA channels handled by the card, the

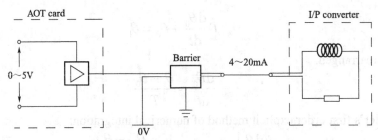

Figure 4.1.5　Analogue output channel.

circuit for which is as depicted in Figure 4.1.5. Again note the barrier for electrical protection.

The sampler is virtual. On a regular basis, under control of the RTOS, values of the AOT output are extracted from the database and routed through to the D/A converter. The sampler is held open long enough for the conversion to take place.

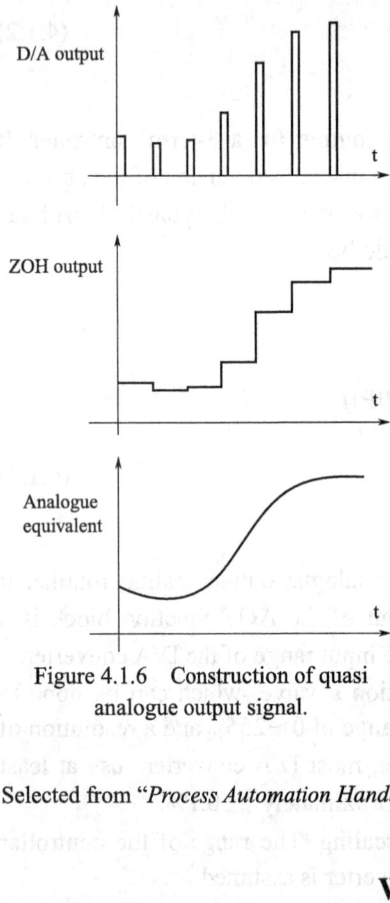

The D/A converter is an integrated circuit chip. It converts the sampled bit pattern into a 0～5 V signal. Since D/A converters are relatively cheap, it is normal practice for each output channel to have its own dedicated D/A converter.

The ZOH holds, or latches onto, the output of the D/A converter in between sampling periods. This effectively converts the pulse output from the D/A converter into a quasi, or piecewise linear, analogue signal that can be output to the I/P converter and thence to the control valve. Figure 4.1.6 depicts the construction of the quasi analogue signal.

Figure 4.1.6　Construction of quasi analogue output signal.

The transmitter V/I provides the scaling and power for signal transmission. The 0～5 V latched signal form the D/A is a very low power, TTL or otherwise, signal. After scaling into a 1～5 V signal it is converted into a 4～20 mA signal.

Selected from "*Process Automation Handbook, Jonathan Love, Springer London,* 2007"

Words and Expressions

1. centrifugal pump　离心泵
2. ZOH (zero order hold)　零阶保持器
3. sampler　['sæmplə]　*n.* 样品检测员，取样器，取样系统
4. dp cell　差压测量元件
5. barrier　['bæriə]　*n.* 隔离器，隔离栅
6. scanning　['skæniŋ]　*n.* 扫描，搜索
7. multiplexer　['mʌltipleksə]　*n.* 多路转换器，多路扫描器，多重通道
8. aliasing　['eilæsiŋ]　*n.* 假频，失真

9. integrated circuit 集成电路
10. scaling ['skeiliŋ] *n.* 定标，换算，定比例
11. quasi ['kwɑːzi] *adj.* 准，伪，拟，半
12. latch ['lætʃ] *v.* 锁住，系固；*n.* 门闩
13. virtual ['vətjuəl] *adj.* 实际上的，现实的，可能的，有效的
14. op-amp (operational amplifier) 运算放大器
15. depict [di'pikt] *vt.* 描述，叙述，画
16. brevity ['breviti] *n.* 简短，简化
17. buffer storage tank 缓冲储罐
18. Euler ['ɔilə] *n.* 欧拉

Exercises

1. *Put the following into Chinese:*

   by means of   analogue to digital converter (A/D)   filtering (FIL)
   sampler   input channel   I/V conversion   op-amp circuit   barrier
   scanning   multiplexer   resolution   scaling   bervity
   discrete device   entity   isolating valve   solenoid valve   I/O interface
   proximity switch   zener diode   threshold value

2. *Put the following into English:*

   离心泵   控制阀   模拟控制电路   计算机控制
   电流压力转换器   零阶保持器   数模转换器   积分电路
   联锁   顺序控制   现场仪表   继电器

Reading Material

Discrete I/O Devices

This chapter explains how a typical discrete device is realised by means of computer control. Discrete devices, sometimes referred to as entities, relate to a system's discrete I/O channels. A device consists of some two to four discrete input and/or output channels that are logically connected. The logic is normally handled by function blocks. Typical applications are in enabling trips and interlocks, discrepancy checking and polling redundant signals. Larger numbers of discrete I/O are normally handled by sequences.

The discrepancy checking of a valve position is used as a vehicle for explaining the operation of devices. The device consists of a discrete output channel which is used for opening an isolating valve, and a discrete input channel connected to a proximity switch used for checking whether the valve is open or not. This is depicted in P&I diagram form in Figure 4.1.7.

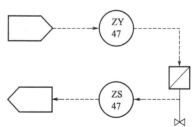

Figure 4.1.7 Representation of an isolating valve as a discrete device.

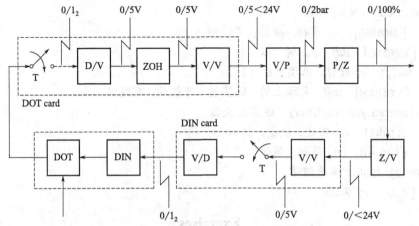

Figure 4.1.8 Block diagram for realisation of discrete device.

The corresponding block diagram is shown in Figure 4.1.8.

This may be considered to consist of four sub systems:

• An output interface consisting of a sampler, discrete to voltage converter D/V, zero order hold ZOH and relay V/V

• Field instrumentation comprising a solenoid actuated pilot valve V/P, pneumatically actuated isolating valve P/Z and a proximity switch Z/V

• An input interface consisting of a voltage converter V/V, sampler and voltage to discrete reader V/D

• Function blocks for handling discrete input DIN and discrete output DOT signals

1. Output Interface

The four elements of sampler, D/V, ZOH and V/V are all realised by the circuits of a DOT card. Assume that the output to the isolating valve is one of a number of 0/24 V channels handled by the card, the circuit for which is as depicted in Figure 4.1.9 Note the barrier for electrical protection.

The sampler is virtual. On a regular basis, under control of the RTOS, the status of the DOT block output is sampled, *i.e.* it is copied from the database into a register. It is usual for all the DOT outputs associated with a card to be stored in the bits of the register and to be "scanned" simultaneously.

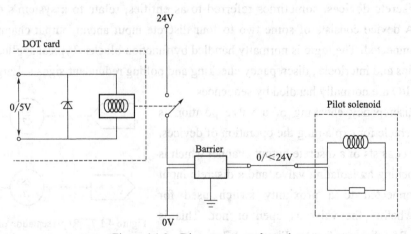

Figure 4.1.9 Discrete output channel.

The D/V conversion of the logical 0/1 in the register into a 0/5 V signal is handled by an op-amp type of circuit. This is then latched by the ZOH in between samples. The relay depicted is electro-mechanical in nature. This, and the transistor based type of relay, are the most common forms of relay used for discrete outputs signals.

2. Field Instrumentation

When the relay is closed, the 24 V power supply is routed through the barrier to the solenoid of a pilot valve. This enables compressed air to be applied to the diaphragm actuator of the isolating valve.

Suppose that the valve is of the air-to-open type and its closed position is of interest. The proximity switch is attached to the yoke of the valve and the magnet to its stem, both being positioned at the closed end of stem travel. Also suppose that the switch is normally open, but is closed by the magnet. Thus, when the valve is shut the output of the proximity switch is approximately 24 V. If the valve is open, fully or otherwise, or if the proximity switch fails, the output is 0 mA.

3. Input Interface

The three elements of V/V, sampler and V/D are all realised by the circuits of a DIN card. Assume that the input from the proximity switch is one of a number of 0/24 V channels handled by the card, the circuit for which is as depicted in Figure 4.1.10.

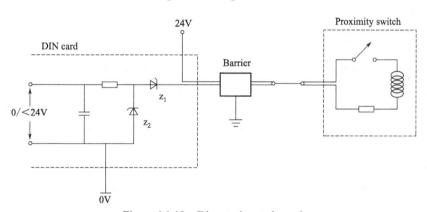

Figure 4.1.10 Discrete input channel.

The two zener diodes would typically have threshold values of z_1=20 V and z_2=25 V. These zeners establish a window through which only voltages of approximately 24 V can pass. This guards against false inputs due to spurious induction effects in the field circuits. Note the RC network for filtering out noise due to bounce on the proximity switch. Again note the barrier for electrical protection.

The V/V conversion concerns scaling the 0/24 V signal into a 0/5 V signal using an op-amp type of circuit. On a regular basis, under control of the RTOS, the 0/5 V signal is sampled, converted into a logical 0/1, and written into a register from which it is read into the database. It is usual for all the inputs associated with a DIN card to be stored in the bits of the register and to be scanned simultaneously.

4. Input Processing

The DIN function block of Figure 4.1.8 represents a discrete input processing routine. Its algorithm operates on the generic data block shown in Table 4.1.1.

Table 4.1.1 Discrete input function and data block

Function block		Datablock	Function block		Datablock
Slot	Description	Value	Slot	Description	Value
①	Block no.	B0027	⑦	Frame/rack/card/channel no.	1/2/4/16
②	Block type	DIN	⑧	Display area	06
③	Tag no.	ZS47	⑨	Alarm priority	0
④	Description	Proximity switch	⑩	Alarm on high	No
			⑪	Alarm on low	No
⑤	Block status	On	⑫	Message code	0
⑥	Sampling frequency	1	⑬	Current status	

The content of these slots is largely self explanatory. Note the following slots in particular:
⑤ If set to off, this would suspend execution of the DIN routine, despite the fact that the input is being sampled. Such a course of action would be appropriate, for example, if there is a hardware fault that causes the input signal to be in a permanent state of alarm.

⑩ and ⑪ These enable alarms to be attached to either state of the discrete input. Neither is used with the proximity switch because of the discrepancy checking on the discrete output to the solenoid valve.

5. Output Processing

The DOT function block of Figure 4.1.8 represents a discrete output processing routine. Its algorithm operates on the generic data block shown in Table 4.1.2.

The content of many of these slots is self explanatory. Note the following slots in particular:
⑦ This identifies the source of the required status of the discrete output corresponding to the valve opening, typically either 0 for shut or 1 for open. The status is normally determined by a sequence or by an operator decision.

⑨ An option for discrepancy checking is provided. For example, following a decision to close the solenoid valve, and allowing a time delay for the valve to close, the input from the proximity switch is checked.

⑩ This identifies the discrete input signal to be used for discrepancy checking.

⑪ A discrete output of 0 should correspond to an input of 1, and *vice versa*. Hence the binary codes of 01 and 10 are specified as acceptable combinations.

⑫ This slot permits the time delay allowed for in the discrepancy checking to be specified.

⑬~⑮ If a discrepancy occurs, it is treated as an alarm for which an area has to be specified, a priority attached and an option to generate messages provided.

These DIN and DOT function blocks have been explained on the basis of their use for discrepancy checking. However, it should be appreciated that the routines are general purpose and are used extensively for handling conventional discrete I/O that are not logically connected.

Table 4.1.2　Discrete output function and data block

	Function block	Datablock		Function block	Datablock
Slot	Description	Value	Slot	Description	Value
①	Block no.	B0270	⑨	Discrepancy checking	Yes
②	Block type	DOT	⑩	Discrepancy input block	B0027
③	Tag no.	ZY47	⑪	Discrepancy criteria	01, 10
④	Description	Isolating Valve	⑫	Discrepancy delay	5
			⑬	Display area	06
⑤	Block status	On	⑭	Alarm priority	0
⑥	Sampling frequency	1	⑮	Message code	0
⑦	Input block	B0470	⑯	Current status	
⑧	Frame/rack/card/channel no.	1/2/7/16			

Selected from "*Process Automation Handbook, Jonathan Love, Springer London*, 2007"

Words and Expressions

1. discrete I/O device　离散输入/输出装置
2. entity　['entiti]　*n.* 实体，实物，组织，机构
3. trip　[trip]　*n.* 断路，跳闸，固定器，自动停止机构
4. interlock　[intə'lɔk]　*n.* 联锁，连接，联锁装置
5. discrepancy　[dis'krepəsi]　*n.* 不同，不一致，差异，偏差，不精确度
6. poll　[pəul]　*n.* 查询，转态，终端设备定时查询
7. vehicle　['viːikl]　*n.* 车辆，运送装置，飞行器
8. isolating valve　隔离阀，隔断阀
9. magnet　['mægnit]　*n.* 磁铁，电磁
10. zener diode　齐纳二极管
11. threshold value　阈值，门限值，界限值
12. spurious　['spjuəriəs]　*adj.* 虚假的，伪的，谬误的
13. bounce　['bauns]　*n.* 脉动，反跳，进回，回波
14. proximity switch　邻近开关
15. solenoid valve　电磁阀
16. generic data　同属数据，同类数据
17. redundant　[ri'dʌndənt]　*adj.* 多余的，冗余的
18. routine　[ruːˈtiːn]　*n.* 子程序，例行程序

4.2 Computer Control System Architecture

> Topics covered in this unit are to describe the different architectures of computer control systems, such as advisory control, supervisory control, direct digital control, integrated control, distributed control, programmable logic controllers, supervisory control and data acquistion, management information systems, computer integrated manufacturing and open systems.

Architecture is the term used to describe the structure of a computer control system. It is directly related to the organisation of the system's I/O channels. New architectures have evolved over the years as the technology of computer control has advanced. This chapter surveys systems architecture and provides a historical perspective. Common terminology used to describe different architectures is explained. Detailed descriptions of systems architecture and terminology are provided by most of the major suppliers in their technical literature.

4.2.1 Advisory Control

Early computer systems were so unreliable that they could not be used for control, so the first systems used were in an off-line advisory mode, as depicted in Figure 4.2.1. The computer system operated alongside the conventional analogue instrumentation which controlled the plant. It was connected up to the input signals by means of an input interface (IIF) and was used for monitoring and data logging purposes only. From a control point of view, the computer system achieved very little and the expenditure could only be justified under some research budget. The first advisory system was installed by Esso at their Baton Rouge refinery in Louisiana in 1958.

Note that double lines with arrows are used to indicate multiple signals.

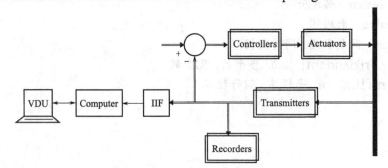

Figure 4.2.1 Advisory control system.

4.2.2 Supervisory Control

Given that the inputs were being monitored, it made sense to put some optimisation programs into the computer and use them to generate set points. These were output to the analogue controllers by means of an output interface (OIF). Hence the so-called supervisory system, as depicted in Figure 4.2.2. Note that when the computer system failed the set points would stay put and the analogue loops would continue controlling the plant. In practice, the optimisation programs were often too complex for the computing power available and their benefits proved to beelusive. Whilst there were some marginal hardware savings, mainly in terms of reduced numbers of analogue recorders, the principal benefits realised were experience and confidence. The first supervisory system was installed by Texaco at their Port Arthur refinery in Texas in 1959.

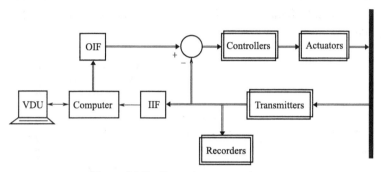

Figure 4.2.2   Supervisory control system.

4.2.3   Direct Digital Control

The next stage of development was to incorporate the computer system within the control loops. This is known as direct digital control (DDC) and is depicted in Figure 4.2.3. DDC enabled the control, display and recording functions to be realised by means of software. All the analogue controllers and recorders, apart from a few retained on critical loops, were replaced by visual display units (VDU), keyboards and printers. Because these were shared between the various loops, this enabled substantial economic benefits in terms of hardware. Given the reliability constraints and the lack of an analogue fall-back position, the early applications had to be on non-critical plant. The first implementation of DDC was on an ICI soda ash plant at Fleetwood in Lancashire in 1962 using a Ferranti Argus system, as reported by Thompson (1964).

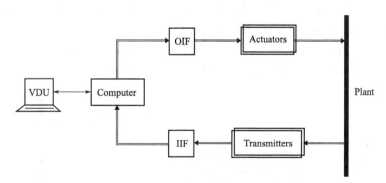

Figure 4.2.3   Direct digital control (DDC) system.

Note that the term DDC initially referred to an architecture which was centralised, or monolithic, in nature. However, over the years, it has become a more generic term and is now synonymous with digital devices being an integral part of the loop.

4.2.4 Integrated Control

This centralised type of architecture was used in particular for the control of complex batch plant. The systems evolved with advances in technology. In particular, from the early 1970s onwards, they became microprocessor based. Initially they were based upon single processors but, with the ever increasing demands for power and functionality, multiple processors became commonplace. Such systems were referred to as integrated control systems (ICS), as depicted in Figure 4.2.4. An ICS essentially consisted of three parts with dedicated links between: a plant interface unit (PIU), a process control unit (PCU) and an operator control station (OCS).

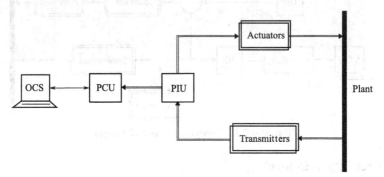

Figure 4.2.4 Integrated control system (ICS).

The PIU handled all the field I/O signals: it was sometimes referred to as a plant multiplexer assembly. The PCU supported all the control software. Note that, although functionally different, the PIU and the PCU were usually housed in the same cabinet. The OCS, often referred to simply as the operator station, was the human interface. An important point to appreciate is that the OCS was more than just a VDU and keyboard and, typically, had a processor which pre-processed signals from the PCU for display purposes.

The obvious drawback to the ICS was that "all its eggs were in one basket" and, when the system failed, control of the plant was lost. Thus, for critical applications, it was necessary to have a dual system with common I/O signals, as shown in Figure 4.2.5, so that the stand-by system could take over when the controlling system failed. Fortunately, it was not usually necessary to have to go to the lengths, not to mention cost, of putting in dual systems.

ICS, as an architecture, fell into disuse as recently as the 1990s.

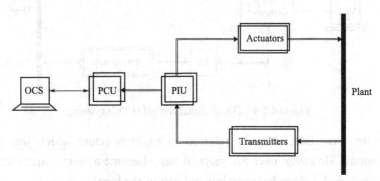

Figure 4.2.5 Dual integrated control system.

4.2.5 Distributed Control

The year of 1975 saw a step change in architecture with the launch by Honeywell of their microprocessor based TDC 2000 system. This was the first distributed control system (DCS) on the market and, in many respects, it became the de-facto standard for the next decade or so. The principal feature of the architecture of a DCS is its decentralised structure, consisting of PIUs, PCUs and OCSs interconnected by means of a proprietary highway. Figure 4.2.6 illustrates a so-called multi-drop type of DCS architecture. Note that the acronyms used are not universal.

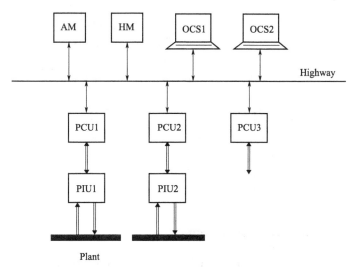

Figure 4.2.6 Multi-drop type of distributed control system (DCS).

The highway provides for communications between the PCUs and the OCSs, with current values and status information being passed from PCU to OCS and control commands in the opposite direction. It is usual for the highway to be dual to provide for redundancy, each PCU and OCS being connected to both highways. In the event of one highway failing, units can continue to communicate over the other. Indeed, this facility enables units to be connected to and removed from the system, one highway at a time, without disrupting operations.

Other modules are invariably connected to the highway, such as history modules (HM) and application modules (AM). Typically, an HM provides bulk memory for archiving purposes which enables much larger quantities of historical data to be stored and processed than is feasible in the memory of a PCU alone. Similarly, an AM enables advanced control packages to be run that require more processor power than is normally available in a single PCU. Such packages would be for optimisation or statistical process control or an expert system for decision support.

The PIUs and PCUs are normally organised on a loca basis, handling the I/O signals and taking the control actions for a relatively self contained area of plant. This is a principal advantage of DCS: it enables processor power to be targeted very effectively. DCS lends itself to the control of continuous plant consisting of relatively autonomous production units. With modern DCSs, a single node consisting of a PIU, PCU and OCS is powerful enough to be considered as an ICS in its own right.

4.2.6 Programmable Logic Controllers

Programmable logic controller (PLC) systems have a different pedigree to PCUs. They emerged within the manufacturing industries as a microprocessor based alternative to hard wired relay logic circuits. Their architecture is not dissimilar to that of DCS systems, to the extent that a PLC has to have a PIU to handle plant I/O and that the PLCs and OCSs communicate over a highway, as depicted in Figure 4.2.7. However, from a software point of view, there are some very important differences.

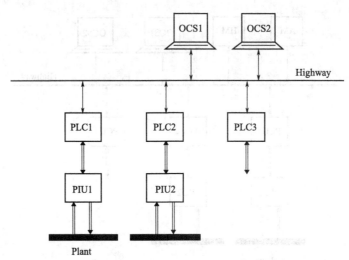

Figure 4.2.7　Programmable logic controller (PIC) system.

Selected from "Process Automation Handbook, Jonathan Love, Springer London, 2007"

Words and Expressions

1. architecture　['ɑːkitektʃə]　n. 体系结构
2. survey　[sə'vei]　n. 综述
3. perspective　[pə'spektiv]　n. 展望，观点
4. advisory control　监督控制，监视控制
5. data logging　数据采集
6. achieve　[ə'tʃiːv]　vt. 获得，完成，实现
7. budget　['bʌdʒit]　n. 预算，预案
8. ESSO　埃索石油公司
9. supervisory control　监督控制
10. optimisation programs　优化程序
11. elusive　[i'luːsiv]　adj. 逃避的
12. direct digital control (DDC)　直接数字控制器
13. soda ash　纯碱
14. centralise=centralize　['sentrəˌlaiz]　n. 集中
15. monolith　['mɔnəuliθ]　n. 整体，单一，一致

16. synonymous [si'nɔniməs] *adj.* 同义的
17. integrated control 集中控制，集成控制
18. drawback ['drɔ:bæk] *n.* 缺点
19. length [leŋθ] *n.* 持续时间，长度
20. distributed control 分散型控制，分布式控制
21. launch [lɔ:ntʃ] *vt.* 提出，开创，开始
22. Honeywell 霍尼威尔公司
23. de-facto standard 事实上的标准
24. acronym ['ækrənim] *n.* 缩写字
25. highway ['haiwei] *n.* 高速公路，公用信息通路
26. programmable logic controller 可编程逻辑控制器
27. pedigree ['pedigri:] *n.* 种类，家谱，由来，起源

Exercises

1. *Put the following into Chinese:*

   architecture   survey   historicalperspective   advisory   control   research budget
   supervisory control   recorder   display   batch plant
   microprocessor   plant interface unit (PIU)   Process control unit (PCU)
   operator control station (OCS)   dual system   decentralised structure
   multi-drop type   history module (HM)   application module (AM)
   advanced control package   supervisory control and data acquistion   data logging
   local area network (LAN)   computer integrated manufacturing (CIM) open system

2. *Put the following into English:*

   不可靠   离线   数据采集   优化程序   直接数字控制   集成控制
   所有鸡蛋放在一只筐子里   分散型（集散型）控制（DCS）   高速公路
   冗余   统计过程控制   专家系统   决策支持系统   可编程逻辑控制器
   制造工业   硬接线继电逻辑电路   网关   管理信息系统   工作站   数据库
   最大处理量   性能优化   最小成本   公用工程   以太网   通信

Reading Material:

Computer Integrated control

Supervisory Control and Data Acquisition

Supervisory control and data acquisition (SCADA) is a term which is ambiguously used to describe a type of application rather than an architecture. Historically, SCADA was mainly associated with utilities and offshore applications but nowadays it is much more commonplace. In general, SCADA systems are used for monitoring and data logging purposes. Their control capability tends to be restricted to adjusting the set points of controllers: supervisory control rather than DDC. Thus SCADA systems have large numbers of inputs and relatively few outputs, as depicted in Figure 4.2.8.

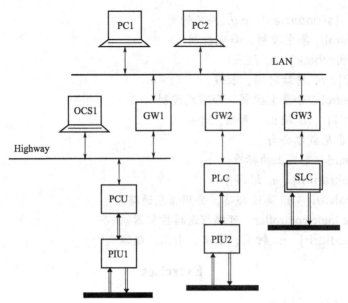

Figure 4.2.8 Supervisory control and data acquisition (SCADA) system.

In terms of hardware, SCADA systems are diverse. Hierarchically speaking, a typical system consists of a local area network (LAN) of personal computer (PC) type operator stations sitting on top of other systems. These other systems may be any combination of DCS nodes, PLCs, single loop controllers (SLC) and "packaged" instrumentation such as analysers. Connections to the network are by means of gateways (GW). These are microprocessor based devices which convert data from the protocol of one highway or network to that of another. Gateways also provide buffering to accommodate the different speeds of communication.

Management Information Systems

A management information system (MIS) typically consists of one or more "host" computers, typically file servers, connected up to the highway of a DCS by means of a gateway to provide access to the field I/O, as depicted in Figure 4.2.9. All the information within the DCS, and other systems connected to the highway, is thus available for storage and manipulation within the host and is typically available at PC type terminals or workstations. Connection of other systems to the highway is by means of other gateways.

The information stored in the database of an MIS is extensive and accessible to personnel beyond those directly concerned with the operation of the DCS. An MIS enables plant wide calculations, on-line, typically using model based methods that would be too complex or too extensive to be carried out within a PCU. Examples of such calculations are of process efficiencies, plant utilisation, materials inventory and utilities consumption.

Computer Integrated Manufacturing

Computer integrated manufacturing (CIM) is in many respects an extension of MIS. The essential difference is that in CIM management information is used for controlling the plant. Thus information flows in both directions between the host and PCUs. For example, production may be scheduled in order to maximise throughput or performance optimised to minimise costs. CIM

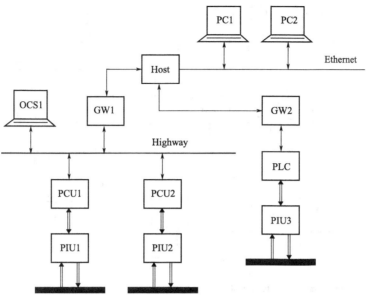

Figure 4.2.9 Management information system (MIS).

calculations are in real-time and have to take into account production requirements, availability of raw materials, plant utilisation, *etc*. It is normal within CIM to adopt a clustered approach, as depicted in Figure 4.2.10. Within a cluster, PCUs and OCSs send data to each other over the highway, such that each cluster can function independently of the others. Thus only data that needs to be transferred from one cluster to another is transmitted over the network.

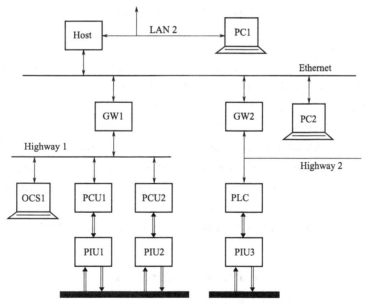

Figure 4.2.10 Computer integrated manufacturing (CIM) system.

Open Systems

The advent of open systems is leading to flatter architectures as depicted in Figure 4.2.11.

In effect, evolution of systems is resolving itself into two distinct domains. The information domain is based upon a network, normally Ethernet, for management information and the control

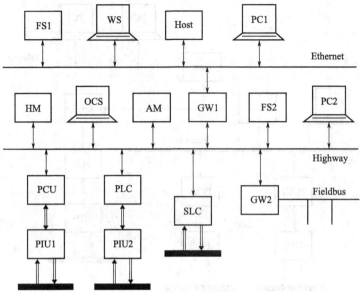

Figure 4.2.11 Open system architecture.

domain consists of devices connected to a highway for control purposes. Central to the concept of an open system is the use of industry standards for communications, databases, displays, *etc.*, which enable integration of non-proprietary equipment. Note the use of workstations (WS) and file servers (FS) on the networks for handling the very large databases associated with management information, communications, *etc*. It is not inconceivable with the advent of real-time Ethernet that evolution will result in just a single domain.

Comments

There are many varieties of architecture and the distinctions between some of them, such as SCADA, MIS and CIM, are rather fuzzy. No particular architecture is "correct" for any given plant, although there are many examples of systems that have been installed that are inappropriate for the application. The golden rule is that the architecture of the system should match that of the plant. For example, as indicated, DCS are appropriate for continuous plant consisting of relatively autonomous production units, SCADA for applications with diverse control systems which need to be co-ordinated, PLCs when there are localised sequencing requirements, and so on.

Selected form "*Process Automation Handbook, Jonathan Love, Springer London*, 2007"

Words and Expressions

1. data acquisition   数据采集，信息采集
2. SCADA (supervisory control and data acquistion)   监控与数采
3. ambiguously   [æmˈbigjuəsli]   *adv*. 多义性地，双值性地，模糊地
4. off shore   离线
5. monitoring   监视控制
6. diverse   [daiˈvəːs]   *adj*. 各种各样的，性质不同的

7. local area network (LAN)　局域网
8. package　['pækidʒ]　*n*. 插件, 组件, 部件, 程序包
9. gateways (GW)　网关
10. protocol　['prəutəkɔl]　*n*. 协议
11. management information systems (MIS)　管理信息系统
12. host computer　主机
13. file server　文件服务器
14. database　数据库
15. plantwide calculation　全厂范围计算
16. process efficiencies　过程效益, 过程效率
17. materials inventory　物料库存量
18. utilities consumption　公用工程消耗
19. computer integrated manufacturing (CIM)　计算机集成制造
20. schedule　['ʃedjuːəl]　*n*. 计划表, 调度表, 方案
21. maximise throughput　最大处理能力, 最大生产能力
22. minimise costs　最小成本
23. real-time　实时
24. cluster　['klʌstə]　*n*. 组件, 插件
25. open system　开放系统
26. flatter　['flætə]　*n*. 扁平槽
27. Ethernet　以太网
28. fieldbus　现场总线
29. golden rule　黄金规则
30. match　[mætʃ]　*vi*. 相适应, 相配
31. autonomous　[ɔː'tɔnəməs]　*adj*. 自主的, 自备的

4.3 Programmable Controllers

Topics coverd in this unit are as follows:
1. The definition of programmable controller
2. The alternatives to programmable controllers
3. An example of industrial application of PLC

4.3.1 Programmable Controllers Defined

The first programmable controller, introduced in 1970, was developed in response to a demand from General Motors for a solid-state system that had the flexibility of a computer, yet could be programmed and maintained by plant engineers and technicians. These early programmable controllers took up less space than the relays, counters, timers, and other control components they replaced, and they offered much greater flexibility in terms of their re-programming capability (Figure 4.3.1). The initial programming language, based on the ladder diagrams and electrical symbols commonly used by electricians, was key to industry acceptance of the programmable controller (Figure 4.3.2).

Because programmable controllers can be programmed in relay ladder logic, it is relatively simple to convert electrical diagrams to the programmable controller program. This process involves defining the rules of operation for each control point, converting these rules to ladder logic, and identifying and labeling outputs (addressing). Today's work force has a mix of engineers—some of whom have been around for a while and are familiar with ladder logic as well as newer engineers more comfortable with computer-centric based programming and control. This has led to a mix of programming technologies that are applied based on user background and application need.

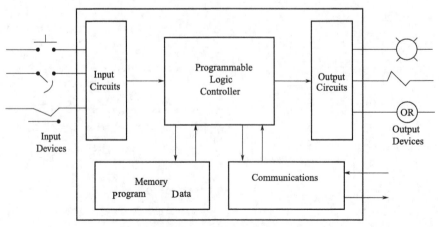

Figure 4.3.1 Basic PLC components.

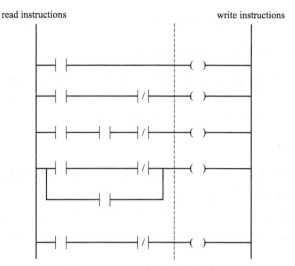

Figure 4.3.2 Relay ladder logic.

Programmable controllers can be place into two categories—fixed and modular. Fixed programmable controllers come as self-contained units with a processor, power supply, and a predetermined number of discrete and analog inputs and outputs. A fixed programmable controller may have separate, interconnectable components for expansion, and it is smaller, cheaper, and easier to install. However, modular controllers are more flexible, offering options for input/output (I/O) capacity, processor memory size, input voltage, and communication type and quantity. Originally, programmable controllers were used in control applications where I/O was primarily digital. They were ideal for applications that were more sequential and more discrete than continuous in nature. Over time, analog and process capabilities were added such that the programmable controller became a feasible solution for batch and process control applications. The evolution of programmable control has increased the options available for control systems that have traditionally relied on alternative technologies. Until the introduction of the micro-programmable logic controller (micro-PLC) in the mid-1980s, relays and single-board computers (SBCs) offered the most common means to increase automation on simple machines and less complex processes. Even though the functionality of the traditional programmable controller often benefited an application, the cost could not always be justified. If cost was not an issue, size often was. Sometimes even small programmable controllers were simply too large to fit in the space allocated for electrical controls.

It wasn't until micro-PLCs were introduced that programmable controllers could economically meet the demands of smaller machines in a more efficient manner than relays and SBCs. These fixed I/O controllers are generally designed to handle 10~32 I/Os in a package that costs less than $300 U.S., making them feasible replacements for even very small panels of relays. In addition, this low-cost controller option has opened the door for many small machine OEMs to apply automated control in places where it wasn't feasible in the past—for instance, one manufacturer uses a micro-PLC as the controller in lottery ticket counting machines. Modular programmable controllers are similar in function to fixed versions, but they physically separate the I/O from the controller. This allows the I/O racks to be distributed closer to the application, where they communicate back to the controller over an industrial network. Modular controllers allow a user to closely match the controller components to the specific application needs.

4.3.2 Alternatives to Programmable Controllers

The success of the programmable controller has spurred innovation in a number of competing technologies. Below is a brief review of these technologies, which may in some cases be successfully applied as an alternative to programmable controllers.

PC-Based Control

Personal computer (PC)-based control is a broad term encompassing not only the controller but all aspects of the control system, including programming, operator interface, operating system, communication application programming interfaces, networking, and I/O. Soft control is the act of replacing traditional controllers with software that allows one to perform programmable controller functions on a personal computer. Soft control is an important development for individuals who have control applications with a high degree of information processing content. For hazardous processes, PC-based control is typically limited to supervisory control in which the PC sends set points for optimization. Regulatory control, sequencing, and interlocks are done in a PLC or distributed control system (DCS).

The operator determines whether the regulatory control system in the PLC or DCS accepts these set points. Typically, the supervisory set points are updated by pulses, so that a loss of the PC signals leaves the set points at last value.

Distributed Control System

A distributed control system is a technology that has evolved to meet the specific needs of process applications such as pulp and paper, utility, refining, and chemical processing. DCSs are generally used in applications in which the proportion of analog to digital is higher than a 60:40 ratio, and/or the control functions performed are more sophisticated. A DCS typically consists of unit controllers that can handle multiple loops, multiplexer units to handle a large amount of I/O, operator and engineering interface workstations, a historian, communication gateways, and an advanced control function is dedicated proprietary controllers. All these are fully integrated and usually connected by means of a communication network. A DCS typically takes a hierarchical approach to control, with the majority of the intelligence housed in microprocessor-based controllers that can each handle 10~1000 inputs and outputs. The advent of Fieldbus has resulted in the development of the field-based DCS (and PLC?) that facilitated both the movement of the control functions to the field and the use of additional measurements and diagnostics from smart instrumentation and control valves.

Relay-Based Control

Relays essentially serve as switching, timing, and multiplying mechanisms for input devices, such as push buttons, selector switches, and photoelectric sensors (Figure 4.3.3). Relays are fairly intuitive; however, as mechanical devices, they do not offer the same programing and troubleshooting flexibility found in modern programmable control systems. Relays are also known for taking up considerable amounts of space, requiring extensive wiring, and needing regular maintenance.

Electromagnet relays and a variety of special purpose components (timers, mechanical counters, cam switches, etc.) can be wired in unique configurations to achieve specific control actions.

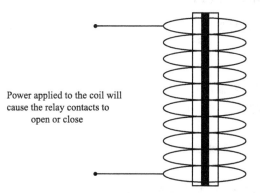

Power applied to the coil will cause the relay contacts to open or close

Figure 4.3.3   Relay logic control

Single-Board Controllers

The first electronic controls on circuit board—or SBCs—appeared in the early 1960s. These "logic modules" were created by placing discrete components, such as transistors, capacitors, and resistors onto boards. These solid-state systems were inherently more reliable than relays because there were no moving parts to wear out. In addition, there are numerous costs associated with installing, operating, and maintaining SBCs above and beyond the initial hardware cost. Because they are not typically available off the shelf, costs for SBCs involve securing the services of an electrical engineer to design the board and test for viability. Still, even today, many original equipment manufacturers choose to design and develop single-board controllers for their own unique machine applications. An SBC is usually very specific to a machine and can be cost effective initially. This is perfectly appropriate when the specific capabilities required by the machine cannot be achieved using standard, off-the-shelf control products.

Although there are many factors that must to be taken into consideration before determining whether a relay, SBC, micro-PLC, or full-size programmable controller is appropriate for the application, the following chart shows how each of the four meet some of the basic application requirements (Table 4.3.1).

Table 4.3.1   Evaluation of control methods for the application.

Application Characteristic	Relay	Micro-PLC	SBC	Full-size Programmable Controllers
Inputs/outputs	1~12 max.	Up to 32	Varies	32~1000s
Timers	Yes	Yes	Yes	Yes
Up/down counters	Yes	Yes	Yes	Yes
High-speed capabilities	No	Yes	Yes	Yes
Data calculations	No	Yes	Yes	Yes
Data acquisition	No	Yes	Yes	Yes
Communications	No	Limited	Yes	Yes
Operator interfaces	Primitive	Variable	Variable	Variable
Memory Size	N/A	1-10K	1-100K	up to 2 Meg

Selected from "*PROCESS/INDUSTRIAL INSTRUMENTS AND CONTROLS HANDBOOK, Gregory K. McMillan and Douglas M. Considine, McGraw-Hill*, 1999"

Words and Expressions

1. programmable controllers　可编程控制器
2. solid-state system　固态系统
3. relay　[ri'lei]　n. 继电器
4. counter　['kauntə]　n. 计数器，计算器
5. timer　['taimə]　n. 定时器，计时器
6. ladder diagram　梯形图
7. programmable logic controller (PLC)　可编程逻辑控制器
8. single-board computer　单板机
9. OEM (original equipment manufacture)　原始设备制造商
10. lottery　['lɔtəri]　n. 彩票
11. modular　['mɔdjulə]　adj. 模块的，标准组件的
12. innovation　[,inəu'veiʃən]　n. 改革，创新，发明
13. spur　[spə:]　n. 刺激，推动
14. encompass　[in'kʌmpəs]　vt. 围绕，拥有
15. operator interface　操作员界面
16. operating system　操作系统
17. PC-Based Control　基于个人计算机控制
18. Distributed control system (DCS)　分散型控制系统，集散型控制系统
19. pulp and paper　制浆与造纸
20. utility　[ju:'tiliti]　n. 公用工程，公用事业设备（如：水、电、煤气）
21. hierarchical approach　递阶方法
22. smart instrumentation　智能仪表
23. diagnostic　[daiəg'nɔstik]　n. 诊断结论
24. Relay-Based Control　基于继电器的控制
25. pushbutton　按钮
26. selector switch　选择开关
27. photoelectric sensor　光电传感器
28. troubleshoot　['trʌbəl,ʃu:t]　n. 寻找故障，发现缺点

Exercises

1. *Put the following into Chinese:*

   relay　　counter　　timer　　flexibility　　ladder diagram
   single-board computers (SBC)　　micro-programmable logic controller (micro-PLC)
   lottery ticket counting machine　　input devices　　PC-Based Control
   soft control　　regulatory control　　utility　　refining　　historian
   smart instrumentation　　field-based DCS　　transistor　　capacitor
   resistor　　OEM　　sump pump　　rung　　contact　　one-shot

2. *Put the following into English:*

   可编程控制器　　编程语言　　梯形逻辑　　低阶控制器　　操作系统

按钮	选择开关	光电传感器	诊断	操作员界面
递阶控制	活水池	低限液位	高限液位	排放
激发	顺序功能图			

Reading Material:

Industrial Applications of PLC

An industrial example requiring simple sequence logic is the effluent tank with two sump pumps illustrated in Figure 4.3.4. There are two sump pumps, A and B. The tank is equipped with three level switches, one for low level (LL), one for high level (LH), and one for high-high level (LHH). All level switches actuate on rising level. The logic is to be as follows:

(1) When level switch LH actuates, start one sump pump. This must alternate between the sump pumps. If pump A is started on this occasion, then pump B must be started on the next occasion.

(2) When level switch LHH actuates, start the other sump pump.

(3) When level switch LL deactuates, stop all sump pumps.

Once a sump pump is started, it is not stopped until level switch LL deactuates. With this logic, one, both, or no sump pump may be running when the level is between LL and LH. Either one or both sump pumps may be running when the level is between LH and LHH.

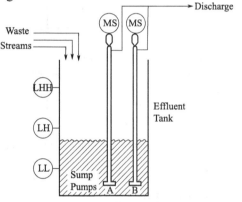

Figure 4.3.4　Effluent tank process.

Figure 4.3.5(a) presents the ladder logic implementation of the sequence logic. Ladder diagrams were originally developed for representing hardwired logic, but are now widely used in PLCs. The vertical bar on the left provides the source of power; the vertical bar on the right is ground. If a coil is connected between the power source and ground, the coil will be energized. If a circuit consisting of a set of contacts is inserted between the power source and the coil, the coil will be energized only if power can flow through the circuit. This will depend on the configuration of the circuit and the states of the contacts within the circuit. Ladder diagrams are constructed as rungs, with each rung consisting of a circuit of contacts and an output coil.

Contacts are represented as vertical bars. A vertical bar represents a normally open contact; power flows through this contact only if the device with which the contact is associated is actuated (energized). Vertical bars separated by a slash represent a normally closed contact; power flows through this contact only if the device with which the contact is associated is not actuated. The level switches actuate on rising level.If the vessel level is below the location of the switch, the normally open contact is open and the normally closed contact is closed. If the level is above the location of the switch, the normally closed contact is closed and the normally open contact is open.

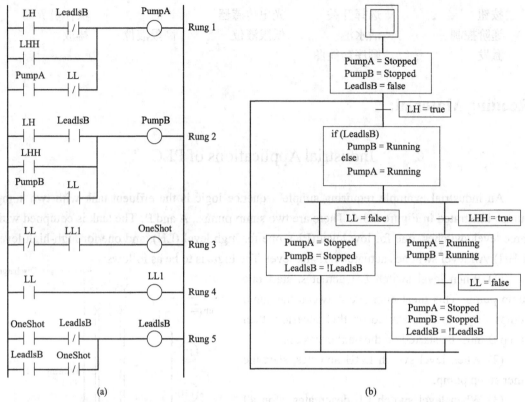

Figure 4.3.5 (a) Ladder logic. (b) Sequence logic for effluent tank sump pumps.

The first rung in Figure 4.3.5(a) is for pump A. It will run if one (or more) of the following conditions is true:

(1) Level is above LH and pump A is the lead pump. A coil (designated as LeadIsB) will be subsequently provided to designate the pump to be started next (called the lead pump). If this coil is energized, pump B is the lead pump. Hence, pump A is to be started at LH if this coil is not energized, hence the use of the normally closed contact on coil LeadIsB in the rung of ladder logic for pump A.

(2) Level is above LHH.

(3) Pump A is running and the level is above LL.

The second rung is an almost identical circuit for pump B. The difference is the use of the normally open contact on the coil LeadIsB.

When implemented as hardwired logic, ladder diagrams are truly parallel logic; i.e., all circuits are active at all instants of time. But when ladder diagrams are implemented in PLCs, the behavior is slightly different. The ladder logic is scanned very rapidly (on the order of 100 times per second), which gives the appearance of parallel logic. But within a scan of ladder logic, the rungs are executed sequentially. This permits constructs within ladder logic for PLCs that make no sense in hardwired circuits.

One such construct is for a "one-shot." Some PLCs provide this as a built-in function, but here it will be presented in terms of separate components. The one-shot is generated by the third rung of ladder logic in Figure 4.3.5(a). But first examine the fourth rung. The input LL drives the output coil LL1. This coil provides the state of level switch LL on the previous scan of ladder logic. This is used in the third rung to produce the one-shot. Output coil OneShot is energized if

(1) LL is not actuated on this scan of ladder logic (note the use of the normally closed contact for LL)

(2) LL was actuated on the previous scan of ladder logic (note the use of the normally open contact for LL1)

When LL deactuates, coil OneShot is energized for one scan of ladder logic. OneShot does not energize when LL actuates (a sligh modification of the circuit would give a one-shot when LL actuates).

The one-shot is used in the fifth rung of ladder logic to toggle the lead pump. The output coil LeadIsB is energized provided that

(1) LeadIsB is energized and OneShot is not energized. Once LeadIsB is energized, it remains energized until the next "firing" of the one-shot.

(2) LeadIsB is not energized and OneShot is energized. This causes coil LeadIsB to change states each time the one-shot fires.

Ladder diagrams are ideally suited for representing discrete logic, such as required for interlocks. Sequence logic can be implemented via ladder logic, but usually with some tricks or gimmicks (the one-shot in Figure 4.3.5(a) is such a gimmick). These are well known to those "skilled in the art" of PLC programming. But to others, they can be quite confusing.

Figure 4.3.5(b) provides a sequential function chart for the pumps. Sequential function charts consist of steps and transitions. A step consists of actions to be performed, as represented by statements. A transition consists of a logical expression. As long as the logical expression is false, the sequence logic remains at the transition. When the logical expression is true, the sequence logic proceeds to the step following the transition.

The basic constructs of sequential function charts are presented in Figure 4.3.6. The basic construct of a sequential function chart is the step-transition-step. But also note the constructs for OR and AND. At the divergent OR, the logic proceeds on only one of the possible paths, specifically, the one whose transition is the first to attain the true condition. At the divergent AND, the logic proceeds on all paths simultaneously, and all must complete to proceed beyond the convergent AND. This enables sequential function charts to provide parallel logic.

In the sequential function chart in Figure 4.3.5(b) for the pumps, the logic is initiated with both pumps stopped and pump A as the lead pump. When LH actuates, the lead pump is started. A divergent OR is used to create two paths:

(1) If LL deactuates, both pumps are stopped and the lead pump is swapped.

(2) If LHH actuates, both pumps are started (one is already running). Both remain running until LL deactuates, at which time both are stopped. The logic then loops to the transition for LH actuating.

Although not illustrated here, programming languages (either custom sequence languages or traditional languages extended by libraries of real-time functions) are a viable alternative for implementing the logic for the pumps. Graphical constructs such as ladder logic and sequential function charts are appealing to those uncomfortable with traditional programming languages. But in reality, these are programming methodologies.

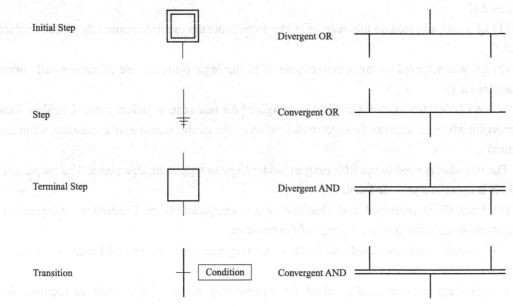

Figure 4.3.6 Elements of sequential function charts.

Selected from "*PERRY'S CHEMICAL ENGINEER'S HANDBOOK*, 8 TH EDITION, *Section* 8: *Process Control*, *THOMAS F. EDGAR. etc.* 2008, *McGraw-Hill Companies*"

Words and Expressions

1. sequence logic 顺序逻辑，程序逻辑
2. effluent tank 污水罐，污水池
3. sump pumps 污水泵
4. coil [kɔil] *n.* 线圈
5. energize ['enədʒaiz] *vt.* 激发，激励，通电
6. rung [rʌŋ] *n.* 梯级，一级
7. one-shot 一次完成，一次启动
8. trick [trik] *n.* 策略，诀窍
9. gimmick ['gimik] *n.* 骗局
10. initial step 开始，初始
11. terminal step 终了
12. transition [træn'ziʃən] *n.* 转换，过渡
13. divergent [dai'və:dʒnət] *adj.* 分叉的，分开的，分支的
14. convergent [kən'və:dʒnət] *adj.* 会聚的，集合的

4.4 Distributed Control System (DCS)

> *Topics covered in this unit are as follows:*
> 1. Introduction and the architecture of DCS
> 2. Operator station
> 3. The physical structure and the card types

4.4.1 Introduction and Architecture of DCS

The year of 1975 saw a step change in architecture with the launch by Honeywell of their microprocessor based TDC 2000 system. This was the first distributed control system (DCS) on the market and, in many respects, it became the de-facto standard for the next decade or so. The principal feature of the architecture of a DCS is its decentralised structure, consisting of PIUs, PCUs and OCSs interconnected by means of a proprietary highway. Figure 4.4.1 illustrates a so-called multi-drop type of DCS architecture. Note that the acronyms used are not universal.

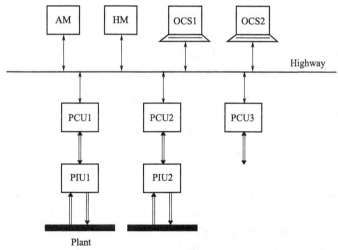

Figure 4.4.1 Multi-drop type of distributed control system (DCS).

The highway provides for communications between the PCUs and the OCSs, with current values and status information being passed from PCU to OCS and control commands in the opposite direction. It is usual for the highway to be dual to provide for redundancy, each PCU and OCS being connected to both highways. In the event of one highway failing, units can continue to communicate over the other. Indeed, this facility enables units to be connected to and removed from the system, one highway at a time, without disrupting operations.

Other modules are invariably connected to the highway, such as history modules (HM) and application modules (AM). Typically, an HM provides bulk memory for archiving purposes which enables much larger quantities of historical data to be stored and processed than is feasible in the memory of a PCU alone. Similarly, an AM enables advanced control packages to be run that require more processor power than is normally available in a single PCU. Such packages would be for optimisation or statistical process control or an expert system for decision support.

The PIUs and PCUs are normally organised on a local basis, handling the I/O signals and taking the control actions for a relatively self contained area of plant. This is a principal advantage of DCS: it enables processor power to be targeted very effectively. DCS lends itself to the control of continuous plant consisting of relatively autonomous production units. With modern DCSs, a single node consisting of a PIU, PCU and OCS is powerful enough to be considered as an ICS in its own right.

There is much similarity in the hardware of different suppliers' systems, whether they are DCS, PLC or otherwise. This chapter provides an overview of various generic aspects of hardware. The emphasis is on developing an understanding of how a system's hardware fits together and of how it relates to the system's functionality. This should be sufficient to enable meaningful dialogue about a systems hardware requirements.

4.4.2 Operator Station

The operator's control station (OCS) is a term which refers to the hardware used by an operator. It typically consists of a colour graphics VDU, a keyboard, and some processor capacity for handling the operators control program (OCP). In essence the OCP is the software with which the operator interacts. It enables access to the system's database and handles the various displays.

The VDU is the primary means of displaying information about the plant being controlled in all but the most rudimentary of systems. Most modern OCSs require high resolution colour VDUs to enable the graphics supported by the OCP to be displayed. Even for the smallest of plants it is usual practice to provide at least two VDUs: on larger plants there are multiple VDUs. First, this provides a measure of redundancy in the event of a VDU failing. And second, it enables different displays to be displayed simultaneously which is often very convenient.

Keyboards are the primary means of manually entering data into a control system. They need to be in some ruggedised form for use in control rooms. Flat panel membrane keyboards are commonly used because they are coffee proof. There has been much effort invested in the design of keyboards. Most have both the standard qwerty alphabetic and numeric keys, and a combination of dedicated and user definable keys. There is a trade off between the number of dedicated keys which make for user friendliness and the number of user definable keys which provide flexibility.

Because process control systems make extensive use of displays, it is necessary to have some form of cursor control. This is typically provided by means of dedicated keys, mouse or trackball. An expensive alternative is use of a touch screen. Note that provision of a touch screen does not obviate the need for a keyboard.

The VDU and keyboard, or alternatives, are often engineered into proprietary desk-type furniture, in which case they are referred to collectively as a console. Again, much effort has been invested by some suppliers in trying to determine the optimum ergonomic layout of consoles in terms presentation of information, access to functions and operator comfort.

For engineering purposes, it is usual to have separate VDUs and keyboards, often located in an office away from the control room. This enables software development to be done off-line. In general, the engineers control program (ECP), through which software development is realised, does not have the same high resolution colour graphics requirements as the OCP and, typically, a PC is used.

The principal peripherals associated with control systems are compact disc (CD) drives and printers. The disc drives are used for system loading and long term archiving of historic data. Normally there will be two printers, one dedicated to event logging and the other for printing out reports, database listings, *etc*. This also provides a minimum level of redundancy. Some printers have dedicated keyboards which may provide emergency backup for the OCS keyboards.

4.4.3 Physical Structure

PIUs, PCUs and PLCs were described in Chapter 38 as being functionally distinct. However, they are not necessarily physically distinct. In practice, systems are built from cards which slot into racks, the combination of cards being determined by the application. The racks, often referred to as bins, cages or files, are mounted in frames which are usually installed in a cabinet. The cabinets typically have self sealing doors at front and back for access. Large systems have several cabinets. Figure 4.4.2 depicts the typical physical structure.

Across the back of each rack is a so-called backplane. This is a printed circuit board (PCB) which has dedicated tracks for the system's buses, *i.e.* the address, control and data buses, and general purpose tracks for power supply and earthing. Each card has a multichannel connector on its back edge which engages in a socket, either directly or by means of a ribbon cable, on the back plane. This extends the buses from the back-plane through to the card, as depicted in Figure 4.4.3.

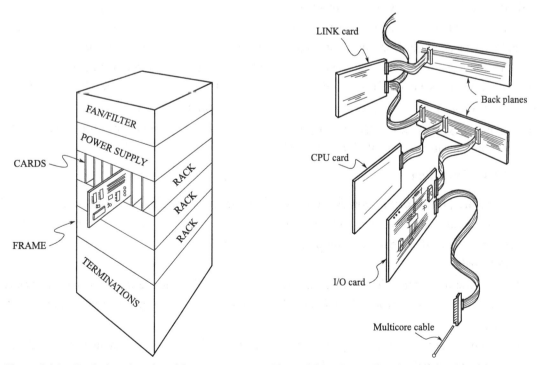

Figure 4.4.2 Typical card, rack and frame structure.   Figure 4.4.3 Connections between cards and back plane.

Slots may be dedicated to a certain type of card, for example a DIN slot for a DIN card, in which case each card will have a keyway, maybe built into the edge connector, to ensure the cards are plugged into the correct type of slot. Otherwise slots may be multipurpose, in which case the type of card in a given slot is established by means of software. Whether slots are dedicated or multipurpose is a function of the design of the backplane.

The back planes are themselves connected to each other to extend the buses from rack to rack and from frame to frame. This is achieved either directly, by means of ribbon cables in a daisy chain, or indirectly by means of LINK cards, also depicted in Figure 4.4.3.

Note the termination rack, power supply and fan shown in Figure 4.4.2.

The termination rack is for handling the I/O signals from the field. These normally arrive at the cabinet *via* multicore cables, having been pregrouped on a like-for-like basis in some separate marshalling cabinets. For example, one multicore cable may carry 4~20 mA current inputs destined for a particular AIN card. Each multicore is either wired into a termination assembly, or is connected *via* a panel mounted multicore socket and plug, to connect up with a ribbon cable. This ribbon cable is connected to the appropriate I/O card by means of an edge connector, again depicted in Figure 4. 4. 3.

Computer control systems are essentially comprised of light current circuits and devices. Their components become hot under normal operation and require cooling. Cabinets are therefore provided with a fan to draw air into the cabinet, through a filter and blow it across the cards.

The power supply to a system is normally either 110 or 240 V a.c. This is rectified to d.c. in a power supply unit (PSU) and regulated at levels appropriate to the device types used on the cards. Typically the PSU supplies power at +24 V, +10 V and ±5 V d.c. Power is distributed from the PSU throughout the cabinet by means of d.c. rails, connections to general purpose tracks on the back-planes and, *via* the edge connectors, to the cards. If the system has several cabinets, it is usual to have a single PSU in one cabinet connected up to the d.c. rails in all the others.

An important point to appreciate is that the PSU is usually sized to provide the power for the computer control system and for all the field instrumentation too. Thus, for example, all the 4~20-mA signal transmission is typically driven by the 24-V system supply. This is a reliability issue. There is no point in providing a high integrity power supply for the computer control system if the power supply for its instrumentation is unreliable.

4.4.4 Card Types

Cards are printed circuit boards with dedicated tracks upon which are mounted a variety of integrated circuit chips, passive and active electronic components. There are essentially three categories of card: I/O signals, systems and communications:

I/O cards

AIN: analogue input cards. These typically handle 8, 16 or 32 analogue input channels per card. There are different types of AIN cards for 4~20 mA, 0~10 V, mV thermocouple signals, *etc.*

AOT: analogue output cards. They handle 4, 8 or 16 analogue output channels per card, the channels normally being of 4~20 mA.

PIN: pulse input cards. For handling pulse input signals from rotary devices such as turbine meters.

DIN: discrete input cards. Typically handle 16 or 32 discrete input signals. The discrete signals are usually in the form of 0/10 or 0/5 V.

DOT: discrete output cards. Normally enable 16 or 32 relays to be operated. There are different types of DOT card according to the power to be handled by the relays.

Note that all I/O cards generally have both active and passive circuits to provide protection against electrical damage. They also provide for significant pre and post processing of I/O signals.

System cards

CPU card. The central processor unit card is the heart of any control system. The functionality of the CPU is described in detail in Chapter 9. The CPU card has the real time clock (RTC) mounted on it. The function of all the other cards is to support CPU activity. Note that in modern control systems there are often several CPUs operating in a multi-processing environment, each CPU being targeted on specific areas of activity.

ROM cards. These cards contain read only memory (ROM) which is inherently permanent. ROM memory is always in the form of chips. Although generically referred to as ROM, there are a number of variations on the theme such as PROM (programmable), EPROM (erasable and programmable) and EAROM (electrically alterable), *etc*.

RAM cards. There cards contain random access memory (RAM) which is not permanent and is often described as being volatile. If the power supply fails the information stored in RAM is lost. For this reason most systems have battery back-up for the RAM which will provide protection for a few hours.

CHECK cards. These essentially check the correct functioning of other cards. They have a diagnostics capability which either intercepts/interprets the transactions between other cards and/or communicates with them directly. It is sensible to have one check card per frame. Not every system has them.

DISC drivers. It is common practice to mount the system's discs, compact or hard, and their drivers in slot based modules and to connect them up to the back-plane as if they were cards. The discs provide bulk memory. There should be at least two separate bulk memory systems to provide for redundancy.

It is normal practice, to make for efficient processing, for the CPU, ROM,and RAM cards to all be within the same rack.

Coms cards

LINK cards. Typically each rack, apart from that housing the CPU, will have one. Link cards may be either active or passive. An active link card receives requests to send/receive data from the CPU and, if the request relates to a card within its rack, will direct the request towards the appropriate card. A passive link card essentially consists of a bus driver and enables extension of the backplane. In effect, any request to send/receive data is repeated to every card connected to the buses.

PORT cards. These are for serial communication with devices, such as the OCS, connected to the highway. They convert the data from the bus system into the protocol of the highway, and *vice versa*. They also provide buffering to accommodate the different communications speeds.

GATE cards, referred to as gateways. They convert data from the protocol of the DCS highway to that of other networks associated with, for example, MIS or CIM. Gateways also provide buffering to accommodate the different communications speeds of the highway and network.

COMS cards. These are for either serial (UART) or parallel communication with peripheral devices connected into the bus structure of the system.

Whereas the functionality of these various cards is reasonably common from one system to another, there is little agreement on the terminology of card types other than for I/O cards. The terminology used in this chapter is representative only.

Selected from "*Process Automation Handbook, Jonathan Love, Springer, London*, 2007"

Words and Expressions

1. DCS(Distributed control system)　集散型控制系统
2. de-facto　[diːˈfæktəu]　*adj*. 事实上的，实际上的
3. respect　[risˈpekt]　*n*. 关系，方面，考虑，遵守
4. decentralised structure　分散型结构
5. PIU　过程转入单元
6. PCU　过程控制单元
7. OCS　操作员控制站
8. HM　历史模块
9. AM　应用模块
10. VDU　可视化单元
11. OCP　操作员控制程序
12. rudimentary　[ruːdəˈmentəri]　*adj*. 基本的，初步的，原始的
13. touch screen　触摸屏
14. ergonomics　[əːgəˈnɔmiks]　*n*. 人机工程学，人体工程学
15. dedicate　[ˈdedikeit]　*vt*. 致力，专用于
16. cabinet　[ˈkæbinit]　*n*. 箱，柜，机壳
17. earthing　接地
18. PCB (printed circuit board)　印刷电路板
19. PSU (power supply unit)　供电单元
20. passive　[ˈpæsiv]　*adj*. 被动的，不活泼的，无源的
21. AIN (analogue input card)　模拟(信号)输入卡
22. AOT (analogue output card)　模拟(信号)输出卡
23. PIN (pulse input card)　脉冲(信号)输入卡
24. DIN (discrete input card)　离散(信号)输入卡

25. DOT (discrete output card) 离散(信号)输出卡
26. RTC (real time clock) 实时时钟
27. peripheral [pə'rifərəl] *adj.* 周边的,外围的

Exercises

1. *Put the following into Chinese:*

   de-facto standard   principle feature   decentralised structure
   colour graphics(VDU)   operators control program (OCP)   rudimentary
   standard qwerty alphabetic keys   dedicated keys   definable keys
   trackball event logging   database listings   printed circuit board(PCB)
   ribbon cable back plean   power supply unit (PSU)   random access memory(RAM)
   link cards   gate cards   remote calibration   HART protocol   fieldbus technologize

2. *Put the following into English:*

   历史模块   应用模块   优化控制   统计过程控制   专家系统
   决策支持系统   操作站   人工输入   鼠标   触摸屏
   插件   机架   输入/输出卡   系统卡   模拟输入卡
   离散输入卡   只读存储器   现场总线   物理层   接线盒

Reading Material:

Fieldbus

The 4～20-mA current loop, used to transmit signals to and from process instrumentation, became an industry *defacto* standard during the latter part of the twentieth century. It was an open standard to the extent that instruments from different manufacturers could be interconnected to form control loops or interfaced with control systems to from I/O channels. The advent of smart, or intelligent, field devices has led to the need to transmit further information, such as range and bias settings for remote calibration and status signals for condition monitoring. Such data has to be transmitted serially. Initially this was realised by means of modulation, with the data being superimposed on the 4～20mA signals on-line, or else with the instrument in an off-line mode. Of the various proprietary protocols and national standards that were established to enable this, the HART protocol became dominant. Latterly transmission has become bus based, with dedicated serial buses, and given rise to the so-called fieldbus technologies.

This chapter first considers HART as a vehicle for introducing fieldbus. That is followed by a potted history of fieldbus. Then comes consideration of the various layers of fieldbus, its configuration, application and management. Finally, the benefits of fieldbus ars summarised. Much of the literature about fieldbus is in the form of journal articles and technical publications. However. an important guide to the application of fieldbus in the process industry was produced by EEMUA(1998).

1. HART Protocol

The highway addressable remote transducer (HART) protocol was developed by the Rosemount company which placed its specification in the public domain in order to encourage other suppliers to add its functionality to their instruments. As a consequence it became the most commonly used protocol based on 4~20mA signals. It is a *de-facto* industry standard, reliable, field proven and in use world-wide. Commitments have been made to its long term support and for its connection into fieldbus. Aspects of the protocol are explained to provide insight to some of the issues involved in fieldbus.

HART is based upon the current transmission of serial messages in the form of a series of 8-bit bytes generated by means of a universal asynchronous receiver and transmitter (UART) type of device. To distinguish between analogue and serial transmission, the logical 0 is deemed to be a current less than 3.8 mA and the logical 1 to be a current greater than 20.5 mA. Remember that to each byte transmitted is added a start bit, a parity bit and s stop bit. The protocol is of a master/slave nature: that is the transmitting device is the master and the receiving device the slave. Its message structure, or frame, is as depicted in Figure 4.4.4.

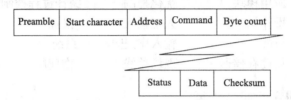

Figure 4.4.4 Message structure of HART protocol.

2. Objectives

It is now well recognised that the 4~20mA standard is too restrictive a medium for intelligent instrumentation. The 4~20 mA wiring does not provide a multidrop capability. The low bus speeds do not permit deterministic sampling for control purposes, although some devices became available with local PID control functionality. Also, the low bus speeds limit transfer of the increasing amounts of data available in field devices.

These constraints have led to the development of fieldbus which is an all digital, two-way, multidrop, high speed communications system for instrumentation. The objective is to provide a single, standard, open, interoperable network protocol for enabling:
- Interconnection of field devices such as transmitters, valves, controllers and recorders.
- Connection of such field devices to PLCs, PCs, I/O multiplexers, *etc*.
- Integration of field devices and control systems within plant wide networks.
- Abstraction of real-time data in a seamless manner.

3. History

The evolution of fieldbus has been tortuous involving various national standards bodies. Several protocols of a proprietary nature have been competing to be adopted as the fieldbus standard but, in effect, they can all be considered to be intermediate stages in its development. The most significant ones are as follows:
- IEC Fieldbus. Two committees were set up by the IEC and ISA in 1985 to work jointly towards a fieldbus standard. The protocol is based upon the physical, data link and application

layers of the OSI seven layer model, described in Chapter 40, together with a user layer. The intent was that the physical layer would embrace all three transmission media: wire, telemetry and fibre optics. The user layer is based on function blocks for process control.

- FIP (factoryinstrumentation protocol). This is a French national standard and has been adopted in Europe by CENELEC as an EN-50170 standard. It is an arbitration (master/slave) based protocol. Chip sets which incorporate the FIP protocol and interface cards are supplied by a number of PLC and PC manufacturers.

- Profibus (process fieldbus). This is a German standard(DIN 19245) which is another of the EN-50170 standards and has the largest installed base of all fieldbus technologies for manufacturing automation worldwide. It is a token passing based protocol. There are two versions: Profibus DP which is a high speed general purpose communications medium, and Profibus PA which was developed specifically for process automation.

- ISP(interoperable systems project). Supported by a consortium of major control system suppliers, this project's intent was to accelerate the establishment of a single international fieldbus standard. It a adopted the IEC/ISA physical layer standard and the user layer specification. The protocol was largely Profibus but incorporated aspects of FIP's synchronisation and the HART device definition language.

- Fieldbus Foundation. This was formed by the merger of WorldFIP and ISP in 1994 and Foundation Fieldbus(FF) now has the largest installed base of all fieldbus technologies for process automation worldwide.

- Fieldbus International, This is a consortium of companies with the Norwegian Government who are developing an alternative transmission system for fieldbus based on FF for sub-sea use. The approach, which uses inductive coupling for connecting devices rather than conventional push fit plugs and sockets, substantially reduces electrical losses. A further bonus is that the maximum number of IS devices per bus is increased from 6 to 30.

Many other protocols have been developed during the period in which fieldbus has evolved. To a large extent these are aimed at other sectors and/or niche markets and many will continue to evolve in their own right. Some of the better known ones are Lonworks, P-NET(Danish origins), CAN(controller area network), DeviceNet, SDS (smart distributed system) and ASI net.

4. Physical Layer

There are three bus speeds specified at the fieldbus physical layer. Focusing on the slowest of these, the 31.25 kbaud rate, this represents the fieldbus replacement for 4~20 mA signals between sensors and actuators. There are three topologies for connecting field devices to the bus, as depicted in Figure 4.4.5. These are trunk with spurs, trunk with splices which is usually referred to as "daisy chain", and tree and branch which is often referred to as "chicken's foot".

By optimising the cable route, the trunk with spurs and/or splices topology will produce the minimum cabling cost solution to an application, albeit with a large number of couplers. However, the potential problems of having to connect in extra instruments if no spare couplers exist mean that this topology will only be attractive to suppliers of packaged equipment, such as compressor sets, where the design is fixed *a priori*.

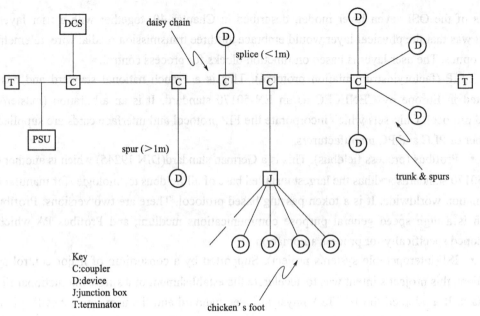

Figure.4.4.5 Topologies for connecting field devices to the bus.

For most applications the tree and branch approach will become the normal topology. This is because of its inherent flexibility: provision can be made in the junction box of the chicken's foot for connecting up extra instruments. Terminations in the junction box should be fitted with isolators to enable individual field devices to be isolated. Each spur from the junction box should be fused to protect the bus from faults in the spur or its attached device.

These topologies may be combined on any single bus, sometimes referred to as a segment, subject to various constraints. The cable length, which is the total length of the trunk and any spurs, depends on the quality of the cabling. The maximum length is 1900m provided shielded, twisted pair(Type A)cabling of 18 gauge(AWG) is used: this maximum is reduced for lesser quality cables.

Selected from "*Process Automation Handbook, Jonathan Love, Springer, London*, 2007"

Words and Expressions

1. range and bias settings   量程和基准设定
2. remote calibration   远程校准，远程校正
3. fieldbus technologies   现场总线技术
4. HART (highway addressable remote transducer)   可编址远程送器
5. deem   [di:m]   vt. 认为，相信
6. parity   ['pæriti]   n. 同等，类似
7. preamble bytes   段首标记，始标
8. multidrop   多站
9. multidrop communications system   多站通信系统
10. IEC Fieldbus   IEC 现场总线

11. FIP   工厂仪表规程
12. Profibus   过程现场总线
13. Fieldbus Foundation   现场总线基金会
14. trunk   [trʌŋk]   *n.* 躯干，中值线
15. spur   [spə:]   *n.* 支线
16. splice   [splais]   *vt.* 拼接
17. daisy chain   菊花链
18. albeit   [ɔ:l'bi:it]   *conj.* 虽然，即便

4.5 Computer Control System Communications(1)

> *The topics of this unit are as follows*:
> 1. What is the message
> 2. The local area networks
> 3. Token systems and communications protocol
> 4. Network access and transmission
> 5. Telemetry and radio communications

Communications, in particular of a digital nature, are fundamental to modern process control systems and some of the concepts have already been encountered in previous chapters. The significance of highways and networks were established in Chapter 38 on systems architecture and various types of communications cards were considered in Chapter 39 on systems hardware.

The technology of communications is vast, embracing different types of networks and transmission media. This chapter, therefore, attempts to summarise some of the more important aspects in relation to process control systems, with an emphasis on the relevant standards and protocols.

4.5.1 Messages

A message is the term loosely used to describe data transmitted over a network. Messages can be transmitted between any two devices, usually referred to as nodes, connected to the network. In practice, depending on the nature of the network, a message consists of a structure known as a frame which contains the data being transmitted. Figure 4.5.1 depicts an IEEE 802 type of frame.

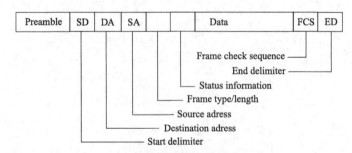

Figure. 4.5.1   IEEE802 type of frame.

As can be seen, the frame consists of a header, the data being transmitted, and a trailer. The header consists of
- A preamble which announces the start of transmission
- A start delimiter which enables the start of the frame to be detected

• The address of the node to which the message is being transmitted: the destination
• The address of the node which generated the message:the source
• The frame type and/or length which enables the destination node to determine how to handle the message
• Status information,such as flags and functional options

The trailer consists of:
• A frame check sequence for checking whether the data transmitted has been received error free
• An end delimiter which enables the end of the frame to be detected

Any device connected to the network must have the necessary hardware and software to be capable of both reading and/or generating such a frame.

4.5.2 Local Area Networks

The most commonly used type of communications system is the local area network (LAN). The IEEE has developed standards for LANs which are generally adhered to by systems suppliers. The three LANs of particular interest for process control purposes are Ethernet, token bus and token ring. The essential difference between them is the method by which messages on the LAN, known as traffic, are controlled.

The IEEE 802.3 standard applies to a LAN type known as the carrier sense multiple access with collision detection (CSMA/CD). The most widespread implementation of CSMA/CD is Ethernet, developed jointly by Xerox, Intel and DEC during the 1980s, although it should be appreciated that Ethernet is not the standard itself. Industrial Ethernet is the technology compatible with the IEEE 802.3 standard that has been designed and packaged to meet the requirements and rigor of industrial applications.

Within an Ethernet system, no one node has priority over another. Thus, before transmitting a message, a node must establish that no other node is using the network. If the network is free then the node can start to send data. If not, it must wait until the other node has completed its transmission: normally there will be minimal delay before an idle condition is detected. When a node transmits, all the other nodes receive the frame and compare the destination address with their own. That node to which the message is directed receives it, the others ignore it.

However, with such a non-priority system, it is possible for two or mode nodes to attempt to start transmitting simultaneously. This is referred to as a collision. If collisions were allowed to occur then the data on the network would become corrupted. Thus the node's hardware contain circuits which recognise the occurrence of collisions and abort transmission. Each node then enters a wait mode before trying again. To reduce the scope of a further collision, each node has a randomised wait period built into its transmission logic. This uncertainty about the delay associated with collisions means that Ethernet transactions are not deterministic with respect to time: the LAN is said to be probabilistic.

Clearly the more nodes there are on a network, the greater the chance of collisions. Also, the longer the network becomes, the more often collisions occur due to the propagation delay between nodes. Both of these factors affect the throughput of the network and thus the response time between nodes. Provided the loading on the network is less than some 30% of the system's capacity, CSMA/CD is the most efficient LAN type. It is easy to see that CSMA/CD will cope well with intermittent operations, such as downloading of programs, file transfer and so on. For this reason Ethernet is commonly used at higher levels in MIS and CIM type applications.

However, for process control purposes, the requirement is to handle many short messages at a relatively high frequency. CSMA/CD would probably cope with normal operating conditions within the 30% of its capacity. However, under abnormal conditions, even if there are only a few nodes, the volume of traffic due to alarms, diagnostics and so on escalates rapidly and leads to a massive increase in the number of collisions. Thus a significant amount of LAN time is spent "timed out" and its performance deteriorates. It is possible, but statistically improbable, that some messages may not get through at all. For this reason token systems are used for control purposes.

4.5.3 Token Systems

Token systems use a mechanism, known as a token, which avoids collisions on the network. It is conceptually equivalent to the baton used in relay races: the nodes take it in turn to hold the token, and only one node can hold the token at a time. The node which currently holds the token may transmit to any other node on the network. It is appropriate to think of the token as being a flag held within the data frame that indicates whether the frame is "free" or otherwise.

The token bus is a LAN, often referred to as a highway, to which the IEEE 802.4 standard applies. Token bus topology, which is essentially the same as for Ethernet, has an open structure as depicted in Figure 4.5.2.

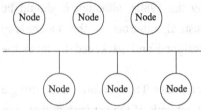

Figure 4.5.2 Open structure of token bus topology.

An empty frame containing a "free" token is passed from node to node in a fixed order. If the node receiving the frame does not have any data to transmit, it is passed on to the next node, referred to as its successor, and so on. In essence, the address of the successor node is loaded into the frame and transmitted. All the other nodes receive the frame and compare the successor address with their own: the successor receives it and the others ignore it. The order of succession is predefined and includes all the nodes on the highway: it is not necessarily the order in which they are physically connected. Although the token bus has an open structure, it can be seen that it is controlled logically as a ring in the sense that the token circulates around all the nodes in a fixed order.

Suppose that an empty frame arrives at a node waiting to transmit data. The token is marked as "busy", the frame is loaded with the address of the source and destination nodes and the data itself, and the frame is transmitted. All the other nodes receive the frame and compare the destination address with their own: that node to which the frame is directed receives it and the others ignore it. The destination node then retransmits the frame to the original source node: in effect, the addresses having been swapped over. The source node then either transmits another frame, if it has time, or else marks the token as "free" and passes it on to its successor.

It is important to distinguish between the two modes of operation. If there are no messages, the empty frame with the "free" token passes around the bus in successor order looking for a message. The time taken for an empty frame to pass around all the nodes is known as the token rotation time. However, when data is being transmitted, it goes directly from source to destination node and back again. The time allowed for this is known as the slot time, and is different from the token rotation time.

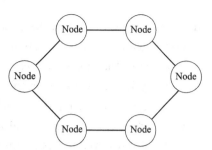

Token passing is most efficient when the network is heavily loaded because there are no collisions: it is inefficient at low loadings since the frame is empty most of the time, but that doesn't matter. Token bus is entirely deterministic because the token rotation time is fixed by the number of nodes and each node's slot time is specified. Also, no single node can monopolise the network. For these reasons token bus is used for real-time control in industry.

Figure 4.5.3 Loop structure of token ring topology.

Token ring is another type of LAN to which the IEEE 802.5 standard applies. It is essentially the same as token bus, except that the ends of the bus are physically connected to form a ring, as depicted in Figure 4.5.3. One obvious advantage of a ring network is that transmission occurs around the ring in both directions which provides for redundancy in the event of it being physically severed.

In some systems, when the token is passed from a node to its successor, the node listens for the successor to either transmit data or pass the token on. If there is no evidence of this, the node assesses the status of the successor and, if a failure is detected, subsequently by passes it.

The process of receiving signals and retransmitting at a node is referred to as repeating. It has the effect of boosting the strength of a signal. Because signals degrade over long distances, *i.e.* they become distorted and pick up noise, repeaters are used to extend the length of a network.

4.5.4 Protocols

The frames transmitted on a network must conform to some form of communications protocol. At its simplest this defines the format of the frames and any control signals that are required to ensure correct data transfer. More complex protocols contain multiple layers which control not only the transmission of the data itself, but also the presentation of that data to and from the applications. The open systems interconnection (OSI) protocol, known as the OSI model, published in ISO 7498-1 (1995) for reference purposes, has seven layers whose functionality is as summarised in Table 4.5.1.

Table 4.5.1 Functionality of OSI Seven Layer Model

Layer	Description	Layer	Description
⑦ Application	User interaction	③ Network	Routes transmission
⑥ Presentation	Translates data	② Data link	Detects errors
⑤ Session	Controls dialogue	① Physical	Connects device
④ Transport	Provides transparency		

The OSI model is generic in that it describes the functionality of an "ideal" protocol and is independent of any physical medium or type of connection. It is designed to cover the most complex communications networks involving world-wide communication of all types and volumes of data transmitted *via* multiple computer systems. Not all seven layers would necessarily exist in any specific protocol. Imagine data being transmitted form a user program in a source computer over a network to a user program in a destination computer. The data travels down the various levels in the source until it reaches the physical layer, is transmitted *via* the physical medium to the destination, and then up through the various layers of the destination to its user program. The functions of each layer are as follows:

• Physical layer: transmits and receives bit patterns over the network. It is concerned with the electronic aspects of the transfer, such as the voltage levels representing binary 0 and 1 and the control signals used for synchronisation, and with the mechanical aspects of plugs and pin assignments.

• Data link layer: makes communications at the physical layer appear to higher layers as though they are error free. It embraces error checking mechanisms and organises for the retransmission of corrupted data.

• Network layer: concerned with routing messages across the network. It takes a message from the transport layer, splits it into "packets," identifies the packets' destinations and organises their transmission.

• Transport layer: hides all the network dependent characteristics from the layers above it, essentially providing transparent data transfer. Thus a user on one computer system can communicate with a user on another without concern for the underlying network being used to transfer the data.

• Session layer: establishes and maintains the communication path between two users of the network during the period of time that they are logically connected.

• Presentation layer: concerns the format of data and handles its encryption and decryption. For example, text may be translated into/from ASCII code, and data may be compressed by using codes for commonly used phrases.

• Application layer: this is the highest level in the model and is the environment in which the user's programs operate.

Many different protocols exist: some are specific to given suppliers and/or systems and others have been defined by bodies such as the International Telegraph and Telephone Consultative Committee (CCITT) and ISO. Protocols can be categorised as being either:

• Master/slave (primary/secondary) communication. The master node is in overall control of the network. Typical of this type of protocol is the ISO high- level data- link control (HDLC).

• Peer to peer communication, as used on most LANs, in which no node has overall control. Perhaps the two best known protocols in this category are General Motors' manufacturing automation protocol (MAP) and the transmission control protocol/internet protocol (TCP/IP) standard.

4.5.5 Network Access

Access concerns gaining control of the network in order to transmit messages. The three layered access model of IEEE 802 is depicted in Figure 4.5.4 and relates to both Ethernet and token bus types of network. The most commonly used access protocol is TCP/IP which has three layers. It is consistent with the two lower layers of the OSI model but doesn't have its full functionality.

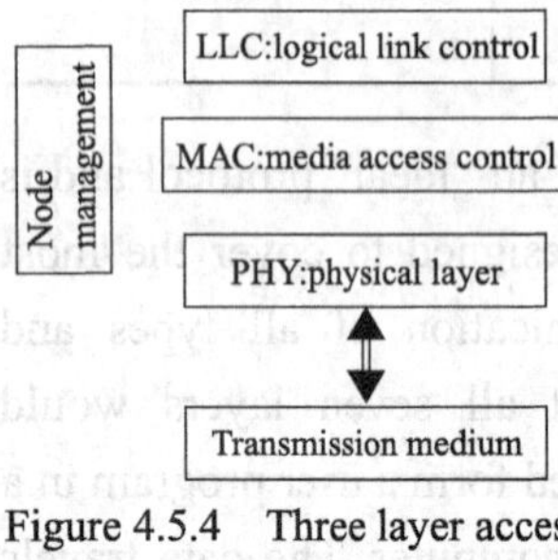

Node management provides the functionality that fragments and/or reconstructs messages into/from frames of data which are of the correct length for transmission. The three layers are:

Figure 4.5.4　Three layer access model of IEEE 802.

• Logic link control (LLC) layer: this puts the source and destination addresses, the data to be transmitted and the checksum into the frame.

• Media access control (MAC) layer: this handles collisions and imposes random waits for Ethernet type LANs, or handles the token/flags and enables repeats for token bus type LANs.

• Physical layer: this handles the encoding and decoding of data, if necessary, and the transmission and/or receipt of messages between nodes.

The hardware interface and software drivers necessary to support these layers of access must be provided by any PORT card to enable its node's access to the network.

Because of the variety of protocols in use, it may not be possible to connect a particular node directly to a network or highway. Incompatibilities are handled by protocol converters, normally referred to as gateways.

Selected from "*Process Automation Handbook, Jonathan Love, Springer, London,* 2007"

Words and Expressions

1. embrace [im'breis] *vt.* 包括
2. message ['mesidʒ] *n.* 信息，情报，报文
3. loose [lu:s] *adj.* 不严格的，大概的
4. node [nəud] *n.* 节点
5. preamble [pri(:)'æmbl] *n.* 段首标记，序言，始标
6. announce [ə'nauns] *vt.* 通报，广播，通知
7. delimiter [di:'limitə] *n.* 定义符，定界符，限制符
8. address [ə'dres] *n.* 地址，称呼
9. flag [flæg] *n.* 标识位，旗码，特征位
10. error free 无差错，无误
11. adhere [əd'hiə] *vi.* 黏附，遵守
12. token bus 令牌总线
13. token-ring network 令牌网
14. collision [kə'liʒən] *n.* 碰撞，冲突
15. rigour ['rigə] *n.* 严格，严密
16. priority [prai'ɔriti] *n.* 优先权，先前
17. mode [məud] *n.* 模式
18. corrupt [kə'rʌpt] *v.* 腐烂
19. randomize ['rændəmaiz] *v.* 形成不规则，使混乱，使随机化
20. deteriorate [ditiəriəreit] *vt.* 变坏，老化，衰退
21. baton ['bætən] *n.* 指挥棒
22. race [reis] *vi.* 竞争
23. successor [səksesə] *n.* 后续符，继承人，继承符
24. monopolise [mə'nɔpəlaiz] *vt.* 独占，得到……专利权
25. open systems interconnection(OSI) 开放式系统内部连接

26. physical layer   物理层
27. data link layer   数据链路层
28. network layer   网络层
29. synchronization   [ˈsiŋkrənaiˈzeiʃən]   n. 同步，同时
30. abort   [əˈbɔːt]   v. 中断，故障，失误
31. transport layer   传输层
32. session layer   对话层，会话层
33. encryption   编码，加密
34. decryption   译码，解码
35. presentation layer   说明层，呈现层
36. application layer   应用层
37. master/slave   主/从
38. TCP/IP (transmission control Protocol/Internet Protocol)   传输控制规程/内部规程
39. access   [ˈækses]   n. 存取，访问，查索
40. carrier   [ˈkæriə]   n. 载体，载波，支座，承重层

Exercise

1. *Put the following into Chinese:*

Message	data transmitted	node	frame	header	trailer
error free	delimiter	token bus	token ring	traffic	Ethernet
idle	non-priority	collision	successor	token circulates
master/slave communication	peer to peer communication	logiclink control(LLC)
Layer	media access control Layer	modem	basedband
pumping stations carrier frequency	radio communication
frequency modulated	troposcopic scatter	satellite

2. *Put the following into English:*

通信	节点地址	目的地址	源地址	局域网	概率
超时	竞争	独占	拓扑	通信规程	物理层
数据链路层	网络层	传输层	对话层	说明层
应用层	TCP/IP 标准	网络存取	宽带	传输	遥测技术
超高频	天线系统	转发器

Reading Material:

Computer Control System Communications (2)

1. Transmission

LANs are available either as broadband or as base band systems:

• A broadband system uses analogue technology, where a modem is used to introduce a frequency carrier signal onto the transmission medium. The carrier signal is modulated by the digital data supplied by the node. Broadband systems are so named because the analogue carrier signals are high frequency: some 10~400 MHz.

• A baseband system uses digital technology. A line driver introduces voltage shifts onto the transmission medium. The voltage changes directly represent the digital data. For example, the RS 232 standard specifies a voltage between +3 and +12V to represent a "0" and between −3 and −12V to represent a "1".

The cabling used for carrying LANS is typically screened copper cable. This may be armoured if it is to be passed through areas where there is a possibility of damage. In many systems dual highways are provided, mainly to increase the security of communication, although some systems use the second highway to increase throughput.

Increasingly, fibre optic cables are being used with networks for communications. This involves converting electrical signals into light pulses before transmission. The advantages of fibre optics include:

• Fibre optics enable longer networks because power loss is very low. Typical distances are 120km without repeaters.

• Because there is no electrical current being carried by the cable, the cable is unaffected by electro-magnetic interference, so it is possible to run fibre optic cables alongside power cables with no adverse effects. Also, there is no induction between different fibre optic channels.

• The absence of electrical energy in the cable makes them particularly useful in hazardous areas, where short circuits are a potential source of ignition.

The principal disadvantages are:
• Limited curvature on bends.
• High skill levels are required for installation and maintenance.
• Cost: the hardware necessary for electrical/optical conversion is expensive, although the advantages gained often outweigh the additional cost.

For all these reasons, fibre optics is an important alternative to conventional copper cabling.

2. Telemetry

Some process industries, such as oil, gas and water, have pipeline networks in which the distances between, say, pumping stations and central control rooms are measured in hundreds of kilometres. In such situations LANs are inappropriate and wide area networks (WAN) may be used. Historically WANs provided their long distance capability by means of modulated frequency techniques through the use of modems. However, with de advent of services such as BT's integrated services digital network (ISDN), digital transmission has become more common.

The transmission medium used in a WAN may be a dedicated private line or one leased from a communications company. Alternatively, the link can be set up temporarily by dialling a connection *via* the public switched telephone network (PSTN). Such transmission is modulated using a carrier frequency in the voice frequency band of 300~400 Hz.

Often the lines used carry several channels of communication. This is achieved by using a technique known as frequency division multiplexing (FDM) for which the carrier frequency required is determined by the rate at which data is to be transferred. Typically this would be 1700 Hz at 1200 baud as specified in CCITT publications.

One modulation technique used in telemetry systems is called frequency shift keying (FSK). In this technique the carrier frequency ω is shifted by the digital data being transmitted. For example, a binary "1" might be represented by $\omega + \Delta\omega$ and a binary "0" by $\omega - \Delta\omega$ where, for a 1200 baud system, $\Delta\omega$ is typically 50 Hz. This technique is depicted in Figure 4.5.5. Other modulation techniques include pulse code modulation (PCM) and phase modulation.

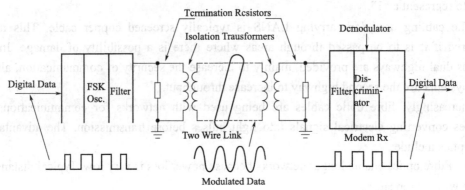

Figure 4.5.5 Frequency shift keying for telemetry.

3. Radio Communications

As an alternative to land lines a telemetry system may use radio communications, or some hybrid of telephone lines and radio channels. The use of radio is similar to using land lines except that the power levels required for signals are higher and transmission delays can be longer.

Radio systems normally use frequency modulated (FM) transceivers operating in the range 450~470 MHz ultra high frequency (UHF) band. At UHF and higher frequencies, radio signals can be made very directional with antenna systems using parabolic reflectors producing very narrow beams. In such systems a line of sight transmission path is required, which may be difficult to achieve in certain terrain.

To overcome obstacles in the transmission path a number of different methods may be used:

• Repeaters. A repeater may be placed on top of a hill or tall building, which is acting as a barrier to communication, to pick up the signal, amplify and retransmit it.

• Troposcopic scatter. Radio energy is directed towards part of the Earth's atmosphere called the troposphere, situated at about 10 km above ground level. This forward scatters the signal to the receiver and thus overcomes any obstacles.

• Satellites. Geo-stationary satellites are increasingly being used for all types of communication and can be used with UHF radio.

4. Telemetry Units

Telemetry systems require a controlling master station at the control centre which will communicate with one or more slaves, known as remote telemetry units (RTU), *via* the selected transmission medium. Because the master station may have to deal with many RTUs using a common link, it scans them on a time division multiplexing (TDM) basis. An RTU may be completely passive, in that it only performs actions when commanded to do so by the master station. Alternatively, an RTU may have a level of intelligence which enables it to perform some functions unsolicited, such as calling up the master station in the event of am alarm.

The messages transmitted between RTUs and master station must adhere to some protocol such as HDLC. A typical message from the master station will indicate the RTU address and the function it is to perform. If data is also to be sent this will be included in the message. The final part of the message will contain checksum information to allow the RTU to check the incoming message for errors. The addressed RTU responds to the command by either reading from or writing to the local instrumentation and /or control systems and returning a message to the master station.

Because of the inherent delays associated with communications used in telemetry systems, realtime functions such as closed loop control are difficult to achieve.

5. Comments

As can be seen, communications is an extensive and complex field. In general it is not necessary for control engineers to have a detailed knowledge of the subject. Control systems are normally supplied with a communications capability adequate for the application, so it is essentially a question of being able to make a sensible specification in the first place. However, when interconnecting two dissimilar system, a surprisingly common problem, a grasp of the principles is essential.

Selected from "*Process Automation Handbook, Jonathan Love, Springer, London*, 2007"

Words and Expressions

1. broadband   ['brɔːd'bænd]   *n.* 宽带，宽波段
2. fiber optic cable   光纤，光缆
3. curvature   ['kəːvətʃə]   *n.* 弯曲，曲率，曲度
4. telemetry   [ti'lemitri]   *n.* 遥测技术
5. modem=modulator-demodulator   调制解调器
6. WAN (wide area network)   广域网
7. temporarily   ['tempərərili]   *adv.* 暂时地，临时地
8. dialling   ['daiəliŋ]   *n.* 拨号，打电话
9. FSK (frequency shift keying)   移频键控
10. UHF (ultra high frequency)   超高频
11. antenna   [æn'tenə]   *n.* 天线
12. parabolic   [pærə'bɔlik]   *adj.* 抛物线的
13. terrain   ['terein]   *n.* 地带，地形，领域
14. barrier   ['bæriə]   *n.* 势垒，阻挡层，屏障
15. tropospheric scatter   对流层散射
16. RTU (remote telemetry units)   远程遥测单元
17. baseband   ['beisbænd]   *n.* 基带，基频
18. armoured   ['ɑːməd]   *adj.* 铠装的，包铍皮的
19. TDM (time division multiplexing)   分时多路传输
20. FM (frequency modulation)   调频
21. PCM (pulse code modulation)   脉冲代码调制

CHAPTER 5 AUTOMATIC CONTROL SYSTEMS

5.1 Mathematical Modeling of Physical Systems

> *After reading the following unit, try to find out the answer for:*
> 1. What is the one of the most important tasks in the analysis and design of Control Systems?
> 2. Try to write the state equations of electric networks.
> 3. What are used to describe translation motion?
> 4. Could you tell the meaning of inertia J.

5.1.1 Introduction

One of the most important tasks in the analysis and design of control systems is mathematical modeling of the systems. In the preceding chapter, we have introduced two most common methods of modeling linear systems namely the transfer function method and the state-variable method. The transfer function is valid only for linear time-invariant systems, whereas the state equations can be applied to linear as well as nonlinear systems.

Although the analysis and design of linear control systems have been well developed, their counterparts for nonlinear systems are usually quite complex. Therefore, the control systems engineer often has the task of determining not only how to accurately describe a system mathematically, but, more important, how to make proper assumptions and approximations, whenever necessary, so that the system may be realistically characterized by a linear mathematical model. It is not difficult to understand that the analytical and computer simulations of any system are only as good as the model used to describe it. It should also be emphasized that the modern control engineer should place special emphasis on the mathematical modeling of systems so that analysis and design problems can conveniently be solved by computers. Therefore, the main objectives of this unit are:

① To introduce some commonly used components in control systems.
② To demonstrate the mathematical modeling of control systems and components.
③ To demonstrate how the modeling will lead to computer solutions.

The intended purpose is to introduce the method of modeling. Since numerous types of control system components are available, the coverage here is by no means exhaustive.

5.1.2 Equations of Electric Networks

The classical way of writing equations of electric networks is based on the loop method or the node method, which are formulated from the two laws of Kirchhoff. A modern method of writing network equations is the state-variable method. Since the electrical networks found in most control systems are rather simple, the subject is treated here only at the introductory level. The state-variable modeling of electric networks can be illustrated by the following example.

Let us consider the *RLC* network shown in Figure 5.1.1(a). A practical way is to assign the current in the inductor L, $i(t)$, and the voltage across the capacitor C, $e_c(t)$, as the state variables. The reason for this choice is because the state variables are directly related to the energy-storage elements of a system. The inductor is a storage for kinetic energy, and the capacitor is a storage of electric potential energy. By assigning $i(t)$ and $e_c(t)$ as state variables, we have a complete description of the past history (via the initial states) and the present and future states of the network.

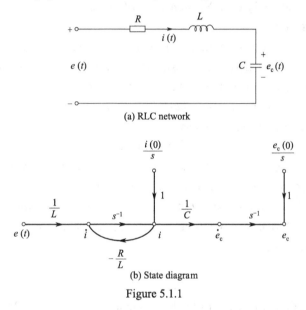

Figure 5.1.1

The state equations for the network in Figure 5.1.1(a) are written by first equating the current in C and the voltage across L in terms of the state variables and the applied voltage $e(t)$. We have

Current in C:
$$C = \frac{de_c(t)}{dt} = i(t) \tag{5.1.1}$$

Voltage in L:
$$L = \frac{di(t)}{dt} = -e_c(t) - Ri(t) + e(t) \tag{5.1.2}$$

In vector-matrix form, the state equations are expressed as

$$\begin{bmatrix} \dfrac{de_c t}{dt} \\ \dfrac{di(t)}{dt} \end{bmatrix} = \begin{bmatrix} 0 & \dfrac{1}{C} \\ -\dfrac{1}{L} & -\dfrac{R}{L} \end{bmatrix} \begin{bmatrix} e_c(t) \\ i(t) \end{bmatrix} + \begin{bmatrix} 0 \\ \dfrac{1}{L} \end{bmatrix} e(t) \tag{5.1.3}$$

The state diagram of the network is shown in Figure 5.1.1(b). Notice that the outputs of the integrators are defined as the state variables. The transfer functions of the system are obtained by applying the SFG gain formula to the state diagram when all the initial states are set to zero.

$$\frac{E_c(s)}{E(s)} = \frac{(1/LC)s^{-2}}{1+(R/L)s^{-1}} = \frac{1}{Cs(Ls+R)} \tag{5.1.4}$$

$$\frac{I(s)}{E(s)} = \frac{(1/L)s^{-1}}{1+(R/L)s^{-1}} = \frac{1}{Ls+R} \tag{5.1.5}$$

5.1.3 Modeling of Mechanical System Elements

Most control systems contain mechanical as well as electrical components, although some systems even have hydraulic and pneumatic elements. From a mathematical viewpoint the descriptions of electrical and mechanical elements are analogous. In fact, we can show that given an electrical device, there is usually an analogous mechanical counterpart mathematically, and vice versa.

The motion of mechanical elements can be described in various dimensions as **translational, rotational**, or combinations. The equations governing the motion of mechanical systems are often formulated directly or indirectly from Newton's law of motion.

Translational Motion

The motion of translation is defined as a motion that takes place along a straight line. The variables that are used to describe translational motion are **acceleration, velocity**, and **displacement**. Newton's law of motion states that the *algebraic sum of forces acting on a rigid body in a given direction is equal to the product of the mass of the body and its acceleration in the same direction*. The law can be expressed as

$$\Sigma \text{ forces} = Ma \tag{5.1.6}$$

where M denotes the mass and a is the acceleration in the direction considered. For translational motion, the following system elements are usually involved.

① **Mass**. *Mass is considered as a property of an element that stores the kinetic energy of translational motion*. Miss is analogous to inductance of electric networks. If W denotes the weight of a body, then M is given by

$$M = \frac{W}{g} \tag{5.1.7}$$

where g is the acceleration of free fall of the body due to gravity. ($g=32.174$ ft/sec^2 in British units, and $g=9.8066$ m/sec^2 in SI units.)

The consistent sets of basic units in British and SI units are as follows:

Units	Mass M	Acceleration	Force
SI	Kilogram(kg)	m/sec^2	Newton(N)
British	slug	ft/sec^2	Pound(lb force)

Figure 5.1.2 illustrates the situation where a force is acting on a body with mass M. The force equation is written

$$f(t) = Ma(t) = M\frac{d^2 y(t)}{dt^2} = M\frac{dv(t)}{dt} \tag{5.1.8}$$

where $v(t)$ denotes velocity.

② Linear Spring.In practice,a linear spring may be a model of an actual spring or a compliance of a cable or a belt.In general, *a spring is considered to be an element that stores potential energy*.It is analogous to a capacitor in electric networks. All springs in real life are nonlinear to some extent.However,if the deformation of the spring is small, its behavior can be approximated by a linear relationship:

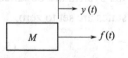

Figure 5.1.2 Force-mass system.

$$f(t)=Ky(t) \qquad (5.1.9)$$

where *K* is the **spring constant**, or simply **stiffness**.

The two basic unit systems for the spring constant are as follows:

Units	Spring Constant *K*
SI	N/m
British	lb/ft

Equation (5.1.9) implies that the force acting on the spring is directly proportional to the displacement (deformation) of the spring. A model of a linear spring element is shown in Figure 5.1.3. If the spring is preloaded with a preload tension of *T*, Eq.(5.1.9) should be modified to

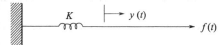

Figure 5.1.3 Force-spring system.

$$f(t)-T=Ky(t) \qquad (5.1.10)$$

5.1.4 Friction for Translation Motion

Whenever there is motion or tendency of motion between two physical elements, frictional forces exist. The frictional forces encountered in physical systems are usually of a nonlinear nature. The characteristics of the frictional forces between two contacting surfaces often depend on such factors as the composition of the surfaces, the pressure between the surfaces, their relative velocity, and others, so that an exact mathematical description of the frictional force is difficult. Three different types of friction are commonly used in practical systems: **viscous friction, static friction, and Coulomb friction.**

5.1.5 Rotational Motion

The rotational motion of a body can be defined as motion about a fixed axis. The extension of Newton's law of motion for rotational motion states that the *algebraic sum of moments or torque about a fixed axis is equal to the product of the inertia and the angular acceleration about the axis*; or,

$$\Sigma \text{ torques} = J\alpha \qquad (5.1.11)$$

where *J* denotes the inertia and α is the angular acceleration. The other variables generally used to describe the motion of rotation are **torque** *T*, **angular velocity** ω, and **angular displacement** θ. The Inertia involved with the rotational motion is as follow.

Inertia. *Inertia, J, is considered to be the property of an element that stores the kinetic energy of rotational motion.* The inertia of a given element depends on the geometric composition about the axis of rotation and its density. For instance, the inertia of a circular disk or shaft about its geometric axis is given by

$$J = \frac{1}{2}Mr^2 \qquad (5.1.12)$$

When a torque is applied to a body with inertia *J*, as shown in Figure 5.1.4, the torque equation is written

$$T(t) = J\alpha(t) = J\frac{d\omega(t)}{d(t)} = J\frac{d^2\theta(t)}{dt^2} \qquad (5.1.13)$$

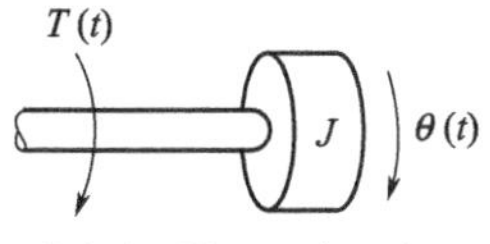

where $\theta(t)$ is the angular displacement, $\omega(t)$ the angular verlocity, and $\alpha(t)$ the angular acceleration.

Figure 5.1.4 Torqueinertia system.

The SI and British units for inertia and the variables in Eq. (13) are tabulated as follows:

Units	Inertia	Torque	Angular Displacement
SI	kg-m^2	N-m	rad
		dyn-cm	rad
British	slug-ft^2	lb-ft	
	lb-ft-sec^2		
	oz-in.-sec^2	oz-in.	rad

Selected from "*Automatic Control Systems, Seventh Edition, Benjamin C. Kuo, Prentice Hall,* 1995"

Words and Expressions

1. mathematical modeling　数学模型
2. time-invariant system　时不变系统
3. electric network　电网络
4. Kirchhoff　克希荷夫
5. inductor　[in'dʌktə]　电感
6. kinetic energy　动能
7. potential energy　势能
8. SFG (signal-flow graph)　信号流图
9. hydraulic　[hai'drɔːlik]　*adj.* 液压的，水力的
10. pneumatic　[njuː'mætik]　*adj.* 气动的
11. translational　[træns'leiʃənl]　*adj.* 平移的，移动的
12. rotational　[rəu'teiʃənl]　*adj.* 旋转的，转动的
13. Newton　牛顿
14. SI (standard international unit)　国际标准
15. British　英制
16. Spring　[spriŋ]　*n.* 弹簧
17. Stiffness　['stifnis]　*n.* 刚性
18. Friction　['frikʃən]　*n.* 摩擦
19. Viscous friction　黏滞摩擦
20. Static friction　静摩擦
21. Coulomb friction　干摩擦
22. Inertia　[i'nəːʃə]　*n.* 惯性
23. Angular velocity　角速度
24. Angular displacement　角位移
25. torque　[tɔːk]　*n.* 转矩，力矩
26. rack [ræk]　*n.* 齿条
27. lead screw　引导丝杆

Exercises

1. *Complete the notes below with words taken from the text above.*

(1) The transfer function is valid_____linear time-invariant systems, _____the state equations can be applied to linear_____nonlinear systems.

(2) Therefore,_____often has the task of determining not only how to_____describe a system_____, but, more important, how to make_____.

(3) It should_____be emphasized_____the modern control engineer place special emphasis_____the mathematical modeling of systems analysis and design problems can conveniently be solved_____computers.

(4) Most control systems contain mechanical____electrical components,_____some systems_____hydraulic and pneumatic elements.

2. *Put the following into Chinese:*

mathematical model	proper assumptions and approximations	
whenever necessary	classical way	hydraulic element
pneumatic element	translational motion	rotational motion
displacement	SI	SFG

3. *put the following into English:*

速度	加速度	电网络方程	机械系统元件模型	质量	线性弹簧	功能
势能	惯性	角速度	角位移	齿条	引导丝杆	传送带

Reading Material

Conversion Between Translational and Rotational Motions and Power Transfer

In motion-control systems it is often necessary to convert rotational motion into translation. For instance, a load may be controlled to move along a straight line through a rotary motor-and-screw assembly, such as that shown in Figure 5.1.5. Figure 5.1.6 shows a similar situation in which a rack-and-pinion is used as a mechanical linkage. Another familiar system in motion control is the control of a mass through a pulley by a rotary motor, such as the control of a printwheel in an electric typewriter (Figure 5.1.7). The systems shown in Figures.5.1.5, 5.1.6, and 5.1.7 can all be represented by a simple system with an equivalent inertia connected directly to the

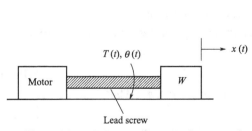

Figure 5.1.5 Rotary-to-linear motion-control system(lead screw).

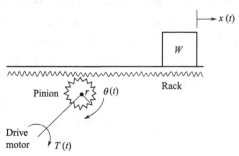

Figure 5.1.6 Rotary-to-linear motion-control system(rack and pinion).

drive motor. For instance, the mass in Figure 5.1.7 can be regarded as a point mass that moves about the pulley, which has a radius r. By disregarding the inertia of the pulley, the equivalent inertia that the motor sees is

$$J = Mr^2 = \frac{W}{g}r^2 \qquad (5.1.14)$$

If the radius of the pinion in Figure 5.1.6 is r, the equivalent inertia that the motor sees is also given by Eq.(5.1.14).

Now consider the system of Figure 5.1.5. The lead of the screw, L, is defined as the linear distance that the mass travels per revolution of the screw. In principle, the two systems in Figure 5.1.6 and 5.1.7 are equivalent. In Figure 5.1.6 the distance traveled by the mass per revolution of the pinion is $2\pi r$. By using Eq.(5.1.14) as the equivalent inertia for the system of Figure 5.1.5, we have

$$J = \frac{W}{g}\left(\frac{L}{2\pi}\right)^2 \qquad (5.1.15)$$

where, in British units,

J=inertia (oz-in.-sec^2) L=screw lead (in.)
W=weight (oz) g=gravitational force (386.4 in./sec^2)

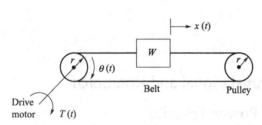
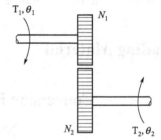

Figure 5.1.7 Rotary-to-linear motion-control system (belt and pulley).

Figure 5.1.8 Gear train.

Gear Trains, Levers, and Timing Belts

A gear train, lever, or timing belt over a pulley is a mechanical device that transmits energy from one part of the system to another in such a way that force, torque, speed, and displacement may be altered. These devices can also be regarded as matching devices used to attain maximum power transfer. Two gears are shown coupled together in Figure 5.1.8. The inertia and friction of the gears are neglected in the ideal case considered.

The relationships between the torques, T_1 and T_2, angular displacement θ_1 and θ_2, and the teeth numbers N_1 and N_2 of the gear train are derived from the following facts:

① *The number of teeth on the surface of the gears is proportional to the radii r_1 and r_2 of the gears; that is,*

$$r_1 N_2 = r_2 N_1 \qquad (5.1.16)$$

② *The distance traveled along the surface of each gear is the same. Thus*

$$\theta_1 r_1 = \theta_2 r_2 \qquad (5.1.17)$$

③ *The work done by one gear is equal to that of the other since there are assumed to be no losses. Thus*

$$T_1\theta_1=T_2\theta_2 \quad (5.1.18)$$

If the angular velocities of the two gears, ω_1 and ω_2, are brought into the picture, Eqs.(5.1.16) through (5.1.18) lead to

$$\frac{T_1}{T_2}=\frac{\theta_1}{\theta_2}=\frac{N_1}{N_2}=\frac{\omega_2}{\omega_1}=\frac{r_1}{r_2} \quad (5.1.19)$$

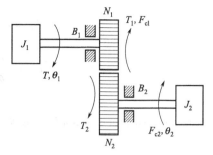

Figure 5.1.9 Gear train with friction and inertia.

In practice, gears do have inertia and friction between the coupled gear teeth that often cannot be neglected. An equivalent representation of a gear train with viscous friction, Coulomb friction, and inertia, considered as lumped parameters, is shown in Figure 5.1.9, where T denotes the applied torque, T_1 and T_2 are the transmitted torques, F_{c1}, and F_{c2}, are the Coulomb friction coefficients, and B_1 and B_2 are the viscous friction coefficients. The torque equation for gear 2 is

$$T_2(t)=J_2\frac{d^2\theta_2(t)}{dt_2}+B_2\frac{d\theta_2(t)}{dt}+F_{c2}\frac{\omega_2}{|\omega_2|} \quad (5.1.20)$$

The torque equation on the side of gear 1 is

$$T(t)=J_1\frac{d^2\theta_1(t)}{dt^2}+B_1\frac{d\theta_1(t)}{dt}+F_{c1}\frac{\omega_1}{|\omega_1|}+T_1(t) \quad (5.1.21)$$

By use of Eq.(5.1.19), Eq.(5.1.20) is converted to

$$T_1(t)=\frac{N_1}{N_2}T_2(t)=\left(\frac{N_1}{N_2}\right)^2 J_2\frac{d^2\theta_1(t)}{dt^2}+\left(\frac{N_1}{N_2}\right)^2 B_2\frac{d\theta_1(t)}{dt}+\frac{N_1}{N_2}F_{c2}\frac{\omega_2}{|\omega_2|} \quad (5.1.22)$$

Equation (5.1.22) indicates that *it is possible to reflect inertia, friction, compliance, torque, speed, and displacement from one side of a gear train to the other*. The following quantities are obtained when reflecting from gear 2 to gear 1:

Inertia: $\left(\frac{N_1}{N_2}\right)^2 J_2$ \qquad Angular displacement: $\frac{N_1}{N_2}\theta_2$

Viscous friction coefficient: $\left(\frac{N_1}{N_2}\right)^2 B_2$ \qquad Angular velocity: $\frac{N_1}{N_2}\omega_2$

Torque: $\frac{N_1}{N_2}T_2$ \qquad Coulomb friction torque: $\frac{N_1}{N_2}F_{c2}\frac{\omega_2}{|\omega_2|}$

Similarly, gear parameters and variables can be reflected from gear 1 to gear 2 simply by interchanging the subscripts in the expressions above.

If a torsional spring effect is present, the spring constant is also multiplied by $(N_1/N_2)^2$ in reflecting from gear 2 to gear 1. Now substituting Eq.(5.1.22) into Eq.(5.1.21), we get

$$T(t)=J_{1e}\frac{d^2\theta_1(t)}{dt^2}+B_{1e}\frac{d\theta_1(t)}{dt}+T_F \quad (5.1.23)$$

where

$$J_{1e}=J_1+\left(\frac{N_1}{N_2}\right)^2 J_2 \quad (5.1.24)$$

$$B_{1e} = B_1 + \left(\frac{N_1}{N_2}\right)^2 B_2 \qquad (5.1.25)$$

$$T_F = F_{c1}\frac{\omega_1}{\omega_1} + \frac{N_1}{N_2}F_{c2}\frac{\omega_2}{|\omega_2|} \qquad (5.1.26)$$

Selected from "*Automatic Control Systems, Seventh Edition, Benjamin C. Kuo, Prentice Hall*, 1995"

Words and Expressions

1. motor-and-screw assembly　马达齿轮付
2. rack-and-pinion　齿条齿轮付
3. typewriter　打字（EP）机
4. drive motor　驱动马达
5. gear train　传动机构
6. gear levers　变速杆
7. timing belts　定时皮带传动

5.2 DC Motors in Control Systems

> *After reading the text below, try to answer the following questions:*
> 1. Why DC motors are one of the most widely used in industrial control systems today?
> 2. What is the basic operational principles of DC motors?
> 3. Could you please give the basic classifications of PM DC Motors.

Direct-current(dc)motors are one of the most widely used prime movers in industry today.Years ago a majority of the small servomotors used for control purposes were of the ac variety.In reality,ac motors are more difficult to control,especially for position control, and their characteristics are quite nonlinear, which makes the analytical task more difficult. Dc motors, on the other hand, are more expensive, because of the brushes and commutators, and variable-flux dc motors are suitable only for certain types of control applications. Before permanent-magnet technology was fully developed, the torque per unit volume or weight of a dc motor with a permanent-magnet (PM) field was far from desirable. Today, with the development of the rare-earth magnet, it is possible to achieve very high torque-to-volume PM dc motors at reasonable cost. Furthermore,the advances made in brush-and-commutator technology have made these wearable parts practically maintenance-free. The advancements made in power electronics have made brushless dc motors quite popular in high-performance control systems.Advanced manufacturing techniques have also produced dc motors with ironless rotors that have very low inertia, thus achieving a very high torque-to-inertia ratio, and lowtime-constant properties have opened new applications for dc motors in computer peripheral equipment such as tape drives, printers, disk drives, and word processors, as well as in the automation and machine-tool industries.

5.2.1 Basic Operational Principles of DC Motors

The dc motor is basically a torque transducer that converts electric energy into mechanical energy. The torque developed on the motor shaft is directly proportional to the field flux and the armature current. As shown in Figure 5.2.1,a current-carrying conductor is established in a magnetic field with flux Φ, and the conductor is located at a distance r from the center of rotation. The relationship among the developed torque, flux Φ, and current i_a is

$$T_m = K_m \Phi i_a \qquad (5.2.1)$$

where T_m is the motor torque (N-m,lb-ft,or oz-in.), Φ the magnetic flux (webers), i_a the armature current (amperes), and K_m is a proportional constant.

In addition to the torque developed by the arrangement shown in Figure 5.2.1, when the conductor moves in the magnetic field, a voltage is generated across its terminals. This voltage, the **back emf**, which is proportional to the shaft velocity, tends to oppose the current flow. The

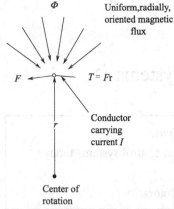

Figure 5.2.1 Torque production in a dc motor.

relationship between the back emf and the shaft velocity is

$$e_b = K_m \Phi \omega_m \qquad (5.2.2)$$

where e_b denotes the back emf (volts), and ω_m is the shaft velocity (rad/sec) of the motor. Equations 1 and 2 form the basis of the dc-motor operation.

5.2.2 Basic Classifications of PM DC Motors

In general, the magnetic field of a dc motor can be produced by field windings or permanent magnets. Due to the popularity of PM dc motors in control system applications, we concentrate on this type of motor. PM dc motors can be classified according to commutation scheme and armature design. Conventional dc motors have mechanical brushes and commutators. However, in one important class of dc motors the commutation is done electronically; this type of motor is called a **brushless dc motor.**

According to the armature construction, the PM dc motor can be broken down into three types of armature design: **iron-core, surface-wound**, and **moving-coil** motors.

Iron-Core PM DC Motors

The rotor and stator configuration of an iron-core PM dc motor is shown in Figure 5.2.2 The permanent-magnet material can be barium-ferrite, Alnico, or rare-earth compound. The magnetic flux produced by the magnet passes through a liminated rotor structure that contains slots. The armature conductors are placed in the rotor slots. This type of dc motor is characterized by relatively high rotor inertia (since the rotating part consists of the armature windings), high inductance, low cost, and high reliability.

Surface-Wound DC Motors

Figure 5.2.3 shows the rotor construction of a surface-wound PM dc motor. The armature conductors are bonded to the surface of a cylindrical rotor structure, which is made of laminated disks fastened to the motor shaft. Since no slots are used on the rotor in this design, the armature has no "cogging" effect. Since the conductors are laid out in the air gap between the rotor and the permanent-magnet field, this type of motor has lower inductance than that of the iron-core structure.

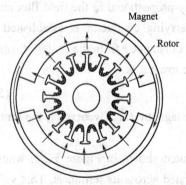

Figure 5.2.2 Cross-sectional view of a permanent-magnet iron-core dc motor.

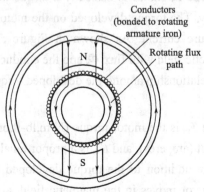

Figure 5.2.3 Cross-sectional view of a surface-wound permanent-magnet dc motor.

Moving-Coil DC Motors

Moving-coil motors are designed to have very low moments of inertia and very low armature inductance. This is achieved by placing the armature conductors in the air gap between a stationary flux return path and the permanent- magnet structure, as shown in Figure 5.2.4. In this case, the conductor structure is supported by nonmagnetic material—usually epoxy resins or fiber glass—to form a hollow cylinder. One end of the cylinder forms a hub, which is attached to the motor shaft. A cross-sectional view of such a motor is shown in Figure 5.2.5. Since all unnecessary elements have been removed from the armature of the moving-coil motor, its moment of inertia is very low. Since the conductors in the moving-coil armature are not in direct contact with iron, the motor inductance is very low; values of less than 100μH are common in this type of motor. The low-inertia and low-inductance properties make the moving-coil motor one of the best actuator choices for high-performance control systems.

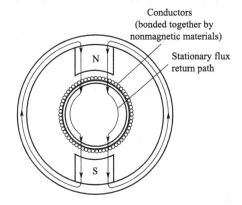

Figure 5.2.4 Cross-sectional view of a moving-coil permanent-magnet dc motor.

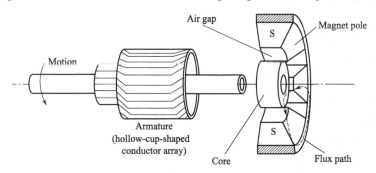

Figure 5.2.5 Cross-sectional side view of a moving-coil dc motor.

Brushless DC Motors

Brushless dc motors differ from the previously mentioned dc motors in that they employ electrical (rather than mechanical) commutation of the armature current. The configuration of the brushless dc motor most commonly used—especially for incremental-motion applications-is one in which the rotor consists of magnets and "back iron" support, and whose commutated windings are located external to the rotating parts, as shown in Figure 5.2.6. Compared to the conventional dc motors, such as the one shown in Figure 5.2.2, it is an "inside-out" configuration. Depending on

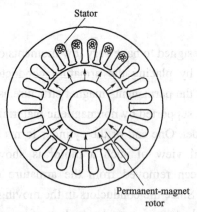

Figure 5.2.6   Cross-sectional view of a permanent-magnet brushless dc motor.

the specific application, brushless dc motors can be used when a low moment of inertia is called for, such as the spindle drive in high-performance disk drives used in computers.

Selected from "*Automatic Control Systems, Seventh Edition, Benjamin C. Kuo, Prentice Hall,* 1995"

Words and Expressions

1. direct-current (DC) motor   直流电动机
2. servomotor   ['sə:vəməutə]   伺服电动机
3. ac motor   交流电动机
4. brush   [brʌʃ]   *n.* 电刷
5. commutator   ['kɔmjuteitə]   整流器
6. variable-flux   变磁力线（磁通）
7. permanent-magnet   *adj.* 永磁的
8. PM dc   永磁直流电动机
9. rare-earth magnet   稀土磁铁
10. maintenance-free   免修的，不需维护的
11. ironless rotor   无铁芯转子
12. armature current   电枢电流
13. back emf   反电动势
14. shaft velocity   转轴速度
15. iron-core   铁芯
16. surface-wound   表面绕线
17. moving-coil   动卷
18. brushless   无电刷的
19. field winding   磁场绕组
20. barium-ferrite   钡铁淦氧磁体
21. rotor   ['rəutə]   转子
22. stator   ['steitə]   *n.* 定子
23. air gap   空（气）隙

Exercises

1. *Complete the notes below with words taken from the text above.*
   (1) _____ are one of the most widely used prime movers in industry today.
   (2) In reality, ac motors _____ difficult to control, _____ Position control, and their _____ are quite _____, _____ makes the analytical task more difficult.
   (3) Today, _____ the development of the rare-earth magnet, _____ possible to achieve very high _____ PM dc motors at _____.
   (4) _____ the armature construction, the PM dc motor _____ into three types of armature design: _____, _____, and _____ motors.

2. *Put the following into Chinese:*

   permanent magnet   brush-and-commutator   inertia
   torque-to-intertia ratio torque transducer   field flux
   armature current   shaft velocity   rotating flux path
   variable-flux   field winding   barium-ferrite

3. *put the following into English:*

   直流电动机   伺服电动机   交流电动机   永磁直流电动机
   稀土磁铁   铁芯永磁电动机   表面绕线直流电动机
   移动线圈直流电动机 无电刷直流电动机   反电动势   转子   定子

Reading Material:

Mathematical Modeling of PM DC Motors

Since dc motors are used extensively in control systems, for analytical purposes, it is necessary to establish mathematical models for dc motors for control applications. We use the equivalent circuit diagram in Figure 5.2.7 to represent a PM dc motor. The armature is modeled as a circuit with resistance R_a connected in series with an inductance L_a, and a voltage source e_b representing the back emf in the armature when the rotor rotates. The motor variables and parameters are defined as follows:

▲ $i_a(t)$=armature current   ▲ L_a=armature inductance
▲ R_a=armature resistance   ▲ $e_a(t)$=applied voltage
▲ $e_b(t)$=back emf   ▲ K_b=back-emf constant
▲ $T_L(t)$=load torque   ▲ ϕ=magnetic flux in the air gap
▲ $T_m(t)$=motor torque   ▲ $\omega_m(t)$=rotor angular velocity
▲ $\theta_m(t)$=rotor displacement   ▲ J_m=rotor inertia
▲ K_i=torque constant   ▲ B_m=viscous-friction coefficient

With reference to the circuit diagram of Figure 5.2.7, the control of the dc motor is applied at the armature terminals in the form of the applied voltage $e_a(t)$. For linear analysis, we assume that the torque developed by the motor is proportional to the airgap flux and the armature current. Thus

$$T_m(t)=K_m(t)\phi i_a(t) \tag{5.2.3}$$

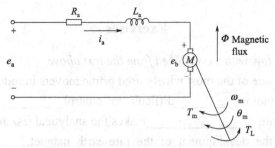

Figure 5.2.7 Model of a separately excited dc motor.

Since ϕ is constant, Eq.(3) is written

$$T_m(t) = K_i i_a(t) \tag{5.2.4}$$

where K_i is the **torque constant** in N-m/A, lb-ft/A, or oz-in./A.

Starting with the control input voltage $e_a(t)$, the cause-and-effect equations for the motor circuit in Figure 5.2.7 are

$$\frac{di_a(t)}{dt} = \frac{1}{L_a} e_a(t) - \frac{R_a}{L_a} i_a(t) - \frac{1}{L_a} e_b(t) \tag{5.2.5}$$

$$T_m(t) = K_i i_a(t) \tag{5.2.6}$$

$$e_b(t) = K_b \frac{d\theta_m(t)}{dt} = K_b \omega_m(t) \tag{5.2.7}$$

$$\frac{d^2\theta_m(t)}{dt^2} = \frac{1}{J_m} T_m(t) - \frac{1}{J_m} T_L(t) - \frac{B_m}{J_m} \frac{d\theta_m(t)}{dt} \tag{5.2.8}$$

where $T_L(t)$ represents a load frictional torque such as Coulomb friction.

Equations (5.2.5) through (5.2.8) consider that $e_a(t)$ is the cause of all causes; Eq.(5.2.5) considers that $di_a(t)/dt$ is the immediate effect due to the applied voltage $e_a(t)$, then in Eq.(5.2.6), $i_a(t)$ causes the torque $T_m(t)$, Eq.(5.2.7) defines the back emf, and finally, in Eq.(5.2.8), the torque $T_m(t)$ causes the angular velocity $\omega_m(t)$ and displacement $\theta_m(t)$.

The state variables of the system can be defined as $i_a(t)$, $\omega_m(t)$, and $\theta_m(t)$. By direct substitution and eliminating all the nonstate variables from Eqs.(5.2.5) through (5.2.8), the state equations of the dc-motor system are written in vector-matrix form:

$$\begin{bmatrix} \frac{di_a(t)}{dt} \\ \frac{d\omega_m(t)}{dt} \\ \frac{d\theta_m(t)}{dt} \end{bmatrix} = \begin{bmatrix} -\frac{R_a}{L_a} & -\frac{K_b}{L_a} & 0 \\ \frac{K_i}{J_m} & -\frac{B_m}{J_m} & 0 \\ 0 & 1 & 0 \end{bmatrix} \begin{bmatrix} \cdot \\ \cdot \\ \cdot \end{bmatrix} + \begin{bmatrix} \frac{1}{L_a} \\ 0 \\ 0 \end{bmatrix} e_a(t) - \begin{bmatrix} 0 \\ \frac{1}{J_m} \\ 0 \end{bmatrix} T_L(t) \tag{5.2.9}$$

Notice that in this case, $T_L(t)$ is treated as a second input in the state equations.

The state diagram of the system is drawn as shown in Figure 5.2.8, using Eq.(5.2.9). The transfer function between the motor displacement and the input voltage is obtained from the state diagram as

$$\frac{\Theta_m(s)}{E_a(s)} = \frac{K_i}{L_a J_m s^3 + (R_a J_m + B_m L_a) s^2 + (K_b K_i + R_a B_m) s} \tag{5.2.10}$$

where $T_L(t)$ has been set to zero.

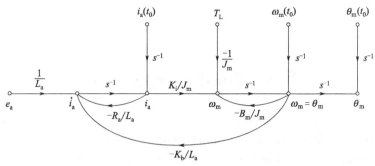

Figure 5.2.8 State diagram of a dc motor.

Figure 5.2.9 shows a block-diagram representation of the dc-motor system. The advantage of using the block diagram is that it gives a clear picture of the transfer-function relation between each block of the system. Since an s can be factored out from the denominator of Eq.(5.2.10), *the significance of the transfer function $\Theta_m(s)/E_a(s)$ is that the dc motor is essentially an integrating device between these two variables.* This is expected, since if $e_a(t)$ is a constant input, the output motor displacement will behave as the output of an integrator; that is, it will increase linearly with time.

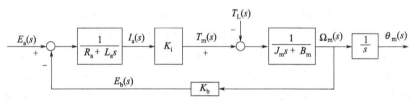

Figure 5.2.9 Black diagram of a dc motor system.

Although a dc motor by itself is basically an open-loop system, the state diagram of Figure 5.2.8 and the block diagram of Figure 5.2.9 show that the motor has a "built-in" feedback loop caused by the back emf. Physically, the back emf represents the feedback of a signal that is proportional to the negative of the speed of the motor. As seen from Eq.(5.2.10), the back-emf constant K_b represents an added term to the resistance R_a and the viscous-friction coefficient B_m. Therefore, *the back-emf is equivalent to an "electric friction," which tends to improve the stability of the motor, and in general, the stability of the system.*

Selected from "*Automatic Control Systems, Seventh Edition, Benjamin C.Kuo, Prentice Hall,* 1995"

Words

1. equivalent circuit diagram 等效电流图
2. cause-and effect equation 因果关系方程
3. frictional torque 摩擦力矩

5.3 Sun-Seeker System

After reading the following unit, try to answer the questions:
1. Could you please give a schematic diagram of sun-seeker control system.
2. How to mount the silicon photovoltaic cells on the space vehicle?
3. What is the principle of tracking the sun for a space vehicle?
4. Please give the black diagram that characterizes all the functional relations of sun-seeker system.

In this section we model a sun-seeker control system whose purpose is to control the attitude of a space vehicle so that it will track the sun with high accuracy. In the system described, tracking the sun in only one plane is accomplished. A schematic diagram of the system is shown in Figure 5.3.1. The principal elements of the error discriminator are two small rectangular silicon photovoltaic cells mounted behind a rectangular slit in an enclosure. The cells are mounted in such a way that when the sensor is pointed at the sun, the beam of light from the slit overlaps both cells. The silicon cells are used as current sources and connected in opposite polarity to the input of an op-amp. Any difference in the short-circuit current of the two cells is sensed and amplified by the op-amp. Since the current of each cell is proportional to the illumination on the cell, an error signal will be present at the output of the amplifier when the light from the slit is not centered

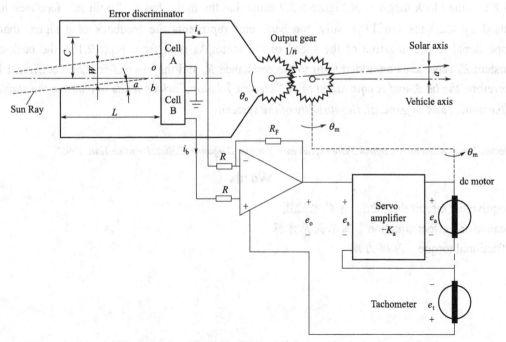

Figure 5.3.1 Schematic diagram of a sun-seeker system.

precisely on the cells. This error voltage, when fed to the servoampli-fier, will cause the motor to drive the system back into alignment. The description of each part of the system is given as follows.

5.3.1 Coordinate System

The center of the coordinate system is considered to be at the output gear of the system. The reference axis is taken to be the fixed frame of the dc motor, and all rotations are measured with respect to this axis. The solar axis or the line from the output gear to the sun makes an angle $\theta_r(t)$ with respect to the reference axis, and $\theta_o(t)$ denotes the vehicle axis with respect to the reference axis. The objective of the control system is to maintain the error between $\theta_r(t)$ and $\theta_o(t)$, $\alpha(t)$, near zero:

$$\alpha(t)=\theta_r(t)-\theta_o(t) \tag{5.3.1}$$

The coordinate system described is illustrated in Figure 5.3.2.

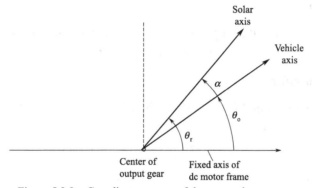

Figure 5.3.2　Coordinate system of the sun-seeker system.

5.3.2　Error Discriminator

When the vehicle is aligned perfectly with the sun, $\alpha(t)=0$, and $i_a(t)=i_b(t)=I$, or $i_a(t)=i_b(t)=0$. From the geometry of the sun ray and the photovoltaic cells shown in Figure 5.3.1, we have

$$oa = \frac{W}{2}+L\tan\alpha(t) \tag{5.3.2}$$

$$ob = \frac{W}{2}-L\tan\alpha(t) \tag{5.3.3}$$

where oa denotes the width of the sun ray that shines on cell A, and ob is the same on cell B, for a given $\alpha(t)$. Since the current $i_a(t)$ is proportional to oa, and $i_b(t)$ to ob, we have

$$i_a(t) = I + \frac{2LI}{W}\tan\alpha(t) \tag{5.3.4}$$

$$i_b(t) = I - \frac{2LI}{W}\tan\alpha(t) \tag{5.3.5}$$

for $0 \leq \tan\alpha(t) \leq W/2L$. For $W/2L \leq \tan\alpha(t) \leq (C-W/2)/L$, the sun ray is completely on cell A, and $i_a(t)=2I$, $i_b(t)=0$. For $(C-W/2)L \leq \tan\alpha(t) \leq (C+W/2)/L$, $i_a(t)$ decreases linearly from $2I$ to zero. $i_a(t)=i_b(t)=0$ for $\tan\alpha(t) \geq (C+W/2)/L$. Therefore, the error discriminator may be represented by the nonlinear characteristic of Figure 5.3.3, where for small angle $\alpha(t)$, $\tan\alpha(t)$ has been approximated by $\alpha(t)$ on the abscissa.

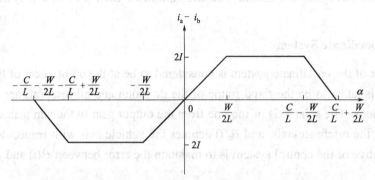

Figure 5.3.3 Nonlinear characteristic of the error discrimina-tor.
The abscissa is tan α but is approximated by α for small values of α.

5.3.3 Op-Amp

The relationship between the output of the op-amp and the currents $i_a(t)$ and $i_b(t)$ is

$$e_o(t) = -R_F [i_a(t) - i_b(t)] \quad (5.3.6)$$

5.3.4 Servoamplifier

The gain of the servoamplifier is $-K$. With reference to Figure 5.3.1, the output of the servoamplifier is expressed as

$$e_a(t) = -K[e_o(t) + e_t(t)] = -Ke_s(t) \quad (5.3.7)$$

5.3.5 Tachometer

The output voltage of the tachometer, e_t, is related to the angular velocity of the motor through the tachometer constant K_t

$$e_t(t) = K_t \omega_m(t) \quad (5.3.8)$$

The angular position of the output gear is related to the motor position through the gear ratio, $1/n$. Thus

$$\theta_o = \frac{1}{n} \theta_m \quad (5.3.9)$$

5.3.6 DC Motor

The dc motor has been modeled in Reading Material 2 of Chapter 5. The equations are

$$e_a(t) = R_a i_a(t) + e_b(t)$$
$$e_b(t) = K_b \omega_m(t) \quad (5.3.10)$$
$$T_m(t) = K_i i_a(t)$$
$$T_m(t) = J \frac{d\omega_m(t)}{dt} + B\omega_m(t)$$

where J and B are the inertia and viscous function coefficients seen at the motor shaft. The inductance of the motor is neglected in Eq.(10). A block diagram that characterizes all the functional relations of the system is shown in Figure 5.3.4.

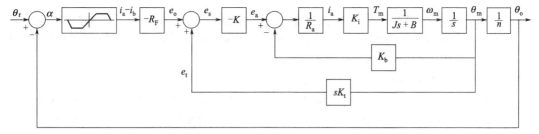

Figure 5.3.4 Block diagram of the sun-seeker system.

Selected from "*Automatic Control Systems, Seventh Edition, Benjamin C. Kuo, Prentice Hall,* 1995"

Words and Expressions

1. sun-seeker system   太阳自导（寻）系统
2. attitude [æti'tju:d]   *n.* 姿态
3. space vehicle   空间飞船
4. track [træk]   *n.* 轨迹，*vt.* 跟踪
5. error discriminator   误差鉴别器
6. rectangular [rek'tæŋgjulə]   *adj.* 直角的
7. silicon [s'ilikən]   *n.* 硅
8. photovoltaic cell   光电池（光生伏打电池）
9. slit [slit]   *n.* 光栅，狭缝
10. rectangular slit   直角光栅
11. enclosure [in'kləuʒə]   *n.* 封装
12. overlap [əuvə'læp]   *vt.* 复盖、重叠
13. op-amp=operational amplifier   运算放大器
14. short-circuit   *n.* 短路电流、漏电电流
15. illumination [ilu:mi'neiʃən]   *n.* 照明（度）
16. alignment [ə'lainmənt]   *n.* 对准
17. abscissa [əb'sisə]   *n.* 横坐标
18. servoamplifier   伺服放大器
19. tachometer [tæ'kɔmitə]   *n.* 转速计

Exercises

1. *Complete the notes below with words taken from the text above.*
    (1) In this section we model_____whose purpose is_____the attitude of a space vehicle _____ it will track the sun with high accuracy.
    (2) The principal elements of the_____are two small_____mounted behind a rectangular slit in an enclosure.
    (3) The cells are mounted in_____that when the sensor_____at the sun,_____of light from the slit overlaps_____.

(4) Since the current of each cell___proportional_____the illumination_____the cell, an error signal will be present_____the output of the amplifier when the light from the slit___centered precisely_____the cells.

2. *Put the following into Chinese:*

sun-seeker   space vehicle   error discriminator   silicon
photovoltaic cell   slit   shut-circuit   illumination
error signal   coordinate system   alignment   rectangular

3. *put the following into English:*

姿态   运算放大器   伺服放大器   横坐标   转速计   放大器

Reading Material:

Design of a Thickness and Flatness Control System for Metal Rolling

Steel or aluminum strip is required to be of a specified thickness and to be flat. We discuss the design of a microprocessor-based controller for this task.

1. Thickness Measurement and Control

In steel or aluminum flat rolling, material of thickness H is entered into a pair of rollers having initial unloaded gap q(Figure 5.3.5).

Entry generates a force F, so that the outgoing strip has thickness

$$h=q+F/M \tag{5.3.11}$$

where M is a stiffness coefficient (see Figure 5.3.6).

For thickness control, q and f are measured by synchro and load cell respectively and Eq(5.3.11) is used to generate an estimate of h, which cannot be otherwise measured without a significant time delay.(A measurement of h by nucleonic gauge is made downstream and is used to "calibrate" Eq(5.3.11).

The thickness control actuator is an electric motor that moves the upper roll vertically to modify q and hence to modify h.

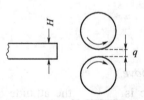
Figure 5.3.5 Steel strip of thickness H about to enter a rool gap of dimension q.

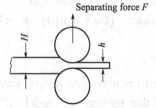
Figure 5.3.6 Steel strip during rolling.

Poor strip flatness is caused by non-uniform elongation across the strip width and flatness is monitored by measuring and comparing tensions at points across the strip width. (Points on the strip width where the elongation has been greatest have lowest tension—see Figure 5.3.7.)

In this application we measure tension at five points, sited symmetrically across the strip width. Let the five tension measurements be denoted $s_{-2}, s_{-1}, s_0, s_1, s_2$ as in Figure 5.3.8. We fit a polynomial of the form

$$s(\omega) = a_0 + a_1 \omega + a_2 \omega^2$$

through these five points, using a least-squares criterion.

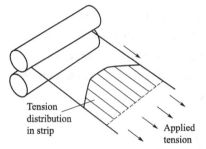
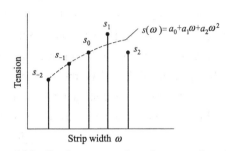

Figure 5.3.7 Non-uniform elongation. Tension is lowest where elongation is greatest.

Figure 5.3.8 Tensions measured at points across the strip width. $s(\omega)$ is a polynomial drawn as a best fit to the five points.

The parameters a_1, a_2 are the measures of flatness with $a_1 = a_2 = 0$ implying perfect flatness. The parameter a_0 is not of interest since it is merely a measure of the mean tension applied during rolling.

For our digital system, we need values of $a_1(kT), a_2(kT)$ for input to the control system and ideally we need the five values $s_{-2}, s_{-1}, s_0, s_1, s_2$ all simultaneously at time (kT), to allow $a_1(kT)$, $a_2(kT)$ to be determined.

2. Flatness Control

Roll bending through fast-acting hydraulic cylinders achieves largely parabolic modification to the roll gap and largely operates on the measured flatness parameter a_2. Roll tilting through electric actuators largely operates on the measured flatness parameter a_1 (Figure 5.3.9).

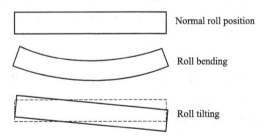

Figure 5.3.9 Flatness actuators operate through roll bending and roll tilting as shown.

3. Control-System Specification

The system is to control h, a_1, a_2 in the strip to remain equal to operator-specified desired values h_d, a_{1d}, a_{2d}. An accuracy of 0.1% is to be aimed for. Closed-loop system bandwidths are to be 6 rad/s or higher. The strip outgoing velocity is 5m/s.

4. Choice of Sampling Interval T for the Control Loops

Using the criterion that sampling frequency ω_s should satisfy $\omega_s \geqslant 10\omega_b$ leads to the requirement $2\pi/T \geqslant 60$ or $T \leqslant 2\pi/60$. We choose $T = 0.1$s.

5. Choice of Input-Signal Scanning Arrangement

Before a control action can be decided upon, the system must be in possession of up-to-date measurements of the parameters h, a_1, a_2. These parameters are calculated from the seven input signals, $q, F, s_{-2}, s_{-1}, s_0, s_1, s_2$, which must therefore be scanned at a much faster rate than every 0.1 s.

Let us first consider the five signals representing strip tensions. Ideally they should be sampled simultaneously, for otherwise they will represent a diagonal scan across the moving strip. At least, we must ensure that the a_1, a_2 parameters cannot change significantly while the s_i signals are being scanned. Let T_s be the time taken to scan the 5 tension signals; then we require that the $a_1.a_2$ parameters do not change significantly over that period.

From the closed-loop bandwidth requirement,

$$\left.\frac{da_i}{dt}\right|_{\max t}=6\text{units/s}, i=1,2$$

(where $a_{i\max}$ has been normalized to unity). This follows since

$$\left.\frac{d\sin\omega t}{dt}\right|_{\max i}=\left.\omega\cos\omega t\right|_{\max t}=\omega$$

Let Δa_i be the change in parameter a_i while the 5 tension meters are scanned—then we require that

$$\left|\frac{\Delta a_i}{a_{i\max}}\right|<0.001$$

Since $a_{i\max}=1$ this implies that

$$\left.\frac{da_i}{dt}\right|_{\max}\times T_s<0.001,$$

or

$$T_s<\frac{0.001}{6}=0.00017$$

therefore the maximum time for connection to each of the s_i signals is $T_s/5=34\mu s$.

Bearing in mind the approximate nature of the bandwidth criterion and the need to allow time for sample acquisition and for switching of input channels, we shall choose an A/D converter with a conversion time of about 25μs.

The input scan therefore requires a total time of 7×25μs+small overheads for acquisition and switching. Computation time and output time complete the cyclic time budget. The total time for the three activities can be kept negligibly small compared with $T=0.1s$, so that the control algorithms may fix their outputs $u(k)$ depending on current inputs $e(k)$ rather than on previous inputs only. The timing diagram of Figure 5.3.10 summarizes the situation.

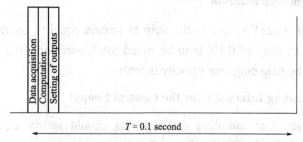

Figure 5.3.10 Computation timing diagram.

6. Choice of Word Lengths

A 0.1% accuracy requirement implies at least 10-bit working. Because we know that there may be an amplification of input quantization noise we choose a 12-bit A/D converter with 16-bit computation and memory followed by 12-bit D/A conversion.

7. Mathematical Models of the Process

The actuators plus the equipment that they drive constitute the dynamics of the process. The models are

$$\frac{h_1(s)}{u_3(s)} = \frac{k_3}{s(1+s)} = G_3(s) \tag{5.3.12}$$

$$\frac{a_1(s)}{u_1(s)} = \frac{k_1}{s(1+s)} = G_1(s) \tag{5.3.13}$$

$$\frac{a_2(s)}{u_2(s)} = \frac{k_2}{s(1+0.1s)} = G_2(s) \tag{5.3.14}$$

8. Control-Algorithm Design

A closed-loop process with undamped natural frequency ω_h has the transfer function

$$\frac{\omega_n^2}{\omega_n^2 + 2\zeta\omega_n s + s^2} = H(s) \tag{5.3.15}$$

(where ζ is the damping factor).

Setting $s = j\omega$ leads to

$$H(j\omega) = \frac{\omega_n^2}{(\omega_n^2 - \omega^2) + j2\zeta\omega_n\omega} \tag{5.3.16}$$

We choose a damping factor $\zeta = 1/\sqrt{2}$, and using this value we obtain $\omega_b = \omega_n$.

In our case, ω_b is given as $\omega_b = 6$ rad/s, so we require

$$\omega_h = 6 \text{ rad/s}$$

To use the z plane loci, we need to express ω_h in terms of $\pi/10T$. i.e. to choose p such that

$$\frac{p\pi}{10T} \approx 6$$

Since $T = 0.1$, this leads to

$$p = \frac{6}{\pi} = 1.91$$

We choose $p = 2$, leading to a somewhat higher bandwidth than required and on the appropriate ζ locus, $\zeta = 0.707$, we find that the necessary z-plane poles are $z = 0.57 \pm j0.28$, and thus

$$H(z) = \frac{N(z)}{(z - 0.57 + j0.28)(z - 0.57 - j0.28)} = \frac{N(z)}{z^2 - 1.14z + 0.403} \tag{5.3.17}$$

with the numerator to be fixed after further consideration.

9. The Complete Scheme

Figure 5.3.11 gives an overview of the designed system. Eight input signals are scanned rapidly and the three output signals are manipulated to bring h, a_1, a_2 to their desired values as input from the operator via the keyboard. The actuators are updated every 0.1s.

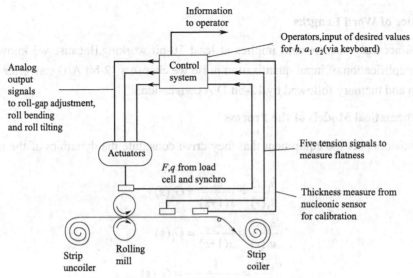

Figure 5.3.11 Overview of the complete scheme.

Selected from "*Applied Digital Control: Theory, Design & Implementation, Second Edition, J. R. Leigh, Prentice Hall*, 1992"

Words and Expressions

1. thickness   [ˈθiknis]   *n.* 厚度
2. flatness   [flætnis]   *n.* 平坦度，不平度
3. metal rolling   金属轧制
4. strip   [strip]   *v.* 拉丝，*n.* 带状物
5. a pair of rollers   一副轧辊
6. gap   [gæp]   *n.* 间隙
7. stiffness coefficient   刚度系数
8. synchro   [ˈsiŋkrəu]   *adj.* 同步
9. nucleonic gauge   核子仪表
10. elongation   [ˌiːlɔŋˈgeiʃən]   *n.* 拉长，延伸
11. tension   [ˈtenʃən]   *n.* 张力，拉伸
12. symmetrical   [siˈmetrikəl]   *adj.* 对称的，平衡的
13. roll bending   轧制弯曲度
14. hydraulic cylinder   液压缸
15. parabolic   [ˌpærəˈbɔlik]   *adj.* 抛物线的
16. roll tilting   轧制倾斜
17. input-signal scanning   输入信号扫描
18. coiler   [kɔilə]   *n.* 卷绕机

5.4 Modern Power Systems

> *During reading the following unit, try to answer the following questions*:
> 1. How many customers of electrical utilities companies in USA?
> 2. How many power plants in USA?
> 3. Please to tell the majority way of power produced.
> 4. What are the future power production methods?

There are well over 80,000,000 customers of electrical utilities companies in the United States today. To meet this demand for electrical power, power companies combine to produce about two million-million ($2,000,000 \times 10^6$) kilowatt-hours of electrical power. This vast quantity of electrical power is supplied by about 4000 power plants. Individual generating units which supply over 1200 megawatts of electrical power are now in operation at some power plants.

Electrical power can be produced in many ways, such as from chemical reactions, heat, light, or mechanical energy. The great majority of our electrical power is produced by power plants located throughout our country which convert the energy produced by burning coal, oil, or natural gas, the falling of water, or from nuclear reactions into electrical energy. Electrical generators at these power plants are driven by steam or gas turbines or by hydraulic turbines, in the case of hydroelectric plants. This chapter will investigate the types of power systems that produce the greatest majority of the electrical power used today.

Various other methods, some of which are in the experimental stages, may be used as future power production methods. These include solar cells, geothermal systems, wind-powered systems, magnetohydrodynamic (MHD) systems, nuclear-fusion systems, and fuel cells.

5.4.1 Electrical Power Plants

Most electrical power in the United States is produced at power plants that are either fossil-fuel steam plants, nuclear-fission steam plants, or hydroelectric plants. Fossil-fuel and nuclear-fission plants utilize steam turbines to deliver the mechanical energy needed to rotate the large three-phase alternators which produce massive quantities of electrical power. Hydroelectric plants ordinarily use vertically mounted hydraulic turbines. These units convert the force of flowing water into mechanical energy to rotate three-phase alternators.

The power plants may be located near the energy sources, near cities, or near the large industries where great amounts of electrical power are consumed. The generating capacity of power plants in the United States is greater than the combined capacity of the next four leading countries of the world. Thus, we can see how dependent we are upon the efficient production of electrical power.

5.4.2 Supply and Demand

The supply and demand situation for electrical energy is much different from other products which are produced by an organization and,then later,sold to consumers.Electrical energy must be supplied at the same time that it is demanded by consumers.There is no simple storage system which may be used to supply additional electrical energy at peak demand times.This situation is quite unique and necessitates the production of sufficient quantities of electrical energy to meet the demand of the consumers at any time.Accurate forecasting of load requirements at various given times must be maintained by utilities companies in order that they may recommend the necessary power plant output for a particular time of the year,week,or day.

5.4.3 Plant Load and Capacity Factors

There is a significant variation in the load requirement that must be met at different times.Thus,the power plant generating capacity is subject to a continual change.For the above reasons,much of the generating capacity of a power plant may be idle during low demand times.This means that not all the generators at the plant will be in operation.

There are two mathematical ratios with which power plants are concerned.These ratios are called load factor and capacity factor.They are expressed as:

$$\text{Load factor} = \frac{\text{Average load for a time period}}{\text{Peak load for a time period}}$$

$$\text{Capacity factor} = \frac{\text{Average load for a time period}}{\text{Output capacity of a power plant}}$$

It would be ideal,in terms of energy conservation,to keep these ratios as close to unity as possible.

5.4.4 Fossil Fuel Systems

Millions of years ago,large deposits of organic materials were formed under the surface of the earth.These deposits,which furnish our coal,oil,and natural gas,are known as fossil fuels.Of these,the most abundant fossil fuel is coal and coal-fired electrical power systems produce about one-half of the electrical power used in the United States.Natural-gas-fired systems are used for about one-fourth of our electrical power,while oil-fired systems produce around 10% of the power at the present time.These relative contributions of each system to the total electrical power produced in the United States are subject to change due to the addition of new power generation facilities and fuel availability.At the present time,over 80% of our electrical energy is produced by fossil-fuel systems.

A basic fossil-fuel power system is shown in Figure 5.4.1.In this type of system,a fossil fuel (coal,oil,or gas) is burned to produce heat energy.The heat from the combustion process is concentrated within a boiler where circulating water is converted to steam.The high-pressure steam is used to rotate a turbine.The turbine shaft is connected directly to the electrical generator and provides the necessary mechanical energy to rotate the generator.The generator then converts the mechanical energy into electrical energy.

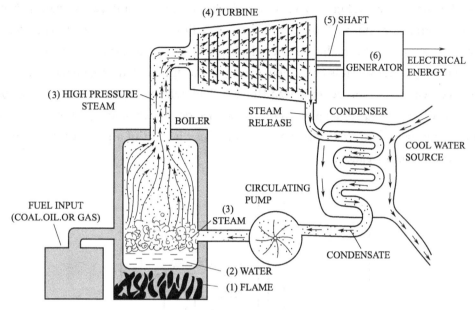

Figure 5.4.1 A basic fossll fuel power system.

Heat from burning fuel (1) changes water in boiler (2) into steam (3), which spins turbine (4) connected by shaft (5) to generator (6), producing electrical energy.

5.4.5 Fossil Fuels

Fossil fuels are used to supply heat by means of their chemical reactions for many different purposes.Such fuels contain carbon materials that are burned as a result of their reaction with air or oxygen.These fossil fuels are used as a direct source of heat when burned in a furnace and are used as a heat source for steam production when used in a power-plant boiler system.The steam that is generated is used for rotating the steam turbines in the power plants.

Fossil fuels vary according to their natural state (solid,liquid,or gas),according to their ability to produce heat,and in the type of flame or heat that they produce.Coal and coke are solid fossil fuels,with coal used extensively for producing heat to support electrical power production.Oil,gasoline,and diesel fuel,which are liquid fossil fuels derived by petroleum processing,are used mostly in conjunction with internal combustion engines.However,oil is used as a heat source for many power plants.Natural gas is the primary gaseous fuel used for electrical power production.

5.4.6 Hydroelectric Systems

The use of water power goes back to ancient times.It has been developed to a very high degree,but is now taking a secondary role due to the emphasis on other power sources that are being developed in our country today.Electrical power production systems using water power were developed for use in the early 20th Century.

The energy of flowing water may be used to generate electrical power.This method of power production is used in hydroelectric power systems as shown by the simple system illustrated in the diagram of Figure 5.4.2 Water,which is confined in a large reservoir,is channeled through a control gate which adjusts the flow rate.The flowing water passes through the blades and control vanes of a hydraulic turbine which produces rotation.This mechanical energy is used to rotate a generator that is connected directly to the turbine shaft.Rotation of the alternator causes electrical power to be produced.However,hydroelectric systems are limited by the availability of large water supplies.Many hydroelectric systems are part of multipurpose facilities.For instance,a hydroelectric power system may be part of a project planned for flood control,recreation,or irrigation.

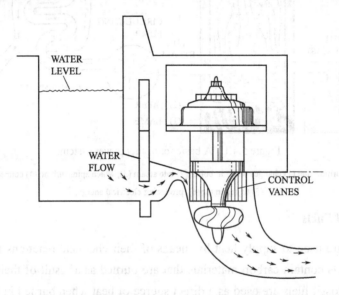

Figure 5.4.2　Drawing of a basic hydroelectric power system.

5.4.7　Nuclear-Fission Systems

Nuclear power plants in operation today utilize reactors which function due to the nuclear-fission process.Nuclear fission is a complex reaction which results in the division of the nucleus of an atom into two nuclei.This splitting of the atom is brought about by the bombardment of the nucleus with neutrons,gamma rays,or other charged particles and is referred to as induced fission.When an atom is split,it releases a great amount of heat.

In recent years,several nuclear-fission power plants have been put into operation.A nuclear-fission power system,shown in Figure 5.4.3,relies upon heat produced during a nuclear reaction process.Nuclear reactors "burn" nuclear material whose atoms are split causing the release of heat.This reaction is referred to as nuclear fission.The heat from the fission process is used to change circulating water into steam.The high-pressure steam rotates a turbine which is connected to an electrical generator.

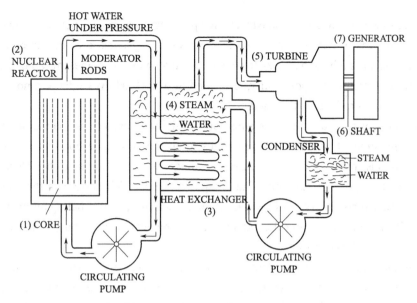

Figure 5.4.3 Drawing illustrating the principles of a nuclear-fission power system.
Nuclear fission in the core (1) of the reactor (2) produces energy in the form of heat, which heats water under pressure. The heat from the water in this primary system is transferred to a secondary stream of water in heat exchanger (3) converting it into steam (4), which spins the turbine (5) connected by shaft (6) to generator (7), producing electricity.

The nuclear-fission system is very similar to fossil fuel systems in that heat is used to produce high-pressure steam which rotates a turbine. The source of heat in the nuclear-fission system is a nuclear reaction while, in the fossil-fuel system, heat is developed by a burning fuel. At the present time, less that 10% of the electrical power produced in the United States comes from nuclear-fission sources. However, this percentage is also subject to rapid change as new power facilities are put into operation.

5.4.8 Potential Power Sources

Solar power is one potential electrical power source. The largest energy source available today is the sun which supplies practically limitless energy. The energy available from the sun far exceeds any foreseeable future need. Solar cells are now being used to convert light energy into small quantities of electrical energy. Possible solar-energy systems might include home heating or power production systems, orbiting space systems, and steam-driven electrical power systems. Each of these systems utilizes solar collectors that concentrate the light of the sun so that a large quantity of heat will be produced. Potentially, this heat could be used to drive a steam turbine in order to generate additional electrical energy.

Geothermal systems also have promise as future energy sources. These systems utilize the heat of molten masses of material in the interior of the earth. Thus, heat from the earth is a potential source of energy for power generation in many parts of the world. The principle of geothermal systems is similar to other steam turbine-driven systems. However, in this case, the source of steam is the heat obtained from within the earth through wells. These wells are drilled to a depth of up to two miles into the earth. Geothermal sources are used to produce electrical energy in certain regions of the western United States.

Wind systems have also been considered for producing electrical energy.However,winds are variable in most parts of our country.This fact causes wind systems to be confined to being used with storage systems,such as batteries.It is possible that wind machines may be used to rotate small generators which could,potentially,be located at a home.However,large amounts of power would be difficult to produce by this method.

Another energy source which has some potential for future use is magnetohydrodynamics (MHD).The operation of an MHD system relies upon the flow of a conductive gas through a magnetic field,thus causing a direct-current voltage to be generated.The electrical power developed depends upon the strength of the magnetic field which surrounds the conductive gas and on the speed and conductivity of the gas.At the present time,only small quantities of electrical energy have been generated using the MHD principle;however,it does have some potential as a future source of electrical energy.

Still another possible energy source is nuclear fusion.This process has not been fully developed due to the extremely high temperatures which are produced as fusion of atoms takes place.A fusion reactor could use tritium or deuterium (heavy hydrogen) as fuels.These fuels may be found in sea water in large quantities,thus reducing the scarcity of nuclear fuel.It is estimated that there is enough deuterium in the oceans to supply all the energy the world would ever need.

If nuclear-fusion reactors could be used in the production of electrical energy,the process would be similar to the nuclear-fission plants which are now in operation.The only difference would be in the nuclear reaction which takes place to change the circulating water into steam to drive the turbines.The major problem of the nuclear-fusion process is in controlling the high temperatures generated.These are estimated to reach 100 million degrees Fahrenheit.

Another energy source which could be used in the future is the fuel cell.This type of cell converts the chemical energy of fuels into direct-current electrical energy.A fuel cell contains two porous electrodes and an electrolyte.One type of fuel cell operates as hydrogen gas passes through one porous electrode and oxygen gas passes through the other electrode.The chemical reactions of the electrodes with the electrolyte either release electrons to an external circuit or draw electrons from the external circuit,thus producing a current flow.

Still another possible alternative power production system utilizes tidal energy.Tidal systems would use the rise and fall of the water along a coastal area as a source of energy for producing electrical power.Coal gasification is yet another process which could be used for future power systems.This process is used to convert the poorer grades of coal into a gas.The use of oil shale to produce fuel is also being considered.

It should be pointed out that many of the future energy sources are direct-conversion processes.For example,the fuel cell converts chemical energy directly to electrical energy and the solar cell converts light energy directly to electrical energy. A more complex transformation of energy takes place in most power plants today.Heat energy is needed to produce mechanical energy which produces electrical energy.This explains the inefficiency of our present systems of producing electrical energy.Perhaps advances in electrical power technology will bring about new and more efficient methods of producing electrical energy.

Selected from "*Electrical Power Systems Technology, Stephen W.Fardo and Dale R.Patrick, Prentice-Hall, 1985*"

Words and Expressions

1. customer   ['kʌstəmə]   *n.* 用户、顾客
2. kilowatt-hours   千瓦时
3. solar cell   太阳能电池
4. geothermal system   地热系统
5. magnetohydrodynamic system   磁流体系统
6. nuclear-fusion   核聚变
7. fuel cell   燃料电池
8. fossil-fuel   矿物燃料
9. nuclear-fission   核裂变
10. three-phase alternator   三相交流发电机
11. hydraulic turbine   水轮机
12. forecast   ['fɔːkɑːst]   *v.* 预报、预测
13. plant load   工厂负荷
14. capacity factor   容量因子
15. idle   ['aidəl]   *adj.* 闲置的；*n.* 停机
16. deposit   [di'pɔzit]   *v.* 沉积
17. furnish   ['fəːniʃ]   *v.* 提供,供给
18. abundant   [ə'bʌndənt]   *adj.* 丰富的
19. burn   [bəːn]   *v.* 燃烧
20. circulating water   循环水
21. high pressure steam   高压蒸汽
22. electrical generator   发电机
23. boiler   ['bɔilə]   锅炉
24. gasoline   ['gæsəliːn]   *n.* 汽油
25. diesel   ['diːzəl]   *n.* 柴油
26. petroleum   [pi'trəuliəm]   *n.* 石油产品
27. internal combustion engine   内燃机
28. large reservoir   大水库
29. blade   [bleid]   *n.* 叶片,桨叶
30. vane   [vein]   *n.* 叶轮
31. flood control   洪水控制
32. recreation   [rekri'eiʃən]   *n.* 再生
33. irrigation   [iri'geiʃən]   *v.* 灌溉
34. bombardment   [bɔm'bɑːdmənt]   *n.* 辐射,轰击
35. neutron   ['njuːtrɔn]   *n.* 中子
36. gamma ray   γ射线
37. foresee   [fɔː'siː]   *v.* 预见

38. orbiting space system   轨迹空间系统
39. molten   (molt 的过去分词)   [ˈməutən]   熔化的
40. well   [wel]   n. 井
41. drill   [dril]   v. 钻井
42. battery   [ˈbætəri]   n. 电池
43. conductive   [kənˈdʌktiv]   a. 导电的
44. tritium   [ˈtritiəm]   n. 氚, 超重氢 3H
45. deuterium   [djuːˈtiəriəm]   n. 氘, 重氢 2H
46. scarcity   [ˈskɛəsiti]   n. 稀少
47. porous   [ˈpɔːrəs]   a. 多孔的
48. electrolyte   [iˈlektrəlait]   n. 电解液
49. tidal energy   潮汐能
50. oil shale   油页岩

Exercises

1. Complete the notes below with words taken from the text above.

    (1) The great majority of our electrical power____produced____power plants_____throughout our country_____convert the energy produced_____,_____or natural gas,_____of water,_____from nuclear reactions_____electrical energy.

    (2) Various other methods, some of_____are in the experimental stages, _____used as future power production methods.

    (3) Fossil-fuel_____nuclear-fission plants utilize steam turbines_____the mechanical energy needed_____the large three-phase alternators which produce_____of electrical power.

    (4) Electrical energy_____supplied at the same time_____is demanded_____consumers.

    (5) Such fuels contain carbon materials_____are burned_____a result of their reaction air _____oxygen. These fossil fuels_____used_____a direct source of heat_____burned _____a furnace_____are used_____a heat source for steam production_____used _____a power-plant boiler system.

2. Put the following into Chinese:

    electrical power   chemical reaction   mechanical energy   power plant
    nuclear-fission   hydraulic turbine   supply and demand
    peak demand times   plant load and capacity factors   deposits
    Natural-gas-fired system circulating water   high-pressure steam
    flood control   irrigation   coal gasification

3. put the following into English:

    千瓦时   太阳能电池   天然气   地热系统   风力系统
    磁流体系统   核聚变系统   燃料电池   矿物燃料   煤和焦炭
    水轮机   发电机   潮汐系统   油页岩

· 220 ·

Reading Material:

Operational Power Control Systems

Basic Control Systems

Electrical power control systems are used with many types of loads. The most common electrical loads are motors, so our discussion will deal mainly with electric motor control. However, many of the basic control systems are also used to control lighting and heating loads. Generally, the controls for lighting and heating loads are less complex.

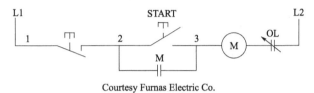

Courtesy Furnas Electric Co.

Figure 5.4.4   A start-stop push-button control circuit with overload protection.

Several power control circuits are summarized in Figure 5.4.4 through 5.4.12. Figure 5.4.4 is a start-stop pushbutton control circuit with overload protection (OL). Notice that the "start" push button is normally open (N.O.) and the "stop" push button is normally closed (N.C.). Single-phase lines L1 and L2 are connected across the control circuit. When the start push button is pushed, a momentary contact is made between points 2 and 3. This causes the N.O. contact (M) to close. A complete circuit between L1 and L2 results that causes the electromagnetic coil Ⓜ to be energized. When the normally closed stop push button is pressed, the circuit between L1 and L2 will open. This causes contact M to open and turn the circuit off.

The circuit B in Figure 5.4.5 is the same type of control as the circuit given in Figure 5.4.4. In the circuit of Figure 5.4.5, the start-stop control of a load can be accomplished from three separate locations. Notice that the start push buttons are connected in parallel and the stop push buttons are connected in series. The control of one load from as many locations as is desired can be accomplished with this type of control circuit.

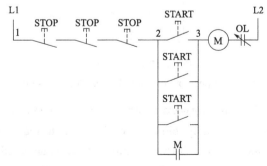

Courtesy Furnas Electric Co.

Figure 5.4.5   A start-stop control circuit with low-voltage protection and control from three locations.

· 221 ·

The next circuit (Figure 5.4.6) is the same as the circuit in Figure 5.4.4 except that a "safe-run" switch is provided.The "safe" position assures that the start push button will not activate the load. A "start-safe" switch circuit often contains a key which the machine operator uses to turn the control circuit on or off.

Figure 5.4.7 is also like the circuit of Figure 5.4.4 but with a "jog-run" switch added in series with the normally open contact (M). In the "run" position,the circuit would operate just like the circuit of Figure 5.4.4.The "jog" position is used so that a complete circuit between L1 and L2 will be achieved and sustained only while the start push button is pressed.With the selector switch in the "jog" position,a motor can be rotated a small amount,at a time,for positioning purposes.*Jogging* or *inching* is defined as the momentary operation of a motor to provide small movements of its shaft.

Courtesy Furnas Electric Co.

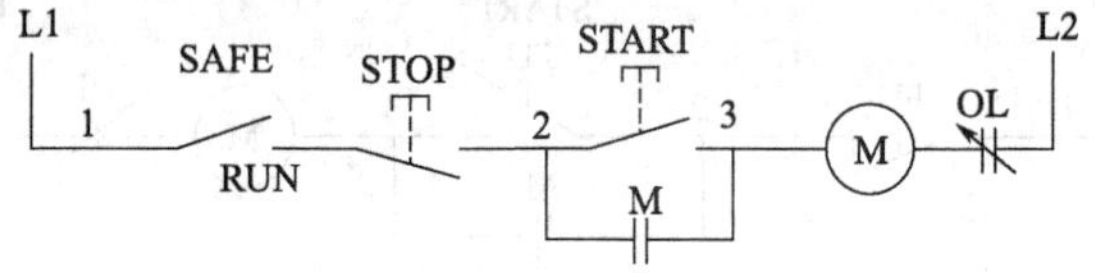

Figure 5.4.6　A start-stop control circuit with a safe-run selector switch.

Courtesy Furnas Electric Co.

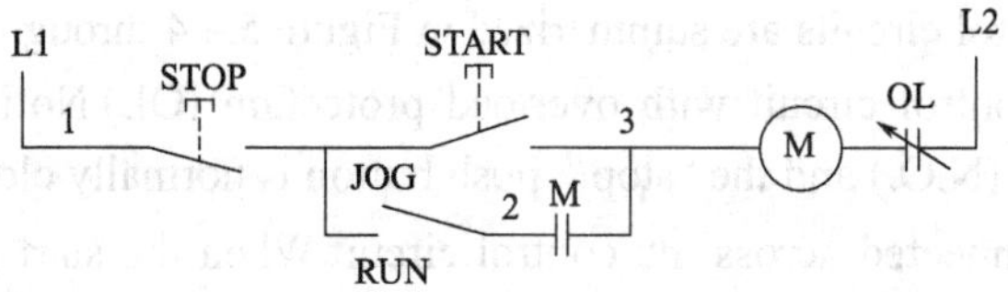

Figure 5.4.7　A start-stop push-button control circuit with a jog-run selector switch.

Figure 5.4.8 shows a circuit that is another method of motor-jogging control.This circuit has a separate push button for jogging which relies upon a normally open contact (CR) to operate.Two control relays are used with this circuit.

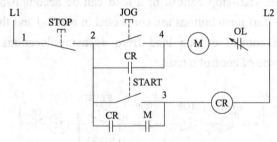

Courtesy Furnas Electric Co.

Figure 5.4.8　A push-button control circuit for start-stop-jogging.

The circuit in Figure 5.4.9 is a forward-reverse push-button control circuit with both forward and reverse limit switches (normally closed switches).When the "forward" push button is pressed,the load will operate until the "forward" limit switch is actuated.The load would,then,be turned off since the circuit from L1 to L2 would be opened.The reverse circuit operates in a similar manner.Two control relays are needed for forward-reverse operation.

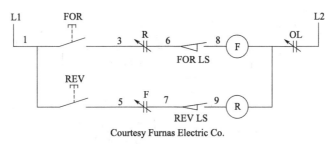

Figure 5.4.9   A forward-reverse push-button control circuit with forward and reverse limit switches.

The circuit of Figure 5.4.10 is the same as the circuit in Figure 5.4.9 except for the push-button arrangement.The forward and reverse push buttons are arranged in sets.Pressing the "forward" push button automatically opens the reverse circuit and pressing the "reverse" push button automatically opens the forward circuit.Limit switches are also used with this circuit.Their function is the same as in the circuit of Figure 5.4.9.In the circuit of Figure 5.4.10,when the "forward" push button is pressed,the top push button will momentarily close and the lower push button will momentarily open.When points 2 and 3 are connected,current will flow from L1 to L2 through coil Ⓕ .When coil Ⓕ is energized,normally open contact F will close and the normally closed contact F will open.The "forward" coil will,then,remain energized.The reverse push buttons cause a similar action of the reversing circuit.Two control relays are also required.

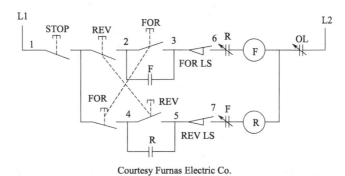

Figure 5.4.10   An instant forward-reverse-stop push-button control circuit.

The circuit of Figure 5.4.11 is similar in function to that of the circuit in Figure 5.4.10.The push-button arrangement of this circuit is simpler.When the normally open forward push button is pressed,current will flow through coil Ⓕ.When the forward control relay is energized,normally open contact F will close and normally closed contact F will open.This action will cause a motor to operate in the forward direction.When the normally closed stop push button is pressed,the current through coil Ⓕ is interrupted.When the normally open reverse push button is pressed,current will flow through coil Ⓡ .When the reverse coil is energized,normally open contact F will close and normally closed contact F will open.This action will cause a motor to operate in the reverse direction,until the stop push button is pressed again.

· 223 ·

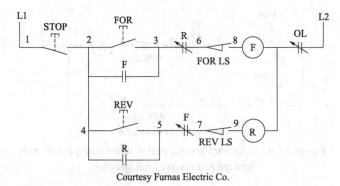

Figure 5.4.11 A forward-reverse-stop push-button control circuit.

Figure 5.4.12 shows a circuit that is another method of forward-reverse-stop control. This control circuit has the added feature of a high-and low-speed selector switch for either the forward or reverse direction. The selector switch is placed in series with the windings of the motor. When the selector is changed from the HIGH position to the LOW position, a modification in the windings of the motor can be made.

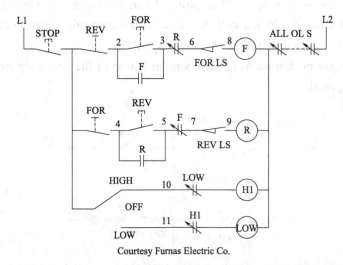

Figure 5.4.12 Push-button control circuit with a high-and low-speed selector switch.

There are many other push-button combinations which can be used with control relays to accomplish motor control or control of other types of loads. The circuits discussed in this section represent some basic power control functions such as start-stop, forward-reverse-stop, jogging and multiple speed control.

Selected from "*Electrical Power Systems Technology, Stephen W. Fardo and Dale R. Patrick, Prentice-Hall, 1985*"

Words and Expressions

1. start-stop pushbutton 启停按钮
2. control circuit 控制电路

3. overload protection (OL)　防超负荷
4. normally open (N.O.)　常开
5. normally closed (N.C.)　常闭
6. contact　[kɔntækt]　*n.* 接触器
7. parallel　[pærəlel]　*adj.* 平行的
8. series　[siəri:z]　*n.* 串联
9. safe-run　安全运行
10. jog-run　精密运行
11. limit switches　限制开关

5.5 Introduction to Industrial Robots

> *After reading the following unit, try to find out the answer for*:
> 1. What is the definition for robots?
> 2. What is the young Rossum says for a working machine?
> 3. What are the main jobs for industrial robots?
> 4. What is the potential by using industrial robots?

Industrial robots became a reality in the early 1960's when Joseph Engelberger and George Devol teamed up to form a robotics company they called "Unimation".

Engelberger and Devol were not the first to dream of machines that could perform the unskilled,repetitive jobs in manufacturing.The first use of the word "robot" was by the Czechoslovakian philosopher and playwright Karel Capek in his play *R.U.R.*(Rossum's Universal Robot).The word "robot" in Czech means "worker" or "slave."The play was written in 1922.

In Capek's play, Rossum and his son discover the chemical formula for artificial protoplasm.Protoplasm forms the very basis of life.With their compound,Rossum and his son set out to make a robot.

Rossum and his son spend 20 years forming the protoplasm into a robot.After 20 years the Rossums look at what they have created and say,"It's absurd to spend twenty years making a man if we can't make him quicker than nature,you might as well shut up shop."

The young Rossum goes back to work eliminating organs he considers unnecessary for the ideal worker.The young Rossum says, "A man is something that feels happy,plays piano,likes going for a walk,and in fact wants to do a whole lot of things that are unnecessary… but a working machine must not play piano,must not feel happy,must not do a whole lot of other things.Everything that doesn't contribute directly to the progress of work should be eliminated."

A half century later,engineers began building Rossum's robot,not out of artificial protoplasm, but of silicon, hydraulics,pneumatics, and electric motors.Robots that were dreamed of by Capek in 1922,that work but do not feel,that perform unhuman or subhuman jobs in manufacturing plants,are available and are in operation around the world.

The modern robot lacks feeling and emotions just as Rossum's son thought it should.It can only respond to simple "yes/no" questions.The modern robot is normally bolted to the floor.It has one arm and one hand.It is deaf,blind,and dumb.In spite of all of these handicaps,the modern robot performs its assigned task hour after hour without boredom or complaint.

A robot is not simply another automated machine.Automation began during the industrial revolution with machines that performed jobs that formerly had been done by human workers.Such a machine,however,can do only the specific job for which it was designed,whereas a robot can perform a variety of jobs.

A robot must have an arm.The arm must be able to duplicate the movements of a human worker in loading and unloading other automated machines,spraying paint,welding,and performing hundreds of other jobs that cannot be easily done with conventional automated machines.

5.5.1 Definition of A Robot

The Robot Industries Association (RIA) has published a definition for robots in an attempt to clarify which machines are simply automated machines and which machines are truly robots.The RIA definition is as follows:

"A robot is a reprogrammable multifunctional manipulator designed to move material,parts,tools,or specialized devices through variable programmed motions for the performance of a variety of tasks."

This definition,which is more extensive than the one in the RIA glossary at the end of this book,is an excellent definition of a robot.We will look at this definition,one phrase at a time,so as to understand which machines are in fact robots and which machines are little more than specialized automation.

First,a robot is a "reprogrammable multifunctional manipulator."In this phrase RIA tells us that a robot can be taught ("reprogrammed") to do more than one job by changing the information stored in its memory.A robot can be reprogrammed to load and unload machines,weld,and do many other jobs ("multifunctional").A robot is a "manipulator".A manipulator is an arm (or hand) that can pick up or move things.At this point we know that a robot is an arm that can be taught to do different jobs.

The definition goes on to say that a robot is "designed to move material,parts,tools,or specialized devices."Material includes wood,steel,plastic,cardboard…anything that is used in the manufacture of a product.

A robot can also handle parts that have been manufactured.For example,a robot can load a piece of steel into an automatic lathe and unload a finished part out of the lathe.

In addition to handling material and parts,a robot can be fitted with tools such as grinders,buffers,screwdrivers,and welding torches to perform useful work.

Robots can also be fitted with specialized instruments or devices to do special jobs in a manufacturing plant.Robots can be fitted with television cameras for inspection of parts or products.They can be fitted with lasers to accurately measure the size of parts being manufactured.

The RIA definition closes with the phrase,"…through variable programmed motions for the performance of a variety of tasks."This phrase emphasizes the fact that a robot can do many different jobs in a manufacturing plant.The variety of jobs that a robot can do is limited only by the creativity of the application engineer.

5.5.2 Jobs for Robots

Jobs performed by robots can be divided into two major categories: hazardous jobs and repetitive jobs.

Hazardous Jobs

Many applications of robots are in jobs that are hazardous to humans.Such jobs may be considered hazardous because of toxic fumes,the weight of the material being handled,the temperature of the material being handled,the danger of working near rotating or press machinery,or environments containing high levels of radiation.

Repetitive Jobs

In addition to taking over hazardous jobs,robots are well suited to doing extremely repetitive jobs that must be done in manufacturing plants.Many jobs in manufacturing plants require a person to act more like a machine than like a human.The job may be to pick a piece up from here and place it there.The same job is done hundreds of times each day.The job requires little or no judgment and little or no skill.This is not said as a criticism of the person who does the job,but is intended simply to point out that many of these jobs exist in industry and must be done to complete the manufacture of products.A robot can be placed at such a work station and can perform the job admirably without complaining or experiencing the fatigue and boredom normally associated with such a job.

Although robots eliminate some jobs in industry,they normally eliminate jobs that humans should never have been asked to do.Machines should perform as machines doing machine jobs,and humans should be placed in jobs that require the use of their ability,creativity,and special skills.

5.5.3 Potential for Increased Productivity

In addition to removing people from jobs they should not have been placed in,robots offer companies the opportunity of achieving increased productivity.When robots are placed in repetitive jobs they continue to operate at their programmed pace without fatigue.Robots do not take either scheduled or unscheduled breaks from the job.The increase in productivity can result in at least 25% more good parts being produced in an eight-hour shift.This increase in productivity increases the company's profits,which can be reinvested in additional plants and equipment.This increase in productivity results in more jobs in other departments in the plant.With more parts being produced,additional people are needed to deliver the raw materials to the plant,to complete the assembly of the finished products,to sell the finished products,and to deliver the products to their destinations.

5.5.4 Robot Speed

Although robots increase productivity in a manufacturing plant,they are not exceptionally fast.At present,robots normally operate at or near the speed of a human operator.Every major move of a robot normally takes approximately one second.For a robot to pick up a piece of steel from a conveyor and load it into a lathe may require ten different moves taking as much as ten seconds.A human operator can do the same job in the same amount of time.The increase in productivity is a result of the consistency of operation.As the human operator repeats the same job over and over during the workday,he or she begins to slow down.The robot continues to operate at its programmed speed and therefore completes more parts during the workday.

Custom-built automated machines can be built to do the same jobs that robots do.An automated machine can do the same loading operation in less than half the time required by a robot or a human operator.The problem with designing a special machine is that such a machine can perform only the specific job for which it was built.If any change is made in the job,the machine must be completely rebuilt,or the machine must be scrapped and a new machine designed and built.A robot,on the other hand,could be reprogrammed and could start doing the new job the same day.

Custom-built automated machines still have their place in industry.If a company knows that a job will not change for many years,the faster custom-built machine is still a good choice.

Other jobs in factories cannot be done easily with custom-built machinery.For these applications a robot may be a good choice.An example of such an application is spray painting.One company made cabinets for the electronics industry.They made cabinets of many different sizes,all of which needed painting.It was determined that it was not economical for the company to build special spray painting machines for each of the different sizes of enclosures that were being built.Until robots were developed,the company had no choice but to spray the various enclosures by hand.

Spray painting is a hazardous job,because the fumes from many paints are both toxic and explosive.A robot is now doing the job of spraying paint on the enclosures.A robot has been "taught" to spray all the different sizes of enclosures that the company builds.In addition,the robot can operate in the toxic environment of the spray booth without any concern for the long-term effect the fumes might have on a person working in the booth.

5.5.5　Flexible Automation

Robots have another advantage: they can be taught to do different jobs in the manufacturing plant.If a robot was originally purchased to load and unload a punch press and the job is no longer needed due to a change in product design,the robot can be moved to another job in the plant.For example,the robot could be moved to the end of the assembly operation and be used to unload the finished enclosures from a conveyor and load them onto a pallet for shipment.

5.5.6　Accuracy and Repeatability

One very important characteristic of any robot is the **accuracy** with which it can perform its task.When the robot is programmed to perform a specific task,it is led to specific points and programmed to remember the locations of those points.After programming has been completed,the robot is switched to "run" and the program is executed.Unfortunately,the robot will not go to the exact location of any programmed point.For example,the robot may miss the exact point by 0.025 in.If 0.025 in.is the greatest error by which the robot misses any point during the first execution of the program,the robot is said to have an accuracy of 0.025 in.

In addition to accuracy,we are also concerned with the robot's **repeatability**.The repeatability of a robot is a measure of how closely it returns to its programmed points every time the program is executed.Say,for example,that the robot misses a programmed point by 0.025 in.the first time the program is executed and that,during the next execution of the program,the robot misses the point it reached during the previous cycle by 0.010 in.Although the robot is a total of 0.035 in.from the original programmed point,its accuracy is 0.025 in.and its repeatability is 0.010 in.

5.5.7　The Major Parts of A Robot

The major parts of a robot are the **manipulator**,the **power supply**,and the **controller**.

The manipulator is used to pick up material,parts,or special tools used in manufacturing.The power supply supplies the power to move the manipulator.The controller controls the power supply so that the manipulator can be taught to perform its task.

Words and Expressions

1. robot　['roubɔt]　n. 机器人
2. team up　合作
3. playwright　剧作家
4. protoplasm　['prəutəuplæz(ə)m]　n. 细胞质
5. emotion　[i'məuʃ(ə)n]　n. 情绪
6. bolt　[boult]　n. 螺栓; v. 用螺检固定
7. deaf　[def]　adj. 聋的
8. blind　[blaind]　adj. 瞎的
9. dumb　[dʌm]　adj. 哑的
10. handicap　[hændikæp]　n. 障碍物
11. boredom　[bɔ:dəm]　n. 讨厌, 厌烦
12. complaint　[kəm'pleint]　n. 意见, 怨言
13. glossary　[glɔsəri]　n. 词汇
14. reprogrammable　重复可编程序
15. cardboard　[kɑ:dbɔ:d]　n. 卡片
16. lathe　[leið]　n. 车床
17. grinder　['graində]　n. 磨床
18. hazardous job　有害工作
19. repetitive job　重复工作
20. toxic fumes　有毒烟气
21. admirably　adj. 极佳的
22. fatigue　[fə'ti:g]　n.v. 疲劳
23. reinvest　[ri:in'vest]　v. 再投资
24. conveyor　[kʌn'veiə]　n. 传送机器
25. spray painting　喷涂, 喷漆
26. punch　[pʌntʃ]　n. 打眼, 冲孔
27. fume　[fju:m]　n. 烟雾, 气体
28. shut up　关闭
29. pace　[peisi]　n. 步调, 速度

30. pallet ['pælit] n. 货架

Exercises

1. *complete the notes below with words taken from the text above.*

(1) A half century later, engineers began building Rossum's robot, not_____artificial protoplasm,_____silicon, hydraulics, pneumatics, and electric motors.

(2) We will look at this definition, one phrase at a time,_____to understand_____machines are in fact robots_____machines are little_____specialized automation.

(3) _____robots eliminate some jobs_____, they normally eliminate jobs_____humans should _____have_____asked to do.

(4) _____to removing people from jobs they_____have_____placed in, robots offer companies the opportunity_____.

2. *Put the following into Chinese:*

industrial robots	artificial protoplasm	manufacturing plants
reprogrammable	multifunctional manipulator	RIA
hazardous jobs	repetitive jobs	rotating or press machinery
robot speed	flexible automation	accuracy and repeatability

3. *put the following into English:*

机器人 剧作家 感觉 情绪 抱怨 增加产率 装货 卸货 移动机器 执行器

Reading Material:

Walking Machine Technology-Designing the Control System of an Advanced Six-Legged Machine

A.Halme and K.Hartikainen

In this chapter design aspects and experiences on walking machines are summarised and critically analysed.Experiences are based on designing the MECANT Ⅰ-machine which is a research and development test-bed for work machine applications in an outdoor environment.Considerations are focused to the mechatronics of the machine and especially to the control system.The control system is based on two level hierarchy and distributed control philosophy which follow the canonical layout Differences between the requirements of engineering design and what nature has realised in animals are considered.

1. Introduction

Legs offer some distinct advantages for vehicles operating in difficult terrain like natural ground or environments designed primarily for man,like buildings with stairs Legs provide more degrees of freedom,which makes the vehicle more flexible in motion and stabilising easier on uneven surfaces.Constructing a successful walking machine,however,is a challenging project and requires special mechanical design knowledge and an extensive on-board computer and software system to provide necessary motion control properties for the machine.Prototype walking machines have been developed this far mainly for research purposes in Japan and USA (some active groups exist also in'Russia).In Europe the research activity has been relatively long until recently.There have been no real commercial successes in making walking machine products so far,although a couple of developments in USA and Japan have been marketed as product prototypes (Odetics,Toshiba).MECANT Ⅰ,shown in Figure 5.5.1,has been developed in the Helsinki University of Technology in a national technology programme on outdoor robotics.It is a research walking machine which probably one of the most advanced presently existing and one of the few which carries all its control and power systems on board.It has been designed as an outdoor test vehicle to study work machine applications in natural environments,like forests.The basic design principles,system structures and the main properties of the machine have been described earlier in ［1］.The details of the motion control principles have been reported in ［2］.The purpose of this is to explain in more detail the hardway and software structure of MECANT and discuss related aspects based on the experiences gained after getting the machine ready and testing it in different conditions. Both structures follow the quite natural distributed philosophy existing in walking machines.

Figure 5.5.1　MECANT I.

2. MECANT

MECANT is a fully independent hydraulically powered six-legged insect type walking machine. It weighs about 1100 kg and its main geometrical dimensions are illustrated in Figure 5.5.2. The legs are all identical,rotating pantograph mechanisms with 3 dof in each. The body is constructed from rectangular aluminium tubes forming a rigid light structure. All components. except the hydraulic cylinders actuating the legs,are commercial ones. The vehicle is controlled remotely via the radio link by the operator using two joysticks.

The motion can be controlled omnidirectionally. The body of the machine is controllable like a free object in the space having all the 6 dof available within the kinematic limits. The leg working volumes overlap both sides of the body making climbing over obstacles possible.

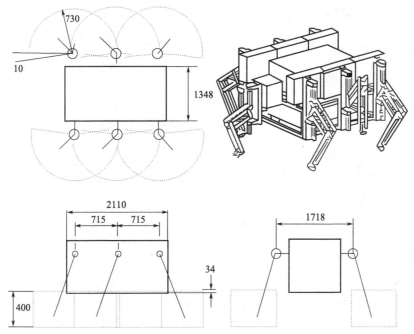

Figure 5.5.2 The mechanical design of MECANT I and its main geometrical dimensions.

Energy, power transmission and actuation systems

MECANT has a fully self-sufficient energy system. The power is generated by a 38kW 2-cylinder ultralight aeroplane engine with air cooling. The hydraulic system is a traditional one including valve-controlled flow system with central pump, oil reservoir and pressure accumulator. the work pressure being about 300 bar. The high speed gas engine is controlled with a fast analogue rpm-controller to adapt to the system load variations. The energy efficiency of the power system is not very high. but the structure is simple and light.

The actuation system in each leg consists of two cylinders and a motor. The cylinders are tailored with bending stress capability and integrated potentiometric position measurement. The hydraulic motor is a commercial one with potentiometric position measurement. All actuators are controlled with proportional valves.

The machine electrical system is a 24V system consisting of a 1.5kW generator. battery backup and stabilised DC-power source giving the different voltage levels needed by the electronics through DC/DC converters.

3. Control Hardware Design

The main principle of the control hardware design has been the use of commercial low-cost components. Another important criterion when selecting the control system hardware was effective software development and testing support. The PC technology offers both the features desired and was thus selected. The availability of real time networking hardware and a supporting commercial operating system gave the opportunity for a modular and distributed control system design with effective software development environment. The control system of MECANT is pictured in Figure 5.5.3.

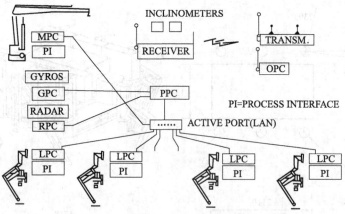

Figure 5.5.3　The control system of MECANT I.

Computer system

The computer system of MECANT is built of seven Intel X86 processors (PC-busboards)connected together with high-speed token-ring network(Arcnet,1 Mbit/s). The computer system configuration supports hierarchical control of the vehicle motion which is the implementation of the supervisory scheme described in reference [1]. According to that scheme the computers are divided into a pilot computer (Intel486/33MHz)and six leg computers (Intel286/16MHz).

The pilot computer assembly can be seen in Figure 5.5.4. The pilot computer has a configuration of an ordinary bus PC. The computer acts as a server computer in the network,i.e.the operating system and control software are loaded into the network from the pilot computer. It also includes a flat panel display(DC-voltage operated)and a PC/AT keyboard for system operation and software development purposes. The pilot computer has a hard disk data storage capacity of 120MBytes.

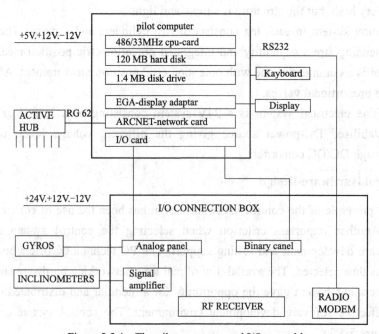

Figure 5.5.4　The pilot computer and I/O assembly.

The leg computer configuration can be seen in Figure 5.5.5. The operating system and the control software are loaded via the computer network. Both the pilot (RAM)each. This is used for on-line data logging purposes.

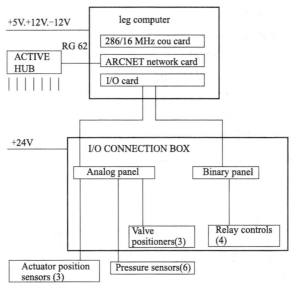

Figure 5.5.5 The leg computer and I/O assembly.

I/O system

The I/O system is distributed between the pilot and leg computers depending on the control responsibilities of the computers according to the supervisory control scheme. The pilot I/O system can be seen in Figure 5.5.4. The pilot computer is responsible for vehicle body motion control,thus pilot computer I/O data include portable operator interface signals and body inclination sensor signals. All leg sensor data are available via computer network at 40 ms intervals. The leg computer I/O system configuration is shown in Figure 5.5.5. The leg computer is responsible for leg motion control. Separate I/O connection boxes are used to make connection modification and maintenance easy. The connection boxes include the I/O interface hardware: isolated analogue and binary output/input panels. In addition the connection box of the pilot computer includes RF receiver,RF modem and inclinometer signal processing electronics and that of the leg computer servo valve positioner electronics.

Minimum sensor configuration implemented into MECANT includes inclinometers,hydraulic actuator pressure and position sensors. Inclinometers are used to measure body attitude,i.e. roll and pitch angle. They are standard oli damped pendulums with LVDT-position sensors. Filtering of the inclinometer signal is necessary in order to remove the high frequency component created by feet stepping cycles. Leg motion control is executed according to actuator position or pressure difference feedback. Potentiometers are used as actuator position sensors which are accurate enough for leg servo purposes. Leg ground contacts and collisions can be detected from hydraulic circuits by pressure sensors. They are also used for actuator force control with limited accuracy.

Selected from "*Advanced Robotics & Intelligent Machines, Edited by J.O.Gray & D.G.Caldwell,Institution of*

Words

1. six-legged machine 六腿机器
2. walking machine 行走机器
3. hierarchy ['haiərɑːki] adj. 分层的
4. canonical [kə'nɔnikəl] adj. 典型的，标准的
5. terrain [te'rein] n. 地带，领域
6. uneven [ʌn'iːvən] adj. 不平的
7. on-board computer 板上计算机
8. prototype [prəutəutaip] n. 原型、样机
9. outdoor robotics 室外机器人
10. design principle 设计原理
11. insect [insekt] n. 昆虫
12. pantograph ['pæntəgrɑːf] n. 比例绘图仪，放大尺，缩放
13. cylinder [silində] n. 汽缸，液压缸
14. radio link 无线电联系
15. joysticks ['dʒɔistik] n. 操纵杆、手柄
16. omnidirectional [ˌɔmnidi'rekʃənəl] adj. 全方位的(全向的)
17. kinematic [kaini'mætik] adj. 运动的，动力学的
18. obstacles ['ɔbstəkəl] n. 障碍物
19. ultralight [ʌltrə'lait] adj. 超轻型
20. potentiometric adj. 电势的，电位的
21. development environment 开发环境
22. token-ring network 令牌网
23. volatile ['vɔlətail] adj. 短暂的
24. volatile memory storage 暂存存储器
25. portable ['pɔːtəbəl] adj. 手提式的
26. inclination [inkli'neiʃən] n. 倾斜角(度)
27. inclinometer [ˌinkli'nɔmitə] n. 倾斜仪
28. pendulum ['pendjuləm] n. 摆动
29. collisions [kə'liʒən] n. 抵触，振动，颠簸

CHAPTER 6 ARTIFICIAL INTELLIGENCE TECHNIQUES AND APPLICATIONS

6.1 Artificial Intelligence Techniques

> *After reading the following unit, try to find out the answer for:*
> 1. List the three AI methods in process control research.
> 2. Describe the applications of expert systems.
> 3. Give some application examples of neural networks.
> 4. Outline the applications of fuzzy control in consumer products.

In recent years there has been intense interest in developing artificial intelligence (AI) techniques for a wide variety of scientific and engineering applications. A comprehensive survey paper provides a thorough review of intelligent systems in process engineering and contains 385 references. The process control research in this area has largely been concerned with three AI methods: knowledge-based systems, neural networks and fuzzy logic.

6.1.1 Knowledge-Based Systems

Knowledge-based systems (KBS), also referred to as expert systems. use a set of 'rules' to perform logical inferences about the state of a process operation or some other activity of interest[①]. An early and highly visible demonstration project, the FALCON project, was a collaborative effort between Du Pont. Foxboro, and the University of Delaware during the period, 1983—1987. The objective was to develop and apply knowledge-based methods for fault diagnosis in a full-scale chemical plant, an adipic acid converter. Although this pioneering project was judged to be only a partial success, it paved the way for many future Du Pont KBS applications.

Stephanopoulos and Han note that industrial applications of KBS systems have largely been concerned with either diagnostic and monitoring activities or supervisory control. Supervisory control applications have included the following problems: complex control schemes; recovery from extreme conditions; and emergency shutdowns. They also describe a number of industrial KBS applications.

A recent trade journal article by Samdani and Fouhy provides an overview of KBS applications in the process industries. They report that "…Du Pont has well quantified the benefits it is reaping from the thousand or so KBS's it has in place". In the same issue, Samdani report that, "… [Du Pont] says that there are about 20,000 more areas of applications yet to be tapped. For every dollar spent in implementing a KBS for process control, the payoff is from six to ten dollars per year".

Future applications of expert systems will be facilitated by real-time KBS which enable the user to integrate plant data and process models in an expert system shell which has a sophisticated graphical interface[2]. This combination provides a powerful vehicle for on-line process monitoring, especially diagnostics and fault detection. At the present time, the most widely used system in the G2 product from the GENSYM Corporation (Cambridge, MA). It has been reported that over 1000 G2 systems have been installed worldwide. In a recent application at a Monsanto-Krummich plant in Illinois, a G2 system provided the framework for a sensor and control loop validation system for over 600 measurement points. The diagnostic system was able to successfully identify a variety of actual faults and is being modified for use in other plants.

The early enthusiasm for KBS has been tempered by the realization that a considerable effort is required to codify the available expertise. Furthermore, if each potential application has a significant number of unique features, it is less feasible to spread the development costs over a large number of projects. Despite this inherent problem, the industrial employment of KBS for applications such as process diagnosis and supervisory control is significant and growing at an impressive rate.

6.1.2 Neural Networks

Neural networks provide a powerful approach for developing empirical nonlinear models for a wide variety of physical phenomena. In the area of process control, they have been used for a variety of traditional activities, such as developing nonlinear dynamic models and control system design. Neural networks also provide a promising approach for pattern recognition problems such as sensor data analysis and fault detection where traditional modeling techniques are not easily applied.

Standard neural network models consist of three layer networks with sigmoidal functions[3] used as the 'activation function' for each neuron in the hidden layer. However, networks which consist of linear combinations of *radial basis functions* offer significant theoretical and computational advantages over the standard neural networks.Furthermore, *a priori* physical information such as known steady-state relations and some types of constrains can easily be incorporated into the otherwise empirical models.

The commercial availability of neural network software for use by non-specialists should continue the current widespread interest in neural network applications for process control. However, at the present time it is difficult to assess the extent to which process control applications of neural networks are being used in industry.

6.1.3 Fuzzy Control Systems

Fuzzy logic provides a conceptual framework for practical problems where some process variables are represented as 'linguistic variables' which have only a few possible values (e.g. very large, large, normal, small etc.). The linguistic variables can then be processed a set of rules. Thus applications of fuzzy logic and fuzzy control can be viewed as special cases of KBS which have fuzzy boundaries for the rules.

Unlike more general KBS and neural nets, fuzzy control strategies have appeared in the control literature for over 20 years. Early process control applications consisted of demonstrations that fuzzy control could be used to control simple laboratory apparatus. In recent years, the success of fuzzy control in Japan, especially in consumer products such as washing machines and camcorders, has generated a new wave of interest. Industrial applications of fuzzy control to process control problems have begun to appear more frequently in Japan and Europe than in the U.S. But even in Japan, a survey has indicated that MPC has been more widely used in the process industries than any of the three AI techniques considered in this section (Yamamoto and Hashimoto 1991).

There has been considerable controversy concerning fuzzy controllers and their relative merits viz. conventional control and model-based control. One of the reasons for this controversy is that there is no theoretical framework for analysing the closed-loop properties of fuzzy control systems. As Stephanopoulos and Han aptly note, 'Using fuzzy controllers takes a lot of testing and/or faith.'

A recent trade journal article provides an overview of fuzzy logic applications in the U.S.. It states, 'Although FL has yet to prove its worth to most ［process］ engineers, particularly in the U.S., vendors believe that it is here to stay, and are steadily commercializing FL-based products.' They report that more than 10,000 FL-embedded PIC controllers have been sold by the Yokogawa Corp. of America. These controllers use FL for auto-tuning. On the other hand, a recent survey of FL applications in engineering cited only a few control applications outside of Japan. Stephanopoulos and Han describe a number of industrial applications of fuzzy control, primarily at the supervisory control level.

Regrettably, a high degree of 'hype' was associated with the initial introduction of these three AI technologies and consequently, early expectations were not always fulfilled. But it is important to keep in mind that these are new approaches for process control and that software still tends to be 'first generation'. As the technology and available software continues to improve, widespread industrial applications are quite likely. Also, the individual AI techniques can be combined to good advantage, for example, by embedding neural networks and fuzzy logic in knowledge-based systems. In particular, neural networks have been proposed for the preliminary screening of data that are analysed further by expert systems in diagnostic and monitoring applications.

Selected from "*A perspective on advanced strategies for process control, Modelling Identification and Control, D.E. Seborg,* 1994"

Words and Expressions

1. neural   ['njurəl]   *adj.* 神经的，神经系统的
2. fuzzy   ['fʌzi]   *adj.* 失真的，模糊的
3. demonstration   ['demən'streiʃən]   *n.* 示范，实证
4. collaborative   [kə'læbərətiv]   *adj.* 合作的
5. diagnosis   ['daiəg'nəusis]   *n.* 诊断

6. adipic acid　　己二酸
7. diagnostic　　[daiəg'nɔstik]　　adj. 诊断的, 特征的; n. 诊断
8. graphical　　['græfikəl]　　adj. 绘图似的, 图解的
9. validation　　[væli'deiʃən]　　n. 确认
10. codify　　['kɔdifai]　　vt. 编成法典, 使法律成文化
11. pattern recognition　　模式识别
12. radial basis functions　　径向基函数
13. sigmoidal　　['sigmɔidl]　　adj. S 字形的, C 字形的
14. neuron　　['njuərɔn]　　n. 神经单位
15. linguistic variable　　语言变量
16. camcorder　　['kʌmkɔːdə]　　n. 可携式摄像机
17. controversy　　['kɔntrəvəːsi]　　n. 争论, 辩论
18. viz　　[viz]　　adv. 也就是, 即
19. commercialize　　[kəˈməːʃəlaiz]　　vt. 使商业化
20. embed　　[im'bed]　　v. 嵌入
21. cite　　[sait]　　v. 引用, 例证
22. hype　　[haip]　　n. 皮下注射, 欺骗, 骗局
23. preliminary　　[pri'liminəri]　　adj. 初步的; n. 初步行动

Notes

① 此句的主体结构是: "Knowledge-based systems (主语) ... use (谓语) a set of 'rules' (宾语) "to perform..."。其中"also referred to ... systems," 是插入语, 补充说明主语。

② enable the user to ...: 使用户有能力做到……;
real-time KBS: 实时知识库系统;
sophisticated graphical interface: 改进了的图像界面实时知识库是专家系统中的一个提高性的软件系统技术。它设置了一个专家系统辅助软件系统。用户可以将来自全厂的数据和过程模型集中到系统中,并通过方便的专用界面来调用、操作和显示。

③ sigmoidal function: sigmid 函数,它是描述一个神经元的总输入与输出之间关系的若干种推荐的函数 (统称为活化函数) 中的一种。其自变量范围是(-∞,+∞), 函数值范围是(0,1),具有连续性。

Exercises

1. *Complete the notes below with words taken from the text above.*

   (1) _____ there has been intense interest in developing artificial intelligence (AI) techniques for a wide variety of _____ applications. A comprehensive survey paper (Stephanopoulos and Han 1994) provides _____ of intelligent systems_____ and contains 385 references. The process control research in this area has _____ concerned _____ three AI methods: _____, _____, _____.

   (2) knowledge-based systems (KBS), also _____ as _____, use a set of 'rules' to perform _____ about the state of a process operation or some

other activity of interest.

(3) _____ provide a powerful approach for developing empirical nonlinear models for _____ of physical phenomena. In the area of process control, they _____ been _____ a variety of traditional activities, _____ developing nonlinear dynamic models and control system design. Neural networks _____ provide a promising approach for _____ problems _____ sensor data analysis _____ fault detection _____ traditional modeling techniques are not easily applied.

(4) Fuzzy logic provides a conceptual _____ for practical problems_____ _____ some process variables are represented _____ linguistic variables _____ have only a few possible values (e.g. very large, large, normal, small etc.). The linguistic variables _____ then _____ processed using _____ of rules. Thus applications of _____ and _____ can _____ viewed _____ special cases of KBS _____ have fuzzy boundaries for the _____.

2. *Put the following into Chinese:*

knowledge based system	neural network	fuzzy logic
logical inference	rule	fault diagnosis
recovery from extreme conditions	emergency shutdown	expert system shell
radial basis function	framework	
intelligent supervisory control	plant wide automation	recipe

3. *Put the following into English:*

人工智能技术	专家系统	故障检测	模式识别
经验模型	洗衣机	柔性	目标
报警管理策略	瓶颈		

6.2 Use Neural Networks for Problem Solving

> *During reading the following unit, you should know:*
> 1. What is a neural network definition?
> 2. How work for neural networks?
> 3. What is the learning process for a neural network?
> 4. The structure and principle of typical back-propagation network.

6.2.1 What Is A Neural Network

Robert Hecht-Nielsen defined a neural network as: "...a computing system made up of a number of simple, highly interconnected processing elements, which process information by its dynamic state response to external inputs".

To put that definition into perspective, consider a serial computer, which is a single central processor that can address data and instructions stored in memory locations. The processor fetches an instruction and any data required by that instruction and saves the results at a specific memory location. In other words, everything happens in a deterministic sequence of operations. In contrast, a neural network is neither sequential nor even necessarily deterministic. It is composed of many simple processing elements that usually do little more than take a weighted sum of all their inputs. Instead of executing a series of instructions, a neural network responds—in parallel—to the inputs given to it. The final result consists of an overall state of the network after it has reached a steady-state condition, which correlates patterns between the sets of input data and corresponding output or target values. The final network can be used to predict outcomes from new input data.

6.2.2 How Neural Networks Work

Neural network technology came from current studies of mammalian brains, particularly the cerebral cortex. Neural networks mimic the way that a human brain copes with an incomplete and confusing information set. Consider how a child learns to identify shapes and colors using a toy consisting of different solid shapes (triangles, squares,circles,and so on) and colors that can be inserted into a box only through correspondingly shaped holes and colors. The child learns about shapes and colors by repeatedly trying to fit the solid objects through these holes by rial-and-error attempts. Eventually, the shapes and colors are recognized, and the child is able to match the objects with the holes by visual inspection. Similarly, neural networks learn by repeatedly trying to match the sets of input data to the corresponding output target values. After a sufficient number of learning iterations, the network creates an internal model that can be used to predict for new input conditions. Just as the child eventually learns to identify shapes and colors, the neural network recognizes the correlative patterns between the inputs and outputs for the corresponding process.

Learning in neural networks can be supervised or unsupervised. Supervised learning means that the network has some information present during learning (training) to tell what the correct answer should be. The network then has a way to find whether or not its input was correct and knows how to apply its particular learning law to adjust itself. This is analogous to the child's learning process in recognizing the shapes and colors of different objects. In contrast, unsupervised learning means that the network has no such knowledge of the correct answer and thus cannot know exactly what the correct output should be. Consider, for instance, how a baby learns to focus its eyes. This skill is not known to newborns. but they acquire it soon after birth. Within a few days, the baby has learned with little or no outside help to associate sets of visual stimuli with objects and shapes. Unsupervised neural networks operate analogously by learning with little or no information about the correct answer for an input pattern.

Although both kinds of learning are important for different applications, for almost all chemical engineering problems supervised learning is sufficient.

Neural networks can learn complex nonlinear relationships even when the input information is noisy and imprecise. Neural networks have made strong advances in the areas of continuous speech recognition and synthesis, pattern recognition, classification of noisy data, nonlinear feature detection, market forecasting, and process modeling. These abilities make the neural network technology very well suited for solving problems in the chemical process industries (CPI).

6.2.3 The Learning Process

A neural network is made up of several interconnected processing elements or neurons, as illustrated in Figure 6.2.1. Each processing element receives a number of inputs X_i, which are assigned weights W_i. From the weighted total input, the processing element computes a single output signal Y. The following four steps, shown in Figure 6.2.2, take place when each neuron is activated or processed:

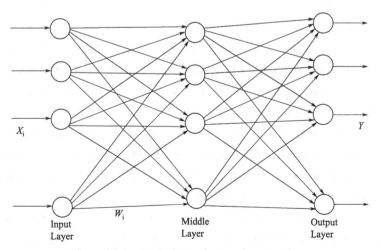

Figure 6.2.1 Typical neural network connections.

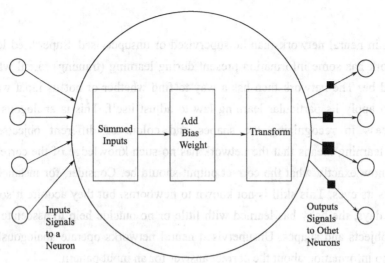

Figure 6.2.2 Processing steps inside a neuron.

① Various signals (inputs of the neuron X_i) are received from other neurons.

② A weighted sum of these signals is calculated.

③ The calculated sum is transformed by a function—that normally, although not always, is fixed for a given neuron at the time the network is constructed.

④ The transformed result (output signal of neuron Y) is sent to other neurons.

What is a learning process in a neuron? Learning implies that the neuron somehow changes its input/output behavior in response to the environment. Because the transfer function usually is fixed, the only way the output from a neuron can be changed due to the input environment is by changing the input weights to the neuron[①]. Thus, the neurons in the network learn by changing the weights on the inputs, and the internal model of the network is embodied in the set of all these weights. Although there are several neural network configurations possible, a particular one known as "back-propagation network" is widely used for chemical engineering applications.

6.2.4 The Back-propagation Network

Back-propagation networks always consist of at least three hierarchical layers of neurons, an input layer, a middle layer (sometimes referred to as a hidden layer), and an output layer. The network is constructed in such a way that each layer is fully connected to the next layer. In other words. every neuron in the input layer will send its output to every neuron in the middle layer, and every neuron in the middle layer will send its output to every neuron in the output layer. The number of neurons in the middle layer can be varied based on the complexity of the problem and the size of the input information. For a given number of inputs, however, if the middle layer is too large, it may not be possible to develop a usable pattern. On the other hand, a middle layer that is too small will drastically extend the number of iterations required to train the network.

*Forward output flow.*In a back-propagation network,a randomized set of weights on the interconnections is used to present the first pattern to the network. The input layer receives the pattern and passes it along to each neuron in the middle layer. Each neuron computes an output signal or activation in the following way. First,the summed output, I_j , is determined by multiplying each input signal times the random weight on that interconnection:

$$I_j = \sum_i W_{i,j-1} X_{i,j-1} + B_j \qquad (6.2.1)$$

This weighted sum is transformed using a function $f(X)$ called the activation function of the neuron. It determines the activity generated in the neuron as a result of an input signal of a particular size. For a back-propagation network and for most chemical engineering applications, the function is a sigmoidal function. A sigmoidal function, as shown in Figure 6.2.3, is continuous, S-shaped, monotonically increasing, and asymptotically approaches fixed values as the input approaches $\pm \infty$. Generally the upper limit of the sigmoid is set to +1 and the lower limit to either 0 or −1. The steepness of the curve and even the exact function used to compute it are less important than the general S-shape. The characteristics of the curve do affect the individual neuron's activity, but the overall network will work well regardless.

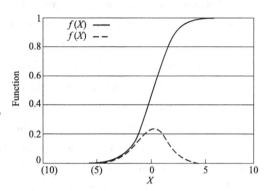

Figure 6.2.3 Sigmoidal function.

The following sigmoidal curve expressed as a function of I_j, the weighted input to the neuron, is widely used:

$$X_j = f(I_j) = 1/[1 + e^{-(I_j + T)}] \qquad (6.2.2)$$

where T is a simple threshold, and X is the input. This transformed input signal becomes the total activation of the middle layer neurons, which, in turn, is used for their output. Following through the network, these outputs are treated as inputs to the output layer. An activation is computed for each output layer neuro using the signals from the middle layer and the sigmoidal function. These activations become output for the network.

Backward error propagation. The computed output from the forward activation is compared to the desired or target output values. Their difference (or error) becomes the basis for modifying the weights: it usually takes several iterations to match the output target values. The principle behind the most widely used back-propagation method is the "delta rule." It iteratively minimizes the average squared error between values of the output neuron and the correct target output values. This is done by first calculating the error gradient δ_j for each neuron on the output layer:

$$\delta_j = X_j (1 - X_j)(T_j - X_j) \qquad (6.2.3)$$

where T_j is the correct target value for output neuron j. the error gradient then is determined for the hidden layers by calculating the weighted sum of error at the previous layer:

$$\delta_j = X_j (1 - X_j) \sum_k \delta_k W_{kj} \qquad (6.2.4)$$

where k is the neuron in the previous layer. Thus the errors are propagated backward one layer. The same procedure is applied recursively until the input layer is reached. This process of back propagating the errors is known as backward error flow. These error gradients are then used to update the network weights:

$$\Delta W_{ji}(n) = \beta \delta_j X_i \qquad (6.2.5)$$

and
$$W_{ji}(n+1) = W_{ji}(n) + \Delta W_{ji}(n) \qquad (6.2.6)$$

where n indexes the iteration number during training and β is the learning rate, which provides the step size during the gradient descent search. Usually a momentum term, which determines the effect of previous weight changes on present changes, in weight space, is included to improve the convergence. The weight change after the nth iteration is:
$$\Delta W_{ji}(n) = \beta \delta_j X_i + \alpha \Delta W_{ji}(n-1) \qquad (6.2.7)$$
where α is a momentum term having a value between 0 and 1.

Thus, back propagation is a gradient descent algorithm that tries to minimize the average squared error of the network by moving down the gradient of the error curve. In a simple system, the error curve is a paraboloid, or bowl-shaped curve, and the network eventually gets to the bottom of the bowl. In real chemical engineering applications, however, the networks is not a simple one-dimensional system, and the error curve is not a smooth bowl-shaped one but, instead, a highly complex, multidimensional, somewhat bowlshaped curve with various valleys and hills. As a result, training the network to find that lowest point becomes more difficult and challenging. There are, as we will now discuss, techniques that are useful in modeling with neural networks for chemical engineering applications.

6.2.5 Training Techniques

Training the neural network to find the lowest point on the complex bowl-shaped error curve often can be made easier by using some combination of the following techniques.

Reinitialize the weights. One way to find the global minimum on the error curve is to start the learning again with a different set of initial weights. This can be achieved by randomly generating the initial set of weights each time the network is made to learn again. Sometimes, if the new starting point is far from the original set of weights, the network moves to a new minimum on the error surface. As a result, the network moves rapidly towards the global minimum.

Add step change to the weights. Sometimes, the network keeps oscillating around a set of weights due to lack of improvement in the error. At this point, all it needs is a slight push to get back on track. This can be achieved by randomly moving the weights to a new position — but not to far from its current one — on the error surface. One way to move the weights is to vary each weight by adding about 10% of the range of the oscillating weights.

Avoid overparameterization. It is very easy to make the mistake of learning with too many neurons in the hidden layer. This causes overparameterization of the model, which then gives poor predictions. One way to avoid this is to design the network with reasonable limits. In general, the number of hidden layer neurons can be determined by the number of learning patterns (cases). Experimenting, however, with a different number of hidden neurons will lead to the correct number.

Change the momentum term. This is the easiest thing to do on any commercial or in-house software. The momentum term α is implemented by adding a fraction of the last weight change to the next set of weights. There are some algorithms that can change the level of this momentum based on the error involved. But, once again, experimenting with different levels will lead to the optimum very rapidly.

Avoid repeated or less noisy data. Repeated or less noisy information makes the network memorize the patterns rather than generalizing their features. Memorization usually implies that the network has only one neuron responding to a particular input pattern. If the network never sees exactly the same input pattern more than once, it has a minimum risk of memorization. This can also be achieved by adding some noise to the training set.

Change the learning tolerance. During training, the learning process stops when the error for all the cases falls below the learning tolerance. If the learning tolerance is too small, the learning process never stops. Therefore, always start with a higher tolerance level and monitor the weight changes with decreasing tolerance levels. By experimenting this way, one can find the tolerance level where there is no significant change in weights anymore.

Increase the hidden layer size. If all fails, increase the number of neurons in the hidden layer to improve the model. In general, a 10% increment does not substantially increase the learning time. Sometimes, this technique in combination with the above techniques can result in an improvement in performance.

Selected form "*Use Neural Networks for Problem Solving*", Chemical Engineering Progress, S.P.Chitra, April, 1993"

Words and Expressions

1. propagation ['prɔpə'geiʃən] *n.* 增殖, 繁殖
2. correlate ['kɔrileit] *n.* 相关物; *v.* 使联系
3. mammalian [mæ'meiljən] *adj.* 哺乳动物的; *n.* 哺乳动物
4. cerebral ['serəbrəl] *adj.* 脑的
5. cortex ['kɔ:teks] *n.* 外皮
6. iteration [itə'reiʃən] *n.* 重复, 反复, 迭代
7. hierarchical [haiərɑ:kikəl] *adj.* 等级的
8. newborn ['nju:bɔ:n] *n.* 婴儿; *adj.* 新生的
9. synthesis ['sinθisis] *n.* 综合, 组织
10. monotonic [,mɔnə'tɔnik] *adj.* 单调的
11. asymptote ['æsimptout] *n.* 渐近线
12. threshold ['θreʃhəuld] *n.* 门槛, 入口, 阀
13. iterative ['itərətiv] *adj.* 重复的, 反复的
14. gradient ['greidjənt] *n.* 倾斜度; *adj.* 倾斜的
15. recursively [ri'kə:sivli] *adv.* 回归地, 递归地
16. descent [di'sent] *n.* 降落, 家系
17. momentum [məu'mentəm] *n.* 动力, 要素
18. convergence [kən'və:dʒəns] *n.* 集中, 收敛
19. algorithm ['ælgəriðm] *n.* 运算法则
20. paraboloid [pə'ræbəlɔid] *n.* 抛物面

21. onedimentional [ˈwʌndiˈmenʃənəl] adj. 一维的
22. multidimentional [ˈmʌltidiˈmenʃənəl] adj. 多维的
23. reinitialize [riːiˈniʃəlaiz] vt. 重新初始化
24. oscillate [ˈɔsileit] v. 振动，使振动

Note

① " the only way ... to the neuron. ": 神经元输出随环境而变的唯一方式是改变神经元的输入权值。

Exercises

1. *Complete the notes below with words taken from the text above.*

    (1) neural network technology _____ current studies of _____ , particularly the cerebral cortex. Neural networks mimic the way _____ a human brain _____ with an incomplete and confusing _____.

    (2) _____ in neural networks can be supervised _____ unsupervised. Supervised learning means _____ the network has some _____ present _____ learning _____ tell _____ the correct answer _____. The network _____ has a way to find _____ its input was correct and knows _____ apply its particular learning law _____ itself.

    (3) learning implies _____ the neuron somehow changes its _____ behavior in response to the environment. _____ the transfer function usually is fixed, _____ the output from a neuron _____ changed _____ the input environment is by _____ the input _____ to the neuron.

    (4) Back-propagation networks always consist of _____ three hierarchical layers of neurons. _____, a _____ (sometimes referred to as a hidden layer), and _____. The network is constructed _____ tat each layer is fully connected to the _____. _____, every neuron in the input layer will send its _____ to every neuron in the _____, and every neuron in the _____ will send its output to every neuron in the _____.

2. *Put the following into Chinese:*

    supervised learning   analogous   speech recognition
    classification of noisy data   market forecasting   nonlinear relationship
    back-propagation network   activation function   sigmoidal function
    delta rule   backward error propagation   momentum term
    overparameterization   tolerance

3. *Put the following into English:*

    大脑   学习   模式   学习过程   神经元   权重
    输入层   隐含层   输出层   收敛   迭代

· 248 ·

6.3 Applications of Fuzzy Logic

> *After reading the following unit, try to answer*:
> 1. What is the major applications of fuzzy logic?
> 2. Describe the classic decision problem in autofocus cameras by using simple rules.
> 3. Outline the image stabilization in camcorders based on if then rules.

Perhaps the most impressive fact about the present success of fuzzy logic is the breadth of application of this paradigm, ranging from consumer products to industrial process control to automotive engineering. Table 6.3.1 illustrates this point in terms of a partial list of applications of fuzzy logic in industrial setting. In brief, we suggest that in each of these applications, in spite of obvious differences in scope and/or manner of implementation. fuzzy logic plays a similarly central role in shaping a suitable rule-based, or *linguistic*, control strategy.

Table 6.3.1 Applications of Fuzzy Logic Control*

Consumer Products	Automotive and Power Generation	Industrial Process Control	Robotics and Manufacturing
• Cameras and camcorders (Canon, Minolta, Ricoh, Sanyo)	• Power train transmission control (GM-Saturn, Honda, Mazda)	• Cement kiln, incineration plant (K.L.Smith, Denmark)	• Electrical discharge machine (Mitsubishi)
• Washing machines (AEG,Shap, Goldstar)	• Engine control (Nissan)	• Refining, distillation, and other chemical processes	
• Refrigerators (Whirlpool)			
• Vacuum cleaners (Phillips, Siemens)			

* In all cases one or a small number of manufacturers are listed according to precedence or visibility.

Further, in the majority of the applications listed in the table, fuzzy logic bridges the gap between *symbolic processing* and *numeric computation*, thereby expanding the domain of application of control engineering to those that have hitherto fallen outside its proper realm. Specifically, we may argue fuzzy logic forms the basis for implementation of control strategies in the *wide sense* to include decision making or supervisory control. We shall see this next in the context of two seminal applications of fuzzy logic in industrial setting.

6.3.1 Modus Operandi of Fuzzy Logic

The distinguishing mark of fuzzy logic, in the context of its use in rule-based systems, is its ability to deal with situations in which one may not be able to make a sharp distinction between the boundaries of application of rules or constraints[①]. Two examples taken from actual instances of application of fuzzy logic control, namely, fuzzy logic-based autofocus mechanisms in cameras and fuzzy logic-based image stabilization in camcorders, clearly illustrate this fact.

6.3.2 Fuzzy Logic-Based Autofocus Camera

The classic decision problem in autofocus cameras is to select the proper object to focus on. The problem is trivially resolved if there is a single object in the field of view. In a typical situation, however, the field of view covers multiple objects whose relative distance from the camera, based on ultrasonic sensor measurements, must in principle be used to select the most plausible object to focus on. A simple approach would be to select the closest object regardless of its location in the field of view. This approach, however, does not produce the desired result, because the relative location of objects in the field of view provides a *context* for the decision process, which if ignored leads to poor picture quality.

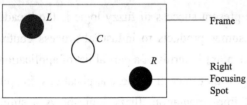

Figure 6.3.1   Autofocus camera proposed by Canon.

An approach developed by Canon and depicted schematically in Figure 6.3.1 illustrates a situation with three focusing spots in the field of view, marked L, C, and R, respectively. The decision process implemented in terms of simple rules of the form

- If C is near, then P_C is high,
- If L is near, then P_L is high,
- If R is near, then P_R is high,
- If L is far, C is medium, and R is near, then P_C is high,
- If R is far, C is medium, and L is near, then P_C is high,

determines the plausibility that L, C, or R should be the proper focusing spot; P_C denotes the plausibility that one must focus on spot C, and so on.

How the final decision is arrived at and what role fuzzy logic plays in the reasoning or inference process is the subject of subsequent sections of this chapter. Roughly speaking, however, at any given instance, sensor readings are used to determine the *degree of activation* of each rule and, in turn, suggest the plausibility of L, C, or R as the focal spot. In doing this, the context for application of each rule is implicitly considered; alternatively, fuzzy logic allows for *blending* of multiple rules representing the multiplicity of points of view in typical decision problem. This is the role that fuzzy logic, as also seen in the next example, universally plays in decision and control problems.

6.3.3 Fuzzy Logic-Based Image Stabilization in Camcorders

There are no structured methods, or algorithms, as it were, for image stabilization in camcorders. The approach often used and outlined here is, as a result, a heuristic one. Specifically, in order to determine whether the present image is a function of movement of the camera or of the movement of objects in the field of view, the camcorder marks certain objects in the field of view as *reference* (Figure 6.3.2). Further, the position of reference objects in two subsequent frames are related in terms of *motion vectors*, whose direction change determines the final outcome of the decision process, which is based on *if, then* rule of the following form:

Figure 6.3.2   Image stabilization via fuzzy logic. The image on the left results from motion of the camera, whereas the one on the right results from motion of the objects in the field of view.

● If motion vectors have different directions and the difference is increasing, then objects are in motion.

● If motion vectors have same directions and the difference is decreasing, then the camera is in motion.

One again the rule set constitutes a fuzzy linguistic decision strategy and, much like the previous example, enables the system to deal with imprecision inherent in the decision process[②].

We can distinguish several features of these cases as paradigmatic of application of fuzzy logic:

● Absence of a readily available algorithm for control;
● Heuristics as the basis for representation of control strategy;
● Use of fuzzy logic as a flexible means of representing this strategy.

Note that, as suggested earlier, the term control here is interpreted in the broad sense and includes decision making and not merely control in its classical sense. Further, the effectiveness of the algorithm is not merely due to application of fuzzy logic. Rather, fuzzy logic enhances the prospects of a linguistic algorithm forming an effective control strategy. In other words, fuzzy logic in and of itself does not solve a problem, just as a hammer in and of itself does not build a building. In the hands of an expert carpenter, it leads to an elegant design; likewise, misused it fails to impress.

Selected from "*Industrial Applications of Fuzzy Logic and Intelligent systems, Edited by John Yen. Reza Langari, Lotfi A.Zadeh, IEEE PRESS*, 1995"

Words and Expressions

1. paradigm   [pærədaim]   *n.* 范例，模范
2. symbolic processing   符号处理
3. numeric computation   数值计算
4. hitherto   ['hiðə'tu:]   *adv.* 迄今，到目前为止
5. modus   ['məudəs]   *n.* 方法，样式
6. operand   [ɔpə'rænd]   *n.* 运算数，操作数

7. trivially ['triviəli] adv. 琐细地，平凡地
8. plausible ['plɔːzəbl] adj. 似真实的，似合理的
9. closest ['kləsist] adj. 最靠近的
10. depict [di'pikt] vt. 描述，描写
11. activation [ækei'veiʃən] n. 使活动，激活
12. focal ['fəukl] adj. 焦点的，在焦点上的
13. implicitly [im'plisitli] adv. 含蓄地，暗中地
14. heuristic [hjuˈristik] adj. 启发式的；n. 启发式教学
15. vector ['vektə] n. 向量，矢量
16. imprecision ['impri'siʒən] n. 不准确，不精确
17. paradigmatic [pærədig'mætik] adj. 模范的，例证的
18. representation ['reprizen'teiʃən] n. 表示法，表现
19. effectiveness [i'fəktivnis] n. 效力
20. elegant ['eligənt] adj. 优雅的，端庄的
21. misuse ['mis'juːz] n.; vt. 误用，滥用

Notes

① in the context of its use in rule-based system: 从它被用于尺规系统的角度来看。
　it is ability ... or constraints: 它能够在人靠自身已不能明确区分尺度和限制的应用界限的情况下发挥效力。
② imprecision inherent in the decision process: 判别过程内部所固有的不精确度。
　inherent in ... : 形容词 inherent 引出介词短语，修饰 imprecision。

Exercises

1. *Complete the notes below with words taken from the text above.*
   (1) Further, in the majority of the applications listed in the table, _____ bridges the gap _____ symbolic processing _____ numeric computation, _____ expanding the domain of application of control engineering _____ have hitherto fallen outside its proper realm. _____ , we may argue fuzzy logic forms the basis for implementation of control strategies in the _____ to include _____ or _____ .
   (2) The classic decision problem in autofocus cameras is _____ the proper object _____ . The problem is trivially resolved _____ is a single object in the field of view.
   (3) There are no structured methods, _____ algorithms, _____ it were, _____ image stabilization in camcorders. The approach _____ and outlined _____ , as a result, _____ . Specifically, _____ determine _____ the present image is a function _____ movement _____ the camera _____ the movement _____ objects in the field _____ view, the camcorder marks certain objects _____ view as reference.

2. *Put the following into Chinese:*
    symbolic processing   numeric computation   decision making
    rule-based system   ultrasonic sensor   image stabilization
    motion vectors   linguistic algorithm   likewise spot

3. *Put the following into English：*
    模糊逻辑   约束   自动聚焦   算法
    吸尘器   发动机控制

6.4 Expert systems

During reading the following unit, try to find out the answer for:
1. What are the applications of expert systems?
2. How many parts an expert system consists of?
3. What is the basic structure of an expert system?

Expert systems is the "hottest" topic in AI today. Prior to the last decade, AI researchers tended to rely on nonknow ledge-guided search techniques or computational logic for problem solving. These techniques were successfully used to solve elementary problems or very well structured problems such as games. However, real complex problems are prone to have the characteristics that their search space tends to expand exponentially with the number of parameters involved. For such problems, these older techniques have generally proved to be inadequate and a new approach was needed. This new approach emphasized knowledge rather than search and has led to the field of knowledge engineering and expert systems. The resultant expert systems technology, limited to academic laboratories in the 1970s, is now becoming cost-effective and is beginning to enter into commercial applications.

Feigenbaum, a pioneer in expert systems, states:

An "expert system" is an intelligent computer program that uses knowledge and inference procedures to solve problems that are difficult enough to require significant human expertise for their solution. The knowledge of an expert system consists of facts and heuristics. The "facts" constitute a body of information that is widely shared, publicly available, and generally agreed upon by experts in a field. The "heuristics" are mostly private, little-discussed rules of good judgment (rules of plausible reasoning, rules of good guessing) that characterize expert-level decision making in the field. The performance level of an expert system is primarily a function of the size and quality of the knowledge base that it possesses.

It has become fashionable today to characterize any AI system that uses substantial domain knowledge as an expert system. Thus, nearly all AI applications to real world problems can be considered in this category, though the designation "knowledge-based systems" is more appropriate.

An expert system consists of:

① A knowledge base (or knowledge source) of domain facts and heuristics associated with the problem

② An inference procedure (or control structure) for utilizing the knowledge base in the solution of the problem

③ A working memory—global database—for keeping track of the problem status, the input data for the particular problem, and the relevant history of what has thus far been done.

A human "domain expert" usually collaborates to help develop the knowledge base. Once the system has been developed, in addition to solving problems, it can also be used to help instruct others in developing their own expertise.

It is desirable, though not yet common, to have a user friendly natural language interface to facilitate the use of the system in all three modes: development, problem solving, and instruction. An explanation module is also usually included, allowing the user to challenge and examine the reasoning process underlying the system's answers. Figure 6.4.1 shows an idealized expert system. When the domain knowledge is stored as production rules, the knowledge base is often referred to as the "rule base," and the inference engine as the "rule interpreter."

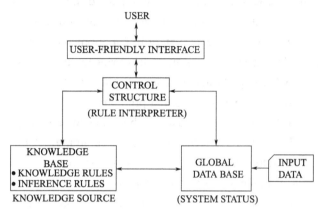

Figure 6.4.1 Basic structure of on expert system.

An expert system differs from more conventional computer programs in several important respects. Duda observes that, in an expert system "...there is a clear separation of general knowledge about the problem (the rules forming a knowledge base) from information about the current problem (the input data) and the methods for applying the general knowledge to the problem (the rule interpreter)." In a conventional computer program, knowledge pertinent to the problem and methods for utilizing this knowledge are all intermixed so that it is difficult to change the program. In an expert system, "...the program itself is only an interpreter (or general reasoning mechanism) and (ideally) the system can be changed by simply adding or subtracting rules in the knowledge base."

The most popular approach to representing the domain knowledge (both facts and heuristics) needed for an expert system is by production rules (also referred to as "SITUATION-ACTION rules" or "IF-THEN rules"). (Frames, semantic networks and object-oriented programming have begun to be important for larger expert systems.) Thus, often a knowledge base is made up mostly of rules that are invoked by pattern matching with features of the task environment as they currently appear in the global database.

In an expert system, a problem-solving paradigm must be chosen to organize and control the steps taken to solve the problem. A common, but powerful, approach involves the chaining of IF-THEN rules to form a line of reasoning. The rules are actuated by patterns (which, depending on the strategy, match either the IF or the THEN side of the rules) in the global database. The application of the rule charges the system status and therefore the database, enabling some rules and disabling others. The rule interpreter uses a control strategy for finding the enabled rules and for deciding which of the enabled rules to apply. The basic control strategies used may be top-down (goal-driven), bottom-up (data-driven), or a combination of the two that uses a relaxation-like convergence process to join these opposite lines of reasoning together at some intermediate point to yield a problem solution. However, virtually all the heuristic-search and problem-solving techniques that the AI community has devised have appeared in the various expert systems.

The uses of expert systems are virtually limitless. They can be used to: diagnose, repair, monitor, analyze, interpret, consult, plan, design, instruct, explain, learn, and conceptualize.

One way to classify systems is by function (e.g., diagnosis and planning). However, existing expert systems indicate that little commonality in detailed system architecture can be detected from this classification. A more fruitmance must be special knowledge, judgment, and experience.

- The expert must be able to explain the special knowledge and experience and the methods used to apply them to particular problems.
- The task must have a well-bounded domain of application.

Using present techniques and programming tools, the effort required to develop a large expert system appears to be converging towards a few man-years, with an initial prototype system often available in less than two months.

Many of the large corporations have formed AI groups to work on expert systems and related AI applications for their organizations. DEC, IBM and Texas Instruments have taken AI to heart and made it a major long-term aspect of their corporations. Many expert systems are being developed and dozens are out in the field in everyday use. Although development of a major AI application is still an arduous task, it is becoming commonplace due to rapidly advancing software and hardware, and the growing number of people with AI training and experience. Many expert system building tools are now available for personal computers. The goal of many of the AI vendors is to integrate AI with more conventional software so that it can become an accepted part of the mainstream software activity. Thus, as enter the 1990s, we can expect AI to be ubiquitous in our society, forming a major element in the decision-making process.

Selected from "Introduction to artificial intelligence, William B.Gevarter etc., Chemical Engineering Progress, Sept., 1987"

Words and Expressions

1. prone [prəun] adj. 面向下的，有……倾向的
2. exponentially [ekspəu'nenʃəli] adv. 指数地
3. designation [dezig'neiʃən] n. 指示，指定，指名
4. expertise [ekspə'ti:z] n. 专门技术
5. pertinent ['pə:tinənt] adj. 相关的，中肯的，切题的
6. intermix [intə'miks] v. 混合，混杂
7. semantic [sə'mæntik] adj. 语义的
8. invoke [in'vəuk] vt. 祈求，恳求，实行
9. actuate ['æktjueit] vt. 开动，促使
10. conceptualize [kən'septjuəlaiz] vt. 使概念化
11. commonality [kɔmə'næliti] n. 公共

12. Well-bounded   严格限制的
13. converge   [kən'və:dʒ]   v. 聚合, 使集合
14. prototype   ['prəutətaip]   n. 原型
15. arduous   ['ɑ:djuəs]   adj. 费力的, 辛勤的
16. commonplace   ['kɔmənpleis]   n. 常事, 老生常谈; adj. 平凡的
17. mainstream   ['meinstri:m]   n. 主流
18. ubiquitous   [ju'bikwitəs]   adj. 无所不在的, 普遍存在的

Exercises

1. *Complete the notes below with words taken from the text above.*
   (1) This new approach emphasized knowledge _____ search _____ has _____ the field of knowledge engineering _____ expert systems. The resultant expert systems technology, _____ academic laboratories in the 1970s, _____ becoming cost-effective and _____ to enter into commercial applications.
   (2) A human "domain expert" usually collaborates _____ help develop the _____ . _____ the system _____ developed, in addition _____ solving problems, _____ can _____ be used to help instruct others _____ eveloping their own expertise.
   (3) In _____ expert system, a problem-solving paradigm _____ be chosen _____ organize _____ control the steps taken _____ solve the chaining of _____ rules _____ form _____ line of reasoning. The rules _____ actuated by patterns (which, depending on the strategy, match either the IF or the THEN side of the rules). _____ the global database.
   (4) Many expert systems are being developed _____ dozens are _____ in the field _____ everyday use. _____ development _____ a major AI application is _____ arduous task, it _____ commonplace _____ rapidly advancing software _____ hardware, _____ the growing number of people _____ AI training and experience. Many expert system _____ tools are now available _____ personal computers.

2. *Put the following into Chinese:*
   last decade   expert system   interpret consult
   plan instruct   explain learn   conceptualize
   global database   domain expert   solving problem
   object-oriented programming   goal-driven
   data-driven

3. *Put the following into English:*
   知识工程   启发式   知识库   推理过程
   规则库   推理机

6.5　AI in Process Control

> *After reading this unit, you should be able to answer*:
> 1. What is the goal of CIM?
> 2. What activities are supported by knowledge base?
> 3. Describe the integration of multiple technologies to build an intelligent system.

CIM is a technology and a concept that is very important to the process industries as well as to general manufacturing industries at large. Its goal is to be able to intelligently integrate, both hierarchically and latitudinally, information, control, process, and analysis extending up from the single process, throughout the plant, and into the corporation. This goal is characterized by requirements that can only be fulfilled by important AI technologies. Problem areas that are particularly important and are natural applications for intelligent software still need a solution.

When bringing new technology into a live operation, it is always necessary to integrate. Given the goals of CIM, integrated intelligent applications and distributed intelligent applications become key methodologies as well as technologies to incorporate and address. It is important in this type of environment to also recognize the need for overall coordination above and beyond the mere computer science functionality of a traditional operating system. This level of cooperation among intelligent applications is central to providing an overall next-generation applications environment. Fundamentally, CIM requires the management of many intelligent application. In both process control and computer integrated manufacturing, time is of great concern. If a loop in a plant becomes unstable or a feed stock becomes contaminated, making a brilliant decision too late is of absolutely no value. Constantly arbitrating between timeliness and intelligence is an absolute requirement in computer-integrated manufacturing and process control. Explicit modeling of the underlying dynamics and time constants with intelligent constraint reasoning is absolutely necessary.

A key application area is the architecture, design, and implementation of intelligent database facilities to support the lofty goals of CIM. There intelligent database facilities should allow a knowledge base or intelligent application to support the following activities:
- Database design
- Database connectivity
- Application generation
- Query optimization
- Data management and modeling
- Performance analysis and tuning

Given the current trends and standardizations in database technology, it is particularly natural and optimal to support structured query language (SQL) as a standard in building intelligent database facilities for the CIM environment. At its heart, much of CIM represents a real-time database environment with a set of supervisory applications built on top of that layer. Artificial intelligence and expert systems are ideally suited not only to address some of the applications, but to provide the overall management, coordination, and facilities associated with CIM down through the layers to direct process control.

Complexities and Requirements

The modern-day manufacturing environment is an exceedingly complex entity with volumes of data and more opportunities to go wrong than to go right. Although there has been much automation at the low levels, and indeed a lot of automation at the highest levels, the intermediate levels are waiting for solutions.

In general, there is an increasing interest in developing intelligent applications as part of an overall process control and management philosophy, incorporating a CIM architecture, with particular interest in interfacing and tightly integrating intelligent applications at the supervision, plant, and corporate level[①]. Most of the receptivity and investment in the real world will take place at the supervision and plant levels. A survey of the process and general manufacturing industries will identify a number of requirements such as:

• Tight integration with existing applications, systems, and communications networks.

• Database connectivity and integration across multiple logical and functional databases with particular attention to relational database technology.

• Interfaces for special-purpose computer environments as well as standard communication protocols and vendor-specific protocols.

• The ability to reason with volumes of data in an online and responsive fashion.

• Highly user-oriented, human-factor-engineered, application user interfaces.

• Application-specific shells requiring no computer science or artificial intelligence to use them.

• Easy construction of large knowledge bases and expert system applications.

• A methodology for phased implementation and cooperation among various intelligent applications. Verification and validation of the underlying knowledge base.

• Minimization of the maintenance burden for an intelligent application.

In addition to the demand for intelligent applications, such as statistical process control, supervisory control, and optimization and scheduling, there is a significant demand for a base technology which could be applied by an enduser to develop an intelligent application. Given the complexities of manufacturing and the goals and requirements of CIM, a knowledge-engineering environment should have the following attributes in order to easily address process control and management problems (see Figure 6.5.1):

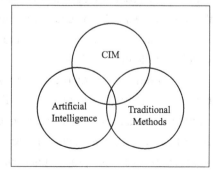

Figure 6.5.1 The Integration of multiple technologies to build intelligent systems.

- Integration facilities
- High performance
- Productivity facilities to ease the burden of development
- Relational database stable storage
- Distributed communications
- An open architecture
- The ability to reuse knowledge and migrate that knowledge across multiple applications
- Multiple knowledge-base modeling techniques, such as objects and rules

The problems that are most important in the process control and management arena tend to have:

- Combinatorially explosive reasoning
- Volumes of data
- Complicated underlying models
- Inexact and mixed formalisms

Because these complexities are purely traditional, highly analytic approaches have failed to provide intelligent solutions. If combinatorially large problems are attached combinatorially, the result is a prohibitively costly and slow solution. It is not uncharacteristic to see people attempting to solve scheduling problems with pure analytic approaches which require tens of hours of computing time on a large multimillion dollar computer to arrive at a single answer (see Figure 6.5.2). More often than not, this answer is obsolete by the time it is presented to the manufacturing floor. The problems have been so severe that by and large automation is provided by people solving problems on the back of the envelope.

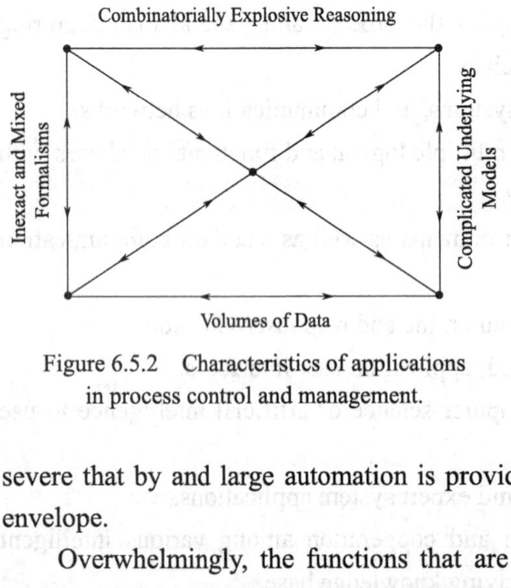

Figure 6.5.2 Characteristics of applications in process control and management.

Overwhelmingly, the functions that are illustrated in this text as opportunities for expert systems and AI technology are currently being performed by human beings. It is some human who usually produces a production schedule or tries to optimize the plant floor. That is not to say that there have not been successful traditional approaches in certain circumstances. But generally, there is a vast pent-up demand for intelligent applications to alleviate the present manual methods which provide the functionality.

Unfortunately, many organizations believe that they can buy CIM like they can buy a loaf of bread. This is really not the case. All too often organizations run out and purchase computers, networks, and databases and interconnect them, only to find that what they have is not CIM, but a collection of computers, networks, and databases. The tough challenge is defining very clearly the applications of interest, their functional requirements, and the associated tasks they must perform in a way that can be implemented in a coherent fashion.

In many ways providing intelligent process control and management is inherently a top-down process that requires an architectural and functional model that can then be implemented using intelligent automation technology. If this were done in a modern plant, it would become obvious that a host of requirements could not be addressed by closed form analytic representation and that artificial intelligence, expert systems, and knowledge-base technology in conjunction with more traditional analytic methodology is the only way to arrive at a set of consistent, integrated, and usable applications.

This book will consistently identify, organization by organization, a number of pervasive problems that are natural candidates for artificial intelligence-based expert system approaches. These include intelligent supervisory control and optimization and intelligent alarm management, scheduling, maintenance, and process modeling.

Supervisory control and optimization adjusts the parametric coefficients in the various traditional control structures throughout the plant. It requires an intelligent system to identify that there is a need to tune, to reason about which tuning method to employ, and then to go ahead and apply the new tuning coefficients. This problem is persuasive and real and its solution requires a high degree of tight integration.

In a plant environment one alarm never goes off. Either 10 alarms go off or no alarms go off. An expert system which would intelligently figure out what is really causing the problem and what to do about it would be of tremendous benefit in the safety and operational functioning of a plant.

Scheduling is a very tough problem because it affects all of the other aspects of the plant environment. The problem is particularly complicated in the batch processing industries, where a finite run of one item is followed by a finite run of another item. Obviously, the ability to properly tune the plant and handle alarms, as well as overall optimal plant utilization, is greatly affected by the schedule of what is produced.

Maintenance is tied into scheduling, alarm management, and tuning. For instance, if a plant is tuned so that its control functions are highly responsive, all things being equal, the components of the plant will be driven much harder than if the plant is highly damped and less responsive.

The process modeling necessary in a plant requires the identification of the best control-oriented abstraction of the process for a particular plant and process. All plants are created unequal and closed form analytic expressions tend to become less important as plant specifics evolve. The ability to have the expertise of a skilled control engineer simultaneously resident with a skilled application engineer to intelligently arrive at the real site-specific process models is of tremendous value.

All of the above problems are exceedingly difficult to solve using purely traditional methods alone. It is by the subtle incorporation of AI theory and technology in applications that already exist and the use of knowledge-based methods in conjunction with traditional analytic techniques to address new application areas that an intelligent process control and management environment can be realized.

Selected from "*AI in Process Control*", Michael Stock, McGraw-Hill Book Company, 1989 "

Words and Expressions

1. latitudinally [ˌlætəˈtjuːdinli] adv. 从纬度而言地
2. extend up 扩充，延伸
3. cooperation [kəuˌɔpəˈreiʃən] n. 合作，协力
4. contaminate [kənˈtæmineit] vt. 弄脏，污染
5. arbitrate [ˈɑːbitreit] v. 仲裁
6. timeliness [ˈtaimlinis] n. 时间性，及时性
7. database connectivity 数据库连通性
8. query optimization 查询最优化
9. standardization [ˌstændədaiˈzeiʃn] n. 标准化，规格化
10. structured query language 结构化查询语言
11. modern-day 现代的，当代的
12. entity [ˈentiti] n. 实体存在
13. receptivity [ˌrisepˈtiviti] n. 感受性，接受能力
14. user-oriented 面向用户
15. human-factor-engineered 人因素驱动
16. verification [ˌverifiˈkeiʃən] n. 确认，查证
17. migrate [maiˈgreit] v. 迁移，移居
18. arena [əˈriːnə] n. 竞技场，活动场所
19. uncharacteristic [ˈʌnˌkæriktəˈristik] adj. 没有特色的
20. obsolete [ˈɔbsəliːt] adj. 陈旧的，过时的
21. overwhelmingly [ˈəuvəˈhwelmiŋli] adv. 压倒性地，无法抵抗地
22. functionality [ˌfʌŋkʃəˈnæliti] n. 机能
23. coherent [kəuˈhiərənt] adj. 黏着的；紧凑的，连贯的
24. conjunction [kənˈdʒʌŋkʃən] n. 联合，并联
25. pervasive [pəˈveisiv] adj. 普遍的，蔓延的
26. site-specific 位置特定的

Note

① 此句主要结构是："there is an increasing interest in ... , with particular interest in ... ." 人们对……的兴趣在增加,特别是对……的兴趣。

Exercises

1. Complete the notes below with words taken from the text above.

   (1) _____ is a technology and a concept _____ very important to the process industries _____ to general manufacturing industries _____. Its goal is _____ intelligently integrate, _____ hierarchically _____ latitudinally, _____, control, _____, and analysis extending up from the single process, _____, and into the corporation.

   (2) The modern-day manufacturing environment is an exceedingly complex entity _____ of

data _____ opportunities to _____ wrong _____ to _____ right. _____ there has been much automation _____ the low levels, _____ indeed _____ automation at the highest levels, the intermediate levels _____ for solutions.

(3) Unfortunately, many organizations believe _____ they can buy CIM _____ they can buy a loaf of bread. This is _____ not the _____. All too often organizations _____ and purchase computers, _____, and databases _____ interconnect them, _____ to find _____ they have is not CIM, _____ a collection of computers, networks, and _____. The tough challenge is defining _____ the applications of _____ , their functional requirements, _____ the associated tasks they must perform _____ that _____ implemented in a coherent fashion.

2. *Put the following into Chinese:*
computer integrated manufacturing   modern-day
management philosophy   user-oriented   shell
validation   relational database   real-time database
intelligent alarm management   maintenance
parametric coefficient   traditional method

3. *Put the following into English:*
统计过程控制   最优化   调度   智能集成   智能软件
标准化   数据库技术   协调   通信规程   数据库

4. *Complete the following close test:*
The success of a manual strategy for _____ abnormal conditions _____ heavily _____ the operator _____ respond correctly to process alarms. However, the operator's response _____ many factors: the number of alarms _____ the frequency of occurrence of abnormal conditions, _____ information is presented to the operator, the complexity _____ the plant, _____ the operator's intelligence, training, experience, _____ reaction to stress. _____ the many factors involved in _____ the appropriate response _____ alarm situation, computational aids for the operator _____ crucial _____ the success of operating complex manufacturing plants. _____ computer-based assistance _____ developed as software systems. These so-called _____ are based _____ emulating the actions_____ a human expert _____ is acknowledged _____ perform the required tasks _____ high level of proficiency. The use of expert systems, also called _____, is a branch _____ artificial intelligence (AI). AI _____ popularly defined _____ the science of enabling computer systems _____ learn, reason, _____ make judgments. _____ expert systems utilize _____ procedures _____ simplify the application _____ inductive _____deductive reasoning _____ to the data base ("knowledge") _____ the system.

APPENDIXES

Appendix 1 Sources of Information in Automatic Control

1. Abstract

EI	Engineering Index
SCI	Science Citation Index
ISTP	Index to Scientific and Technical Proceedings
ISR	Index to Scientific Reviews
CA	Chemical Abstracts
SA	Science Abstracts

日本科学技术文献速报

2. Society for Automatic Control

IFAC International Federation of Automatic Control
  国际自动控制联合会

IEEE Institute of Electrical and Electronics Engineers
  电气与电子工程师协会

IEE Institute of Electrical Engineers
  电气工程师协会

IFIP International Federation for Information Processing
  国际信息处理联合会

IFORS International Federation of Operational Research Societies
  国际运筹学会联合会

IFSR International Federation for Systems Research
  国际系统研究联合会

ACC American Control Conference
  美国控制会议

IAPR International Association for Pattern Recognition
  国际模式识别学会

SIAM Society for Industrial and Applied Mathematics
  工业及应用数学学会

Chinese Association of Automation
  中国自动化学会

AIChE American Institute of Chemical Engineers

美国化学工程师协会
ASME American Society of Mechanical Engineers
　　美国机械工程师学会
ISA Instrument Society of America
　　美国仪表学会

3. Journals

Applied Artificial Intelligence　　应用人工智能
Artificial Intelligence　　人工智能
ASC Cybernetics Forum　　美国控制论学会论坛
Assembly Automation　　装置自动化
Automatica(IFAC)　　自动学
Automatic Control & Computer Sciences　　自动控制与计算机科学
Automation　　自动化
Engineering Applications of Artificial Intelligence　　人工智能工程应用
Expert Systems With Applications　　专家系统应用
CAD/CAM Technology　　计算机辅助设计与制造技术
Canadian Controls & Instrumentation　　加拿大控制与仪表应用
CIM Technology　　计算机集成制造系统技术
Computer-Aided Design　　计算机辅助设计
Computer-Aided Engineering　　计算机辅助工程
Computer-Aided Engineering Journal　　计算机辅助工程杂志
Computer world O.A.　　计算机世界：办公自动化
Control and Computers　　控制与计算机
Control and Instrumentation　　控制与仪表应用
Control Engineering　　控制工程
Control Engineering Practice　　控制工程实践
Cybernetics　　控制论
Cybernetics & Systems　　控制论与系统
Digital Systems for Industrial Automation　　工业自动化数字系统
I&CS(Instruments and Control Systems)　　仪表与控制系统
IEEE Control Systems Magazine IEEE　　控制系统杂志
IEEE Expert　　IEEE 专家系统杂志
IEEE Transactions on Automatic Control　　IEEE 自动控制汇刊
IEEE Transactions on Information Theory　　IEEE 信息论汇刊
IEEE Transactions on Pattern Analysis and Machine Intelligence
　　IEEE 模式识别与机器智能汇刊
IEEE Transactions on Systems, Man & Cybernetics
　　IEEE 系统、人与控制论汇刊
IEE Proceedings-D: Control Theory and Applications
　　IEE 控制理论与应用汇刊

英文名称	中文名称
Industrial Robot	工业机器人
Industrial Robots International	国际工业机器人杂志
Instruments & Control Systems	仪表与控制系统
Information & Control	信息与控制
Information Processing & Management	信息处理与管理
International Journal of Control	国际控制杂志
International Journal of Modelling & Simulation	国际建模与仿真杂志
International Journal of Robotics & Automation	国际机器人学与自动化杂志
Journal of Cybernetics & Information Science	控制论与信息科学杂志
Journal of Dynamic Systems, Measurement & Control	动态系统、计测与控制杂志
Journal of Process Control	过程控制杂志
Journal of Intelligent System	智能系统杂志
Journal of Robotic Systems	机器人系统杂志
Large-Scale Systems-Theory and Applications	大系统理论与应用
Mathematical Modelling	数学模型
Mathematics & Computers in Simulation	仿真数学与仿真计算机
Measurement & Control	测量与控制
Optimal Control Applications & Methods	最优控制应用与方法
Pattern Recognition	模式识别
Robotics	机器人学(英国)
Robotics & Computer-Integrated Manufacturing	机器人学与计算机集成生产
Sensors and Actuators	传感器与执行器
Sensors Review	传感器评论
SIAM Journal on Control & Optimization	SIAM 控制与最优化杂志
Simulation	仿真
Systems, Computers, Controls	系统、计算机、控制
Transactions of the Institute of Measurement and Control	英国测量与控制学会汇刊
Artificial Intelligence in Engineering	工程中的人工智能工程
Computers & Chemical Engineering	计算机与化学工程
Computer & Control Engineering Journal	计算机与控制工程杂志
Chemical Process Control	化工过程控制
Computer & Industrial Engineering	计算机与工业工程
Computers in Industry	计算机在工业中应用
Computer Modeling and Simulation in Engineering	工程中计算机模型与仿真
Control and Dynamic System	控制与动态系统
Dynamic and Control	动态与控制
Engineering Applications of Artificial Intelligence	人工智能在工程中应用
Fuzzy Systems and Artificial Intelligence	模糊系统与人工智能
IEEE Transactions on Fuzzy Systems	IEEE 模糊系统汇刊
IEEE Transactions on Neural Networks	IEEE 神经网络汇刊
IEEE Transactions on Robotics & Automation	IEEE 机器人与自动化汇刊

International Journal of Adaptive Control and Signal Processing
自适应控制信号处理国际杂志
International Journal of Intelligent Systems　智能系统国际汇刊
International Journal of Pattern Recognition and Artificial Intelligence
模式识别与人工智能国际汇刊
International Journal of Robust & Nonlinear Control
International Journal of Systems Science　系统科学国际杂志
Instrumentation in the Chemical & Petroleum Industries　化工与石化工业中的仪表
ISA Transactions　ISA 汇刊
AIChE Journal　AIChE 学报
Canadian Journal of Chemical Engineering　加拿大化学工程学报
Chemical Engineer　化学工程师
Chemical Engineering　化学工程
Chemical Engineering Progress　化工进展
Chemical Engineering & Technology　化学工程与工艺
Chemical Processing　化工过程
Chinese Journal of Chemical Engineering　中国化学工程学报(英文)
ACTA Automatica　中国自动化学报(英文)

Appendix 2　总词汇表 (INDEX)

abbreviate　v. 缩写，简化
abort　v. 中断，故障，失误
abrasive　adj. 具有磨蚀性的
absclssa　n. 横坐标
absolate pressure　绝对压力
absolute stability　绝对稳定性
abundant　adj. 丰富的
accelerometer　n. 加速度表
access　n. 存取，访问
accommodate　vt. 调节，提供，适应
accounting　n. 统计，计算
accumulator　n. 积聚者，累加器
accuracy　n. 精(确)度，准确度
ac motor　交流电动机
acc of gravity　重力加速度
achieve　vt. 完成，实现
Acoustic thermometry　声测温技术
acoustical　adj. 声学的；听觉的
acquisition　n. 获取，采集，探测，显示
acronym　n. 缩写字
activation　n. 使活动，激活
actuate　vt. 开动，促使
actuator　n. 执行器
adaptive　adj. 适合的，适应的
adaptive control system　自适应控制系统
adaptive loop　适应性环路
adaptive system　自适应系统
address　n. 地址，称呼
adhere　vi. 黏附，遵守
adipic acid　己二酸
admirably　adj. 极佳的
advisory control　监督控制
aforementioned　adj. 上述的，前述的
agitate　v. 搅动
aileron　n. 副翼
AIN (analogue input card)　模拟（信号）输入卡
aircraft　n. 航空器，飞行器
air gap　空（气）隙
albeit　conj. 虽然，即使
algebraic　adj. 代数的，代数学的

algorithm　n. 运算法则，算法
aliasing　n. 假频，失真
align　v. 结盟，使结盟
alignment　n. 对准
allowable　adj. 可允许的
allure　n. 引诱，吸引；vt. 魅力
alternative　n. 选择；adj. 选择性的，二中选一的
aluminum oxide　n. 氧化铝
AM　应用模块
ambient variation　环境变化
ambiguously　adv. 多义性地，模糊地
amibent　adj. 周围的，外界的
ample　adj. 充足的，丰富的
amplitude　n. 振幅，振荡
analog　n. 模拟量，相似体
analogous　adj. 类似的
analytic　adj. 分析的，解析的
analytical　adj. 分析的
analyzer　n. 分析器
anarchy　n. 混乱
anesthesia　n. 麻醉，麻痹
angles　n. 幅角
Angular displacement　角位移
Angular velocity　角速度
announce　vt. 通报，广播，通知
antenna　n. 天线
anticipate　vt. 预期，占先
anti-reset windup　防积分饱和
AOT (analogue output card)　模拟（信号）输出卡
a pair of rollers　一副轧辊
application　n. 应用，应用程序
application layer　应用层
approximation　n. 近似值
apt　adj. 倾向于
arbitrary　adj. 任意的
arbitrate　v. 仲裁
architecture　n. 结构
arduous　adj. 费力的，辛勤的
arena　n. 竞技场，活动场所

armature current 电枢电流
armoured *adj.* 铠装的, 包铍皮的
ascertain *vt.* 确定, 调查, 弄清
assertion *n.* 要求
assign *vt.* 分配, 指派
assumption *n.* 假设, 假定
asteroid *adj.* 星状的; *n.* 小行星
asymptote *n.* 渐近线
atmospheric pressure 大气压
attenuate *v.* 削弱
attitude *n.* 姿态
auctioneer *vi.* 最大脉冲输出
audit *v.; n.* 检查, 决算, 查账
automatic calibration 自动校准
automatic control 自动控制
autonomous *adj.* 自主的, 自备的
autotuning *n.* 自动整定
available time 空闲时间
axes *n.* 轴, 轴线, 轴心
back emf 反电动势
ball valve 浮球阀
bandpass *adj.* 带通的
bandwith *n.* 带宽; 误差范围
barium-ferrite 钡铁淦氧磁体
barometric *adj.* 气压的, 大气的
barrier *n.* 隔离器, 隔离栅
baseband *n.* 基带, 基频
basically *adv.* 基本上, 主要地
batch operation 批操作, 批处理
batch process 批处理
baton *n.* 指挥棒
battery *n.* 电池
beam *n.* 横梁, 秤杆, 天平梁
belows *n.* 风箱; 波纹管; 弹簧皱纹管; 膜盒
beryllium copper 铍青铜
be compatible with 与…一致; 与…兼容
be inferior to 较…差, 在…下面
be prone to 倾向于
Bernoulli equation 伯努利方程
bevel *n.* 斜角, 斜边
bidirectional *adj.* 双向的
bifurcation *n.* 分叉, 分歧
bimetallic strip 双层金属片, 双金属片
bipolar *adj.* 两极的, 双极的
bistable *n.* 双稳定
black-box model 黑箱模型

blade *n.* 叶片, 桨叶
blind *adj.* 瞎的
boiler 锅炉
boiler drums 锅炉汽包
boiling point 沸点
boldface *n.* 黑体字
bolt *n.* 螺栓, *v.* 用螺检固定
bombardment *n.* 辐射, 轰击
boolean *adj.* 布尔的
boost *n.; vt.* 推进, 提高, 促进
bore *n.* 腔, 中心孔
boredom *n.* 讨厌, 厌烦
bottleneck *n.* 瓶颈
bounce *n.* 脉动, 反跳, 进回, 回波
Bourdon tube 弹性金属曲管; 波登管
brass *n.* 黄铜
brevity *n.* 简短, 简化
British 英制
broadband *n.* 宽带, 宽波段
brush *n.* 电刷
brushless 无电刷的
brute-force 强力
bubble *n.* 水泡, 气泡
budget *n.* 预算
buffer *n.* 缓冲器
buffer storage tank 缓冲储罐
buoyancy *n.* 浮力, 浮动性
burdensome *adj.* 繁重的, 艰难的
burn *v.* 燃烧
butterfly valve 蝶阀
cabinec *n.* 箱柜, 机壳
calibration *n.* 刻度, 标度; 标准
camcorder *n.* 可携式摄像机
cancellation *n.* 相消, 删去
candidate *n.* 候选人, 投考者
canonical *adj.* 规范的
cantilever *n.* 悬臂梁
capacitance *n.* 容量, 电容
capacitive probe 电容电极
capacitor *n.* 电容器
capacity factor 容量因子
capillary *adj.* 毛细的; *n.* 主细管
capsule *n.* 小盒, 膜盒, 容器
capture *v.* 获取
cardboard *n.* 卡片
carrier *n.* 载体, 载波, 支座, 承重层

cartridge n. 弹药筒
casecade n. 串级
catalyst n. 催化剂
catalyst activity 催化作用
catalytic adj. 催化的
categorize vt. 把……分类, 将……归类
cause and effect equation 因果关系方程
caution n.; vt. 警示, 警告
cavity n. 内腔, 中空
celsius adj. 摄氏的
centipoise 厘泊 (黏度单位), 10^{-2} 泊
centistoke 厘池 (动力黏度单位)
centralise n. 集中
centrifugal pump 离心泵
centrifuge n. 离心(分离)机
ceramic beaded 陶制珠状的
cereal adj. 各类的
cerebral adj. 脑的
characteristic equation 特征方程
chart n. 图表, 曲线
chip n. 晶片, 碎片
chip select pulse 选片脉冲
chromatograph vt. 套色复制
chromatography n. (印刷)套色板
circuitry n. 电路, 线路
circulating water 循环水
circumvent vt. 躲避; 避免
cite v. 引用, 例证
clamp n. 夹板, 压板, 夹紧
classical adj. 经典的
client n. 顾客, 客户
clinical adj. 临床的
clock cycle 时钟周期
clock wise adj. 顺时针的
closed-loop stability 闭环稳定性
closest adj. 最靠近的
cluster n. 组件, 插件
codify vt. 编成法典, 使法律成文化
coefficient n. 系数
coherent adj. 黏着的; 紧凑的, 连贯的
coil n. 卷; vt. 环绕
coiler n. 卷绕机
collaborative adj. 合作的
collisions n. 抵触, 振动, 颠簸
combinatorial adj. 组合的
commercialize vt. 使商业化

commonality n. 公共
commonplace n. 常事, 老生常谈; adj. 平凡的
commutator n. 整流器
compactness n. 致密, 紧密
comparison n. 比较, 对照, 比喻
compensation n. 补偿
competition n. 竞赛, 竞争
complaint n. 意见, 怨言
complement n. 补足物; vt. 补足
complex variable 复变量
complex-conjugate pairs 共轭复数对
complicate vt. 使复杂
compromise n. 折衷, 综合平衡
computationally adv. 计算上地
computer integrated manufacturing (CIM) 计算机集成制造
comunication protocol 通信协议
concentration n. 浓度
concentric adj. 同心的
conceptualization n. 概念化
conceptualize vt. 使概念化
condensate n. 冷凝物
conductive a. 导电的
conduit n. 导管
configuration n. 结构, 形态, 配置
conjecture n.; v. 推测, 猜想
conjunction n. 联合, 并联
constant n. 常数, 恒量
constraint n. 强制, 局促
constricting hole 节流孔
consultant n. 顾问
contact n. 接触器
container n. 容器
contaminate vt. 弄脏, 污染
contamination n. 污染, 污染物
continuous-time signal 连续时间信号
continuty equation 连续方程
contour n. 轮廓
contractor n. 承包者, 合同户
control circuit 控制电路
control configuration 控制组态
control law 控制法则
controller gain 控制器增益
controller tuning 控制器整定
control strategy 控制方案
control torque 控制转矩

control valve 控制阀
controversy n. 争论, 辩论
convenient adj. 方便的, 便利的
converge v. 聚合, 使集合
convergence n. 集中, 收敛
conveyor n. 传送机器
convolution 回旋, 旋转
cooperation n. 合作, 协力
coordinate n. 坐标; adj 同等的; v. 使协调
correlate n. 相关物; v. 使联系
correlation n. 相关, 相关性, 相互关系, 交互作用
corrosion n. 侵蚀, 腐蚀状态
corrosive adj. 腐蚀性的, 生锈的
corrugated adj. 波纹状的
corrugated tube 波纹管
corrupt v. 腐烂
cortex n. 外皮
cost function n. 成本函数
Coulomb friction 干摩擦
counter n. 计数器
counterclockwise adj. 逆时针的
covariance function 协方差函数
criterion n. 判据, 准则
cross-correlation method 互相关法
crossover operation 交叉操作
cross-sectional area 横截面
CRT 阴极射线管
crucial adj. 决定性的
crude adj. 天然的, 粗糙的
cruise missile n. 巡航导弹
crux n. 症结
cubic adj. 立方的
cubic meter n. 立方米
cumulative flow 累计流量
current source 电流源
curvature n. 弯曲, 曲率, 曲度
customer n. 用户, 顾客
cutoff frequency 切断频率
cutoff rate 切断速率
Cv number 阀流通能力
cycle n. 周期, 循环
cylinder n. 汽缸, 液压缸
daily cycle 日常周期性变化
daisy chain 菊花链
damp v. 阻尼; 衰减
damper n. 阻尼器, 调节板, 制动器, 风门, 气闸

damping ratio 衰减率
dangerous adj. 危险的
dasheol line 虚线
data-acquisition instrument 数据获取仪
data link layer 数据链路层
data logging 数据采集
database connectivity 数据库连通性
DCS (Distributed Control System) 集散控制系统
dead time 滞后
deaf a. 聋的
debug v. 调试
decay ratio 衰减比
decentralised structure 分散型结构
decoder n. 解码器, 译码器
decryption 译码, 解码
dedicate vt. 致力, 专用于
deduce vt. 推论, 演绎出
deem vt. 认为, 相信
deemed adv. 值得依赖地
de-facto standard 事实上的校准
deficiency n. 不定, 故障
deflection n. 偏转, 偏移, 偏角
deformation n. 变形, 扭曲
degradation n. 降低; 降解
delay time 滞后时间
delimeter n. 定义符, 定界符, 限制符
delivery n. 递送
demise n. 死亡, 让位
demonstration n. 示范, 实证
denominaton polynomial 分母多项式
denote vt. 指示
dense adj. 密集的, 稠密的
depict vt. 描述, 描写
deposit v. 沉积
derioative adj. 引出的; n. 衍生物
descent n. 降落, 家系
describe vt. 描述, 描绘
designation n. 指示, 指定, 指名
design principle 设计原理
detector n. 发现者; 探测器
deteriorate vt. 变化, 老化, 衰退
deterioration n. 变坏, 恶化; 退化
deterministic part 确定性的部分
detrimental adj. 有害的
deuterium n. 氘, 重氢 2H
development environment 开发环境

deviate v. 偏离
deviation n. 偏差
diagnosis n. 诊断
dial n. 表盘，表面，指针，刻度盘
diaphragm n. 隔膜；光圈；膜片，膜盒
dielectric n. 绝缘体，电介质
dielectric constant 介电常数
diesel n. 柴油
differential equation 微分方程
differential pressure 差压
digester n. 蒸煮
digital controller 数字控制器
digitization n. 数字化
digitize vt. 将……数字化
dilute vt. 冲淡，稀释；adj. 淡的
dimensional adj. 尺寸的，量纲的，因次的
DIN (discrete input card) 离散（信号）输入卡
diode n. 二极管
Dirac delta function 迪拉克δ函数
direct-current (DC) motor 直流电动机
direct-digital-control 直接数字控制
disable v. 使残废，使无效
discrepancy n. 偏差，不精确度
discrete adj. 离散的，不连续的
discrete-data 离散数据
discrete I/O device 离散输入/输出装置
discrimination n. 差别，歧视
disparate adj. 不同的，不等的，不相称的
dispense vt. 分发，分配
disposal n. 处理，安排
dissect v. 切成碎片；仔细研究；解剖
dissimilar adj. 不相似的，不同的，不一样的
distillation n. 蒸馏
distinct pole n. 孤立极点
distort vt. 使……变形，弯曲，扭曲
distortion n. 失真，变形
distributed control 分布式控制
disturbing torque 干扰转矩
divergent adj. 分支的
diverse adj. 各种各样的
diversify vt. 使多样化，使变化
divert v. 转移
divide by 用……除以
division n. 分界线；刻度线
dominant adj. 主要的
doom vt. 注定要

DOT (discrete output card) 离散（信号）输出卡
double integrator 双积分器
double seating 双座
downstream adj.; adv. 下流的(地)；顺流的(地)
dp cell 差压测量元件
drastic adj. 激烈的
drawback n. 不利点，缺点
drill v. 钻井
drive motor 驱动马达
drum n. 室
dumb adj. 哑的
duplicate vt. 加倍，复写，复制
durability n. 耐久性
duration n. 持续时间
earthing 接地
eccentric adj. 古怪的
ecology n. 生态学
economical failure 经济不可行
EEPROM 电可擦写可编程只读存储器
effectiveness n. 效力
effluent tank 污水罐，污水池
elaborate adj. 详细的，精确的
elasticity n. 弹性，弹力
elbow n. 肘,弯管接头，弯管流量计
electrical generator 发电机
electric network 电网络
electrode n. 电极
electrolyte n. 电解液
elegant adj. 优雅的，端庄的
elevate vt. 升高，增加
elongate adj. 拉长的，延伸的
elongation n. 拉长，延伸
elude vt. 避免
elusive adj. 逃避的
embed v. 嵌入
embrace vt. 包括
emission n. (光、热)散发
emotion n. 情绪
empirical modeling 经验模型
empirical adj. 经验主义的；以经验为根据的
emulate vt. 效法，尽力赶上，竞争
enclosure n. 封装
encode v. 编码，译码
encompass vt. 围绕，拥有
endogenous adj. 内生的，内源的
endow v. 捐赠；赋予
energy balance 能量平衡

energy factors 能量因素，品质因素
energy losses 能量损失
energize vt. 激发，激励，通电
enhance vt. 提高，加强
entail vt. 需要，必须
enthalpy n. 焓，热函
entity n. 实体，实物，组织，机构
entrain v. 以气泡形式存在
entrapment n. 截留，收集
entrust v. 委托
enumerate vt. 列举，枚举
equal percentage 等百分比
equilibrium n. 平衡点，平衡状态
equivalent adj. 等价的，相等的
equivalent circuit diagram 等效电流图
erase vt. 抹去，擦掉
ergonomics n. 人机工程学，人体工程学
erosion n. 腐蚀，侵蚀
error criterion n. 误差标准
error discriminator 误差鉴别器
error free 无差错，无误
essence n. 基本，本质
esthetic adj. 感觉的
esthetics n. 美学
estimate converge 估计收敛
Ethernet 以太网
Euler n. 欧拉
evaluate n. 评估，评价
evaporator n. 蒸发器，脱水器
even adj. 偶的
exception n. 除外，例外
exogenous adj. 外生的，外源的
exothermic adj. 放热的
exothermic catalytic reaction 放热催化作用
expansion n. 扩张，膨胀，延长
expertise n. 专门技术
explicit adj. 外在的，清楚的
explicitly adj. 明白的
exploratory adj. 探查的，调查的
exponent n. 说明书，指数
exponentially adv. 指数地
exponential response n. 指数响应
extend up 扩充，延伸
extension n. 扩展，扩充
extract n. 提取物；vt. 提取，摘录
extractor n. 提取器

extrapolate vt. 推断
extrude v. 挤压；突出
e.m.f 电动势
facilitate vt. 帮助，使容易，促进
fast fourier transform 快速傅里叶变换
fatigue n; v. 疲劳
feasibility n. 可行性，现实性
feedback control 反馈控制
feedforward control 前馈控制
fiber optic cable 光纤，光缆
fidelity n. 保真度
fieldbus 现场总线
Fieldbus Foundation 现场总线基金会
field test 现场测试，现场试验
field winding 磁场绕组
file sever 文件服务器
filter n. 滤波器
FIP 工厂仪表规程
flag n. 标识位，旗码，特征位
flammable adj. 易燃的，可燃性的
flange n. 凸缘，边缘；法兰
flatness n. 平坦度，不平度
flatter n. 扁手槽
flexibility n. 弹性，适应性
flexible member 柔性部件
flip flop 触发器，触发电路
float n. 浮体，浮标
flood control 洪水控制
flooding n. 泛滥；溢流
flowing adj. 流动的
flowmeter n. 流量计
flowsheet n. 工艺流程图
flow nozzle 测流嘴
flow patterns 流型，流动型式
flow rate 流速
fluctuation n. 波动，不稳定
FM (Frequency modulation) 调频
foam n. 泡沫
focal adj. 焦点的，在焦点上的
force-balance pressure transmitter 力平衡压力变送器
forcing signal 强迫信号
forecast v. 预报、预测
foresee v. 预见
former n. 样板，模型，线图框架
formulation n. 阐明，描述
fossil-fuel 矿物燃料

fraction n. 部分;分数
fragile adj. 易碎的, 脆的
freezing point 凝点
frequency-domain 频率域
frequency response 频率响应
friction n. 摩擦
frictional torque 摩擦力矩
FSK (frequency shift keying) 移频键控
fuel cell 燃料电池
full-bore ball valve 穿孔球阀
full-scale 满尺度, 满量程
fume n. 烟雾, 气体
functionality n. 机能
furnish v. 提供, 供给
future control action 未来控制行为
future tracking error n. 未来的跟踪错误
fuzzy adj. 失真的, 模糊的
gage pressure 标准压力
gain n. 增益
gamma ray γ射线
gap n. 间隙
garn-soaking kettle 纱浸泡桶, 染缸
gasoline n. 汽油
gateways (GW) 网关
gauge n. 量表, 标准尺
gauge pressure 表压
gear n. 齿轮
gear levers 变速杆
gear train 传动机构
generalized predictive controller 广义预测控制器
generator n. 发电机, 生产者
generic data 同类数据
genetic adj. 遗传的, 起源的
geothermal system 地热系统
gimmick n. 骗局
globe valve 球形阀
glossary n. 词汇
golden rule 黄金规则
gradient n. 倾斜度; adj. 倾斜的
granularity n. 粒度, 间隔尺寸
graphical adj. 绘图似的, 图解的
graphically adv. 图形地
grinder n. 磨床
gripper n. 夹子, 夹具
grounded adj. 接地的
guideline n. 方针

hamper n. 阻碍物; vt. 阻碍
handicaps n. 障碍物
HART (highway addressable remote transducer) 可编址运程变送器
hazardous adj. 危险的, 冒险的
hazardous job 有害工作
heater n. 加热器
heat exchanger 热交换器
heat loss 热损失
heat sink n. 散热片, 散热装置
helical adj. 螺旋状的
helix n. 螺旋管, 螺旋弹簧
hermetic adj. 密封的
heterogeneous adj. 异种的, 异质的
heuristic a. 启发式的; n. 启发式教学
hexadecimal adj. 十六进制的; n. 十六进制
hierarchical adj. 等级的
hierarchical approach 递阶方法
hierarchy a. 分层的; n. 层次
high-level language 高级语言
high-order model 高阶模型
high-order system 高阶系统
high pressure steam 高压蒸汽
highway n. 高速公路, 公用信息公路
histogram n. 直方图, 频率曲线
hitherto adv. 迄今, 到目前为止
HM 历史模块
hog v. (使)拱(弯、扭)曲, 变形
hollow adj. 空心的, 中空的
horizontally adv. 水平地
host computer 主机
human-factor-engineered 人因素驱动
humble adj. 低级的
humidity n. 湿度
hurdle n. 障碍; vt. 越过, 克服
hybrid n. 混合物; adj. 混合的
hydraulic adj. 水力的, 液动的
hydraulic actuator 液动执行机构
hydraulic cylinder 液压缸
hydraulic turbine 水轮机
hydrocarbon-to-oxygen n. 碳氢化合物的氧化
hydrostatic adj. 流体静力学的, 静水力学的
hype n. 皮下注射, 欺骗, 骗局
hypothesis n. 假说, 假定
hypothetical adj. 假设的, 假定的
hysteresis n. 滞后

identifiable subspace 可辨识子空间
identification *n.* 辨识
idle *adj.* 闲置的；*n.* 停机
IEC Fieldbus IEC 现场总线
IEEE-488 communication performance IEEE-488 通信操作
IEEE-488 controller IEEE-488 控制器
ignition *n.* 点火，点燃
ignore *vt.* 不管，忽略不计
illumination *n.* 照明（度）
imaginary axis *n.* 虚轴
immerse *vt.* 浸没，沉入
immunity *n.* 免疫，免疫性
impedance *n.* 阻抗，全电阻
imperfect *adj* 半完成的，减弱的；*n.* 未完成体
implement *n* 工具；*vt.* 使生效，执行
implementation *n.* 工具；安装，启用
implicit *adj.* 隐含的，内含的
implicitly *adv.* 含蓄地，暗中地
impractical *adj.* 不实用的，不切实际的
imprecision *n.* 不准确，不精确
Impulse Response Model 脉冲响应模型
inclination *n.* 倾斜角（度）
inclinometer *n.* 倾斜仪
inconsequential *adj.* 无意义的，不重要的
inconsistency *n.* 不一致，不调和
increment *n.* 增加，增量
incremental *adj.* 增加的；*n.* 增量
indicate *vt.* 显示，指示
indirect *adj.* 间接的
inductance *n.* 感应系数，自感应
induction *n.* 感应现象
inductor 电感
inequality *n.* 不等式
Inertia *n.* 惯性
inertial *adj.* 惯性的
inevitable *adj.* 不可避免的
infancy *n.* 初期，幼年
inferential control 推理控制
infinite *adj.* 无穷大
ingredient *n.* 成分，配料，组成部分
inherent *adj.* 固有的，内在的，本征的
intial step 开始，初始
inject *vt.* 注射
inlet *n.* 入口，进口
innovation *n.* 改革，创新

input-signal scanning 输入信号扫描
insect *n.* 昆虫
insertion *n.* 插入，安置
instantaneously *adv.* 同时地
instruction register 指令寄存器
instrumental *adj.* 仪器的，可作为手段的
instrumentation *n.* 仪器
insulate *v.* 绝缘
integral square 求平方积分
integrate *v.* 使成整体；求……积分
integrated circuit 集成电路
integrated control 集中控制
intelligence *n.* 智力，情报
intelligent supervisory control 智能监控
intense demand 强烈要求
intercept *v.* 截止
interconnect *vt.* 使相互连接
interface *n.* 接触面，流口；分界面
interlock *n.* 联锁，连接，联锁装置
intermix *v.* 混合，混杂
internal combustion engine 内燃机
internal model control 内部模型控制
intersect *v.* 相交，交叉
interviewee *n.* 被接见者，被访问者
initial value 初始值
intrinsically *adv.* 本质上
intuition *n.* 直觉
intuitive *adj.* 直觉的
intuitively *adv.* 直觉地
invar *n.* 镍铁合金，殷钢
inverse *adj.* 逆的，相反的
inverse *z*-transform *z*-逆变器
invoke *vt.* 祈求，恳求，实行
IPTS 国际实用温标
iron-core 铁芯
ironless rotor 无铁芯转子
iron nickel alloys 铁镍合金
irrelevant *adj.* 不相关的，不切题的
irrespective *adj.* 无关的，没关系的
irrigation *n.* 灌溉，冲洗
irrigation *v.* 灌溉
isolate *v.* 使隔离，使孤立
isothermal *n.* 等温线；*adj.* 同温的
iteration *n.* 重复，反复，迭代
iterative *adj.* 反复的
jog-run 精密运行

joysticks　*n.* 操纵杆、手柄
junction　*n.* 接触点，接触端
kernel　*n.* 核心，中心
keypad　*n.* 键区
keystroke　*n.* 键击
kilogram　*n.* 千克，公斤
kilopascal　*n.* 千帕斯卡 (压强单位)
kilowatt-hours　千瓦时
kinematic　*adj.* 运动的,动力学的
kinetic energy　动能
Kirchhoff　克希荷夫
laborious　*adj.* 艰苦的, 费力的
ladder diagram　梯形图
lag　*vi.* 落后；延缓
lagging edge　后沿下降边, 后沿
laminer flow　层流
laplace transform　拉普拉斯变换
large reservoir　大水库
latch　*n.* 门闩; *v.* 抓住，占有
lathe　*n.* 车床
latitudinally　*adv.* 从纬度而言地
launch　*vt.* 提出，开创，开始
lead screw　引导丝杆
least-squares method　最小二乘法
level measurement　物位测量
liaison　*n.* 联络
limit switches　限制开关
linear configuration　线性结构
linear quadratic Gaussian　线性二次型高斯
linear quadratic regulator　线性二次型调节器
linearity　*n.* 线性
linguistic variable　语言变量
liquid-in-glass thermometer　*n.* 充液管式温度计
liter　*n.* 公升
literally　*adv.* 逐字的, 按照字面上的
live zero　实际零点，实时零点
load cell　荷重元件, 载荷传感器
local area network (LAN)　局域网
loci　*n.* 轨迹 (pl.locus)
longevity　*n.* 长寿命, 耐久性
loop tuning　回路整定
loose　*adj.* 不严格的, 大概的
lottery　*n.* 彩票
lower limit value　下限值
low-order system　低阶系统
low-pass filter　低通滤波器

magnesium oxide　*n.* 氧化镁
magnet　*n.* 磁铁，电磁
magnetic flowmeter　磁性流量计
magnetohydrodynamic system　磁流体系统
magnitude　*n.* 大小，幅值
mainframe　*n.* 主机
mainstream　*n.* 主流
maintenance-free　免修的,不需维护的
malfunction　*n.* 故障; *vi.* 发生故障
mammalian　*adj.* 哺乳动物的; *n.* 哺乳动物
management information systems (MIS)　管理信息系统
mandatory　*adj.* 命令的, 强制的
manifest　*vt.* 表明, 显示
manifold　*adj.* 各种各样的, 形形色色的
manipulate　*v.* 处理
manipulator　*n.* 机械手
manual control　手动控制，人工控制
margin　*n.* 阈；限度；范围
marginal　*adj.* 边缘的, 末端的
master controller　主控制器
master/slave　主/从
match　*vi.* 相适应，相配
material inventory　物料库存量
mathematical modeling　数学模型
matrix　*n.* 矩阵
maximise costs　最小成本
maximise throughput　最大处理能力，最大生产能力
maximum likelihood method　极大似然法
maximum overshoot　最大超调
mean　*n.* 平均(数), 平均(值), 中值
mechanical linkage　机械连接
mechanism　*n.* 机构，机理，结构
media　*n.* 媒体
Mercury　*n.* 汞，水银，水银温度计
message　*n.* 信息, 情报, 报文
metabolism　*n.* 同化作用, 新陈代谢
metal rolling　金属轧制
methodology　*n.* 方法学, 方法论
metric unit　公[米]制单位
minimum variance-stochastic control　最小差异随机控制
microcomputer　*n.* 微型计算机
microelectronic　*n.* 微电子学
migrate　*v.* 迁移，移居
millivolt　*n.* 毫伏
minicomputer　*n.* 小型计算机
minimum variance criterion　最小差异准则

missile *n.* 飞弹, 火箭
misuse *n.*; *vt.* 误用, 滥用
mixing ingredients 混合配料
mode *n.* 模式
model predictive casecade control 模型预测串级控制
model-based controller 基于模型的控制器
model structure 模型结构
modem=modulotor-demodulator 调制解调器
moderate *adj.* 中等的, 适度的
modern-day 现代的, 当代的
modification *n.* 修正, 修饰, 修改
modular *adj.* 模块的, 标准组件的
modulate *v.* 调制; 调节
modus *n.* 方法, 样式
moisture *n.* 潮气, 潮湿
mole *n.* 摩尔
molecular *adj.* 分子的
mole flow rate 摩尔流率
molten (molt 的过去分词) 熔化的
moment of inertia 惯量瞬时
momentum *n.* 动力, 要素
monitor *n.* 监视器
monolith *n.* 整体, 单一, 一致
monolithic *adj.* 独立的, 完整统一的
monopolise *vt.* 独占, 得到……专利权
monotonic *adj.* 单调的
motivation *n.* 动机
motor *n.* 马达, 电动机
motor-and-screw assembly 马达齿轮付
motor relay 电动继电器
moving-coil 动卷
multidimentional *adj.* 多维的
multidrop 多站
muttidrop communications system 多站通信系统
multiple *adj.* 复合的
multiplex *adj.* 多样的; *v.* 多重发信
multiplexer *n.* 多路转换器, 多路扫描器, 多重通道
multiplicative *n.* 乘法, 乘子
multiplying factor 乘号
multitask *n.* 多任务; *vt.* 使多任务化
multivariable *n.* 多变量
mutation rate 交配率
necessitate *vt.* 需要, 迫使
negative feedback 负反馈
negligible *adj.* 可以忽略的, 微不足道的
nest *vt.* 组合

network systems interconnection (OSI) 开放式系统内部连接
neural *adj.* 神经的, 神经系统的
neuron *n.* 神经单位
neutron *n.* 中子
newborn *n.* 婴儿, *adj.* 新生的
Newton 牛顿
node *n.* 节点
noise immunity 噪声抗御性
nonconductive *adj.* 不传导的, 不导电的
nonlinearity *n.* 非线性度, 非线性
nonrigorous *adj.* 不严密的
nonsingular *adj.* 非奇异的, 满秩的
nonvolatile *adj.* 永久的, 非挥发性的
normalized model 标准化模型
normally closed (N.C.) 常闭
normally open (N.O.) 常开
notation *n.* 记号法, 表示法
notch *n.* 槽口; 凹口
notorious *adj.* 名声极坏的
nozzle *n.* 管口, 喷嘴
nuclear-fission 核裂变
nuclear-fusion 核聚变
nucleonic gauge 核子仪表
nullify *vt.* 使无效, 废弃
numerator polynomial 分子多项式
numerator *n.* 分子
numeric computation 数值计算
numerous *adj.* 众多的, 大量的
obsolete *adj.* 陈旧的, 过时的
obstacles *n.* 障碍物
obstruction *n.* 阻碍, 障碍物
occurrence *n.* 发生
OCP 操作员控制程序
OCS 操作员控制站
odd *adj.* 奇的
OEM (Original Equipment Manufaturing) 原始设备制造商
off shore 离线
oil shale 油页岩
omnidirectional *adj.* 全方位的（全向的）
on-board computer 板上计算机
onedimentional *adj.* 一维的
one-shot 一次完成, 一次启动
ongoing *adj.* 前进的; *n.* 前进
opaque *adj.* 不透明的, 不传动的

· 277 ·

op-amp=operational amplifier　运算放大器
open system　开放系统
operand　n. 运算数, 操作数
operating system　操作系统
operator interface　操作员界面
optimal　adj. 最优的, 最佳的
optimisation programs　优化程序
optimize　vt.; vi. 使完善, 优化
optimizer　n. 最佳化器, 优化器
orbit　n. 轨道
orbiting space system　轨迹空间系统
order　n. 指令, 命令; 次序; 阶
orders of magnitude　数量级
orient　n. 东方; vt. 定……的方位
orifice　n. 孔, 口
oscillate　v. 振动, 使振动
oscillatory　adj. 振动的
outdoor robotics　室外机器人
output variance　输出变异
outstrip　v. 超过
oval　adj. 椭圆形的
oven　n. 烘箱, 烤炉, 干燥箱
overflow　vi. 溢出, 溢流
overlap　n.; vt. 重叠, 相交
overload protection (OL)　防超负荷
override switch　过载开关
override　v.; n.越限, 超驰, 过载
overshoot　n. 超调
oversimplify　vt. 过于简化
overview　n. 纵览
overwhelmingly　adv. 压倒性地, 无法抵抗地
oxidize　v. 氧化, 生锈
pace　n. 步调, 速度
package　n. 套装软件, 包裹
packing box　密封盒, 填料盒
pad　v. 填补, 衬垫
pallet　n. 货架
pantograph　n. 比例绘图仪, 放大尺, 缩放
parabolic　adj. 抛物线的
parabolic shape　抛物线形
paraboloid　n. 抛物面
paradigm　n. 范例, 模范
paradigmatic　adj. 模范的, 例证的
parallel　adj. 平行的
parameter variation　参数摄动
parameter　n. 参数

parity　n. 同等, 类似
partial fraction expansion　部分分式展开
partial　adj. 部分的, 偏的
particle　n. 粒子, 质点, 颗粒
Pascal　帕斯卡
passive　adj. 被动的, 无源的
pattern recognition　模式识别
PC-Based control　基于个人计算机控制
pedal　n. 踏板
pedigree　n. 种类, 家谱, 由来, 起源
pellet　n. 颗粒, 粉末
pendulum　n. 摆动
penetrate　v. 刺穿, 穿透
perceive　v. 感知, 察觉
perceptible　adj. 明显的
perfect control　完美控制
peripheral　adj. 周边的, 周围的, 肤浅的
permanent-magnet　adj. 永磁的
perpendicular　adj. 垂直的, 正交的
perspective　n. 展望, 观点
pertinent　adj. 相关的, 中肯的, 切题的
perturbation　n. 干扰
pervasive　adj. 普遍的, 蔓延的
petroleum　n.石油产品
phase plane　相平面
phase　n. 相角, 相位
phosphor bronze　磷青铜
photoelectric sensor　光电传感器
photovoltaic cell　光电池（光生伏打电池）
physical component　物理组件
physical layer　物理层
physical modeling　物理模型
pictorial　adj. 图示的
piezoelectric　adj. 压电的
pilot static tube　测量静力管, 导向静力管
PIN (pulse input card)　脉冲（信号）输入卡
pitot tube　n. 皮托管
PIU　过程控制单元
pivot　n. 枢轴, 支点, 杠杆
plague　n. 麻烦, 灾害
plant　n. 车间, 工厂, 系统
plant load　工厂负荷
plantwide　厂域, 工厂范围
platinum　n. 铂, 白金
plausible　adj. 似真实的, 似合理的
playwright　剧作家

pliable　　*adj.* 易弯的，可弯的
plot　　*n.* 情节，图；*vt.* 绘图
PM dc　　永磁直流电动机
pneumatic actuator　　气动执行机构
pneumatic diaphragm actuator　　气动薄膜执行器
pneumatic　　*adj.* 气动的
poise　　*n.* 平衡剂，缓冲剂，泊（黏度单位）
pou　　*n.* 查询，转态，终端设备定时查询
polymerization　　*n.* 聚合
polynomial　　*n.* 多项式；*adj.* 多项式的
porous　　*a.* 多孔的
port　　*n.* 汽门，出口，入口，孔，空气口
portable　　*adj.* 手提式的
positioner　　*n.* 定位器
positive feedback　　正反馈
positive integer　　正整数
postulate　　*v.* 假定，要求
potential　　*n.* 潜力；*adj.* 潜在的
potential energy　　势能
potentiometer　　*n.* 电位计，分压计，电位器
potentiometric　　*adj.* 电势的，电位的
powder　　*n.* 粉末
power　　*n.* 幂
practitioner　　*n.* 专业人员；老手
pragmatic　　*adj.* 实用主义的，活跃的
preamble bytes　　段直标记，始标
precise　　*adj.* 精确的，准确的
predefine　　*v.* 预定义
predetermine　　*vt.* 预定，预置
predictive control　　预测控制
predictor　　*n.* 预估器
preliminary　　*adj.* 初步的；*n.* 初步行动
prerequisite　　*adj.* 先决条件的，首先的
pressure drop　　压力降
pressure regulator　　压力调节器
pressure-spring thermometer　　压力弹簧式温度计，压力式温度计
pressurized container　　带压容器，带压储罐
prevail　　*vi.* 发生；流行
primary element　　主元件
priority　　*n.* 优先权，先前
probabilistic　　*adj.* 概率的
process control　　过程控制
processefficiences　　过程效率
productivity　　*n.* 生产力
Protibus　　过程现场总线

program counter　　程序计数器
programmable controllers　　可编程控制器
programmable logic controller　　可编程逻辑控制器
programmed adaptation　　可编程自适应
prohibitively　　*adv.* （价格）高得吓人的
pronate　　*v.* 使伏下，伏下
prone　　*adj.* 面向下的，有……倾向的
propagate　　*v.* 繁殖；宣传，传播
propagation　　*n.* 增殖，繁殖
propeller　　*n.* 推进器
proportional band　　比例带
proportional plus derivative　　比例加微分
proportional plus integral　　比例加积分
protocol　　*n.* 协议
protoplasm　　*n.* 细胞质
prototype　　*n.* 样机；标准，范例
proximity　　*n.* 近似，接近
proximity switch　　邻近开关
prudent　　*adj.* 谨慎的，精明的
psi　　磅/每平方英寸
PSU (power supply unit)　　供电单元
pulley　　*n.* 滑轮
pulp　　*n.* 纸浆
pulp and paper　　制浆与造纸
pulse　　*n.* 脉冲
pulse-transfer　　脉冲传递
pump　　*n.* 泵
punch　　*n.* 打眼，冲孔
purging　　*n.* 清洗，净化
pursue　　*vt.* 追赶，追求
pushbutton　　*n.* 按钮
quadratic　　*adj.* 二次的，二次型的，二次项的
quality　　*n.* 质量
quantitative　　*adj.* 数量的，定量的
quantize　　*v.* 量化
quasi　　*adj.* 准，伪，拟，半
query optimization　　查询最优化
race　　*vi.* 竞争
rack　　*n.* 齿条
rack-and-pinion　　齿条齿轮付
radial basis functions　　径向基函数
radiation　　*n.* 发射，放射，放射线
radio link　　无线电联系
randomize　　*v.* 使混乱，使随机化
range　　*n.* 范围

range and bias settings　量程和基准设定
rare-earth magnet　稀土磁铁
ratio　n. 比率, 比值
ratio control　比率控制
rational function　有理函数
readability　n. 可读性; 分辨率
readout　n. 读出器
realistically　adv. 实际地
realm　n. 区域
reboiler　n. 重沸器
receptivity　n. 感受性, 接受能力
recommendation　n. 推荐, 建议
recreation　n. 再生
rectangular　adj. 矩形的, 成直角的
rectangular slit　直角光栅
recur　n. 重复; 递归
recursive estimation　递推估计
recursive　adj. 循环的, 递归的
recursively　adv. 回归地, 递归地
redundancy　n. 过多, 累赘
redundant　adj. 多余的, 冗余的
reflux　n. 回流; 分馏
register　n. 登记表, 自动记录器
regular interval　规律性时间间隔
regulator　n. 调整者, 调整器
reinitialize　vt. 重新初始化
reinvest　v. 再投资
relative stability　相对稳定性
relay　n. 中继, 接力(电工)继电器; v. 转播
Relay-Based Control　基于继电器的控制
reload　v. 重新加载
remote calibratcon　远程校准, 远程校正
remote control　远距离控制
repetitive job　重复工作
representation　n. 表示法, 表现
reprogrammable　重复可编程序
reprogramme　v. 重新编程
residence time　滞留时间
residue　n. 残余物, 剩余物
resilient　adj. 有回弹力的, 有弹性的
resistance　n. 电阻, 阻抗
resistive　adj. 电阻的, 抵抗的
resolution　n. 分辨率, 清晰度
resonant peak　n. 共振尖峰
respect　n. 关系, 方面, 考虑, 遵守
restriction　n. 限制, 约束

retard　v. 延迟
retrieval　n. 恢复, 修补
reverse engineering　反转工程
Reynolds number R　雷诺数 R
ricipe　n. 食谱, 处方
rigidity　n. 刚性, 刚度, 硬度
rigorous　adj. 严格的
rinse　v. 漂洗
rise time　上升时间
robot　n. 机器人
robotics　n. 机器人学
robust　adj. 鲁棒性的
robustness　n. 健壮性, 鲁棒性
rod　n. 拉杆, 连杆
roll bending　轧制弯曲度
roll tilting　轧制倾斜
root contours　根轨线
root mean square (RMS)　均方根
rotameter　n. 转子流量计, 转子式测速仪
rotary valve　旋钮阀
rotational　adj. 旋转的, 转动的
rotor　转子
router　n. 路由器
routine　n. 子程序, 例行程序
routinize　v. 程序化; 惯例化
RTC (real time clock)　实时时钟
RTD　热电阻
rudder　n. 方向舵
rudimentary　adj. 基本的, 初步的, 原始的
rugged　adj. 坚固的
rung　n. 梯级, 一级
RTU (remote telemetry units)　远程遥测系统
safe-run　安全运行
salient　adj. 显著的
sampled unit ramp　单位采样的斜坡函数
sampler　n. 样品检验员, 取样器, 取样系统
sampling instant　抽样瞬间
sampling period　n. 采样周期
sand-water slurry　n. 沙水浆
saturable reactor　饱和电抗器, 饱和式磁力仪, 饱和扼流圈
saturation　n. 饱和, 饱和度
saunders-patent　桑托斯专利
scaling　n. 定标, 换算, 定比例
scanning　n. 扫描, 搜索
scarcity　n. 稀少

scenario *n.* 假定; 情节; 方案
schedule *n.* 时间表, 进度表
schematic *adj.* 概要的; 图解的
scratch *n.* 初稿, 草稿
scrutinize *v.* 仔细检查, 核查
seal *n.; v.* 密封
secondary element 二级元件
secondary-storage system 二次储存系统
segment *n.* 片段, 部分; *vt.* 分割
segmental *adj.* 部分的
selector switch 选择开关
self-operating 自力式操作, 自力式控制
self-tuning adaptive controller 自整定适应控制器
self-tuning regulator 自整定式调节器
semantic *adj.* 语义的
semiconductor *n.* 半导体
semipermanent *adj.* 非永久性的, 暂时性的
sense *n. v.* 感受; 检测
sensitivity *n.* 灵敏度
sensor *n.* 传感器
sensor layer 会话层
sequence logic 顺序逻辑, 程序控制
sequential *adj.* 继续的, 后果的
sequentially *adv.* 继续地, 从而
series *n.* 串联
servoamplifier 伺服放大器
servomotor *n.* 伺服电动机
set point *n.* 设定值, 给定值
settling time 建立(置位, 稳定)时间
SFG (signal-flow graph) 信号流图
shaft *n.* 连接轴
shaft position 轴位
shaft velocity 转轴速度
sheath 鞘; 护套
short-circuit *n.* 短路电流, 漏电电流
shutoff *n.* 阀门, 栓, 开关
shut up 关闭
sight glass 玻璃液面计, 观察玻璃, 观察孔
sigmoidal *adj.* S 字形的, C 字形的
signal processor 信号处理器
silicon *n.* 硅
simplicity *n.* 简单
simplify *vt.* 单一化, 简单化
simulated annealing method 模拟退火法
simultaneously *adv.* 同时地
sine-wave *n.* 正弦波

single-board computer 单板机
single seating 单座
single technique 单一性技术
sinusoidal *adj.* 正弦波的
SI (standard international unit) 国际标准
site-specific 位置特定的
six-legged machine 六腿机器
sketch *v.* 拟定, 勾画
slave controller 从属控制器
sleek *adj.* 光滑的
slew *n.* 旋转; *v.* 使旋转
slit *n.* 光栅, 狭缝
slope *n.* 斜率; 倾斜
sludge *n.* 污泥, 污水, 沉积物
sluggish *adj.* 迟缓的, 迟滞的
slurry *n.* 泥浆
smart instrumentation 智能仪表
smith predictor technique 史密斯预估器技术
snugly *adv.* 贴身地, 紧挨着
soda ash 纯碱
solar cell 太阳能电池
solenoid *n.* (电)螺线管
solenoid valve 电磁阀
solidify *adj.* 充实的, 固化的, 充满的
solid-state system 固态系统
sonic *adj.* 音速的
sophisticated *adj.* 复杂的, 高级的; 非常有经验的
space vehicle 空间飞船
spark *n.* 火花
span *n.* 跨距, 跨度; 量程
specific weight 密度
specification *n.* 规格, 详细说明书
spectral density *n.* 谱密度
spectral *adj.* 光谱的
spectrometry *n.* 分光计, 分光仪
spectrophotometer *n.* 分光光度计
spectroscopy *n.* 光谱学, 波谱学
spectrum *n.* 谱, 系列
sphere *n.* 范围; 球体, 球形
spherical *adj.* 球形的, 圆的
spin *v.* 旋转
s-plane s 平面
splashing *n.* 喷溅物
splice *vt.* 拼接
split 迁移
split-range control 滑动区间控制

spray painting 喷涂,喷漆
spurious *adj.* 虚伪的, 伪的, 谬误的
Spring *n.* 弹簧
spar *n.* 刺激，推动支线
stain gauge 应变仪，应变电阻片
stainless steel 不锈钢
stability augmentation *n.* 稳定性增益
standard deviation *n.* 标准偏差
standard *n.* 标准
standardization *n.* 标准化，规格化
start-stop pushbutton 启停按钮
startup *n.* 启动
start-up *vi.* 启动
state-of-the-art 技术水平, 科学发展动态, 现代化的
state-space model 状态空间模型
state-space representation 状态空间描述
Static friction 静摩擦
static-system 静态系统
stationary *adj.* 静止的, 平稳的
statistical quality control (SQC) 统计质量控制
statistical-estimation-problem 统计学估计问题
stator *n.* 定子
steady-state *n.* 稳态
stem *v.* 滋生，产生
step-function 阶跃函数
stepper motor 步进电机
stiff *adj.* 刚性的
Stiffness *n.* 刚性
stiffness coefficient 刚度系数
stimulus *n.* 刺激, 激励
stirred-tank *n.* 搅拌槽
stirrer *n.* 搅拌器
stochastic approximation method 随机近似理论
stochastic *adj.* 随机的
stoke *n.* 存料, 原料, 库存, 股票
stoichiometric *adj.* 化学计算的
storage tank *n.* 存储器
strain gauge 应变仪, 拉力计
strainer *n.* 过滤器
strategic *adj.* 战略上的
strategy *n.* 策略
streamline *adj.* 流线型的
stretch *vt.* 伸长, 拉长, 展开
strip *n.* 拉丝, 带状物
stroke *n.* 行程, 冲程
structured query language 结构化查询语言

sturdy *adj.* 坚固的
suboptimally *adv.* 亚最佳地, 次优地
subroutine *n.* 子程序
subscript *n.* 下标
subsequent modification 后修正
subset *n.* 子集
substantial *adj.* 实质上的, 有内容的
subtract *v.* 减去
subtraction *n.* 减少
successive *adj.* 连续的
successor *n.* 后续符, 继承人, 记录符
sufficiently exciting 充分激励的
sump pumps 污水泵
sun-seeker system 太阳自导（寻）系统
superheater *n.* 过热器
supervision *n.* 监督管理
supervisory *adj.* 管理的, 监督的
supervisory control 监督控制
surface-wound 表面绕线
surge capacity *n.* 谐振能力
survey *n.* 综述
susceptible *adj.* 灵敏的, 易感的, 易受影响
swirl *n.* 漩涡
switch *n.* 开关, 交换机; *vt.* 转变, 转换
symbolic processing 符号处理
symbolic *adj.* 代号的, 象征的
symmetrical *adj.* 对称的, 平衡的
synchro *adj.* 同步
synchronization *n.* 同步, 同步化
synchronize *v.* 使同步, 同时发生
synonym *n.* 同义字
synthesis *n.* 综合, 组织
syrup *n.* 浆, 糖浆, 糖汁
system identification 系统辨识
systematic *adj.* 有系统的, 体系的
systematically *adv.* 有条理地, 系统地
tachometer *n.* 转速计
tackle *n.* 工具, 装备; *vt.* 处理
tactical *adj.* 战术的
tangent *n.* 切线; 正切
taper *n.* 圆锥形
target value *n.* 目标值
TCP/IP (transmission control/protocol/Internet protocol) 传输控制规程/内部规程
TDM (time division multiplexing) 分时多路传输
team up 合作

technical success　技术可行
tedious　*adj.* 乏味的，沉闷的
Teflon ring　聚四氟乙烯填圈，特氟隆填圈
telemetry　*n.* 遥测技术
temporarcty　*adv.* 暂时地，临时地
tension　*n.* 紧张，压力；*vt.* 使紧张
tentative　*adj.* 试验性的，尝试性的
terminal step　终了
terminology　*n.* 专有名词，术语
terrain　*n.* 地带，领域
textile　*adj.* 纺织的，织成的
theorem　*n.* 定量，原理
theoretical　*adj.* 理论的
theoretically　*adv.* 理论上
thermal-noise　*n.* 热噪声
thermocouple　*n.* 热电偶
thermodynamics　*adj.* 热力学的
thermoelectric effect　热电势效应
thermography　热像仪
thermometer　*n.* 温度计，温度表
thermostat　*n.* 自动调温器，温度调节装置
thermowell　*n.* 热电偶套管，测温插套
thickness　*n.* 厚度
three-phase alternator　三相交流发电机
threshold　*n.* 门槛，入口，阀
threshold value　阈值，门限值
throttle　*v.* 扼杀
thumb　*n.* 拇指；*vt.* 笨拙处理
tidal energy　潮夕能
tie　*v.* 结；约束
tightly couple　紧耦合
time constant　时间常数
time interval　时间间隔
time-consuming　耗时的
time-delay　*n.* 时间滞后
time-domain　时间域
time waveform　时间波形
time-invariant system　时不变系统
timeliness　*n.* 时间性，及时性
timeout　*n.* 工间休息
timer　*n.* 计时器，定时器
time-series model　时间序列模型
timing　*n.* 定时；时序；同步
timing belts　定时皮带传动
token bus　金牌总线
token-ring network　令牌网

torque　*n.* 转矩，力矩
total flow　总体流量
touch screen　触摸屏
tow　*n.* 拖曳所用之绳；*vt.* 拖曳
toxic　*adj.* 中毒的，有毒的，有害的
toxic fumes　有毒烟气
track　*n.* 轨迹；*vt.* 跟踪
trail and error　试差法
trajectory　*n.* 轨道；轨线
transceiver　*n.* 无线电收发器，收发器
transducer　*n.* 传感器
transient　*n.* 暂态；*adj.* 短暂的，易变的
transient response　瞬时响应
transition　*n.* 转换，过渡
translational　*adj.* 平移的，移动的
transmit　*vt.* 传送
transmitter　*n.* 传送器；变送器
transparent　*adj.* 透明的，明晰的
transport layer　传输层
trap　*n.* & *vt.* 捕获，收集，截留，使分离
traverse　*vi.* 横过，通过，往返运动，上下来回
tray　*n.* 塔盘
triangular　*adj.* 三角形的
trick　*n.* 策略，诀窍
trip　*n.* 断路，跳闸
triple point　三态点
tritium　*n.* 氚，超重氢 3H
trivially　*adv.* 琐细地，平凡地
tropospheric scatter　对流层散射
troubleshooting control loop　故障排除控制回路
true value　真值
truncated　*adj.* 削去尖角的，截短的
trunk　*n.* 躯干，中值线
tuning rules　*n.* 整定规则
turbine　*n.* 涡轮
turbulence　*n.* 湍流
turbulent　*adj.* 汹涌地，狂暴的
turbulent flow　湍流
two-edged　*adj.* 双刃的
typewriter　打字（EP）机
ubiquitous　*adj.* 普遍存在的
UHM (ultra high frequency)　超高频
ultimate　*adj.* 最终的；临界的
ultralight　*adj.* 超轻型
ultrasonic　*adj.* 超音速的；超声的
unauthorized　*adj.* 未经认可的

unbiased　*adj.* 无偏的，没有偏见的
uncharacteristic　*adj.* 没有特色的
unconstrained　*adj.* 自由的，无约束的
undamped　*adj.* 无阻尼的，无衰减的
underestimate　*vt.* 看轻，低估
underlying theory　支撑性的理论
undetected grade　未发现的级别
uneven　*adj.* 不平的
unified　*adj.* 统一的
uninterrupted　*adj.* 不停的，连续的
unipolar　*adj.* 单极的
unique　*adj.* 独特的，独一无二的
unit matrix　单位矩阵
unity　*n.* 一致，联合
update　*vt.* 更新，修正，校正
upper limit value　上限值
upset　*n.*; *v.* 混乱，扰乱
user-oriented　面向用户
utility　*n.* 公用工程，公用事业设备
vacum　*n.* 真空，真空度，真空状态
vague　*adj.* 含糊的，不清楚的
validate　*v.* 使有效，确认，验证
validation　*n.* 验证，确认
valve　*n.* 阀
vane　*n.* 叶轮
vaporizer　*n.* 蒸馏器
variable-flux　变磁力线（磁通）
variable speed pump　可变速泵
variation　*n.* 变化量
vat　*n.* 大桶
VDU　可视化单元
vector　*n.* 向量，矢量
vehicle　*n.* 车辆，运送装置，飞行器
velocity　*n.* 速率，速度
vena contracta　缩脉，收缩断面
vendor　*n.* 卖主，商家
vent　*v.* 排放，排出
venturi tube　*n.* 文丘里管
verbal　*adj.* 口头的
verification　*n.* 确认，查证
verisimilitude　*n.* 逼真

versatile　*adj.* 通用的，万能的
vertically　*adv.* 垂直地
vessel　*n.* 容器，导管
via　*prep.* 经由；经过
vibration　*n.* 振动，颤动
vice versa　*adv.* 反之亦然
violation　*n.* 违反，违背
virtually　*adv.* 实际上
viscosity　*n.* 黏质，黏性
Viscous friction　黏滞摩擦
visual　*adj.* 可视的，可见的，光学的
visualization　*n.* 使看见，使清楚呈现
vital　*adj.* 重要的
viz　*adv.* 也就是，即
volatile　*adj.* 挥发性的；*n.* 挥发物
volatile memory storage　暂存存储器
voltage　*n.* 电压，伏特数
voltage level　电压电平
volumetric　*adj.* 测定体积的
WAN (wide area network)　广域网
walking machine　行走机器
watt　*n.* 瓦特
waveform　*n.* 波形
weeping　*n.* 渗漏；分泌
weld　*v.* 焊接
well　*n.* 井
Well-bounded　严格限制的
wetting　*n.* 浸湿，润湿
Wheatstone bridge　索斯登电桥
white-noise　白噪声
winding　*adj.* 卷绕的；*n.* 线圈，绕组
wire-wound resistor　绕线电阻，线绕电阻
workload　*n.* 工作量
yaw　*n.*; *vi.* 偏航，侧滑
yoke　*n.* 支架
zener diode　齐纳二极管
zero mean　零均值
zero-order hold　零阶保持
zinc　*n.* 锌
ZOH　零阶保持器

REFERENCES

[1] 王树青, 韩建国.工业自动化专业英语. 修订版.化学工业出版社, 2001.
[2] Dale E.Seborg, Thomas F.Edgar Duncan A.Mellichamp.Process Dynamics and Control.Second Edition. John Wiley & Sons Inc.2004.
[3] Jonathan Love.Process Automation Handbook.Springer-Verlag London Limited 2007.
[4] Benjamin C.Kuo.Automatic Control Systems.Seventh Edition.Prentice-Hall.Inc.1995.
[5] Norman A.Anderson.Instrumentation for Process Measurement and Control.Chilton Company, 1998.
[6] Douglase O.J.deSa.Applied Technology and Instrumentation for Process Control.Taylor & Francis, 2004.
[7] Alan S.Morris.Measurement and Instrumentation Principles.Butterworth-Heinemann, 2001.
[8] William C.Dunn.Fundamentals of Industrial Instrumentation and Process Control. McGraw——Hill,2005.
[9] Thomas F.Edgar, Cecill L.Smith,F.Greg Shinskey,George W.Gassman,Andrew W.R.Waite, Thomas J.Mcavoy, Dalee.Seborg. Perry's Chemical Engineers Handbook.Eighth Edition. Secon 8:Proces Control.MeGraw-Hill, 2008.
[10] Gregory, K, McMillan Editor-in-chief, Doughas M.Considine Late Editor-in-chief. Process/Industrial Instruments and Controls Handbook.MeGraw-Hill, 1999.
[11] Stephen P.Boyd, Craing H.Barratt.Linear Controller Design.Prentice-Hall,Inc.1991.
[12] Bernard Frideland.Advanced Control System Design.Prentice Hall Inc.1996.
[13] Rurl Johan Astrom and Tore Haggland.Automatic Tuning of PID Controllers.ISA,1991.
[14] Battikha N.E..The Condensed Handbook of Measurement and Control.Instrument Society of America, 1997.
[15] Camacho E.F., C.Bordons.Model Predictive Control in The Process Industry.Sping Verlag, 1995.
[16] C.Brosilow,N.Markale.Model predicitve Cascade control and its Implications for Classical and IMC Cascade Control.Annual AIChE Meeting, Miamsi,1992.
[17] Michael stock.AI in Process Control.NewYork,McGraw-Hill Book Company, 1989.
[18] D.E.Seborg.A perpective on advanced strategies for process Control.Modelling Identificaiton and Control,1994.
[19] S.P.Chitra.Use Neural Networks for problem Solving.Chemical Engineering Progress,April, 1993.
[20] John Yen,Reza Langari, Lotfi A.Zadeh.Industrial Applications of Fuzzy Logic and Intelligent Systems.IEEE PRESS, 1995.
[21] William B.Gevearter etc..Introduction to Artificial Intellogence.Chemicla Engineering Progress,Sept., 1987.
[22] J.R.Leigh.Applied Dingital Control:Theory, Design & Implementation.Second Edition. prentice-Hall,1992.
[23] W.Fardo,Dale R.Patrick.Electrical Power Systems Technology.Prentice-Hall, 1985.
[24] J.O.Gray,D.C.Caldwell.Advanced Robotics & Intelligent Machines.Institution of Electrial Engineers, London, 1996.
[25] D.Seborg,T.Edgar.Process Dynamics and Cotrnol.John wiley & sons ,1989.